Public Sector Housing Law

Public Sector Housing Law

by D.J. Hughes, LL B

Lecturer in Law,
University of Leicester

London
Butterworths
1981

England London	Butterworth & Co (Publishers) Ltd 88 Kingsway, WC2B 6AB
Australia Sydney	Butterworths Pty Ltd 586 Pacific Highway, Chatswood, NSW 2067 Also at Melbourne, Brisbane, Adelaide and Perth
Canada Toronto	Butterworth & Co (Canada) Ltd 2265 Midland Avenue, Scarborough, M1P 4S1
New Zealand Wellington	Butterworths of New Zealand Ltd 33 – 35 Cumberland Place
South Africa Durban	Butterworth & Co (South Africa) (Pty) Ltd 152 – 154 Gale Street
USA Boston	Butterworth (Publishers) Inc 10 Tower Office Park, Woburn, Mass. 01801

ISBN Casebound 0 406 60061 9
           Limp 0 406 60060 0

Printed and bound in Singapore by
Singapore National Printers (Pte) Ltd.

Preface

I make no apology for the appearance of this book on the law of housing. For some years the law on this subject has not been so closely examined as planning law or the law of compulsory purchase. This is an oversight on the part of lawyers because, for most people, houses and flats are rather more important than the land on which they stand. Certainly there is a great body of law relating to the public regulation and provision of housing. Those books that have attempted to examine either the whole, or aspects, of housing law, excellent though they are, have inevitably suffered from the march of time and the fact that housing law is often the outward manifestation of housing policy which itself changes rapidly from government to government. I therefore perceived the need to adopt an entirely new approach to the subject largely based on the premise that this is one area of law and practice where local discretion is likely to be replaced increasingly by central control, as expressed in legislation such as the Housing (Homeless Persons) Act 1977 and the Housing Act 1980.

The work is intended to be a textbook: but a textbook for whom? Housing law is increasingly taught in Universities and Polytechnics at diploma, undergraduate and postgraduate degree levels. It is taught in law degrees and as part of courses leading to qualifications in housing and estate management. It is for such students that this book is intended. The book has been written so as to make it useful to people undertaking courses where law is either their main subject or a component part of their discipline.

I have tried to bear in mind that this is an introductory work and not a learned exposition of the whole of a vastly complicated subject. I have eschewed the use of footnotes — the ultimate academic heresy! It seems to me that if a reference is worth making it is worth making in the text, and that if references to further reading are desired then they can be made at the end of each chapter: I have included them in detailed 'further reading' lists.

As I have been writing I have been made aware by a number of local government officers of the need they feel for an introductory study of housing law. I have tried to bear this need in mind, and to write a book that will be of service to those engaged in the work of local government.

Those concerned with the administration of housing have accepted the need for considerable time and resources to be devoted to in-service training and continuing education. It has been my intention to produce a book that will be an aid in such work. I will be well satisfied if this volume finds a place on the shelves of local authority housing and legal departments. Elected members of local authorities might also consider it time well spent to read a book dealing with the legal framework of their housing functions. The book may also serve a purpose as an introductory guide for practitioners and workers in legal advice and law centres who have to deal with a growing number of cases involving points of municipal housing law.

Despite these purposes the primary function of the book is to serve as an introductory text. Accordingly it is necessary to give some description of the scheme of the work. If it is not to become a dry-as-dust paraphrase of statutory provisions housing law cannot be divorced from its wider social economic and political setting. These considerations have affected the way in which I have written. The book begins with an introductory chapter designed to set housing law in its wider setting, and to attempt some elucidation of the complicated legalites whereby housing finance is controlled. I have attempted to repeat this pattern in the subsequent chapters. Wherever possible each chapter begins with the statement of the wider issues affecting the particular area of law under consideration: occasionally it has been necessary to provide introductory material to parts of some chapters. After this introduction the law is examined in greater detail. I have included a number of quotations from statutes, so that the book can be of maximum use to those whose time and ease of access to library facilities are limited.

A wise elder statesman in the world of local government once told me that he had always enjoyed his work as housing chairman of his local authority because 'housing is about people'. This book has not been possible without the help and advice of many people. My thanks are due to: Christine Driver, Jean Kenyon and Barbara Goodman for coping with the original manuscript when it came to be typed; to my colleagues at the Faculty of Law of the University of Leicester for their constant help, encouragement, advice and forbearance when I have sounded like a long playing record of housing law; to the countless officials in both central and local government who have courteously answered my questions; to my students who have cheerfully served as guinea pigs for parts of this book delivered as lectures; to my publishers for giving me the chance to write this book; and finally to my mother, who decided that I should become a lawyer, and again to my teachers, colleagues and students for bearing so well with the fruits of her decision! This book is affectionately and respectfully dedicated to them all.

i.o.d.g.   David Hughes
Within the Octave of St. Michael 1980

Addendum

Through the kindness of my publishers I have been able to amend the text of this book at proof stage so as to bring it up to date as at 25 January 1981. Most of the necessary changes have been accommodated in the body of the text, but two important homelessness cases I have thought it best to comment on here as both require more than a passing mention.

The decision of the Court of Appeal in *R v Slough Borough Council, ex parte London Borough of Ealing* [1981] 1 All ER 601 goes somewhat further than the decision of the Divisional Court considered below at page 185. Shaw LJ stated that the law relating to homelessness has become a sort of 'merry-go-round' so that a person's entitlements can vary according as to how he boards it by making applications for aid to a number of authorities. The decision makes it clear that if a local authority, having come to their own decision that a person who has applied to them for aid is unintentionally homeless, consider that that person has a local connection with the area of another authority, then they are entitled to notify that other authority of their findings and conclusions. The notified authority are then under a duty to secure that accommodation becomes available for the homeless person indefinitely notwithstanding that they had previously determined that he was homeless intentionally. The effect to this ruling is that there will be circumstances where the decision of one authority will overrule that of another, and, in cases where the issue of local connection is raised, the decision of the notifying authority will be able to override an earlier decision of the notified authority.

An equally important decision on the issue of intentional homelessness is *Lewis v North Devon District Council* [1981] 1 All ER 27. The applicant, a married woman, lived with a farm worker (who was not her husband) and a child of her marriage as a family in a house provided by the man's employer. The man became unhappy in his job and left it, with the result that the couple were forced to vacate the house. When an application by the man to the local housing authority for accommodation under the Housing (Homeless Persons) Act 1977 for himself and the applicant was refused on the ground that by giving up his job he had become homeless intentionally, the applicant made an application in her name. She made it clear in her application that the man and her child were members of her household and would share any accommodation provided. The housing authority refused her application on the ground that, by acquiescing in the man's decision to leave his job knowing that they would then have to vacate the house provided by his employer, she had herself become homeless intentionally. The applicant applied for judicial review of the authority's decision, contending that, in deciding whether she had become homeless intentionally within the meaning of that term in section 17 of the 1977 Act, it was her conduct alone which ought to be considered by the housing authority. The authority contended that where one member of a family unit became homeless intentionally the whole family was to be treated as being homeless intentionally, with the result that rejection of an application by one member of the family because of intentional homelessness was sufficient reason to reject any further application by another member on behalf of the family. The authority submitted that if the position were otherwise a husband could make the family homeless intentionally and then the wife could successfully apply for accommodation under the 1977 Act.

It was held that on the true construction of section 17 of the 1977 Act a woman who lived with a man who became homeless intentionally was not necessarily barred by his conduct or by the fact that he might benefit undeservingly if she were given accommodation from being entitled to the relief available under that Act to a person who had not become homeless intentionally. However, since the policy of the 1977 Act required a housing authority to consider the family unit as a whole they were entitled to take into account the conduct of other members of the family and could assume, in the absence of contrary evidence, that the applicant was a party to that conduct. Since the housing authority had concluded that the applicant had acquiesced in the decision by the man she was living with to become homeless intentionally by giving up his job, they were entitled to take the view that the applicant had herself become homeless intentionally. The application would accordingly be dismissed.

The decision would appear to establish:

1   That in the case of multiple applications for aid from different members of one family a local authority are entitled to consider the conduct of all the members of the family, and are also entitled to assume, in the absence of contrary evidence, an act of intentional homelessness on the part of one of them is an act to which the others are party;

2   That there may be cases where a family's second applicant is not so tainted with intentional homelessness, though in such cases the burden of proving non-acquiescence in the intentional act will rest on the second applicant. But it may be enough to show that at the time of the act of intentional homelessness the second applicant was acting in good faith, being truly unaware of some relevant fact affecting the situation. [See further: Andrew Arden, 'The Homelessness Case' (1981) LAG Bulletin 17.]

25 January 1981   DJH
                                              The Conversion of St. Paul

Contents

Preface v
Table of Statutes xv
List of Cases xxv
Commencement Table xxxi

Introduction 1
The law as the child of policy 3
The wider debate on housing 4
The argument on tenure 4
The serfs or citizens issue 5
The Housing Act 1980 9
The erosion of local housing autonomy 10
Capital for local authority house building 11
The new system of capital expenditure control 14
Other controls over local authority house building 18
The control of recurrent housing expenditure: the role of housing
    subsidies 20
The new subsidy system 21
Whither local housing autonomy? 24

Part I: The public provision of housing 29

Chapter 1   The general housing powers and duties of local
               authorities and new town corporations 31
The housing authorities 32
The duty to provide housing 34
The acquisition of land for housing purposes 37
Compulsory purchase of land 41
The acquisition of ancillary rights 43
Enforcing the duties of local authorities 45
The provision of housing in new areas 45
Town development 46
The new towns 48

The ownership of housing in the new towns   49
The effect of the transfer of new town housing   51
Housing management powers in new towns   52
The effect of the 'right to buy' provisions of the Housing Act 1980   52

Chapter 2   The sale of council houses   54
Introduction   54
The former law   54
The history and development of the sales policy   55
The background to the modern law and policy on sales   57
The 'right to buy' under the Housing Act 1980   60
The price to be paid for the house or flat   65
Exercising the right to buy   66
Completing the transfer   67
The right to a mortgage   67
The amount to be left outstanding   68
Exercising the right to a mortgage   69
The terms of the mortgage   70
Miscellaneous points   71
The terms of the freehold sale or long lease   71
Restrictions on resale   75
The powers of the Secretary of State   77
Other powers of sale   78
Selling land for starter home schemes   81
Acquisition and improvement for sale   82
Shared ownership schemes   83

Chapter 3   The management of council housing   86
Allocation policies   86
Residence qualifications   88
Selection schemes   91
Reform   95
Racial and sexual discrimination in housing allocation   96
Tenure of council houses   99
The rights of secure tenants   101
Security of tenure   103
Tenant participation in housing management   107
Other rights of secure tenants   108
Variation of terms and publicity   110

Chapter 4   Rents and rent rebates for municipal houses   113
Rent pooling   115
Reasonable rents   117
Increasing rents   118
Rent arrears   119

An action for the rent ('rent action')   121
Distress   122
Eviction   125
Administrative practices for dealing with rent arrears   128
Rent rebates   129
The model rent rebate scheme   130
The calculation of rebate   132
Rebate examples   133
Administrative procedures concerning rebates   134

Chapter 5   Municipal housing, matrimony and mortgages   138
The council house as the matrimonial home   138
The rights of a non-tenant wife   139
Domestic violence   140
The rights of the parties on the break-up of a marriage   144
Other housing problems arising after marital break-up   146
Mortgages   147
Local authority mortgage interest rates   149
Local authority lending in practice   150
Co-operation between local authorities and the building societies   152
Local authority mortgage guarantee powers   155
Other local authority mortgage powers   156
The local authority's power as a mortgagee   156
Local authority home purchase assistance powers   157
Miscelleneous points   158
Option morgages   159
The right to opt for subsidy   160
Extending the right to opt   161
The end of the option   162
Guarantees for large mortgage advances   162

Chapter 6   Homelessness   164
Causes and numbers   164
The new law   169
Who are 'the homeless'?   169
Initial contact with the local authority   171
The duties owed to the homeless   174
The duty to accommodate   186
Duties of notification   188
Offences   189
Protecting the property of the homeless   190
Challenging decisions made under the Act and enforcing the
    duties   190
Other provisions to aid the homeless   192

Part II: Repairs, housing standards and remedies 195

Chapter 7   The landlord's obligation to repair and maintain 197
Landlord's obligations in tort 198
Liability under the Occupiers Liability Act 1957 204
Liability for breach of the Building Regulations 205
Landlord's obligations in contract 205

Chapter 8   The individual sub-standard house: problems and
             remedies 220
The requirements of the Housing Act 1957 221
The standard of fitness 221
The duties of local authorities 222
The duty where the house can be made fit at reasonable expense 223
The duty where the house cannot be made fit at reasonable
  expense 225
Other powers for dealing with houses which cannot be made fit 227
The appeals procedure 229
Well maintained payments 230
The mandatory character of the requirements of the legislation 231
Supplementary powers to prevent houses becoming unfit 232
The requirements of the Public Health Act 1936 235
The definition of 'statutory nuisance' 235
The procedures for taking action in respect of a statutory
  nuisance 236
The taking of action in respect of statutory nuisances by private
  citizens 239
The relationship between the Housing and Public Health Acts 241
The individual sub-standard house in private ownership 241
The sub-standard older house in local authority ownership 242
The sub-standard modern council-built house 243
Miscellaneous powers to deal with sub-standard housing 244
The position in Greater London 247

Chapter 9   Clearance procedures, compulsory purchase and
             rehousing 249
The development of the law 249
The old procedure by way of clearance order 251
The modern procedure by way of compulsory purchase 251
The assessment of compensation 261
The purchase price of the land 261
Well maintained payments 264
Disturbance payments 267
Other powers to assist displaced occupiers 268

Home loss payments   269
The fate of the land after acquisition   270
Rehousing displaced residents   271
Rehabilitation of houses in clearance areas   272

Chapter 10   Improvement policies   276
History   276
How many unsatisfactory houses are there?   280
House renovation grants   283
Certificates of future occupation   285
The payment of grants   286
Residence conditions   287
Other grant conditions   288
Enforcing the grant conditions   289
The individual grants   290
Area improvement   296
Housing action areas   296
General improvement areas   299
Priority neighbourhoods   300
Compulsory improvement   301
Compulsory improvement outside improvement areas   304
An assessment of improvement policies   305

Chapter 11   Multi-occupancy and overcrowding   308
Introduction   308
The supervision of multi-occupation by planning control   310
The supervision of multi-occupation under the Housing Acts   312
The definition of multi-occupation   313
Local authority powers   314
Overcrowding   329
Enforcement and remedial powers and duties of local authorities   333

Chapter 12   Municipal housing: the rôle of the Commission for Local Administration   335
The creation of the Commission and its terms of reference   335
Procedure before the Commission   337
Revised operating procedures   339
The effectiveness of the Commission in providing a remedy   341
An assessment of the work of the Commission   344
Future reforms   345
Overseeing the overseers   348

Index   351

Table of Statutes

References in this Table to "*Statutes*" are to Halsbury's Statutes of England (Third Edition) showing the volume and page at which the annotated text of the Act will be found.

PAGE

Acquisition of Land (Assessment of Compensation) Act 1919 . . 249

Acquisition of Land (Authorisation Procedure) Act 1946 (6 *Statutes* 154) 41

Administration of Justice Act 1970 (40 *Statutes* 390)

s 40 128

Agricultural Holdings Act 1948 (1 *Statutes* 685) 101

Arbitration Act 1950 (2 *Statutes* 433)

s 32 75

Artizans and Labourers Dwellings Act 1868 249

Artizans' and Labourers' Dwellings Improvement Act 1875 . . . 249

Attachment of Earnings Act 1971 (41 *Statutes* 791) 121

s 6, 15 122

Charities Act 1960 (3 *Statutes* 589) . 61

Children and Young Persons Act 1963 (17 *Statutes* 699)

s 1 . . . . 121, 147, 193

Chronically Sick and Disabled Persons Act 1970 (40 *Statutes* 766)

s 3 (1) 35

Compulsory Purchase Act 1965 (65 *Statutes* 281)

s 1 (1) 260

4 259

5 259

(1) 258

6, 9 259

23 (1), (2), (6) 259

Sch 5 259

Control of Pollution Act 1974 (44 *Statutes* 1191)

Sch 2 . . . . 238, 239

PAGE

Criminal Law Act 1977 (47 *Statutes* 142)

s 60 240

Defective Premises Act 1972 (42 *Statutes* 1395) 203

s 1 201

(1), (4) 200

(5) 200, 201, 202

3 202

(1) 202

(2) 202, 203

(3) 202

(4), (5) 203

4 . . . . 202, 211

(1) 202

(6) 204

6 204

(3) 201, 202

7 (2) 200

Distress for Rent Act 1689 (9 *Statutes* 511) 123

s 1 123

Domestic Proceedings and Magistrates' Courts Act 1978 (48 *Statutes* 730)

s 16 (2) − (4) 143

18 144

Domestic Violence and Matrimonial Proceedings Act 1976 (46 *Statutes* 713) 140, 141

s 1 (1) 141

2 (1) 142

4 139

Education Act 1944 (11 *Statutes* 153) 100

s 81 131

Health and Safety at Work etc. Act 1974 (44 *Statutes* 1083) . . . 205

s 71 205

PAGE

Home Purchase Assistance and Housing Corporation Guarantee Act 1978 (48 *Statutes* 718)

s 1 157
  (5) 158
  2 (4) 158

Homes Insulation Act 1978 (48 *Statutes* 726)

s 1 306

House Purchase and Housing Act 1959 (16 *Statutes* 314)

s 3 149
  13 34

Housing Act 1930 (16 *Statutes* 41) . 249

Housing Act 1935 (16 *Statutes* 43) . 113, 276, 331

Housing Act 1936 (16 *Statutes* 46)

s 79 (1) 55

Housing Act 1949 (16 *Statutes* 83) . 3, 31, 276

Housing Act 1952 55

Housing Act 1957 (16 *Statutes* 109) . 11, 14, 32, 33, 34, 51, 57, 61, 79, 82, 148, 168, 186, 206, 221, 222, 237, 241, 250, 268, 273, 275, 279, 300, 304, 325

s 1 32
  4 . . . . . 221, 243, 251, 293, 301
  5 252
  (1) 252
  6 . . . . 211, 218
  (1), (2) 211
  9 . . . . . 231, 234, 243, 295
  (1) 223, 224, 225
  (1A) . . . 232, 233, 234, 280
  (1B) 234
  (1C) 234
  (2) 224
  10 (1) 224, 225
  (3), (5), (7) 224
  11 (1) 224, 225
  (3) 224
  12 224
  16 . . . . . 231, 232, 243, 246, 272
  (1) 225
  (3) 225
  (4) 226, 230
  (5) 226
  17 242
  (2) 228

PAGE

Housing Act 1957—*contd*

s 19 . . . . 226, 228
  20 228
  (1)–(3) 229
  21 227
  22 (1), (4) 226
  23 227
  24 227
  27 227
  (1) 227, 228
  (3) 227
  (5) 228
  28 227
  29 228
  (2) 228
  30 (1) 230
  37 230
  39 232
  (1) 231, 233
  (2) 223
  42 (1) 251, 253, 254
  43 . . . . 251, 273
  (1) 255
  (2) 262
  (3), (5) 256
  44 251
  45 (2) 255
  46 242
  47 270
  48 . . . . 242, 270
  49 273
  50 255
  54 242
  59 (1), (2) 261
  60 (1) 264
  62 261
  72 246
  76 334
  77 . . . . 330, 333
  78 . . . . 331, 333
  (4) 332
  80 . . . . 331, 333
  81 333
  83 333
  85 . . . . 38, 333
  (2), (3) 333
  87 . . . . 38, 329, 331, 332
  90 321
  91 . . . . 34, 35, 45
  92 . . . . 35, 36, 46
  (1) 35
  93 . . . . 35, 36, 37
  94 35

PAGE

Housing Act 1957—*contd*

s 95 . . . . 35, 37
96 . . . . . 37, 39, 44, 81
97 (1), (2) 41
98 44
99 45
104 . . . . 54, 78, 81, 83, 156
   (1) 55
   (2) 56
   (4) 85
   (5), (6) 78
   (9) 83
104A 78, 79
104B 78, 79, 80
104C 78
105 . . . . . . 37, 39
   (4), (4A) 39, 40
107 36
110A 40
111 86
   (1) 117
113 (1A) 118
   (2) 86
   (3) 129
   (5) 83, 144
126 32
136 – 138 11
149 (1) 36
157 251
   (2) 222
159 322
165 36
189 252
   (1) 221
Sch 2, Pt I . . . 230, 264, 265
   Pt II 266
Sch 3 273
   Pt I 256
   Pt II 263
   Pt III 262, 263
Sch 4 258
Sch 6 . . . . . 106, 330
Sch 7 41
Sch 8 11
Housing Act 1961 (16 *Statutes* 327). 20, 72, 217
s 12 . . . . . 315, 323, 324
13 . . . . . . 314, 323
   (4) 316
14 . . . . 316, 319, 323, 325
15 . . . . 294, 302, 317, 318, 319, 320, 323, 325

PAGE

Housing Act 1961 — *contd*

s 15 (1) 302
16 . . . . 318, 319
18 319
19 . . . . 320, 322, 323, 325
   (9) 322
   (11) 320
21 323
22 . . . . 323, 324
   (4) 324
23 (6) 323
25 227
26A 320
32 . . . . 111, 203, 211, 213, 214, 217, 218, 242, 243
   (1) 212, 213, 214
   (3) 212, 213, 215
   (4) 213
33 . . . . . 213, 242, 243
Housing Act 1964 (16 *Statutes* 362) . 277, 296, 301
s 65 319
67 323
73 (1) 324
74, 77 325
78 326
79 . . . . . 325, 326, 327
80 326
82 . . . . 325, 326
83, 86 326
Housing Act 1969 (16 *Statutes* 496) . 277, 299
s 17 – 19 22
28 299
29 300
   (3) 255
29A, 30 – 33, 37 300
58 323
   (1) 313
61 319
63 326
64 323
   (7) 324
66 . . . . 230, 265
67 264
70 . . . . 35, 45, 222, 251, 318
71 221
72 232
Sch 4 . . . . . . 230, 265
Sch 5 266
Sch 8 328
Housing Act 1971 (41 *Statutes* 745)
s 1, 2 22

	PAGE
Housing Act 1974 (44 *Statutes* 405) .	39, 110, 159, 160, 267, 268, 269, 271, 273, 278
s 36	296
(4)	298
37, 39, 41, 43 − 45 . . .	298
46, 47	299
56	283
57	284
(6), (6A)	285
58	291
59	285
60 (1) − (5)	286
61	290
(4), (4A), (5) . . .	291
62	291
63	292
64	292
(7)	292
65	292
66	293
67	292
(3)	293
(5)	320
68	293
69	294
(2)	294
69A, 70, 70A	294
71	295
(4)	295
71A	295
72	295
73	287
(3)	287
74	287, 288
75	287, 290
(6)	286
76	287, 290
77	290
78	296
79	22
80	285
82 (1) − (3)	286
(6)	287
85	301
(3)	302
87, 88	302
89	303, 304
90, 91	303
93, 94	304
99	302
100	156, 304
101	304

	PAGE
Housing Act 1974 — *contd*	
s 103A	275, 301
104	234
(1)	305
105	11, 298
108 (1)	251
(2)	264
(3)	251
114 (1), (1A), (2) . . .	273
114A, 115	275
125 (1)	217
(2)	218
126	39, 75
129	294
(3)	288
130	251, 269
(1)	271
Sch 6	291, 293, 295
Sch 9	264
Sch 10	273, 275
Sch 13	269, 271
Sch 15	251
Housing Act 1980 . .	9, 21, 63, 66, 77, 78, 79, 80, 83, 90, 99, 110, 111, 125, 139, 145, 155, 159, 160, 279, 284, 295, 305, 306, 310
s 1	60
(1)	67
2 (1) − (3)	61
(4)	52, 61, 62
3	60
(4)	60
4	62
(2)	62
5	66
(1)	71
6	63, 66
7	63, 66
8	78
9 (1)	67, 68, 70
(2) − (5)	68
10	66, 69
11	66, 67
(2)	67
(5)	67, 69
12	69
(1)	70
(2)	69
(4)	69, 70
13, 14	71
15	62, 63, 65
16	69

PAGE

Housing Act 1980—*contd*

s 16 (1). 67
  (3)−(5) 69
  (6). 69, 70
  (7). 69
  (8). 69, 70
  (9)−(11). 67
17 71
18 . . . . 70, 71
19 . . . . 75, 78
20 67
21 71
  (2). 68
23 . . . . . 77, 78, 319
24 77
25 60
27 (1). 62
  (3). 61
28 99
29 . . . . . 71, 101, 102
30 . . . . 101, 102, 109
31 . . . . . 101, 102
  (2). 102
32 103
33 103
  (2). 103
34 103
  (1). 103
  (2), (3) 105
35 (1), (2) 108
36 108
37 . . . . . . 108, 144
  (1) 144
38, 39 110
40 110
41 . . . . . . 110, 217
42, 43 107
44 (1), (2), (5), (6) . . . 94
46 90
47, 48 101
50 (2) 60
  (3) 62, 102
80 218
81−83 109
86 (1) 103
87, 89 106
91, 92 78
93 . . . . 39, 81
94 83
95 40
97 21
98 (2) 22
101 23
102 24

PAGE

Housing Act 1980—*contd*

s 102 (1)−(3). 24
106 284
  (4) 289
108 82
109 301
110 149
  (1) 70
  (11), (12) 150
111 155
112 156
113 157
114 161
  (3), (4) 161
115 161
117 24
  (2) 136
119 131
  (1) 128
134, 135 114
136 74
137 81
140 83
146 321
149 234
Sch 1, Pt I 52, 61
Sch 2 . . . 71, 72, 73, 74, 75
Sch 3 100
Sch 4, Pt I 103
  Ground 1−6 . . . . 103, 104
    7 . . . 103, 104, 106
    8−12 . . . 103, 104
    13 . . . . 104, 105
  Pt II 105
Sch 12 . . . 285, 286, 291, 292,
                293, 318
Sch 13 . . . . 298, 299, 300
Sch 15 129
Sch 19 73
Sch 23 . . . . 316, 320, 324
Sch 24 . . . . 294, 318, 319
Sch 25 . . . 34, 100, 119, 145,
                273, 301
Sch 26 . . . 34, 37, 83, 253, 283

Housing (Amendment) Act 1973 (43
    Statutes 521)
s 2 55

Housing Finance Act 1972 (42 *Statutes*
    557) . . . 10, 20, 116, 128
s 12 113
18 129
  (4). 129
20, 21 129
24 129

PAGE

Housing Finance Act 1972—*contd*
s 24 (6) 130
  25 129
    (3) 131
  63 (1) 116
  90 − 91A 73
  93 (1) 53
Sch 1 114
Sch 3 . . . . 129, 130, 131, 132,
                133, 134, 135
Sch 4 . . . . 129, 130, 134, 135,
                136

Housing (Financial Provisions) Act
  1958 (16 *Statutes* 271) . . . 32
s 9 34
  43 . . . . 148, 158
  45 155
  54 151
Housing (Homeless Persons) Act 1977
  (47 *Statutes* 34) . . 11, 59, 100,
                164, 165, 169, 172
s 1 (1) 169
  (2) 170, 238
  (3) 170
  2 (1), (2) 172, 173
  3 186
    (1) 171
    (2) 171, 172
    (3) 172
    (4) . . . 100, 172, 190, 191,
                192
  4 . . . . 86, 186
    (1), (2) 174
    (3) . . . 100, 174, 179, 180,
                190
    (4) 174, 190
    (5) . . . 174, 182, 187, 190
  5 . . . . 86, 186, 190
    (1) 182, 184
    (3), (4) 184
    (5), (6) . . . 100, 184, 185
    (7), (8) 184, 185
    (11) 184
  6 (1) 186, 187
  7 190
    (1) 190
  8 (6) 190
  9 (1) 185
  11 189
    (2) − (4) 189
  16 . . . . 176, 188
  17 . . . . . . 175, 176, 177
    (2) 175
    (4) 177, 179

PAGE

Housing (Homeless Persons) Act 1977—
  contd
s 18 (1) 182, 183
    (2), (3) 183
  19 (1) 175
Housing of the Working Classes Act
  1885
s 12 211
Housing Rents and Subsidies Act
  1975 (45 *Statutes* 622, 826) . . 10,
                21, 117
s 1 (3) 114
  2 22
  3 24
  4 22
  11 (1) 118
  15 (5) 118
  17 269
Sch 5 . . . . . . 114, 269, 273
Housing Repairs and Rents Act 1954 277
Housing Subsidies Act 1967 (16
  Statutes 450) 20, 159
s 24 160
    (2A) 160, 162
    (3) 161
    (3A) 160, 162
  24A (1) 162
  26 161
  27 (1) 159
  30 162
Housing, Town Planning, &c. Act
  1909 (16 *Statutes* 21) . . . 20, 31
Industrial and Provident Societies
  Act 1965 (17 *Statutes* 33) . . 61
Industrial Injuries and Diseases (Old
  Cases) Act 1975 (45 *Statutes*
  1319) 131
Inheritance (Provision for Family
  and Dependants) Act 1975 (45
  Statutes 493)
s 2 76
Inner Urban Areas Act 1978 (48
  Statutes 1493) 305
Land Compensation Act 1961 (6
  Statutes 238) 161
s 5 . . . . 262, 267
  10 262
  32 268
Sch 2 228
Land Compensation Act 1973 (43
  Statutes 170, 528) 334
s 29 269
  30 (1) 270
  32 270
    (6) 270

PAGE

Land Compensation Act 1973 — *contd*
s 37 267
  (3) 268
  38 268
  39 . . . . 86, 238, 271, 272
    (1) 271, 302
  43 268
  50 263
Land Compensation (Scotland) Act
  1973) 271
Sch 2 269
Land Registration Act 1925 (27
  Statutes 778) 67
Landlord and Tenant Act 1927 (18
  Statutes 451)
s 19 (2) 109
Landlord and Tenant Act 1954 (18
  Statutes 553, 726) 101, 129
s 1 284
  37 268
Landlord and Tenant Act 1962 (18
  Statutes 615)
s 1 333
Law of Distress Amendment Act
  1888 (9 *Statutes* 532) 123
s 5 123
Law of Property Act 1925 (27 *Statutes*
  341) 157
s 54 (2) 206
  84 36
  101 (1) 156
Leasehold Reform Act 1967 . . . 83
Litigants in Person (Costs and
  Expenses) Act 1975 (45 *Statutes*
  1639) 240
Local Authority Social Services Act
  1970 (40 *Statutes* 991)
Sch 1 100
Local Government Act 1972 (42
  Statutes 841) 45
s 112 223
  193 (2) 36
  194 . . . . 32, 100
    (3) 45
  195 . . . . 167, 192
Sch 13 11
Sch 22 32
Sch 23 . . . . 167, 192
Sch 29 223
Local Government Act 1974 (44
  Statutes 403, 637) . . . 335, 348
s 24 348
  (5) 347
  25 (1) 335

PAGE

Local Government Act 1974 — *contd*
s 26 337
  (1) 336
  (6) 339
  29 338
  30 (4) 347
  31 . . . . 341, 347
  32 (1) 347
  (3) 344, 347
  34 (3) 336
  37 150
Local Government Act 1978 (48
  Statutes 855) . . . 342, 347, 348
s 1 342
Local Government (Miscellaneous
  Provisions) Act 1976 (46 *Statutes*
  247, 707, 958)
s 8 (1) 226
  9 36
  13 44
  16 324
Local Government, Planning and
  Land Act 1980 . . . 14, 34, 37,
    39, 305
s 32 270
  71 14
  72 . . . . 14, 17
  73 . . . . 17, 18
  75 16
  (1) 15
  (5) 15
  76 14
  78 . . . . 17, 18
  79 18
  (2), (3) 18
  94 38
  93, 95, 99 38
  114 270
  116 37
  118 41
  153 34
Sch 6 287
Sch 12 14
Sch 13 18
Sch 16 38
Sch 32 306
Local Government (Scotland) Act
  1975 348
Lodging Houses Act 1851 31
London Building Acts (Amendment)
  Act 1939 (20 *Statutes* 136) . . 247
London County Council (General
  Powers) Act 1958 (20 *Statutes*
  385) 247

PAGE

London Government Act 1963 (20
    Statutes 448)
s 21 32
    (3), (4) 33
    (11) 34
    22 (1) 34
    (2) 32, 34
    (5) 34
    23 (3) 33
Magistrates' Courts Act 1952 (21
    Statutes 181)
s 42 237
Matrimonial Causes Act 1973 (43
    Statutes 539)
s 24 . . . . . . 76, 102, 108, 139,
                            144
    (1) 144
Matrimonial Homes Act 1967 (17
    Statutes 139) . . . 106, 139, 140
s 1 139
    (1) 140
    (5) 100
    7 (1), (2) 145
National Assistance Act 1948 (23
    Statutes 636) 166, 327
s 2 (1) 166
    21 167
    (1) 167, 169, 192
    36 (1) 167
    17 166
National Loans Act 1968 12
National Parks and Access to the
    Countryside Act 1949 (24 *Statutes*
    65) 48
s 87 76
New Towns Act 1946 48
New Towns Act 1959 (36 *Statutes*
    65) 49
New Towns Act 1965 (36 *Statutes*
    374) 38
s 1 (1), (2) 48
    2 49
    3 49
    (2) 52
    7 (2) 49
    18 52
    35 50
    36 . . . . 50, 52
    37 50
    (3) 52
    38, 39, 41 50
Sch 1, 3 49
Sch 10 52

PAGE

New Towns (Amendment) Act 1976
    (46 *Statutes* 1845) 50
s 2 50
    3 50
    (3) 51
    (6) 50, 51
    5 (2) 50
    6 - 8 51
Nuisances Removal etc. (1846) . . 210
Occupiers' Liability Act 1957 (23
    Statutes 792)
s 2 (1) 204
    3 (1) 204
Parliamentary Commissioner Act
    1967 (6 *Statutes* 822)
s 11 (3) 344
Powers of Criminal Courts Act 1973
    (43 *Statutes* 288)
s 35 240
Prevention of Damage by Pests Act
    1949 (26 *Statutes* 408) . . . 244
s 2 - 4 245
Prices and Incomes Act 1968 (16
    Statutes 489)
s 12 119
Protection from Eviction Act 1977
    (47 *Statutes* 661) 312
Public Health Act 1875 (26 *Statutes*
    38) 210
Public Health Act 1936 (26 *Statutes*
    189) 205, 221, 235, 237,
                            279, 327
s 48 243
    58 246
    83 (1), (1A) 245
    91 236
    92 236
    (1) 235
    93 . . . . . . 236, 237, 239
    94 . . . . . . 236, 238, 239
    (1) 237
    (2) 237, 238
    (3) 240
    (6) 238
    95 236
    (1) 238
    96 . . . . 236, 239
    97, 98 236
    99 . . . . . 8, 238, 239, 240,
                        242, 243, 244
    100 239
    235, 236 327

PAGE

Public Health Act 1936—*contd*
s 238 – 244 328
    246 . . . . 327, 329
    247 329
    322 240
    343 . . . . . . 235, 328
      (1) 235, 237
Public Health Act 1961 (26 *Statutes*
    500) 205, 279
s 24 . . . . 246, 247
    35 245
Public Health (Recurring Nuisances)
    Act 1961 (26 *Statutes* 620)
s 1 (1) 239
    3 (1) 239
    26 239
Public Works Loans Act 1875 (22
    Statutes 746) 12
Race Relations Act 1976 (46 *Statutes*
    389)
s 1 (1) 97, 99
    3 (1) 97
    21 (1), (2) 97
    71 97
Rent Act 1968 (18 *Statutes* 777) . . 269
Rent Act 1977 (47 *Statutes* 387) . . 101,
            105, 125, 204, 269,
                289, 319
s 101 . . . . . . 332, 333
    147 122
Sch 15, Pt. II. 105
Sch 23 55
Rent (Agriculture) Act 1976 (46
    Statutes 50) 284, 289
Sch 8 145
Sex Discrimination Act 1975 (45
    Statutes 221) 138
s 1, 30 99
Small Dwellings Acquisition Act 1899
    (165 *Statutes* 10) 34
s 1 147

PAGE

Small Tenements Recovery Act 1838
    (18 *Statutes* 421) 125
Social Security Act 1975 (45 *Statutes*
    1071)
s 37A (8) 132
Social Security Act 1980
    Sch 5 . . . . . . 167, 192
Supplementary Benefits Act 1976 (46
    Statutes 1046) 128
s 14 (3) 128
Town and Country Planning Act
    1947 (36 *Statutes* 22) 48
Town and Country Planning Act
    1959 (36 *Statutes* 48)
s 46 47
Town and Country Planning Act
    1968 (40 *Statutes* 301)
s 30 260
Sch 3 260
Town and Country Planning Act
    1971 (41 *Statutes* 1571) . . . 275
s 22 79
    (1) 310, 311
    (2) 310
    (3) 310, 311
    40 (1) 42
    52 81
    192 270
    270 42
Town Development Act 1952 (36
    Statutes 25)
s 1 46
    2 47
    3 48
    5, 6 47
    7, 8 46
    9, 13, 21 47
Tribunals and Inquiries Act 1971 (41
    Statutes 248)
s 12 41

List of Cases

PAGE

Abingdon Rural District Council v
O'Gorman (1968) 122
Adeoso v Adeoso (1981) 142
Alexander v Mercouris (1979) . . 210
American Cynamid Co v Ethnicon
Ltd (1975) 192
Andresier v Minister of Housing and
Local Government (1965) . . . 37
Annicola Investments Ltd v Minister
of Housing and Local Government
(1968) 252
Anns v Merton London Borough
Council (1977) 198, 205
Arden v Pullen (1842) 199
Asco Developments Ltd v Lowes
(1978) 208
Ashridge Investments Ltd v Minister
of Housing and Local Government
(1965) 254
A-G ex rel. Rivers-Moore v Ports-
mouth City Council (1978) . . . 40,
41, 274
A-G ex rel. Lilley v Wandsworth
London Borough Council (1980) . 193
Attridge v LCC (1954) 40, 41

Backhouse v Lambeth Borough
Council (1972) 116
Bacon v Grimsby Corpn (1950) . . 231
Bainbridge, Re, South Shields
(D'Arcy Street) Compulsory Pur-
chase Order 1937 (1939) . . . 252
Ball v LCC (1949) 197
Bass Charrington (North) Ltd v
Minister of Housing and Local
Government (1971) 256
Bathavon Rural District Council v
Carlile (1958) 119
Batty v Metropolitan Property Reali-
sations Ltd (1978) . . . 198, 205

PAGE

Belcher v Reading Corpn (1950) . 117
Betts v Penge UDC (1942) 235
Billings (AC) & Son v Riden (1958) . 198
Birmingham Corpn v Minister of
Housing and Local Government
and Habib Ullah (1964) . . . 311
Bishop Auckland Local Board v
Bishop Auckland Iron Co (1882) . 236
Blamires v Bradford Corpn (1964) . 259,
344
Bottomley v Bannister (1932) . . 197
Brent London Borough Council v
Greater London Council (1980) . 33
Bristol Corpn v Sinnott (1918) . . 237
Bristol District Council v Clark
(1975) 95, 126
British Anzani (Felixstowe) Ltd v
International Marine Management
(UK) Ltd (1979) . . . 208, 209, 210
British Railways Board v Herringion
(1972) 226
Broadbent v Rotherham Corpn
(1917) 226
Brown v Liverpool Corpn (1969) . 213
Buswell v Goodwin (1971) . . . 212
Butler, Re, Camberwell (Wingfield
Mews), No. 2 Clearance Order
1936 (1939) 252

Camden Nominees v Forcey (1940) . 208
Campden Hill Towers v Gardner
(1977) 213, 218
Cannock Chase District Council v
Kelly (1978) 95, 99, 126
Cavalier v Pope (1906) 197
Charsley v Jones (1889) 206
Chertsey UDC v Mixnam's Properties
Ltd (1965) 312

PAGE

Chorley Borough Council v Barratt
  Developments (North West) Ltd
  (1979) 252, 329
Clarke v Taff Ely Borough Council
  (1980) 203
Cleethorpes Borough Council v
  Clarkson (1978) 126
Cocker v Cardwell (1869) 236
Cole v Harris (1945) 100
Coleen Properties v Minister of
  Housing and Local Government
  (1971) 255
Conron v LCC (1922) 36
Cooper v Wandsworth Board of
  Works (1863) 127
Coventry City Council v Cartwright
  (1975) 235, 240
Cunard v Antifyre Ltd (1933) . . 198

Davis v Foots (1940) 197
Davis v Johnson (1979) 142
De Falco v Crawley Borough Council
  (1980) 176, 177, 179,
                            181, 192
Delahaye v Oswestry Borough Council
  (1980) 180
De Rothschild v Wing RDC (1967) . 303
Devereux v Liverpool City Council
  (1978) 215
Donoghue v Stevenson (1932) . 197
Dudlow Estates Ltd v Sefton Metro-
  politan Borough Council (1978) . 231,
                                      232
Duffy v Pilling (1977) 311
Dyson v Kerrier District Council
  (1980) 180, 181

Ealing Corpn v Ryan (1965) . . . 310
Eckersley v Secretary of State for the
  Environment and Southwark
  London Borough Council (1977) . 253
Elliott v Brighton Borough Council
  (1979) 224
Elliott v Southwark London Borough
  Council (1976) 273
Ellis Copp & Co v Richmond-upon-
  Thames London Borough Council
  (1976) 231
Evans v Collins (1964) 117

PAGE

FFF Estates Ltd v Hackney London
  Borough Council (1981) . 303, 305
Fawcett v Newcastle-Upon-Tyne City
  Council (1977) 299
Fletcher v Ilkeston Corpn (1931). . 229
Foster v Day (1968) 216
Francis v Cowcliffe Ltd (1977) . . 218

Gill & Co v Secretary of State for the
  Environment (1978) 257
Goddard v Minister of Housing and
  Local Government (1958) . . . 254
Goodrich v Paisner (1957) . . . 311
Gosling v Secretary of State for the
  Environment (1975) 256
Gould v Times Square Estates Ltd
  (1975) 240
Granada Theatres Ltd v Freehold
  Investments (Leytonstone) Ltd
  (1959) 72
Great Western Rly Co v Bishop
  (1872) 236
Green v Eales (1841) 216
Green (HE) and Sons v Minister of
  Health (No. 2) (1948) 37
Greg v Planque (1936) 214
Guinness Trust (London Fund) v
  Green (1955) 329

Hall v Manchester Corpn (1915) . 45,
                                      222
Harrington v Croydon Corpn (1968) 303
Harris v Birkenhead Corpn (1976) . 226
Hart v Rogers (1916) 209
Hart v Windsor (1844) 199
Hewitt v Rowlands (1924) 216
Hillbank Properties Ltd v Hackney
  London Borough Council (1978) . 233,
                                      234
Hoggard v Worsborough UDC (1962) 264
Honig v Islington London Borough
  (1972) 319
Hopkins v Smethwick Local Board of
  Health (1890) 127
Hopwood v Cannock Chase District
  Council (1975) 213
Horgan v Birmingham Corpn (1964) 319
Hunter v Manchester City Council
  (1975) 266

PAGE

Inworth Property v Southwark London Borough Council (1977) . 231

Jeune v Queen's Cross Properties Ltd (1974) 217
Johnson v Leicester Corpn (1934) . 226

Lally v Kensington and Chelsea Royal Borough (1980) 178
Lambeth London Borough Council v Stubbs (1980) 237
Leeds Corpn v Jenkinson (1935) . . 117
Lee-Parker v Izzet (1971) 207, 208, 209
Lewis v North Devon District Council (1981) vii
Lipson v Secretary of State for the Environment (1977) 311
Liverpool City Council, Re a complaint against (1977) 344
Liverpool City Council v Irwin (1977) 206
Logsden v Booth (1900) 327
Logsdon v Trotter (1900) 327
LCC v Hankins (1914) 327
Luby v Newcastle-Under-Lyme Corpn (1965) 117
Lurcott v Wakely and Wheeler (1911) 72

McCarrick v Liverpool Corpn (1947) 211
McVittie v Bolton Corpn (1945) . . 246
Malton Board of Health v Malton Manure Co (1879) . . . 235, 236
Meravale Builders Ltd v Secretary of State for the Environment (1978) . 36
Middleton v Hall (1913) 211
Milford Properties v Hammersmith London Borough Council (1978) . 314
Miller v Wandsworth London Borough Council (1980) . 178, 180
Mint v Good (1951) 203
Morgan v Liverpool Corpn (1927) . 222

National Coal Board v Neath Borough Council (1976) . 234, 236

PAGE

Neale v Del Soto (1945) 100
Newham London Borough v Patel (1979) 215
Northwood Flat Dwellers and Tenants Association v Knowsley District Council (1974) 244
Nottingham Corpn v Newton (1974) 237, 241

O'Brien v Robinson (1973) . . . 211
Okereke v Brent London Borough Council (1967) 313
Oppenheimer v Minister of Transport (1942) 259
Otto v Bolton and Norris (1936) . 197

Pembery v Lamdin (1940) . . . 214
People's Hostels Ltd v Turley (1938) 327
Perry v Garner (1953) 245
Pocklington v Melksham UDC (1964) 227
Practice Direction (1978) 142
Proudfoot v Hart (1890) 217

Quiltotex Co Ltd v Minister of Housing and Local Government (1966) 252

R v Beverley Borough Council, ex parte McPhee (1978) . . . 189, 191
R v Bolton Recorder, ex parte McVittie (1940) 246
R v Bristol City Council, ex parte Browne (1979) . . . 184, 187, 188
R v Bristol Corpn, ex parte Hendy (1974) 272
R v Corby District Council, ex parte McClean (1975) 269
R v Epping (Waltham Abbey) Justices, ex parte Burlinson (1948) . . . 240
R v Epsom and Ewell Corpn, ex parte R.B. Property Investments (Eastern) (1964) 226
R v Hillingdon London Borough Council, ex parte Royco Homes Ltd (1974) 36

PAGE

R v Hillingdon London Borough Council, ex parte Slough Borough Council (1980) . . . . . vii, 185

R v Hillingdon London Borough Council, ex parte Streeting (1980) 183

R v Kerrier District Council, ex parte Guppy's (Bridport) Ltd (1976) . 231, 241, 242

R v Local Comr for Administration for the North and North East Area of England, ex parte Bradford Metropolitan City Council (1979). 340

R v Newham East Justices, ex parte Hunt (1976) 236

R v Oxted Justices, ex parte Franklin (1976) 236

R v Penwith District Council, ex parte Hughes (1980) 180

R v Secretary of State for Home Affairs, ex parte Ostler (1977) . 258

Ravenseft Properties v Davstone (Holdings) Ltd (1980) 214

Rawlence v Croydon Corpn (1952) . 223

Regan v Regan (1977) 144

Robbins v Jones (1863) 197

Rollo v Minister of Town and County Planning (1948) 49

Ryall v Kidwell (1914) 211

Saddleworth UDC v Aggregate and Sand Ltd (1970) 243

Salford City Council v McNally (1976) . . . 235, 240, 241, 242, 271

Sarson v Roberts (1895) 206

Savoury v Secretary of State for Wales (1974) 253

Sevenoaks District Council v Emmott (1980) 126, 127

Sharpe v Manchester Metropolitan District Council (1977) 199

Sheldon v West Bromwich Corpn (1973) 211

Shelley v LCC (1949) 86

Silbers v Southwark London Borough Council (1978) 314

Simmons v Pizzey (1979) . . 313, 320

Sleafer v Lambeth Metropolitan Borough Council (1960) . . . 206

Smith v Cardiff Corpn (1954) . . 118

PAGE

Smith v Cardiff Corpn (No. 2) (1955) 118

Smith v East Elloe RDC (1956) . . 258

Smith v Marrable (1843) . . 206, 211

Southwark London Borough Council v Williams (1971) 167

Sovmots Investments Ltd v Secretary of State for the Environment (1979) 43, 44

Sparham-Souter v Town and Country Developments (Essex) Ltd (1976) . 205

Springett v Harold (1954) 235

Stidworthy and Stidworthy v Brixham UDC (1935) 226

Summerfield v Hampstead Borough Council (1957) 117

Summers v Salford Corpn (1943) . 222

Surplice v Farnsworth (1884) . . 207

Sutherland v CR Maton & Son Ltd (1976) 198

Talisman Properties Ltd v Hackney London Borough Council (1978) . 233

Taylor v Liverpool Corpn (1939) . 198, 204

Thornton v Kirklees Metropolitan Borough Council (1979) . 191, 192

Tickner v Mole Valley District Council (1980) 179

Travers v Gloucester Corpn (1947) . 197

Tusting v Kensington and Chelsea Royal Borough (1974) 244

Uttoxeter Urban District Council v Clarke (1952) 40, 41

Victoria Square Property Co Ltd v Southwark London Borough Council (1978) 228, 229

Wahiwala v Secretary of State for the Environment (1977) 254

Warren v Keen (1954) . . . 216, 217

Watson v Minister of Local Government and Planning (1951) . . . 35

PAGE

White v St. Marylebone Borough
  Council (1915) 252
Williams v Wellingborough Borough
  Council (1975) 156
Wilson v Finch-Hatton (1877) . . 206
Wolkind v Ali (1975) 312
Wyness v Poole District Council
  (1980) 181

PAGE

Youngs v Thanet District Council
  (1980) 177, 178, 180

Zaitzeff v Olmi (1952) 330
Zbytniewski v Broughton (1956) . . 333

Commencement Table

The Housing Act 1980

The following provisions came into force on the day the Act was passed.

8 August 1980	Sections 90 to 105 (Powers to dispose of land and housing subsidies)
"	Section 108 (Disposal of houses after improvement)
"	Sections 112 and 113 (Vesting of mortgaged property by local authorities)
"	Sections 134 and 135 (Working Balances in Housing Revenue Accounts and creation of Housing Repairs Accounts)
"	Section 137 (Avoidance of certain unauthorised disposals)
"	Section 140 (Exclusion of shared ownership schemes from Leasehold Reform Act 1967)
"	Sections 150, 151, 152(2), 153, 154 and 155 (Interpretation, commencement, extent and other supplemental provisions)

Under section 153 of the Housing Act 1980, Chapter I, Part I of the Act came into force eight weeks after the date on which the legislation was passed, that is 3 October 1980. Chapter II was also in force on that date. The following provisions (those relevant to municipal housing powers) came into force on the date shown. (All outstanding provisions were expected to be in force by April 1981.)

3 October 1980	Part III (Tenants' repairs and improvements)
"	Part IV (Jurisdiction and procedure)
"	Section 145 and Schedule 23 (Revised penalties for offences in connection with houses in multiple-occupation)

3 October 1980	Section 146 (Overcrowding in a house in multiple-occupation)
"	Section 152(1) (Certain amendments and repeals)
27 October 1980	Section 107 and most of Schedule 12 (Amendments to Part VII of the Housing Act 1974 dealing with grants payable by local authorities towards the cost of works for the improvement and repair of dwellings and houses in multiple-occupation)
"	Section 147 and Schedule 24 (Local authority powers in respect of the provision of means of escape from fire in houses in multiple-occupation, and to replace section 16 of the Housing Act 1961 and section 60 of the Housing Act 1969)
"	Section 152(1) and (3) (Certain specified appeals and amendments)
11 November 1980	Section 115 (Enables elderly persons obtaining loans on the security of their homes in order to purchase annuities to obtain subsidies on the interest payable under the Housing Subsidies Act 1967)
28 November 1980	Section 149 (Extended power for local authorities to require the repair of houses in such condition as to interfere materially with the personal comfort of occupying tenants)
"	Section 152(1) and (3) (Certain specified repeals and amendments)
15 December 1980	Section 106 and consequential provisions of Schedule 12 (Enabling certain tenants with security of tenure to apply for grants under Part VII of the Housing Act 1974 in respect of house improvement and repairs)
"	Section 107 and the remaining paragraphs of Schedule 12 (Enabling the Secretary of State to prescribe 'appropriate percentages' for grants under Part VII of the Housing Act 1974, and to amend circumstances in which repairs grants are available)

15 December 1980   Section 109 and Schedule 13 (Amending the Housing Acts 1969 and 1974 with regard to general improvement areas, housing action areas and priority neighbourhoods)
Section 152(1) and (3) (Certain repeals and amendments)

The Local Government, Planning and Land Act 1980

Part VIII (Capital Expenditure of Local Authorities) is to be brought into force by an appointed day order made in the form of a statutory instrument.

The Local Government, Planning and Land Act 1980 (Commencement No. 2) Order 1980 S.I. No. 1893 brought into force sections 72(1) and (2), 73 and 74 enabling the Secretary of State to make or withdraw specifications of amounts of prescribed expenditure, to give directions of amounts of prescribed expenditure, or to give directions for the year commencing 1 April 1981 and subsequent years. These came into force on 11 December 1980. Sections 71, 75(5), 76, 84 and Schedule 12 also came into force on 11 December 1980. The remainder of Part VIII comes into force on 1 April 1981.

Part X (Land Held by Public Bodies) came into force with the passing of the Act, but its implementation with respect to individual authorities depends on orders made by the Secretary of State. The Local Government, Planning and Land Act 1980 (Commencement No. 1) Order 1980 S.I. No. 1871 brought Part X of the Act into force in the following district and London borough councils on 31 December 1980.

Birmingham	Newcastle-under-Lyme
Bradford	Newcastle upon Tyne
Bristol	Preston
Coventry	Salford
Dudley	Sefton
Ealing	Stockport
Gateshead	Stoke
Leeds	Trafford
Liverpool	Wandsworth
Manchester	Wirral
Middlesbrough	

Section 104 (Assessment of Development Land) came into force on the passing of the Act.

Part XVI (Urban Development) came into force on the passing of the Act, but the creation of urban development areas and corporations depends on orders being made by the Secretary of State. The London Docklands Development Corporation (Area and Constitution) Order 1980 and the Merseyside Development Corporation (Area and Constitution) Order 1980 were laid before Parliament on 27 November 1980 to come into operation in 1981 one day after being approved by Parliament.

Part XVII (Enterprise Zones) came into force on the passing of the Act but the designation of individual zones depends on the preparation and approval of schemes by the appropriate authorities.

Introduction

The purpose of this introduction is to familiarise the reader with the content of the book, to say what it is about and also what it does not cover. As this is a 'law' book it cannot deal in great detail with the history, economics and philosophy of housing as an aspect of social policy.

Nevertheless as housing law cannot be studied in a traditional 'black letter' fashion but can only be understood in its wider social, political and economic context some initial mention must be made of the policy issues and debates that have done so much to form and, some would say, *deform* the law. These wider policy issues will be discussed in some detail subsequently in this Introduction. The *economics* of council housing will not be dealt with in great detail as the present author is neither an accountant nor an economist. The use of central government subsidies and loan sanction powers as means of *control* over local authorities will be discussed, and there is a later chapter on rent for municipal housing, but beyond that I have not thought it safe to go. Likewise there is a geographical limitation on the ambit of the book in that it relates to municipal housing functions in England and Wales. Scotland and Northern Ireland have their own housing systems and their own housing problems which are better dealt with by those having first-hand experience of local situations.

As the title states this is a book about the rôle local authorities play in relation to housing. Accordingly this work will *not* deal with the private rented sector, nor, in general, with the law relating to the private owner-occupier, nor with the building societies, except in so far as their operations directly concern and involve local authorities. Neither will this book concern itself with the functions of housing associations, which is something on which a brief word of explanation must be given. First, a volume of this size cannot hope to do full justice to its subject matter if it spreads its field of discussion and inquiry too far: the housing association movement could not have been included without making the book either superficial, if kept to a manageable length, or unwieldy if proper coverage had been accorded to housing associations. Second, it is arguable that housing associations with all their diversity require

1

separate treatment in a book directed solely to their own development and current operations. Finally it is the present author's belief that the housing association movement does not have a sufficiently close connection with municipal housing law to be included in this book. Many local authorities, it is true, co-operate with housing associations by making financial and technical assistance available, and in return often refer applicants for housing to such bodies. However, housing associations have their own history and governing structures and must really be regarded as a 'third force' with regard to rented housing filling the area between the private landlord and the public rented sectors.

The concern of this book then is with the powers and duties of public authorities with regard to housing. These will be considered generally under two main headings: first, the functions of local authorities as *providers* of homes and the relationships between them and the persons who look to them for accommodation, and second, the task that has been committed to local authorities to oversee housing repair and public health standards, not just in relation to their own properties but also with regard to owner-occupied and privately rented dwellings. This division is mirrored in the structure of the work which consists of two parts. The first deals with the housing provision powers of local authorities, their general rôle as landlords, and their responsibilities with regard to the homeless. The second part deals with local authority responsibilities to enforce housing and public health standards with regard to sub-standard properties, though I have been somewhat pragmatic and included in this part local authority repairing obligations arising out of their capacity as landlords. This second section of the book also includes a chapter on the increasingly important part being played by the Commission for Local Administration in England (the 'local ombudsman'). I think it entirely proper that a book on the powers and duties of local authorities should conclude with a discussion of a most important part of the machinery set up to govern the governors.

Those governors are presently one of the two great sources of accommodation in this country. At the end of the First World War about 90 per cent of the housing stock was privately rented, and nearly all the rest was owner-occupied, with very little local authority housing. In 1977 'Housing Policy: a Consultative Document', Cmnd. 6851, revealed that well over 50 per cent of all houses were owner-occupied, some 30 per cent or more were in the public sector and only 15 per cent were privately rented. The 1980 figures from the Government Statistical Service showed that in 1979, the last year for which figures are currently available, 55 per cent of dwellings were owner-occupied, 32 per cent were rented in the public sector, leaving a seemingly inexorably shrinking private rented sector of 13 per cent. Within the public sector local authorities are the main providers of housing. In addition to their present tenants it has been estimated that there are over one million other households registered on their housing waiting lists. (See *Roof*, October 1976, p. 135.) The 1969 Report of the Central Housing Advisory Committee on Council Housing Purposes Procedures and Priorities (The Cullingworth Report, HMSO 1969) stated that each year local authorities allocated about 350,000 houses, over 200,000 to households living in the private sector and about 145,000 to council tenants transferring to different houses. The vast importance of local authorities simply as providers of accommodation can thus be easily appreciated.

The law as the child of policy

The law relating to the provision of this municipal accommodation, and also to the other housing functions of local authorities, is the child of housing policy, and also housing politics. It is sadly a truism that housing has become a political football in this country, though, speaking of analogies, the present author prefers the symbolism of a clock whose pendulum has come to describe an ever increasing arc with the passage of time and the widening divergence of views between the major political parties. In the years since the end of the Second World War the Conservative Party has come increasingly to stand for owner-occupation as the dominant housing tenure and the philosophy of the 'property owning democracy'. There are also a number of Conservatives who would like to see a revival in the fortunes of the private landlord. This preference for a mixture of private renting and for increasing owner occupation, if necessary by the widespread sale of municipal housing, tends to lessen the housing rôle of local authorities and even to reduce it to what is essentially a welfare service designed to meet the needs of those who cannot afford to be owner-occupiers. The traditional stance of the Labour Party has been to see municipal housing as having a wider social rôle to play. Traditional Labour policy, especially in the post-war years of the Atlee Government, has seen council housing as being for all who want it and not just for one particular social class, a policy embodied in the Housing Act 1949. The Labour Party has also tended to favour municipalisation of houses, especially at the expense of the private landlord.

The political issues surrounding housing have been made more complex by the fact that both major parties while in power have tended to veer between dogmatism and pragmatism on housing issues. Pragmatism has been particularly evident under Labour administrations, especially as they have tended to be dominated by the right wing of the Labour Party which has come to accept the Conservative view of owner-occupation as the normal and natural form of land tenure to the exclusion of all others. Indeed there are some commentators who would argue that a Labour administration in this country has yet to pursue a truly left-wing socialist housing policy: see Stephen Merrett, *State Housing in Britain* Chap. 11. However, leaving aside the rights and wrongs of left versus right housing policies, an even more serious allegation can be made against governments of all political colours, and that is the continual use of the housing system as an economic regulator and a prime target for public spending cuts, disrupting patterns of investment and development. See Chris Holmes, 'Housing Expenditure: How It Breaks Down', and Chris Trinder, 'Housing Expenditure: Who Benefits Most', *Roof*, May 1976, pp. 72 – 76 and 81 – 84 respectively.

The wider debate on housing

The debate on housing has not been confined to the political parties. Over the past few years we have lived through a remarkable period in which the basic philosophy of municipal housing law, policy and practice has come under increasing scrutiny and attack. The debates have been drawn from a wide spectrum of political opinion and from an equally wide range of academic and vocational disciplines. The debate has not just been confined to municipal housing and has ranged across housing policy generally, but it has been at its most fierce in relation to council housing.

The argument on tenure

There has been a fear that there could be a growth of class distinction based on the tenurial difference between owner-occupiers and council tenants. As B.T. Robson said in *Urban Social Areas* at p. 41: '. . . That one is dealing with virtually separate sub-markets can be seen in the flows of households between each of the tenure types . . . . The two categories of owner-occupiers and council renters provide distinct end-points to the various moves between tenure types: flow moves into them, but once a household lives in either type it rarely moves out . . . . These tenure categories play an important rôle in structuring social areas within towns and also in allocating resources within society'. Of course it may be possible to over-emphasise the divisive nature of tenurial differences. Official sources tend to discount such fears, and one study has said: 'There have been fears expressed that, as the private rented sector diminishes in size, English housing will become "polarised" between the owner-occupied and local authority sectors. The data presented in this article shows little evidence of any serious accentuation of differences between the two growing sectors. The similarities between households in these sectors are more marked than the differences,' see 'Housing Tenure in England and Wales: the present situation and recent trends' in *Social Trends 1979* (HMSO) pp. 10 – 19.

Of course official utterances are not invariably to be regarded as unanswerable. The well paid council house tenant may be as well-off and comfortable as his owner-occupier neighbour, and there may be little to choose between their homes and standards of living. But that ignores the less well-off tenant, the tenant who lives on a less desirable estate, or in a poorer old house, or in an unpopular tower block. It has been pointed out by more than one authority that it is *relative* deprivation that is the cause of many current problems. As D.V. Donnison said in *The Government of Housing* (Penguin, 1967) p. 350: 'The problem arises from the mixture of squalor and affluence, the persistence of bad housing conditions within a generally improving situation, and the degrading human conflicts fostered by these contrasts'.

There is evidence that we are not moving towards a situation where decent accommodation will be *reasonably* cheaply available for all; the present law relating to the provision of housing by local authorities may not be helping, and furthermore it *may* be perpetuating divisions in our society which could in the future prove serious.

The serfs or citizens issue

There came, a few years ago, a number of calls to *give* council tenants their houses, and many people became unhappy about the system of council housing. [Thus on 21 June 1975 Peter Walker called for council houses to be given to their tenants; see also *The Times*, 24 July 1975, p. 2, reporting the Conservative Selsdon Group proposals advocating the same transfer. From a different point in the political spectrum Colin Ward called for the transfer of council estates to Tenants Co-operative, Co-ownership Schemes — see *Tenants Take Over*, (Architectural Press, 1974). See also the views of Frank Field as expressed in *Do we need Council Houses?* (C.H.A.S., 1976). For a contrary view see Bernard Kilroy, 'Council Housing is Beautiful', *Roof*, May 1976, pp. 67 – 68, and also Frank Field, 'Again, I ask, do we need Council Housing?', *Roof*, July 1976, p. 101.] It is not certain that turning council tenants into 'property owning democrats' would automatically produce a housing utopia, nor is it self-evidently right to hand over to private control assets purchased and provided by public funds. Furthermore it should be noted that once one makes a man an owner-occupier one confers on him a great power, which remains substantially unaffected by legislation, and that is the power to alienate his house — at the highest price he can get! It may well be that, remembering the disastrous house price boom of 1972 – 73 and substantial increases in house prices ever since, the nation should be considering house price control for present owners, rather than increasing the number of owners by handing over council houses to their tenants. Nevertheless some fundamental re-examination of the legal and tenurial position of council housing became essential by the late 1970's. Why?

First, as we have already seen, local authorities are collectively the greatest landlords in the country. The two largest groups of housed people in this country are those living in owner-occupied property and those living in council owned property — yet the rights and liabilities of these two groups are very different. In *1962* Professor Lafitte said, 'within ten years we shall urgently need new forms of housing tenure combining the advantages, but not the drawbacks, of the owner-occupation and the council tenantry between which we are becoming increasingly divided', see 'Social Policy in a Free Society', reprinted in *Social Welfare in Modern Britain* (Ed. by Butterworth and Holman) (Fontana, 1975) p. 55. Housing associations and the Housing Corporation may go some way to providing those new forms of tenure, but we must not expect too much of them, see *Municipal and Public Services Journal*, 4 July 1975, pp. 875 – 876. I have already referred to the importance of the form of tenure in formalising and sustaining social divisions, and so if we wish to move towards a society free from divisions, and if we cannot look to housing associations to provide a real 'bridge' between owner-occupiers and council tenants, then it would seem essential to examine modifications of the law relating to council housing so as to give its occupiers a greater say in the determination of decisions relating to their homes, without necessarily handing over to them the fee simple.

Second, vis-a-vis his local authority a tenant or potential tenant is in a very weak position legally. In general terms no one has the *right* to be housed just as he wishes. The insertion of one's name on the housing list is likewise no guarantee of housing. When council housing is being allocated, or a tenant requests a transfer to another council house the broad general discretionary powers of the local authority come into play. It is, of course, well known that local authorities use a variety of schemes to help them in the exercise of this discretion, and these will be examined in greater detail in due course. But it should be a matter for public concern that there are often odd policy biases in these schemes which seem to be subject to no legal control or central governmental direction. There can be little doubt that some local authorities have graded tenants and potential tenants, and placed them in houses according to their social desirability. [The allegations come from too many sources to be ignored — see B.T. Robson, *Urban Social Areas* pp. 48 – 49 (quoting D.A. Kirkby (1971) 42 Town Planning Review 250 – 268 and J. Tucker, *Honourable Estates* (1966)); *The Shelter Report on Slum Clearance* (1975) pp. 23 – 28; R. Holman, 'Poverty:

Consensus and Alternatives', (1973) British Journal of Social Work, vol. 3, No. 4, reprinted in *Social Welfare in Modern Britain* p. 403 (see especially p. 413); Colin Ward, *Tenants Take Over* pp. 16 – 18; and Norman Lewis, 'Council Housing Allocation: Problems of Discretion and Control' in (1976) Public Administration, vol. 54, p. 147.] And of course there is a considerable body of evidence as to the discriminatory attitudes adopted in the past by some housing authorities towards coloured immigrants. Not only is this undesirable, leading as it can to a concentration of socially inadequate families and individuals in particular areas, it is a method of proceeding which bears no resemblance to allocation according to need. [See: Ernest Krausz, *Ethnic Minorities in Britain* (Paladin, 1971) Chap. 4; W.W. Daniel, *Racial Discrimination in England* (Penguin, 1968) Chap. 11; Clifford Hill, *How Colour Prejudiced is Britain?* (Panther, 1967) p. 111; Deakin, *Colour Citizenship and British Society* (Panther, 1970) Chap. 6; Lester and Bindman, *Race and Law* (Penguin, 1972); David J. Smith, *Racial Disadvantage in Britain* (Penguin, 1977) Part III; and Smith and Whalley, *Racial Minorities and Public Housing* (P.E.P., 1975).] To be fair, it must be stressed that many, if not indeed most, local authorities *now* adopt liberal and progressive administrative policies with regard to their tenants. Nevertheless, attention must be drawn to the often paternalistic and, sadly, sometimes negligent ways in which housing powers have been used. As Fred Berry has said in *Housing: The Great British Failure* p. 105: 'The council tenant in short was, and is, considered an inferior being for whom inferior and segregated housing should be provided if any is to be provided at all'. This paternalism dates back to the very beginning of public housing provision. As Enid Gauldie in *Cruel Habitations* (George Allen and Unwin, 1974) concludes at p. 310: 'by the time the idea of compulsorily subsidised housing had been realised, it was almost too late for anything but wholesale destruction of a centuries old environment, for the meanest replacement of it by the cheapest houses, the barest amenities, the bleakest layout . . . the idea that working people should in any way participate in the planning of the environment that is to be the setting for their lives is a new and to some people a startling one even in 1973. Poor Law thinking continued to affect the planning of council housing long after the Poor Law itself was dead'. A paternalist view of the exercise of legal power sometimes continues, as Colin Ward has shown in Chapter 1, 'Serfs or Citizens', of *Tenants Take Over*. The existence of this attitude was admitted at the Royal Society of Health's 1975 Conference where Mr K.J. Campbell spoke of both the polarity between owner occupancy and municipal tenancy (a polarity greater here than in any other country of which he was aware) and the fact that there is a 'deep rooted habit in British local government of thinking *for* people and governing *for* them rather than through them'. At the same conference Mr P.J. Dixon said, 'the blind acceptance of each new architectural fad . . . and *a total disregard of the views of those privileged to live in the "units of accommodation"* provided, have combined to produce some of the most unattractive, unloved and even unwanted dwellings that have ever been produced'.

Turning to maintenance the evidence mounted throughout the period under discussion that a great deal of council housing — much of it new or recent — was declining into poor condition as a result of the failure of local authorities to maintain it. In some cases the decline has been so serious as to render the premises 'prejudicial to health or a nuisance' contrary to section 92(1)(a) of the Public Health Act 1936. One must sympathise with the economic plight of local authorities, and realise the effect of government restrictions on maintenance programmes, but the sad fact remains that all over the country council owned property has declined in condition at an alarming rate, and until the recent use of section 99 of the Public Health Act 1936, there seemed little hope of legal redress for tenants. [For evidence of the widespread existence of poor conditions in modern council property see: *Coventry Council Houses: The New Slums* (Shelter, 1974); *The Report on the Sandfields Estate, Port Talbot* (Shelter Community Action Team, 1975); Colin Ward, *Tenants Take Over*, especially pp. 27 – 35 and 68 – 69; *Homes Fit for Heroes* (Shelter, 1975); *A State of Disrepair: Report of a Survey of Council Housing in Colchester* (Colchester C.P.A.G., 1976); John Darwin, 'Build Cheap Now — Pay More Later', *Roof*, May 1979, pp. 82 – 84 and John McQuillan and Nick Finnis, 'Ways of Seeing Damp', *Roof*, May 1979, pp. 85 – 89.] Even when it was established that a *criminal* sanction under the public health legislation is available to individuals against a defaulting local housing authority, the courts, as we shall see, have been wary of granting contractual remedies to tenants. It is easy to say that tenants should resort to self help, but the problem is often too large for the resources of individuals, and why, it can reasonably be asked, should they bother to do anything about the problems when they have no real degree of control over their own environment, and the local authority frequently seems remote, unwilling to listen, or even intransigent? [On the feeling of distance between local authorities and their tenants see the Shelter Report *Slum Clearance* pp. 23 – 28, see also *Coventry Council Houses: The New Slums* (Shelter, 1974) pp. 34 – 35. Even where a local authority has been prepared to give financial assistance to a tenant wishing to improve his home, the scale of generosity has varied vastly from place to place — see *The Times*, 16 July 1975, reporting the different attitudes of London Boroughs towards giving grants for the decoration of council housing.]

To sum up so far, for a variety of reasons the law relating to council housing became subject to numerous criticisms. First of all its tenurial basis may confirm the mythical divisions between the supposedly 'subsidised' council tenant and the 'poor mortgaged' ratepayer. [For the real facts see Berry, *Housing: The Great British Failure* pp. 108 – 109.] Second, the law subjects potential and actual council tenants to the discretionary selection and allocation powers of the local authority which are subject to little legal control. Third, the law subjects the council tenant to the great managerial powers of his local authority with, in the past, few opportunities for the redress of grievances. Fourth, despite the official central government lip service given to the notion of public participation, council tenants have been given very little say in the control and management of their homes and their immediate environment. Fifth, local housing authorities have been subject to very little central control in relation to these great discretionary powers of selection, allocation and management. *Housing Policy,* Cmnd. 6851, the consultative paper on future developments in housing, accepted that there would have to be changes in both law and practice, and the then government accepted the need for a 'tenants' charter'.

The Housing Act 1980

It was against this background of increasing debate and dissatisfaction that the Housing Act 1980 emerged. The success of this new law of housing will depend very much on how effective it is in meeting the criticisms mentioned above. However, it is the present writer's belief that the 1980 Act only deals with some of these problems. The provisions of Part I, Chapter II of the legislation, the 'tenants' charter', confer a number of new and important rights on individual municipal tenants, but do not go nearly as far as many critics would have wished in relation to tenant involvement and participation in housing management. With regard to selection and allocation procedures the new law makes no radical changes.

The truly wide reaching alterations are those contained in Part I, Chapter I, the 'right to buy' provisions. The Conservative Government have committed themselves to a major new departure in both legal and policy terms by introducing a form of 'compulsory purchase in reverse'. This forced sale of local authority assets is a most controversial issue and, whether one agrees with it or not, it has to be seen as a piece of dogmatic and overtly politically motivated legislation. It is most odd that the years of debate about the tenurial basis of municipal housing should have produced a sadly simplistic governmental response which will not lead to the development of the longed-for new land tenures, but rather will serve only to strengthen the ranks of the dominant land-holding group within society, i.e. the owner-occupiers. The 1980 Housing Act enshrines the current housing orthodoxy that owner-occupation is self-evidently good and desirable for as many as can afford it, coupled with the government's determination to effect a massive transfer of wealth from the public to the private sector. It seems somewhat sad that yet another opportunity has been missed for attempting at least a degree of tenurial experimentation. Tenant co-operatives, equity-sharing schemes, co-ownership and condominiums (as on the American pattern) all need legislation before their usefulness can be tried out in this country, yet the 1980 Act ignores them in favour of the continued prescription of doses of owner-occupation.

The danger is that only the most pleasant and socially desirable council houses will be purchased under the terms of the new law, leaving local authorities with less attractive properties with which to meet the needs of those who cannot, or do not wish to, become owner-occupiers. This can only lead to an increase in that undesirable social polarisation according to housing tenure referred to earlier. It is, moreover, in less desirable council houses, the older properties, those situated on socially stigmatised estates, and in the tower blocks where the largest number of repair problems and design and construction defects are likely to occur.

It is hard to escape the conclusion that the provisions of the Housing Act 1980 are, with some exceptions, *exactly the wrong response* to the mounting criticisms of housing law and practice heard over the preceeding years.

The erosion of local housing autonomy

It has been argued above that one of the central issues in the debate on the law and practice of municipal housing has been that of the control of local discretion, and that there has been considerable dissatisfaction with the lack of accountability of local authorities with regard to this issue. In one sense this debate remains current in that, despite the introduction of the tenants' charter, the individual is still, on the whole, in a weak position vis-à-vis the discretionary powers of his local authority. But when attention is turned to the relationship between central and local government a very different picture emerges. The last few years have seen the definite, if gradual, erosion of local autonomy in housing matters and its replacement by an ever increasing degree of control. This process has been carried on by the Act of 1980 despite its cosmetic removal of certain minor controls. It is arguable that the forced sale of council houses is the greatest imposition of central policy on local discretion to date.

The Housing Finance Act 1972, which was an attempt to introduce new 'fair' rents for council houses everywhere, was undoubtedly a major inroad into local discretion. Though this legislation was largely repealed by the Housing Rents and Subsidies Act 1975, those provisions relating to rent rebates were left in force, and so there remains a mandatory requirement for all local authorities to operate a rent rebate scheme for their tenants. Some people also view the Housing (Homeless Persons) Act 1977 as a further erosion of local autonomy in that it places a statutory duty on local authorities to provide accommodation for certain groups of homeless persons. Another 'legal' reduction in local discretion was introduced by section 105 of the Housing Act 1974 which provided that local authorities should not incur expenditure in connection with the provision of dwellings by conversion or the carrying out of improvements and associated repairs without the approval of the Secretary of State. The object of this provision was to introduce a strategic system of control whereby the Secretary of State could direct local investment *away* from the improvement of existing council houses and *towards* the conversion and improvement of acquired properties.

These reductions in the amount of discretion enjoyed by local authorities are, however, of comparatively little importance when contrasted with central requirements as to municipal house building standards and control over housing finance.

Capital for local authority house building

Local authorities require loan sanction from the Secretary of State before raising money for housing purposes. The detailed rules on borrowing generally are now found in Schedule 13 to the Local Government Act 1972. Sections 136 and 137 of the Housing Act 1957 (which must be read subject to the terms of the above Schedule) are also relevant in this context. Section 136 grants a general power to local authorities to borrow for the purposes of Part II of the 1957 Act, in so far as it relates to the execution of repairs and works by them, and also with regard to Part III (clearance and re-development). Local authorities also have power to borrow for the purposes of Part V of the 1957 Act, but where a local authority propose to execute such purposes outside their own area their borrowing is made subject, by section 137, to ministerial approval.

Section 138 of the Act of 1957 allows local authorities to exercise their borrowing powers by means of an issue of local housing bonds, which, in accordance with Schedule 8 to the Act, must be secured upon all the rates, property and revenue of the issuing authority, and must be issued for periods of not less than five years. However, such bonds may not be issued without ministerial consent. In 1977 bonds accounted for 27.7 per cent of the capital debt of local authorities in Great Britain. The Ministry of Housing and Local Government Circular No. 19/59 gives a general consent to the issuing of local housing bonds.

Approval for loan finance may be withheld or given subject to restrictions whenever central government feels it necessary to reduce or contain public spending. Indeed, recently, control over local authority borrowing has become an important part of the government's general economic managerial rôle.

The vast majority of money used in the construction of council housing is in fact borrowed, and loan finance rather than money raised from taxation is an enduring feature of our municipal housing system. The loans themselves come from many sources. On the open money market finance is raised by mortgage loans, stock, local bonds, negotiable bonds and temporary loans. Some money is obtained internally from superannuation funds and from revenue balances temporarily used for capital purposes. The rest comes from the Public Work Loans Board which in 1977 supplied 37.4 per cent of capital finance for housing.

The Public Works Loans Board derives its powers from the Public Works Loans Act 1875 and the National Loans Act 1968. Nearly all its lending is to local authorities requiring money for purposes sanctioned by central departments. The Board's funds are derived from the National Loans Fund and the rates of interest are fixed by the Treasury. At one time local authorities were required to raise all their loan finance through the Board but this requirement ended in 1953, since when its importance as a source of loan finance has declined.

For our present purposes, however, the important point to make is that new council house construction is dependent on finance being raised, for which central loan sanction will be required, and, as has been said above, central control over local borrowing has become an important feature of the economic policy of successive governments.

Because of the amount of time taken up in negotiating loan sanction for individual projects, and to introduce more freedom for local authorities, new procedures were introduced in 1971 (and see Department of the Environment Circular No. 66/76). These divided all local authority expenditure into two major categories, 'key sector schemes' and 'locally determined schemes'. For the latter an allocation is made annually within which authorities have freedom to borrow and spend in so far as the law does not impose other restrictions. Within the key sector loan sanction is still required for individual projects. The key sector covers most of the major capital expenditure. For instance in 1978/79, *before the recent public spending cuts*, the key sector in housing accounted for £1,921.4 million, while the locally determined sector accounted for only £27 million. Thus municipal capital spending on housing has continued overwhelmingly to require project by project approval before loan sanction has been forthcoming. In order to obtain such sanction authorities have had to comply with central standards and requirements.

During the 1970's it became apparent that these established methods of control were by themselves insufficient to cope with the problems of capital outlay. *Housing Policy*, Cmnd. 6851 proposed a new system of planning capital expenditure the main element of which was to be: 'A reasoned capital budget covering the local authority's own capital spending plans — related to its broad housing strategy — for the coming four years'. It was argued that this new system would allow local authorities greater flexibility to alter their spending both within financial years and also from one year to another, while at the same time allowing central government greater freedom to forecast capital needs and to relate these to total public spending.

Department of the Environment Circular No. 18/77 looked forward to the introduction of Housing Investment Programmes (HIPs) which would be subject to loan sanction approved by the Secretary of State. The same circular made virtually all housing work fall within the key sector for capital sanction purposes and also instructed local authorities to adhere to the overall cash limits laid down in approvals. However, within the total amount of capital sanctioned for expenditure various block allocations were introduced within which local authorities were allowed an element of local flexibility by resort to virement (i.e. the power to switch a proportion of expenditure between capital projects) and tolerance (i.e. the power to anticipate expenditure up to a predetermined limit). This system continued in operation for some years, but in November 1979 the Secretary of State and the Housing Consultative Council agreed a new system of *single* block allocations within which greater freedom of manouevre would be allowed to local authorities. The new block allocation will cover *all* local authority capital spending, not just housing, and will allow for the switching of funds between capital projects. It will therefore be the case that housing may be in competition for capital with other local services.

Department of the Environment Circular No. 63/77 introduced HIPs on which central decisions on capital allocations were to be based. From 1978 – 79 onwards HIPs were designed, 'to enable local authorities to present co-ordinated analyses of housing conditions in their area and to formulate coherent policies and programmes of capital spending on public housing. Within the framework of national policies and resources available, this system will enable local authorities to produce solutions that accord most closely to their assessment of local need'. The constituent elements of a HIP are:

1) a brief narrative description of the general housing strategy and situation of the given authority;

2) a fuller numerical statement about levels of population, households and the housing stock;

3) a financial statement about past expenditure and proposals for the ensuing four years.

To these, authorities are invited to add their proposals for capital spending divided into the following heads:

1) new house building, including the acquisition of land under Part V of the Housing Act 1957;

2) slum clearance and acquisition of land under Part III of the 1957 Act;

3) improvement programmes for municipally owned dwellings;

4) acquisition of newly built and existing dwellings for continued housing use;

5) private sector improvement grants;

6) gross lending to private citizens for house purchase and improvement; and

7) gross lending to housing associations.

Circular 63/77 counselled against over ambitious housing programmes and urged local authorities to operate in a spirit of financial realism. Moreover it stated that local authorities should be wary of committing themselves to expenditure in excess of their current commitments, and hinted darkly at the imposition of cash limits on those authorities who wished to increase their housing expenditure. It is quite clear that HIPs have been and are subjected to careful scrutiny in order to assess their public expenditure implications. Strict control over local capital spending has been a feature of central policy and most proposals for capital spending have required individual project approval, particularly those within heads 1 to 4 above.

The new system of capital expenditure control

Part VIII of the Local Government, Planning and Land Act 1980 goes much further than the statements contained in circulars, and introduces legal limits on the capital *expenditure* powers of local authorities. For the future not just the power of local authorities to borrow will be controlled — the power to spend what has been borrowed will be controlled. Housing authorities fall within the scope of this new legislation under section 71 and Schedule 12. As from a date to be specified by the Secretary of State, the 'appropriate minister' (i.e. the Secretary of State) will be under a duty, under section 72 of the Act, to specify for each relevant authority (that is district councils and London Boroughs) an amount of prescribed expenditure for the year, such specification to be given before the year begins (section 76). Thereafter an authority may make in that year payments in respect of prescribed expenditure not exceeding the sum of:

1) the ministerially specified amount referred to above; plus

2) a sum equal to 10 per cent of that sum, or such other percentage as is centrally specified; plus

3) any amount of prescribed expenditure specified for the year by the Secretary of State in addition to the sum specified in (1) above;

4) an amount for the year equal to the authority's net capital receipts, or to such proportion of them as may be centrally specified;

5) an amount for the year equal to the authority's profits from a trading undertaking.

This provision places a 'ceiling' on expenditure beyond which local authorities may not go.

The definition of 'net capital receipts' is contained in section 75 of the Act. In general such receipts are:

1) any sums received by an authority before or after the commencement date in respect of disposals of land, vehicles, vessels, plant and machinery, etc.;

2) sums received by way of repayment of grants and advances of a capital nature, for example a mortgage repayment;

3) sums received by way of payment for a leasehold interest in, or licence to occupy land.

Under section 75(5) of the Local Government, Planning and Land Act 1980, however, regulations may be made:

1) to vary the amounts capable of being treated as 'net capital receipts' according to the class of assets disposed of;

2) to state that any sum received before a specified date shall not be treated as received, and that sums spent before a specified date shall not be treated as spent;

3) to vary the classes of assets counted as giving rise to capital receipts on disposals; and

4) to treat any sum as a capital asset even though it falls outside the definition in section 75(1).

The effect of this new Act will be to give central government the power to exercise a continuing year to year control over what a local authority will be able to spend by way of capital. The power to make supplementary capital allocation under section 72(3)(c) and that of making regulations under section 75(5) of the new local government legislation will enable central government to make considerable modifications in the capital spending of local authorities. Some such modifications were outlined by Mr John Stanley, the Minister of State for Housing, on 24 April 1980 in a speech to the Institute of Housing. Thus from 1 April 1981 it is proposed that individual local authorities will be able to increase their new single block allocation for capital spending for *all* services by amounts equivalent to the capital receipts which they receive in the course of the year.

There will be special arrangement for 'housing capital receipts' which are certain *cash* sums that accrue to a local authority from the disposal of certain assets. It is proposed that:

1) Where a local authority are in receipt of money representing the sale price of a dwelling or a share of the equity therein, and where the dwelling was before sale a Housing Revenue Account dwelling available for letting, they shall be able to augment their total capital allocation by 50 per cent of those receipts;

2) a similar rule will apply to repayments of *principal* sums left outstanding by way of mortgage on such dwellings;

3) a similar rule will apply to repayments of grants and advances of a capital nature with regard to house purchase or improvement in the private sector.

Additional expenditure under a HIP allocation increased by applying capital receipts in the way described will be regarded admissible for subsidy on the same basis as all other HIP expenditure.

An example of increased housing capital receipts

The proposals for the use of housing capital receipts mean that from 1981/82 each local authority will be able to increase their housing capital expenditure by the equivalent of 50 per cent of the cash receipts from council house sales in that year plus 50 per cent of any accumulated unspent receipts in hand on 1 April 1981. The definition of housing capital receipts given above means that the more council house sales are financed other than by local authority mortgages (in other words by personal savings or by private sector mortgages) the greater will be the financial benefit to the local authority. Under the new single block HIP it will be up to local authorities to decide to what use to put their housing capital receipts. They could be used to build, for example, new elderly persons' wardens schemes. They could be used to provide mortgage loans to priority buyers in the private sector. They could be used to finance new housing association projects.

The following is an example of how an authority might benefit in 1981/82 from their capital receipts from council house sales in 1980/81. Assume an authority sell 200 houses in 1980/81 at an average price after discount of £9,000 and all sales are completed in the year; assume further that on average 30 per cent of the purchases are privately financed by personal savings and private sector mortgages. This would give the local authority capital receipts of £540,000 in 1980/81. If by 1 April 1981 these receipts remained 'unspent', as stated earlier, the authority would be entitled to spend £270,000 in addition to their HIP allocation for 1981/82.

However, it will be noted that the sums involved are, by the standards of public expenditure, very small indeed. The increase in the amount of local discretion contained in these new administrative arrangements on capital control cannot be said to be great, and some might call it a mere sop to offended local feelings.

Where an authority exceed their capital expenditure limit in any given year by more than the permitted 10 per cent the 'penalty' will be in general a reduction in the amount of prescribed expenditure for the next year equal to their excess spending.

Further ministerial powers to control capital spending are to be found in section 73 of the 1980 Act. In relation to projects of national or regional importance the Secretary of State may specify that:

1) a specified amount of the aggregate prescribed expenditure under section 72 may only be spent on such a project; or

2) that no part of the aggregate may be spent on a specified project.

Where the Secretary of State comes to the opinion that a local authority have failed, or are likely to fail, to keep within the boundaries of permitted expenditure, he may use his powers under section 78 of the Act to direct that the authority shall not:

(a) make any payment in respect of prescribed expenditure, if that payment, added to the other payments on prescribed expenditure, would exceed that authority's capital expenditure limit for that year;

(b) enter into any contract for the carrying out of, or undertake, any construction or maintenance work (i.e. any building or engineering work in the construction, improvement, maintenance or repair of buildings and other structures) the cost of which would exceed an amount specified by the Secretary of State; and

(c) enter into any contract under which they would incur liability to pay a sum or sums, the amount of which exceeds the amount specified in the direction.

Section 79 of the Act states that it shall not be, in general, beyond the powers of an authority to make a payment or enter into a contract leading to their exceeding their prescribed capital expenditure limit. But section 79(2) states that such a contract or payment will be ultra vires if made in contravention of a direction under sections 73 and 78. However, to protect other contracting parties, section 79(3) declares that a transaction between a local authority and another person is not void merely because it contravenes such a direction. Neither is such a person required to inquire before entering into a contract with a local authority whether they have been made subject to such a direction.

The capital expenditure of the Greater London Council is also made subject to new central controls which may be found in Schedule 13 to the Local Government, Planning and Land Act 1980.

It can be argued that the new law represents a greater degree of freedom and control for local authorities to determine their own priorities *within overall capital expenditure ceilings*. But the fact remains that these ceilings are set by central government. In fact the new system of control ensures that local authorities will rarely be able to spend their own money on capital projects without overall central supervision.

For the future a HIP allocation will be only one component in an authority's single block capital expenditure allocation (although, as we have seen, authorities may increase such allocations by the amount of their capital receipts) and they may use on housing whatever proportion of their allocation they think fit. A block borrowing approval — i.e. permission to incur debt will — accompany the allocation. However, capital projects involving municipalisation of houses or the acquisition of land for housing development will continue to need special approval.

Other controls over local authority house building

The Parker Morris standards

In addition to the above financial hurdles, local authorities have been required to conform with the Parker Morris Committee house building standards. These were made a pre-condition for loan sanctions and subsidisation under the Housing Acts for all public sector housing built after 1968 by the Ministry of Housing and Local Government Circular

No. 36/67, *Housing Standards, Costs and Subsidies*. However, at the same time the circular also made use of a 'housing cost yardstick' which stated that subsidies would not be paid on design schemes exceeding certain centrally laid down norms on building costs. As Stephen Merrett points out in *State Housing in Britain* p. 105: 'the new design regime was a combination of mandatory minima in terms of space and heating [The Parker Morris standards] and mandatory maxima in terms of permitted cost [the Housing Cost Yardstick]. The local authority architect was handed his circular and thrust out onto the high wire'. The sad result is that the Parker Morris standards, which were regarded by their author as a minimum requirement which should be gradually exceeded in practice, have tended to become a maximum standard reflecting both the increased cost of housebuilding and also the restrictive effect of the Housing Cost Yardstick.

It would certainly seem that the imposition of the Parker Morris standards led to a *decrease* in local authority housebuilding as there has been less money available and this has had to be used to build fewer but higher quality houses. In *Housing and Public Policy* p. 75, Stewart Lansley states: 'There is the question of whether to go for quality or quantity. The higher the standard of new housing, the fewer households can be rehoused; the better the quality of rehabilitation, the fewer houses can be improved. Opting for quality means larger benefits for a smaller number. In the past 20 years, policy makers seem to have gone for quality, at least in the public sector. By way of example, it has been estimated that the provision of houses to Parker Morris standards resulted in a loss of over 94,000 houses over the period 1964 to 1969, or about 10 per cent of the total number of local authority dwellings built in this period. While the adoption of high standards means a lower rate of obsolescence, it may be one reason why we continue to suffer from a housing shortage'.

From time to time there were statements from central government indicating consideration of a general departure from the Parker Morris standards, for example at p. 78 of *Housing Policy*, Cmnd. 6851. Finally on 22 January 1980 the Secretary of State announced that, with effect from 1 April 1981, local authorities would no longer be required to conform with either the Parker Morris standards or the Housing Cost Yardstick. The reasoning behind this change of policy is that the *strategic* controls over capital expenditure outlined above, and those over housing subsidies to be examined shortly, enable central government to concentrate on the overall control of the economic implications of municipal housing rather than local detailed construction issues which it is now thought best to leave to individual authorities.

In one sense the past effectiveness of the Parker Morris standards and the Housing Cost Yardstick in placing constraints on the freedom of local authorities was due to the fact that they existed behind the veil of the housing and local government legislation. But their real significance was that they represented central government's 'power of the purse'. If local authorities were not prepared to comply with the centrally adopted house building norms then the Minister could use his power given under legislation to starve them of finance. But as we have seen, and shall see, other more effective financial controls are now available. The economic power of government is a most effective governing instrument; a power that is particularly potent with regard to subsidies.

The control of recurrent housing expenditure: the role of housing subsidies

Housing Subsidies were introduced by the Housing, Town Planning &c. Act 1919 and have remained an essential feature of public housing provision ever since, though the form and nature of those subsidies has varied greatly with the years. Subsidies are just as important to the continuing health of the municipal housing stock as loan capital is to its creation. This can be readily understood when the composition of local authority current housing expenditure is examined. A local authority's housing operations, as brought to account in the 'Housing Revenue Account', have as their income rents and subsidies, and as their expenditure interest on loans, and the costs of repair, maintenance and management. As we have seen above the money for actually *building* houses is capital expenditure and so forms no part of the housing revenue account. However, the *interest* payable on such borrowed capital forms a large part of a local authority's recurrent expenditure and so of the need for subsidisation.

Before 1967 subsidies were given as fixed annual payments over a number of years for each completed house, irrespective of its cost. The amount payable were simply varied by legislation, though the Housing Act 1961 did introduce some allowance for variations between local authorities with extra subsidies for those who faced especially high housing costs. The Housing Subsidies Act 1967 introduced a new system of subsidies to cover not only the special costs associated with building on expensive sites or in areas of subsidence, but also to provide local authorities with a 'cushion' against high interest rates by having the subsidies related to the interest rates actually payable. In return for these more generous subsidies the government introduced controls to which reference has been made above; the Parker Morris standards and the Housing Cost Yardstick.

The new subsidy system proved extremely complex to operate, sometimes wasteful in its operation and inequitable in its distribution. The 1970 Conservative Government introduced another subsidy system in the Housing Finance Act 1972. Local authorities were placed under an obligation to pay rent rebates to their more needy tenants, and were expected, in the first instance, to find that money from their own resources. Subsidies were payable to cover rent allowances payable to *private* sector tenants, slum clearance programmes, and in respect of rising costs to those local authorities whose expenditure was outstripping their income. These new subsidies were coupled with the introduction of 'fair' rents for council houses — and these were generally rather higher than the old 'reasonable' rents. The measure was one of the most politically controversial introduced by what was a generally contro- versial government. Another new subsidy system, designed to undo what the 1972 Act had done, was introduced by the Housing Rents and Subsidies Act 1975.

This Act was designed also to be an interim measure. It restored the power of local authorities to charge 'reasonable' rents, and on the subsidy side made the following major subsidies payable:

1) An annual lump sum representing a consolidation of the *actual* subsidies paid for 1974 − 75 under the 1972 Act;

2) a sum to meet 66 per cent of loan charges on new expenditure on house building, the acquisition of houses or land, or improvements;

3) a sum to cover 33 per cent of the extra costs incurred since 1974 on refinancing earlier borrowing; and

4) a sum to meet 75 per cent of the cost of rent rebates.

The new subsidy system

The Housing Act 1980, Part VI introduces yet another new housing subsidy system which replaces the interim system of the 1975 Act. The new system is based on deficit financing. Local authorities will be expected to balance their books with regard to housing expenditure and any shortfall will have to be borne by income from increased rents and rates. The 1980 Act also gives the Secretary of State much greater discretion than he has had before to determine subsidy levels. The heart of the system is the equation introduced by section 97 of the Act whereby the amount of subsidy payable depends upon the difference between the sum of the 'base amount' (BA) (i.e. the previous year's subsidy, if any) *plus* the 'Housing Costs Differential' (HCD) (which is a sum to be determined annually by the Secretary of State) minus the 'Local Contribution Differential' (LCD) (another sum largely to be determined by the Secretary of State). HCD will have two basic elements in actuality:

1) Debt charges on capital expenditure, a figure that will not be easily

predicted under the new single block allocation system whereby capital can be switched between projects;

2) Maintenance and management costs which will have to be computed in consultation between the Department of the Environment and the local authority associations, bearing in mind central insistence on the need for economy and the fact that maintenance and management costs inevitably vary between different parts of the country.

This figure overall will probably be determined according to the difference between what local authorities actually spent in the previous year and what, it is thought, they *should* be able to spend in the current year. Both HCD and LCD will be largely determined by consultation between central and local authorities, but it would seem that some increase in local funding from rents and/or rates will be inevitable.

Where the equation BA + HCD − LCD produces a negative figure no housing subsidy will be payable to the authority concerned for that year of account. Effectively this means that the government will determine each council's subsidy entitlement by taking what it received in the previous year, if anything, adding to that all the authority's increased housing costs, and then subtracting an amount which it is expected will be derived from rents and rates (which may have to be increased accordingly) to cover some of these increased costs.

For the first year of operation of the new subsidy system, 1981 − 82, the 'base amount' is the aggregate of:

1) the amount of subsidy payable in 1980 − 81 under section 2 of the Housing Rents and Subsidies Act 1975; plus

2) the amount, if any, of any expanding towns subsidy paid under section 4 of the 1975 Act; plus

3) any contribution made under the Housing Act 1969, ss. 17 to 19, the Housing Act 1971, ss. 1 and 2, and the Housing Act 1974, s. 79.

In 1981 − 82 this figure, when computed, will be the first element in the section 97 equation, and will be modified by the addition of the housing costs differential and the subtraction of the local contribution differential to produce the subsidy payable to any given authority. In 1982 − 83 the subsidy figure so produced will be the new base amount for the calculation of subsidy, and so on for the subsequent years. A further measure of central control over subsidies is contained in section 98(2) of the Housing Act 1980 which grants power to the Secretary of State to adjust the 'base amount' either generally or in the case of individual authorities, if he is of the opinion that the circumstances require it. Such an adjustment may be up or down. [The housing subsidy payable to new town corporations, etc., is, according to section

101 of the Act, to be calculated, with appropriate modifications, broadly on the same basis as for other local authorities.]

What clearly emerges is that the new subsidy system will take greater account of local factors in many ways, it will also give central government much greater ability to vary subsidies, possibly even between neighbouring authorities. Though it would be politically unwise for any government to interfere too closely with the detailed working of local government, any subsidy system based so much on yearly changes in the costs and incomes of individual authorities must run the danger of seeming to grant over mighty powers of direction and determination to central government. As Steve Schifferes has written in 'Housing Bill 1980', *Roof*, January 1980, pp. 10 – 14, at p. 12: 'the new deficit system involves a scrutiny of the management and maintenance expenditure for the first time. These costs are much higher for inner city authorities than elsewhere, but the Government has shown interest in imposing a ceiling. This could mean a freeze on increasing management and maintenance in these areas, or it could particularly affect those authorities that are trying to increase their services. It will certainly mean that after 1981 – 82 councils will have to justify carefully to central government their decisions to provide substantially increased or improved management and maintenance services'.

So much will depend on a consideration of local factors in the determination of the local contribution differential that there will no longer be any real national basis for determining subsidies. This is evidence of the ever growing power of central government vis-à-vis the individual local authority. Other problems inherent in the new subsidy system include the fact that a break is made with the long standing principle that a local authority should know its financial commitments in advance of entering into building programmes. There is a danger that subsidies could be reduced using the '1980 Act equation' in an attempt to cut public spending. One other danger is that local authorities could one day be faced with massive and unforeseen repair bills arising out of the premature obsolescence of much modern council housing, for example, tower blocks of flats, due to constructional and design defects. The new subsidy system may not be able to cope with such situations.

In reply to the above criticisms it can be argued that the former subsidy systems have all broken down. From 1919 to 1961 flat rate contributions were made, but they could not take account of rising prices and local differences. Throughout the 1960's and 70's attempts were made to base the subsidy system on legal rules contained in legislation. That system also has broken down under the attack of persistently high rates of inflation. It may be that a subsidy system based on a wide measure of central discretion is the only workable way forward for the future. Nevertheless it will certainly bring about the danger of increased central control of local affairs and may lead to a yearly argument between central and local government as to the amounts of subsidies payable.

It should be noted that the modified rent rebate subsidy, introduced by section 3 of the 1975 Act, which covers a proportion of the standard amount of rent rebates will continue to be separately payable. This money will not form any part of the computation of the ordinary housing subsidy. Section 117 of the Housing Act 1980 makes the amount of subsidy payable to a local authority in respect of rent allowances and rebates 90 per cent of the standard amount of allowances and rebates payable by them. Finally note should be taken of section 102 of the Housing Act 1980 which provides:

'(1) Where any subsidy has been paid to any local authority or other body under this Part of this Act, and it appears to the Secretary of State that —

   (a) the purpose for which it was paid has not been fulfilled or not completely or adequately or not without unreasonable delay; and
   (b) that the case falls within rules published by him;

he may recover from the authority or other body the whole or such part of the payment as he may determine in accordance with the rules, with interest from such time and at such rate as he may so determine.

(2) A sum recoverable under this section may be recovered either as a simple contract debt or by withholding or reducing housing subsidy payable in any year or in successive years.

(3) The withholding or reduction under this section of housing subsidy payable to a local authority or other body for any year shall not affect the authority's or other body's base amount for the following year'.

This power enables the Secretary of State to recover any subsidy paid to a local authority where it appears to him that there has been a failure to achieve the purpose for which the money was paid, or where there has been unreasonable delay in achieving that purpose.

Whither local housing autonomy?

By now it should be clear that the new housing and local government legislation marks a further, and most important, stage in a process whereby the effective control over both capital and recurrent expenditure on housing has passed from local to central government. In 1973 Richard Buxton in *Local Government* drew attention to the increasing control exercised by Whitehall over the town hall. He wrote at p. 71 – 72: '. . . a wide range of capital projects, the essential vehicles of policy change, can be, and are, controlled by Whitehall by means of the power to prevent the borrowing of money . . . . The need for ministry consent effectively deprives . . . councillors of much of their influence . . . . In recent years it has not been unknown for house or school-building programmes to be altered at very short notice, and for local authorities to be required to provide Whitehall with answers on priority and policy questions with a rapidity which has made it difficult for the issues even to be submitted to committees and councils, let alone to be properly considered by them . . . . The erratic nature of the relations between central and local government is in a large part explicable by the use which has been made of the loan sanction system as a means of controlling spending in the economy as a whole'.

In the years that have passed since these words were written some attempts, such as the introduction of HIPs, have been made to restore some freedom of action to local authorities, but in the main they have been cosmetic. The control of finance and capital has passed increasingly from local to central bodies, something that is more than confirmed by the latest legislation. The result is not happy. We have a municipal housing system which is much more amenable to the dictates of central government than to the desires of local communities and individuals. The criticisms made of council housing earlier in this introduction stand: with regard to the individual the local housing authority is in a powerful, perhaps over powerful, position. However, as between local and central government the latter has far too much power.

It would be easy here to go on and decry all levels of government and to state that what will be found in the following chapters will be a handbook for those who are the defenders of tenants' rights. It is hoped that the book will be useful for such people but it is not intended *just* for them. Champions of underdogs frequently attack middle dogs rather than directing their attention to the real villians of the dog fight. There *is* a great deal to criticise in local authority housing practice and in the way in which housing law is administered. But it must not be forgotten that much of that law and practice is determined by central government, and that the mind of central government changes in confusing and contradictory ways. Local authorities are caught between the legitimate wants and needs of communities and the dictates and directives of an over-powerful central administration. Over the last few years local authorities have been made subject to increased statutory duties while not being given resources commensurate to these new responsibilities.

In this connection the findings of the House of Commons Environment Committee First Report July 1980, H.C. 714 should be briefly noted. That Committee concluded that:

1) the Local Government, Planning and Land Act would lead to a reduction in the discretion enjoyed by local authorities;

2) allowing local authorities to add 50 per cent of the capital receipts from the sale of council houses to their capital investment programmes will be of very limited effect since an average of between five and ten houses will need to be sold in order to build one replacement, and that in any case receipts from sales are likely to be unevenly spread across the country;

3) the new subsidy system will lead to a very large reduction in net general subsidies to local authority tenants, and larger rent increases;

4) a reduction in local authority capital investment in housing is likely to produce a need for accommodation which the private sector will not be able to meet, and that by the mid 1980's there will be a cumulative shortfall of some half a million dwellings. In 1975/6 the English local authorities completed 105,600 new dwellings, by 1983/84 the estimate is that they will only complete some 61,300.

It is an obvious truism to state that this country's housing problem will not be solved until society devotes the necessary social, political and economic resources to the problem, and that it is impossible to solve the issue merely by putting laws on the statute book. Nevertheless the lawyer can play some real part in trying to bring about better housing conditions. In the first place he can expose the political policy biases implicit in much of our housing law and practice, and he can show how extremes of policy, be they from the right or the left, work confusion. Second, he can work for a system of laws that will produce a just and equitable division of housing resources within society, though it must be admitted that the debate on what is 'just and equitable' will probably, and quite rightly, never be ended. That is no bad thing for the law must adapt itself to the ever-changing needs of society. Finally he can discharge the traditional lawyer's rôle of seeking justice for individuals in individual situations. It is the author's hope that the present work can make some contribution with regard to the tasks outlined above.

Further reading

Each chapter of this book will conclude with a 'further reading' list of books which either give more detailed treatment of the subject matter contained therein or place it in its wider social, economic and political context. In writing this introduction, for example, the following books and papers have been found particularly helpful:

Berry, F., *Housing: The Great British Failure* (Charles Knight, 1974)
Buxton, R., *Local Government* (2nd edn, Penguin Books, 1973)
Cullingworth, J.B., *Essays on Housing Policy* (George Allen and Unwin, 1979)

Lansley, S., *Housing and Public Policy* (Croom Helm, 1979)

Merrett, S., *State Housing in Britain,* (Routledge and Kegan Paul, 1979)

Murie, Niner and Watson, *Housing Policy and the Housing System* (George Allen and Unwin, 1979)

Housing Policy: A Consultative Document (Cmnd. 6851, HMSO, 1977)

Aughton, H., 'More controls on council subsidies and less on projects?', *Roof*, September/October 1980, p. 134.

First Report from the Environment Committee Session 1979 – 80, *Enquiry into Implications of Government Expenditure Plans 1980 – 81 to 1983 – 84 for the Housing Policies of the Department of the Environment*, 24 July 1980, H.C. 714 (HMSO)

The reader should also note that the best general reference works on housing law and practice are: *The Encyclopedia of Housing Law and Practice* (Sweet & Maxwell) and *Social Welfare Law* (Ed. by D.W. Pollard) (2 volumes, Oyez). Whittaker, *Handbook of Environmental Powers* (The Architectural Press) is a useful, quick reference guide to housing and other environmental legislation down to 1975.

The local government and town planning journals frequently carry articles on housing law and practice, and useful articles are often to be found in the Legal Action Group Bulletin, The Journal of Planning and Environmental Law, The Journal of Social Welfare Law and The Conveyancer. However, the best general housing magazine is *Roof*, which is published bi-monthly by Shelter.

Part I
The public provision of housing

Chapter 1

The general housing powers and duties of local authorities and new town corporations

The Lodging Houses Act 1851 was the first legislation having as its main object the housing of working people, though its scope was limited, as it allowed local authorities to purchase land and to erect or purchase and repair buildings suitable for lodging houses. Within these houses the sexes were to be segretated. Other legislation followed at regular intervals until the Housing, Town Planning &b. Act 1909, but as Stephen Merrett shows in *State Housing in Britain* Appendix 2, pp. 320 – 321, very little use was made of these powers, and the number of houses *completed* each year by local authorities ran only into the hundreds. With the end of the Great War came a governmental commitment to the building of 'homes fit for heroes'. Between 1919 and 1925 a series of legislative measures imposed duties on local authorities to survey the needs of their areas, to make and carry out plans for the provision of the houses needed and introduced the principle of exchequer subsidies for municipal housing. This legislation was followed by an immediate increase in the number of local authority dwellings completed each year, though Lloyd George's 1918 promise of half a million working class homes in three years was not fulfilled.

More housing legislation in the 1930's increased both the powers and duties of local authorities, particularly with regard to slum clearance areas, the residents displaced therefrom and overcrowding. During this period very considerable numbers of council houses were completed, and 1939 saw the completion of 121,653 municipal homes. The Second World War reduced house building drastically, and, of course, also led to the destruction of many other houses as a result of enemy action. In the later years of the war and the immediate post war years much legislation was passed to stimulate municipal house building. The great social reforms of the late 1940's were expressed in housing terms by a massive boost for municipal housing, and a widening of local authority responsibilities to house all members of the community, and not just the working classes, in the Housing Act 1949. In 1953 local authorities completed 229,305 houses, and for 1954 the figure was 223,731, figures they have never attained since. Most of the previous Housing Acts were

31

repealed and replaced by the Housing Act 1957 and the Housing (Financial Provisions) Act 1958, though hardly a year has gone by since without some major alteration, extension or replacement of housing legislation. It cannot be too often repeated that as this legislation is, in essence, no more than the ritual expression of housing policy, the law bears witness in its tangled provisions to the 'to-ing and fro-ing' of policy between governments of different political colours. The Housing Acts are now a terrifying agglomeration of powers and duties, provisos and replacements and intertwined provisions through which even the lawyer finds it hard to make his way. It is perhaps a little too much to hope, given the conflict of views as to the purpose of municipal housing between the major political parties, that early order will be imposed on the chaos, though this is a most devoutly to be prayed for goal. Until that happy day when we have an agreed national housing policy and a clear and coherent set of statutory provisions relating to it we must make the best use of what we have!

This and the subsequent chapters in Part I will attempt to elucidate the law and practice relating to the provision, control, management and disposal of the houses provided and acquired by local authorities under housing legislation.

The housing authorities

Outside Greater London the principal housing authorities are the district councils, see section 1 of the Housing Act 1957 as amended by paragraph 1 of Schedule 22 to the Local Government Act 1972. County councils have only certain reserve powers under section 194 of the Act of 1972, such as to undertake the provision of housing on behalf of a district or districts within their area, following a request from such councils, provided the Secretary of State gives his approval. County councils have power under section 126 of the Housing Act 1957 to provide homes for persons employed or paid by them, for example school caretakers. In the Greater London Council area the position is more complex. The Common Council is the housing authority for the City of London. In the rest of the metropolis responsibility has been divided between the Greater London Council and the London Boroughs. The London Boroughs are, under section 21 of the London Government Act 1963, the principal housing authorities within their areas. By section 22(2)(a) of the London Government Act 1963 applicants for housing resident in a London Borough are to make their application to that borough, whether or not they are actually applying for housing there. Each borough must keep a register of such applications, together with any application made to the Greater London Council and passed on by them to the borough. London Boroughs are not permitted to exercise their powers to provide housing under Part V of the Housing Act 1957 outside Greater London without ministerial consent (section 21(3) of the 1963 Act), but they may, under section 21(10), agree amongst themselves to exercise their powers on each other's behalf and to share the task and costs of providing houses.

The Greater London Council has some housing functions, being a housing authority in its own right for the purposes of providing accommodation, for the whole of its area, see section 21(4) of the London Government Act 1963. The Greater London Council also inherited the former housing powers of the London County Council, though this is for a limited period only, and can be ended by the Secretary of State making an appointed day order to take away all or some of these powers. The Greater London Council has not exercised any powers in relation to overcrowding or multi-occupation since 1965, see the Greater London Council (Housing Powers) Order (S.I. 1965 No. 1835). The role of the GLC as a housing authority is thus arguably diminishing. The council may not exercise its power to provide housing accommodation by development or redevelopment of land in a London Borough except with the consent of that borough, or, if that consent is withheld, with the consent of the Secretary of State, unless the accommodation is provided by them in connection with a development plan relating to an area of comprehensive development, or to rehouse persons displaced by them in the exercise of any of their powers. Furthermore section 23(3) of the 1963 Act provides for the transfer of housing land and accommodation from the Greater London Council to the London Boroughs. Since 1971 a number of such transfers have been made, the most recent major transfer being made under the Greater London Council (Transfer of Land and Housing Accommodation) Order 1980 (S.I. 1980 No. 320) which came into force on 31 March 1980. This particular scheme preserves the Greater London Council's right to nominate tenants to the transferred accommodation for a ten year period.

The housing management powers of the Greater London Council are soon to be brought to an end, though this has not been without opposition from some of the London Boroughs. In *Brent LBC v Greater London Council* (1980) *Times,* 13 October a number of London Boroughs sought judicial review of a request made by the Greater London Council to the Secretary of State on 19 May 1980 to make a transfer under section 23(3) of the London Government Act 1963, of its remaining 100,000 houses to various boroughs. The boroughs objected to the proposed transfer but the Court of Appeal held that they could grant no remedy. The proper way to oppose such a transfer is for the objecting borough to make submissions to the Secretary of State under the consultative arrangements of section 23(3). That is the only safeguard, and the boroughs may not block the transfer process by recourse to the courts because in the end the decision on transfer must be made by the Minister.

The Greater London Council also has the following functions:

1) A power under section 21(11) of the 1963 Act to agree with district councils whose areas lie outside but adjacent to or in the vicinity of Greater London, for the provision in such areas by the Greater London Council of housing to meet the special needs of such other councils, or for the provision by them of housing within their areas to meet the Greater London Council's needs, and for the making of consequential financial agreements;

2) A duty to maintain, under section 22(1), records of the housing needs of Greater London;

3) A duty to receive applications, under section 22(2)(b) for accommodation from persons who are *not* resident in any London Borough, and to transmit these on to such London Boroughs as they think appropriate;

4) A duty to establish and maintain, section 22(5), facilities for the exchange of housing in Greater London, and

5) To provide mortgage finance under the Small Dwellings Acquisition Act 1899, Part V of the Housing Act 1957, section 9 of the Housing (Financial Provisions) Act 1958, and section 13 of the House Purchase and Housing Act 1959.

Part XVI of the Local Government, Planning and Land Act 1980 provides for the creation of new corporations to regenerate urban areas, for example London's docklands. The powers of such corporations are to be modelled upon those of the new town development corporations. Under section 153 of the Act the Secretary of State may provide by order that such a corporation may assume total and exclusive or shared housing powers under the Housing Acts within its area or in any part thereof.

The duty to provide housing

This is contained in Part V of the Housing Act 1957. (All references hereafter are to this Statute unless otherwise stated.)

Section 91 provides that it shall be the duty of every local housing authority to consider the housing conditions in and the needs of their district with respect to the provision of further housing accommodation. Such authorities were subject to a ministerial power to require periodic reviews of their housing needs and conditions, but this requirement has been repealed by Schedule 26 to the Housing Act 1980.

The housing needs of a district are not confined to the needs of its inhabitants. In *Watson v Minister of Local Government and Planning* [1951] 2 KB 779, [1951] 2 All ER 664 where the appellant claimed that the local authority had no power to make a compulsory purchase order on his land because they required it partly to house persons from *outside* their area, Devlin J said, at p. 783: 'It cannot be right . . . that in considering the needs of a district a local authority should stop short at a street which is immediately beyond their district and which is badly overcrowded and the inhabitants of which might more conveniently be rehoused on the other side of the boundary. It seems to me that a local authority must, when considering the needs of their district look at the districts immediately adjacent'. Thus the needs of persons in adjacent districts who could conveniently be housed within a local authority's area may also be taken into account. Likewise section 3(1) of the Chronically Sick and Disabled Persons Act 1970 requires local authorities to take into account the special needs of chronically sick and disabled persons in discharging their section 91 duty.

Local authorities must themselves review from time to time the housing information with which they have been presented about their district, whether that has been provided by their own officers or otherwise, and a further duty to review unfit houses, clearance areas, houses in multiple occupation, general improvement areas and housing action areas was imposed by section 70 of the Housing Act 1969.

Section 92 provides:

'(1) A local authority may provide housing accommodation —
  (a) by the erection of houses on any land acquired or appropriated by them,
  (b) by the conversion of any buildings into houses,
  (c) by acquiring houses,
  (d) by altering, enlarging, repairing or improving any houses or buildings which have, or an estate or interest in which has, been acquired by the local authority'.

Any house so erected, converted or acquired may subsequently be altered, enlarged, repaired or improved, and must be provided with a fixed bath in a bathroom (except in so far as is otherwise permitted in *particular* cases by ministerial consent, for example in relation to old people's accommodation under Ministry of Housing and Local Government Circular No. 18/57.) Supplementary powers to fit out and furnish section 92 accommodation are granted by section 94, and powers to provide meals, refreshments, including the sale of alcoholic liquors for consumption with meals, laundry facilities and services are granted by section 95.

Section 93 provides that the local authority may, with ministerial consent, provide along with housing accommodation, shops, recreation grounds and other land or buildings which the minister considers would benefit the occupants of the housing provided, a power wide enough, according to the opinion of Peterson J in *Conron v LCC* [1922] 2 ChD 283 at 297, to cover the provision of public houses so long as they are 'conducted on the most improved lines'.

Section 9 of the Local Government (Miscellaneous Provisions) Act 1976 permits the making of byelaws with respect to the use of any land held under section 93, and *not* covered by buildings or within the curtilage of a building or forming part of a highway.

The Greater London Council and the London Boroughs also have power to provide and maintain commercial premises along with housing accommodation. Section 107 grants powers to lay out public streets, roads and open spaces on land acquired for housing purposes. In *Meravale Builders Ltd v Secretary of State for the Environment* (1978) 36 P & CR 87 it was held that this power only entitles a local authority to build such roads as fairly and reasonably relate to the provision of housing accommodation, and not to create new major roads, interchanges and extensions which have a purpose independent of housing. Section 149(1) requires local authorities to have regard to 'the beauty of the landscape or countryside, the other amenities of the locality, and the desirability of preserving existing works of architectural, historic or artistic interest' when proposing to provide housing.

The power to provide section 92 accommodation may be used outside an authority's district, but only after they have given notice to their county council, and also, where they propose to act outside their county, to the council of the county where they propose to act, see section 193(2) of the Local Government Act 1972. The obligation to provide housing cannot, in effect, be transferred to private shoulders by attaching a condition to a grant of planning permission that the developer must grant the first right to occupy dwellings he wishes to build to persons on the local authority waiting list, see *R v Hillingdon London Borough Council ex parte Royco Homes Ltd* [1974] QB 720, [1974] 2 All ER 643.

To deal with the problem of a restrictive convenant standing in the way of the conversion of, for example, a large old house, into smaller units of accommodation, a local authority may use section 84 of the Law of Property Act 1925 under which the Lands Tribunal may discharge or modify restrictive covenants affecting freehold land. With regard to leasehold properties acquired by a local authority, section 165 of the 1957 Act confers power on the county court to vary the terms of the lease if they prohibit or restrict conversion of the property. The local authority *must* prove either that, because of changes in the character of the neighbourhood of the house it cannot be readily let as a single house, but could be if it were, for example, divided into two or more flats or bed sitting rooms, or that planning permission has been granted for such a conversion into separate dwellings.

The acquisition of land for housing purposes

Section 96 provides:

'A local authority shall have power under this part of this Act —
  (a) to acquire any land, including any houses or buildings thereon, as a site for the erection of houses,
  (b) to acquire houses or buildings which may be made suitable as houses, together with any lands occupied with the houses, or buildings, . . .
  (c) to acquire land [for the purposes of sections 93 and 95]
  (d) to acquire land for the purpose of the carrying out thereon . . . of works for the purpose of, or connected with, the alteration, enlarging, repair or improvement of an adjoining house'.

A number of points should be noted about this section. First, the power is very wide. In *HE Green and Sons v Minister of Health (No. 2)* [1948] 1 KB 34, [1947] 2 All ER 469, a building company had acquired land in 1938, on which they laid down sewers and roads and built 22 houses. The Second World War stopped further work and shortly after peace returned the local authority made a compulsory purchase order on the site. This was held to be within the words of the statute. In *Andresier v Minister of Housing and Local Government* (1965) 109 Sol Jo 594 it was held that a local authority may use its powers to acquire houses with a view to improving them as housing accommodation, even if that work does *not* result in a net increase in the amount of available accommodation.

Second, some attention must be given to section 105, most of which has been repealed by Schedule 26 to the Housing Act 1980. This provision has in the past imposed certain powers and duties on local authorities. They have had a power, with the consent of the Minister, to sell or exchange land for other land better adapted for housing purposes, either with or without paying or receiving any money for equality of exchange. They have had power to sell or lease land to any person on condition that he will undertake an approved house building and estate development scheme.

The Local Government, Planning and Land Act 1980 introduces very different provisions to deal with the problem of securing the development of land for residential purposes. The new approach favours development by private, as opposed to municipal, enterprise. The thrust of the new legislation is away from acquisition and towards the *disposal* of land by local authorities. Accordingly it is necessary to postpone discussion of those provisions of section 105 of the Housing Act 1957 still in force until after consideration has been given to the new law as contained in the Local Government, Planning and Land Act 1980. Section 116 grants power to the Secretary of State to direct county and district councils, the Greater London Council and the London

Boroughs to make assessments of land in their areas which, in their opinion, is available and suitable for development for residential purposes. In particular the Secretary may direct them to have prior consultations with other authorities, with builders, developers and others, and about producing reports of their assessments and making copies available to the Public. Part X of the Act introduces further reaching procedures and section 93(1) of and Schedule 16 to this statute apply its provisions to, inter alia, county and district councils, the Greater London Council, the London Boroughs, the Common Council of the City of London, the Commission for the New Towns, a development corporation established under the New Towns Act 1965, or one of the new urban development corporations established under the Act. The Secretary of State may by order direct that the provisions of Part X shall be operable in any district or London Borough specified in the order, see section 94 of the Local Government, Planning and Land Act 1980. Section 95 empowers the Secretary of State to compile and maintain a register of land:

1) of which the freehold or leasehold belongs to one of the authorities specified above;

2) which is situated either in an area in which Part X of the Act is in operation, or which is adjacent to such land, and

3) which, in the Secretary's opinion, is not being used or sufficiently used for the performance of the authority's undertaking.

Section 97 of the Act empowers the Secretary of State to discover from authorities information as to their land holdings, and he is to send, under section 96, a relevant authority a copy of any register of land made under the Act for their area. This they must make available for public inspection at all reasonable hours, together with facilities for allowing the public to obtain copies of information contained in the register.

The real 'teeth' of Part X are contained in sections 98 and 99. The Secretary of State is empowered to direct a specified authority to take steps which he may specify to dispose of land registered by him under Part X. Before issuing such a direction, the Secretary of State must give the relevant authority notice of the proposed direction and its contents. They then have 42 days or such longer period as may be allowed in which to make representations as to the content of the direction or why it should not be made. Where such representations are made the Secretary of State may not proceed to make the direction *unless* he is satisfied that the land in question can be disposed of in the manner in which and on the terms and conditions on which he proposes that is shall be disposed of without serious detriment to the ability of the authority in question to perform their functions. Thus a housing authority owning land which the Secretary of State concludes is being underused may find themselves being directed to offer it for sale.

In such circumstances county and district councils, the Greater London Council, London Borough councils or the Common Council of the City of London may be able to rely on section 126 of the Housing Act 1974. This provides that if such an authority and a person having an interest in land in their area become parties to an instrument executed for the purpose of carrying out works on or developing the land, and that instrument contains a covenant on the part of any person having an interest in land, then that covenant is to be enforceable against any person deriving title from the original covenantor. This provision is a departure from the normal rule that positive covenants are not enforceable against successors in title. Furthermore the provision allows the local authority in a case of breach of covenant, without prejudice to any other method of enforcement, to enter on the land and carry out the works which the other covenanting party has failed to do. They may also recover their expenses from him. Presumably a housing authority directed to sell land under the Local Government, Land and Planning Act 1980 could enter into such a covenant under the Housing Act 1974 to secure that land sold by them was still used for housing purposes. But it should be noted that this provision only applies to those covenants expressly made subject to it.

Section 93 of the Housing Act 1980 declares that the power of a local authority to acquire land for housing purposes under section 96 of the 1957 Act, includes power to acquire land for the purpose of disposing of any houses erected or to be erected thereon, and power to dispose of the land to a person who intends to provide housing on it.

It is necessary now to return to considering the remaining provisions of section 105 of the Housing Act 1957.

Section 105(4) and (4A) provide that where a local authority acquire a building which may be made suitable as a house, they are forthwith to secure that the building is made suitable, either by doing work themselves, or by selling or leasing it to some other person on condition that he does the work. In those cases where they do the work themselves they are under a further duty to ensure, as soon as practicable after the acquisition or the completion of the necessary work as the case may be, that the house or building is used as housing accommodation. Such buildings are often acquired as a consequence of use of local authority powers to deal with unfit housing (see Chapters 8 and 9 below). In some cases such buildings are used for accommodation purposes, for example as short life housing, see Bob Widdowson, 'Short Life Ghettoes', *Roof*, March 1977, pp. 42 – 45. But in some areas older houses, once acquired, are simply boarded up and left unused, or subjected to the process known as 'prior demolition' and the properties have been demolished and the sites left vacant for many years before redevelopment, see Ron Bailey, 'Grabbing the Smashers', *Roof,* July 1978, pp. 99. Over the years the courts have interpreted section 105(4) and (4A) so that they cannot be used to prevent such a waste of housing resources.

In *Uttoxeter Urban District Council v Clarke* [1952] 1 All ER 1318 a local authority made a compulsory purchase order on an estate which contained a large old house converted into a private hotel. They then used the house for administrative and social service purposes. It was held that there was no obligation on the local authority to convert the old house into suitable dwellings. That obligation was said to arise only where a local authority acquires a house for *conversion,* and does not arise in relation to houses merely acquired as part of an estate. In *Attridge v LCC* [1954] 2 QB 449, [1954] 2 All ER 444 a local authority compulsorily acquired a site for the purposes of building a housing estate. There was already a bungalow on the land which could have been used as housing accommodation, but they wished to demolish this in order to construct a road giving access to the housing estate. It was held that where a local authority acquires a site, the fact that there are already buildings on it which might be used as dwellings does not in any way restrict the local authority in the proper development of their estate plans. Finally in *A-G ex rel. Rivers-Moore v Portsmouth City Council* (1978) 36 P & CR 416 the local authority had acquired a number of old houses using their compulsory purchase powers. It was alleged that due to the council's neglect these houses became unfit. The local authority subsequently declared the area a clearance area and proposed to demolish the houses. It was alleged, inter alia, that the local authority were in breach of their duty under section 105(4A) to secure the speedy use of acquired premises as housing accommodation. The Court held the duties imposed by section 105(4) and (4A) are not of infinite duration, and a local authority is bound to deal with houses as they are and not as they once were. Even though the houses had become unfit as a result of municipal inaction, provided the council could honestly say that they were in bad condition and unfit for human habitation, having outlasted their reasonable life by years, they could be properly included in a demolition area.

Section 95 of the Housing Act 1980 inserts section 110A into the 1957 Act. This provides that, where a local authority have acquired or appropriated land for the purposes of Part V of that Act, they may not put any part of the land consisting of a house, or part of a house, to any other purpose without ministerial consent. The relationship of this new provision to section 105(4) and (4A) should be noted. The new requirement is that where land has been appropriated or acquired for housing purposes, houses on that land shall not be put to any other purpose without ministerial consent. It is *not* a requirement that such houses shall not cease to be used as accommodation. This provision does not overturn the decisions in *A-G ex rel. Rivers-Moore v Portsmouth City Council*, where houses were simply left empty; in *Uttoxeter Urban District Council v Clarke* where the property acquired was not at the time of acquisition a house but a hotel; nor in *Attridge v LCC* where the house was acquired so that it could be demolished prior to the building of other houses.

Compulsory purchase of land

Section 97 provides:

'(1) Land . . . may be acquired by a local authority by agreement, or they may be authorised to purchase land compulsorily . . . by the Minister . . .

(2) A local authority may, with the consent of, and subject to any conditions imposed by, the Minister acquire land . . . notwithstanding that the land is not immediately required [for housing purposes]. Provided that a local authority shall not be authorised to purchase any land compulsorily [for housing purposes] unless it appears to the Minister that it is likely to be required . . . within ten years from the date on which he confirms the compulsory purchase order'.

The procedure to be followed is further contained in Schedule 7. This provides that the procedure is to be that laid down by the Acquisition of Land (Authorisation Procedure) Act 1946.

Very briefly this means that the local authority has to make the compulsory purchase order in draft, describing the land to be acquired by reference to a map. Thereafter the authority must serve notice on owners, lessees and occupiers except tenants for a month or less, of the land stating times and places where the order and map can be seen, and granting at least 21 days for the making of objections. The Minister's power to direct that the notices be displayed on boards on the land is repealed by section 118 of the Local Government, Planning and Land Act 1980. Additionally the same information must be advertised in the local press for two successive weeks. If any objections are received, unless they are such as can be dealt with when the issue of compensation is being settled, they must be heard either at a public local inquiry, or, more rarely, at a hearing before an inspector appointed by the Secretary of State. The procedure at any inquiry is governed by the Compulsory Purchase by Public Authorities (Inquiries Procedure) Rules (S.I. 1976 No. 746). After the inquiry or hearing the inspector will make his report and this will be considered by the Secretary of State when he decides whether or not to confirm the order. The Secretary may confirm the order with or without modification, or refuse to confirm it. By section 12 of the Tribunals and Inquiries Act 1971 the Secretary of State must state the reasons for his decision in any case where an inquiry has been, or could have been, held. Where an order is confirmed notice must again be given in the local press, and further notices must be served on those owners, lessees and occupiers who were previously notified. These notices must state the times and places where the confirmed order and maps can be inspected. The order will normally come into operation on the day on which the announcement of its confirmation first appears in the local press. The validity of the order can then be challenged during a six week period, but not otherwise, in the High Court by a person aggrieved on the grounds either that the order is ultra vires or that the procedure followed in its making has been faulty. If no challenge is made the acquiring authority may then proceed to serve notice to treat on the affected landholders and thereafter proceed to take possession.

(Readers requiring a fuller exposition of compulsory purchase procedure are referred to Keith Davies, *The Law of Compulsory Purchase and Compensation* (3rd edn.) Chaps. 3 and 4.)

Confirmation by the Secretary of State of a compulsory purchase order will normally be dependent on the necessary planning permission being obtained for the proposed development. Section 40 of the Town and County Planning Act 1971 provides:

'(1) Where the authorisation of a government department is required by virtue of an enactment in respect of development to be carried out by a local authority . . . that department may, on granting that authorisation, direct that planning permission for that development shall be deemed to be granted . . . .'

In practice local authorities are expected to obtain planning permission. Under section 270 of the Town and Country Planning Act 1971 the Secretary of State has made the Town and Country Planning General Regulations (S.I. 1976 No. 1419). A local authority seeking planning permission must now follow the following procedure:

1) Pass a resolution to seek permission for the proposed development;

2) Place a copy of the resolution and relevant plans in the public register of planning applications;

3) Give all persons having a 'material interest' in the land notice of the proposal;

4) Where the proposed development consists of any matter that would need to be published in the case of a normal planning application, give notice in local newspapers, and give any other publicity that would be required in the case of an ordinary planning application;

5) Wait for the expiry of the period allowed for the making of representations against the proposal, which must be at least 21 days;

6) If any representations are received, they must be considered;

7) Unless the Secretary of State has required the local authority to apply to him for planning permission for the proposed development, they may pass a second resolution, this time to carry out the development, at which point permission for the development is deemed to be granted.

(A more general discussion of this topic will be found in A.E. Telling, *Planning Law and Procedure* pp. 250 – 254.)

The acquisition of ancillary rights

On the whole the procedure for acquiring land compulsorily and then obtaining the necessary planning permission to develop it though somewhat attenuated is not over complex. But it can contain pitfalls of an unexpected nature. In *Sovmots Investments Ltd v Secretary of State for the Environment* [1979] AC 144, [1977] 2 All ER 385 such a pitfall was encountered. This case arose out of the disquiet that has surrounded the tower block known as 'Centre Point' ever since it was completed in 1967. The development has three parts: a tall tower meant to be used as offices; a bridge block intended for use as shops and showrooms; and a wing block consisting of a basement car-park surrounded by four floors of offices and shop units which itself supports stilts which in their turn support a six storey block of 36 maisonettes, access to which was provided by lifts and staircases. The services for the whole of this wing block were common, and the electricity, water and sewerage services were all shared and incapable of separation. The local authority, Camden LBC, wishing to alleviate the housing shortage in their area, made a compulsory purchase order on the maisonettes in 1972 as they were unoccupied. This was in due course confirmed, and was said to include all the access ways to the dwellings.

The question then arose of whether the local authority had also acquired all the ancillary rights necessary for them to make use of the maisonettes, for example use of emergency fire escapes, use of goods lifts and rubbish chutes, a right of support from the unacquired shop units and stilts below the maisonettes, a right to use the service facilities, and a right of access to the outside of the building in order to allow window cleaning and repair. The House of Lords held that the powers of a local authority, being strictly limited by statute, did not allow them to compel the grant of ancillary rights over land which was not being acquired. Before the attempted compulsory purchase Centre Point was a single unit held in entirety by Sovmots Investments Ltd. The purported acquisition would have divided the block and given the local authority a 'flying leasehold'. This would have been utterly useless to them unless its acquisition carried with it the ancillary rights mentioned above. As they had, apparently, no power to compel the grant of such rights they could not use the maisonettes for housing purposes, and as they only had power to make the compulsory purchase order to acquire property for housing accommodation, they could not acquire the block of maisonettes at all. The House of Lords added that even if a local authority have power to force the grant of ancillary rights, any such rights required must be clearly specified in the compulsory purchase order.

In these circumstances local authorities should rely on section 13 of the Local Government (Miscellaneous Provisions) Act 1976 which provides that where a local authority is authorised to purchase land compulsorily that the Secretary of State may also authorise them by such an order to purchase compulsorily such 'new rights' as are specified in the order. 'New rights' are rights which were not in existence when the order specifying them was made, but otherwise they are not defined by the Act, though easements and those rights of a like kind which caused the trouble in the *Sovmots* case are within the meaning of the phrase. Department of the Environment Circular No. 26/77, Appendix 1M points out that when reliance is placed on this new provision:

1) The purpose for which the new rights are required must be the same as for the land made subject to the compulsory purchase order itself;

2) The compulsory purchase order should contain a statement of the reasons for needing the new right, and also information about its nature and extent; and

3) Each new right should be separately referenced and made easily identifiable in the order and its accompanying map.

In many of our larger towns and cities there are empty tower blocks speculatively built for commercial occupation that has never materialised. Frequently these towers stand empty and forlorn above shops and showrooms and form part of the same development. Provided these empty properties are capable of being made suitable as houses within section 96(b) of the 1957 Act, section 13 of the 1976 Act now opens the way for local authorities to acquire the unused parts by compulsory purchase procedure and also to acquire the necessary ancillary rights needed in order to use the converted properties as housing accommodation. Of course, the financial issues involved in the compulsory acquisition of such buildings may preclude any such action being taken.

Supplementary provisions

Section 98 permits a local authority who have acquired the right to enter and take possession of a house following its compulsory purchase to authorise any person in occupation of the house at that time to continue his occupation, subject of course, to the rights of the local authority. Section 99 allows the appropriation for the purpose of providing housing accommodation, of any land or houses which are for the time being vested in a local authority or at their disposal.

Enforcing the duties of local authorities

The default powers of the Secretary of State whereby local residents could complain to central government if a local housing authority failed to fulfil their statutory duties, with a view to persuading the Secretary of State to undertake the work himself, were repealed with effect from 1 April 1974 under the Local Government Act 1972. This leaves few possibilities of legal action open to individuals or groups dissatisfied with their local authority's response to a bad housing situation in the district. Section 91 of the 1957 Act and section 70 of the Housing Act 1969 place local authorities under statutory duties to carry out reviews of their housing performance and functions. They could be ordered to discharge these functions by way of an order of mandamus, but it would not be appropriate for a court to order any particular mode of discharge of local authority housing functions, see generally, *Hall v Manchester Corpn* (1915) 84 LJ Ch 732 per Lord Atkinson at 741. An approach may be made to the county council who may, under section 194(3) of the Local Government Act 1972, undertake the provision of housing accommodation subject to the approval of the Secretary of State. Another method of bringing legal pressure to bear is for a person who has suffered *particular injustice* as a result of municipal mishandling of housing obligations to initiate a complaint to the local ombudsman (see Chapter 12, below). Nevertheless it must be said that this is an area where the law is loath to become too involved, preferring to leave such matters to the political judgment of the local electorate on polling days.

The provision of housing in new areas

Many of our older large towns and cities, particularly before the creation of the large new districts by the Local Government Act 1972, had insufficient land within their areas to provide all the new housing they required. This led to the development of the concept of 'overspill' whereby the surplus population from older urban areas was rehoused in new developments in rural areas reasonably adjacent to their former home towns. Such large scale movements of population have been resisted by employers, by the host areas and sometime by those to be rehoused themselves. Local authorities have power as we have seen to provide housing outside their areas under section 92 of the 1957 Act, but the immediate post war years saw the development of two policies designed to provide much more comprehensive powers to develop housing in new areas, as part of general central policy to effect a material rise in the health and housing standards of urban dwellers. One policy was to expand existing smaller towns, the other was to create entirely new communities in rural areas.

These policies met with considerable difficulties when they came to be implemented. The problems facing the great West Midlands cities of Birmingham and Coventry in finding sufficient space in rural areas to house their surplus population have been chronicled by Neal Roberts in *The Reform of Planning Law* pp. 41 – 43. The saga of the new towns can be found in Frank Schaffer, *The New Town Story* and, as he points out at page 17, these new communities faced their own special problems even before they could be truly created: 'Unpredictable, too, was the strength of opposition, even after Parliament had given its blessing. Legal action in the courts, local resistance or non-co-operation, under-mining of industrial confidence, and the cries of the Jonahs who insisted that the towns would never be built or would be the biggest white elephants of all time — all these forces combined to try to stifle the idea at birth. The new towns have been called the miracle of the century. The real miracle is that they ever got off the ground'.

Town development

The Town Development Act 1952 was passed to facilitate, as its first section as amended provides: 'development in a . . . district . . . which will have the effect, and is undertaken primarily for the purpose, of providing accommodation for residential purposes (with or without accommodation for the carrying on of industrial or other activities, and with all appropriate public services, facilities for public worship, recreation and amenity and other requirements) the provision whereof will relieve congestion or over-population outside the county comprising the district or districts in which the development is carried out'. The Act is directed to the development of existing small towns. Section 7 of the 1952 Act as amended provides that the Greater London Council, the council of a district which is not itself a 'receiving district' (i.e. already a district in which such development is being carried out), or a water authority may participate in town development schemes. This participation involves an agreement between an authorised authority, as defined above, and a receiving authority to co-operate in town development. The combined effect of sections 7 and 8 of the Act is to allow agreement as to agencies, the transfer of land, the undertaking of works and the making of payments between the authorities. Of course an authority cannot participate in town development without the consent of the receiving authority. If the latter are unable or unwilling to agree to a development proposal, and the Secretary of State concludes that such action is required but is being prevented or hampered by the receiving authority, he may, under section 9 of the 1952 Act, make an order providing for their participation. Such orders must be approved in draft by Parliament unless the local authorities concerned otherwise give their assent.

Supplementary provisions

Section 13 of the Act of 1952 provides that where the carrying out of town development has led to houses or land being held by an authority whose continued holding thereof would be contrary to the interests of good local government, in the opinion of the Secretary of State, or that other circumstances call for change, and that the terms of the town development agreement do not make sufficient provision to deal with the problem, he may make an order, subject to Special Parliamentary procedure, providing for, inter alia, the transfer of land, the right to receive subsidy payments and the payment of other monies. Section 5 of the Act allows the Secretary of State to authorise a receiving district to exercise, for the purposes of town development, those powers, within or outside their area, which they normally use only for the benefit of their own area. Section 6 of the 1952 Act empowers the Secretary of State to authorise the compulsory acquisition of land for the purpose of town development, even though it has not been designated by a development plan as subject to compulsory acquisition. The land need not be immediately required provided it will be required within ten years, see section 46 of the Town and County Planning Act 1959. After consulting with the relevant authorities the Secretary of State may authorise the acquisition of land by an authority other than that of the receiving district. Of course, for the actual carrying out of development on any acquired land the developing authority must still obtain planning permission, see section 21 of the 1952 Act. Where a receiving district objects to town development on planning grounds there is a ministerial undertaking (H.C. Debs, 12 June 1952, Vol. 502, col. 620) that a public local inquiry will be held if that district so desires.

The Secretary of State also has power under section 2 of the Town Development Act 1952 to make, with Treasury approval, contributions towards the expenses arriving out of *substantial* works of town development in connection with the cost:

1) of acquiring land for town development;

2) of site preparation and other preliminary works;

3) of providing social, cultural and recreational buildings;

4) of providing water and sewerage facilities and other payments to water, river and drainage authorities arising out of town development.

When giving an undertaking to make such payments the Secretary of State may impose such conditions as appear to him to be expedient for securing the intended scheme of town development, see section 3 of the 1952 Act.

The new towns

The first modern new towns legislation was the New Towns Act 1946, part of a famous trio along with the Town and Country Planning Act 1947 and the National Parks and access to the Countryside Act 1949 that did so much to bring about radical changes in land use in mid-twentieth century Britain. The first 'new town' was Stevenage which was designated on 11 November 1946, followed shortly by Crawley, Hemel Hempstead, Harlow, Hatfield, Welwyn Garden City (which had been previously begun by Ebenezer Howard the originator of the 'garden city' concept), Basildon and Bracknell. These were the ring of new towns around London. Newton Aycliffe and Peterlee in Durham were founded about the same time to meet local housing needs and to diversify industry. Corby was designated a new town in 1950, and then several years elapsed before the designation of Skelmersdale in 1961, Telford, 1963, Redditch, 1964, Runcorn, 1964, Washington, 1964, Milton Keynes, 1967, Peterborough, 1967, Northampton, 1968, Warrington, 1968 and Central Lancashire in 1970. There are other new towns in Wales, Scotland and Northern Ireland. It will be noted that in many recent cases the towns are not 'new' at all. Peterborough and Northampton in particiular are centuries old as urban centres, but in all cases a massive expansion of housing and opportunities for employment has been planned, together with, in nearly all cases, a great reconstruction of the old inner urban areas and central shopping zones.

The present legislation is the New Towns Act 1965, section 1 of which provides:

'(1) If the Minister is satisfied, after consultation with any local authorities who appear to him to be concerned, that is expedient in the national interest that any area of land should be developed as a new town by a corporation established under this Act, he may make an order designating that area as the site of the proposed new town.

(2) An order under this section may include in the area designated as the site of the proposed new town any existing town or other centre of population . . . .'

The consultation required is not specified by the Act, and can take various forms, but it must be such as to allow a proper exchange of views. There must be a flow of information from central government to enable local authorities to give advice, and they must be also given a proper opportunity to tender that advice, see *Rollo v Minister of Town and County Planning* [1948] 1 All ER 13. The procedure to be followed in designating a site is laid down in Schedule 1 to the 1965 Act and follows the usual planning pattern of advertising the designation, allowing for the making of objections, the holding of a public local inquiry if any are made, followed by the final decision as to whether to proceed, subject to an appeal to the courts on a point of law. The decided cases indicate that where such an appeal is made the courts are unwilling to interfere too much with ministerial discretion.

Once the site of the new town has been designated, its development is undertaken by a development corporation established by orders made under section 2 of the 1965 Act. Each corporation consists of a chairman, deputy chairman and up to eleven members appointed ministerially after due consultation with those local authorities who appear to be concerned. Wide powers are conferred on development corporations by section 3 of the Act in order to help them achieve their statutory duty to lay out and develop the new town in accordance with the proposals they have made to the Secretary of State and had approved by him. These powers include power to acquire land and to undertake building work. Land may be acquired by agreement or compulsorily within or adjacent to the site of the new town. Section 7(2) of and Schedule 3 to the 1965 Act govern the compulsory purchase procedure within new towns. This has the effect that where an objection is made to a compulsory purchase order made in connection with a new town that there will, in general, be *no* public local inquiry, and objections will be dealt with on the basis of written submissions, or by a private hearing before an inspector at which the objector and the acquiring authority will both be heard.

The ownership of housing in the new towns

The founding fathers of the new towns did not envisage that the development corporations should be permanent bodies. Their original scheme was that after a period of years the development corporations should be wound up and their assets transferred to those local authorities in whose areas new towns were situated. However, by the mid 1950's serious doubts were emerging as to whether this policy would be implemented, and some of the development corporations themselves were not enthusiastic at the prospect of their demise and loss of identity within the normal local government system. The New Towns Act 1959 created the Commission for the New Towns, to take over the assets and liabilities of each development corporation as it completed its programme, and this body now functions under the New Towns Act 1965, ss. 35 to 38 and 41. Transfers to the Commission are made by the Secretary of State by orders when he is satisfied that the development corporation has substantially achieved the purposes for which it was set up. (The history of the debate on this issue, inter alia, will be found in J.B. Cullingworth and V.A. Karn, *The Ownership and Management of Housing in the New Towns* (Ministry of Housing and Local Government, 1968).)

Section 39 of the New Towns Act 1965 also allowed development corporations, subject to ministerial approval, to transfer to a local authority any part of their undertaking. The New Towns (Amendment) Act 1976 now goes much further than this. The Secretary of State has power under section 2 of this Act to give directions to new town corporations, the Commission for the New Towns and district councils to consult over the transfer of housing and associated property. Before the Secretary of State can give such directions *one* of three conditions has to be satisfied:

1) An order was made before the commencement of the 1976 Act with respect to the new town under section 41 of the 1965 Act transferring property of the development corporation to the Commission for the New Towns;

2) The site of the new town was first designated not less than fifteen years before the date of the Secretary of State's directions;

3) The Secretary of State, after consulting the new town corporation involved, formed the opinion that the development of the new town has been substantially completed, or would not be detrimentally affected by making a transfer scheme.

Even where the Secretary of State gives no directions, a new town corporation or district council may, provided the site of the new town was designated more than fifteen years previously, request that consultations should take place with a view to a transfer scheme being made.

It will be seen that the present law favours the transfer of the new town housing stock to the ordinary local authorities. Indeed section 3 of the 1976 Act gives power to the Secretary of State to give further directions after the consultations have taken place as to the making of a transfer scheme. The directions may include a requirement as to time, and though the time allowed for making a transfer scheme may be extended under section 5(2) of the 1976 Act, the Secretary of State may, with Treasury Consent, make a scheme himself if the authorities still fail to agree within the time allowed. Section 3(6) states the matters to be included in a transfer scheme: the property subject to the scheme must be so described that the scheme, once approved, provides a good title to the property; the scheme must confer on the new town corporation or the Commission for the New Towns a right to nominate tenants; it must include a statement of the financial arrangements involved in the transfer, and finally it must safeguard the interests of the staff of the parties. If the Secretary of State is satisfied with the scheme he may approve it, with or without modification. If he does not approve the proposals he may refer them back to be renegotiated and re-submitted within a new time limit. He may, of course, reject the proposals outright in which case he may, with Treasury Consent, make his own transfer scheme, after giving the parties an opportunity to comment on his proposals. Directions under section 3(3) of the New Towns (Amendment) Act 1976 may also require the development corporation and the district council concerned to enter into management arrangements in respect of buildings and other land within the district in which the corporation has an interest, but which are not being transferred, whereby the district council will undertake the management of such property.

After consultations have been held on a transfer scheme the Secretary of State may decide, under section 8 of the 1976 Act, not to require that such a scheme be made, provided he gives the parties notice of his decision and the reasons for it, and keep the situation under review to see if further consultation should take place. Either party is also able to initiate further consultations once three years have elapsed from the Secretary of State's decision.

The effect of the transfer of new town housing

Section 6 of the 1976 Act provides that the actual transfer occurs on 1 April of each relevant year. Transferred land is treated as having been acquired under Part V of the Housing Act 1957 unless the Secretary of State directs otherwise. Department of the Environment Circular No. 5/77, Part IV counsels development corporations and district councils to harmonise their housing policies as to rents and management before effecting a transfer scheme. Even after a transfer scheme has been implemented a new town corporation or the Commission for the New Towns as the case may be retains the right under section 7 of the 1976 Act to nominate tenants in respect of transferred housing. As seen above such nomination rights have to be included in a transfer scheme by virtue of section 3(6) of the 1976 Act, section 7 provides for the length of time during which they are to be exercised to be decided by agreement, subject to certain statutory minimum periods; for example, where a development corporation transfers its housing the right to nominate lasts from the day on which the houses vest in the district council until the date when the Secretary of State vests their other property in the Commission for the New Towns under Schedule 10 of the New Towns Act 1965. Department of the Environment Circular No. 5/77 contains a model transfer scheme.

Housing management powers in new towns

Before housing in new towns is transferred to a district council its ownership, management and control are vested in the relevant development corporation or the Commission for the New Towns as the case may be. Section 3(2)(a) of the 1965 Act confers the general power to acquire, hold, manage and dispose of land. However, this general power is subject to limitations. Section 18 of the Act states that a development corporation shall not have the power to transfer the freehold of any land or grant a lease of land for a term of more than 99 years without the consent of the minister. In the case of the Commission for the New Towns under sections 36 and 37(3) of the 1965 Act they may dispose of land freely, provided it is to supply the site of a house which the transferee has agreed to occupy as his residence. Otherwise they too require ministerial consent, either specific or general, for the disposal of land freehold or on a lease for more than 99 years.

The effect of the 'right to buy' provisions of the Housing Act 1980

Section 2(4) of the Housing Act 1980 provides that the right to buy does not arise in any of the circumstances mentioned in Part I of Schedule I to the Act, i.e. where the landlord is, inter alia, a development corporation or the Commission for the New Towns, *and*

1) the dwelling is held by it for purposes *not* corresponding to those for which dwelling-houses are held by local authorities under Part V of the 1957 Act; (that is the dwelling is held for purposes other than housing accommodation) and

2) the landlord, or on appeal the Secretary of State, is of the opinion that the right to buy ought not to be capable of being exercised with respect to the dwelling-house.

The effect of Schedule 1, paragraph 2(b) is that the 'right to buy' provisions apply unless the landlord, or the Secretary of State on appeal; is of the opinion that the right to buy ought not to be capable of being exercised.

Finally it should be noted that new town authorities have the same power as other local authorities under section 93(1) of the Housing Finance Act 1972 to make payments to assist their tenants with removal expenses.

Further reading

Cullingworth, J.B. and Karn, V.A., *The Ownership and Management of Housing in the New Towns* (Ministry of Housing and Local Government, 1968).

Roberts, N.A., *The Reform of Planning Law* (Macmillan, 1976).

Schaffer, F., *The New Town Story* (Paladin, 1972).

Social Welfare Law (Ed. by D.W. Pollard) (Oyez) paras. B.101 – B.227 and B.376 – B.450.

Chapter 2

The sale of council houses

Introduction

The sale of council houses has been an issue ever since municipalities first began to provide housing. It is no new subject for debate both nationally and locally, and central and local policies have varied greatly from time to time and place to place. It has been the subject of fierce and often bitter controversy in town halls and at Westminster. Against this background of controversy a number of council houses have been sold. In the period 1953 – 59 some 14,000 council dwellings were disposed of; between 1959 and 1972 sales reached over 150,000, and in 1972 alone 60,000 were sold.

Over the years the main planks in the arguments used by both the Conservative and Labour parties for and against the sale of council houses have remained fairly constant. The principal difference seems to be that the Labour party is prepared to allow the sale of council houses, provided that such sales are not to the disadvantage of the community, and provided that they do not impair the ability of housing authorities to meet their other obligations, while the Conservatives have favoured the idea that local authorities should be under an obligation to give tenants the right to buy. During most of this period of debate, which has lasted from 1951 until the present day, the form of the law remained constant, in that local authorities had a *power* to sell their houses subject to ministerial consent. That consent was varied from time to time but the basic law, which was to be found in section 104 of Part V of the Housing Act 1957, remained fundamentally unchanged for many years. What is dramatically new in the debate is the new law giving certain persons the *right* to purchase council houses and stating that local authorities shall be unable to prevent the exercise of that right. The *power* to sell has been transformed into a *duty* to sell, and the *privilege* of being able to purchase has been transmuted into a *right*.

The former law

Part V, section 104 of the Housing Act 1957, as amended by Schedule

54

23 to the Rent Act 1977 and section 2 of the Housing (Amendment) Act 1973, provided:

'(1) Where a local authority have acquired or appropriated any land for the purpose of this Part of the Act, then, without prejudice to any of their other powers under this Act, the local authority may, with the consent of the Minister, sell or lease any houses on the land or erected by them on the land, subject to such covenants and conditions as they may think fit to impose in regard to the maintenance or use of the houses and upon any such sale or on the grant of any such lease they may, if they think fit, agree to the price or any premium being paid by instalments or to a payment of part thereof being secured by a mortgage of the premises'.

The crucial words were: '. . . The local authority *may*, with the consent of the minister, sell or lease any houses on the land or erected by them on the land'. These created the power of sale, but also made it subject to a measure of central supervision. Obviously therefore the form in which the Minister gave his consent was of considerable importance. The Department of the Environment, inheriting the attitudes of the old Ministry of Housing and Local Government, traditionally did not interfere over much with the housing powers and policies of local authorities. The result was that in so far as there was any central articulation of a sales policy for council houses that it was somewhat circumspect and not too promotional. There was a reliance on exhortation and advice, coupled with a reluctance to interfere with or take away local autonomy.

The history and development of the sales policy

During the period from 1945 – 51 the Minister did not give his consent to the sale of council housing pursuant to his powers under section 79(1)(d) of the Housing Act 1936. There had been sales before 1939 but the World War broke the link with earlier precedents and there seems to have been a conscious political decision after 1945 not to allow sales of council houses. Great changes came about with the return to power of the Conservatives in 1951. The Housing Act 1952 included provisions to facilitate the sale of council houses, such as the repeal of the old 1936 Act requirement to sell houses only at the best price obtainable. This Act also granted local authorities the power to limit the price at which a house sold by them could subsequently be resold for a period of up to five years after disposal, and also gave them the power to reserve a five year right of pre-emption for themselves. The Act was followed by Ministry of Housing and Local Government Circular No. 64/52 which, in effect, gave a general ministerial consent, in accordance with the terms of the Act, to sales to sitting tenants, or, in the case of unoccupied houses, to persons in need of a house for their own exclusive use. No allowance was made in the circular for discount sales. The wording of this circular was mild, restrained and certainly not promotional. It was not revised until 1960 despite the enactment of the 1957 Housing Act. In view of the non-promotional nature of the legislation and the guidance contained in the circular it is not surprising that there were few council house sales in the 1950's.

On 1 March 1960 Ministry of Housing and Local Government Circular No. 5/60 replaced No. 64/52. For the first time local authorities were encouraged to consider the aspirations of those of their tenants who had the means to become owner-occupiers. A sales policy was encouraged insofar as it was compatible with other obligations. The circular also gave a wide discretion as to the prices which could be charged for council houses on sale, though there were no fixed discounts as such and a minimum price level was set. These changes in policy can be seen as a limited move to bring council house sales policy more in line with the dominant Conservative philosophy of 'the property owning democracy'. Circular No. 5/60 remained in force and virtually unamended until 1 April 1967 when it was replaced by Ministry of Housing and Local Government Joint Circular No. 24/67. This pointed out that any substantial development of sales in areas with pressing social need for rented accommodation would be wrong. Indeed the new circular seemed to reprove some authorities who had gone far beyond the cautious policies advocated by Circular No. 5/60. Local authorities were exhorted to have regard to the effect sales might have on the available housing stock and the Housing Revenue Account. The new advisory policy was that where the demand for rented accommodation could be said to be falling off then consideration could be given to a sales policy which would not cause financial or managerial problems. Deference was still shown to local autonomy by leaving the general consent to sales in force. Restrictions were imposed mainly by reason and persuasion.

Much greater changes were wrought by Ministry of Housing and Local Government Circular No. 42/68 which withdrew the previous circular *and* the general consent to the sale of council houses. The terms in which this circular was phrased made much more use of the very loose terminology of section 104(2) of the Housing Act 1957, in that the ministerial consent given differentiated between different areas of the country. In the conurbations of Greater London, Merseyside, South East Lancashire and the West Midlands, sales were to be limited to one-quarter of the total housing stock in an authority's area. In other areas the 1967 consent was renewed. This circular showed that central government was prepared to exert greater control over council house sales and to restrict them by quota if it thought fit. Circular No. 42/68 was destined to be short lived. It was soon replaced by Ministry of Housing and Local Government Circular No. 54/70 which was introduced by the new Conservative Government, and which was concerned with the policy of encouraging the spread of home ownership. It stated that: 'progress can be made towards meeting the desires of those tenants who wish to own their homes without conflicting with the needs of the homeless and the inadequately housed'. The 1968 quota restrictions were removed and full discretion to dispose of council houses was conferred in a new general consent. Discount sales were again allowed provided there were restrictions on resale. Department of the Environment Circular No. 56/72 urged those authorities who were not utilising their sale powers to do so, and said: 'unless the local circumstances are quite exceptional, a local authority who deny their tenants the opportunity to own the house which they have made their home would be failing to exercise their powers under . . . the Housing Act 1957 in a manner which is appropriate to the present circumstances'. The same circular also urged local authorities to sell on the most advantageous 20 per cent discount terms.

The return to power of the Labour Party in 1974 led to the issue of Department of the Environment Circular No. 70/74. Inter alia this stated that local authorities should see it as their first duty to provide an adequate supply of houses for renting, and that they should not therefore indulge in an indiscriminate sales policy. It continued that in the large cities it would be wrong generally to sell houses. The general consent to sales was not withdrawn and the circular contended itself with expressing the policy of the new government in exhortatory fashion only. No doubt the drafters of the circular were happy to use this sort of wording as many large urban areas were at the time controlled by Labour councils who would be unlikely to make much use of their powers of sale. No more concrete restrictions on sale were imposed at that time.

The background to the modern law and policy on sales

At the beginning of 1979 local authorities had a general power to sell their houses, and this was coupled with a general governmental consent for the power to be exercised, though other statements of an admonitory and exhortatory nature counselled against its use. This left a vast amount to be decided at the discretion of individual authorities whose sales policies might be determined by their political colour. There was also the knowledge that a general election could not be far away and this led both major political parties to indulge in bellicose statements with regard to housing policy. While the Conservatives had for some time talked of 'the sale of the century', the Labour Government's own consultative document *Housing Policy,* Cmnd. 6851, disapproved of a general sales policy and declined to introduce a statutory right for tenants to buy. In March 1979 government policy was taken ever further when the Secretary of State announced further restrictions on the sale of council houses. (See H.C. Debs., 1979, vol. 963, cols. 933 – 934.) These restrictions became effective as from 17 March 1979 being contained in letters sent from the Department of the Environment to chief executives; but they were not to last long. The incoming Conservative Government had made much of their promise to sell council houses during their successful election campaign. It came as no surprise, when on 17 May 1979, the new Secretary of State for the Environment, Mr Heseltine, together with his Minister of State, Mr Stanley, made major policy statements on future council house sales policy in Parliament (H.C. Debs., 1979, vol. 967, cols. 408 et seq. and 535 et seq.) The Secretary of State began by stating a number of reasons why the government favoured the sale of council houses. These included:

1) The gap that had opened increasingly between owner-occupiers and council tenants, because of the vast capital increase in value of owner-occupied dwellings, which had made the council tenant relatively much worse off;

2) The fact that owner-occupiers are much more mobile than council tenants who may often seem to be the prisoners of their environment; and

3) The lack of freedom of choice, especially with regard to the conditions of tenancies, prevailing in the public sector.

To these reasons we may add that which stemmed from the dominant Conservative Party policy that there should be a massive reallocation of wealth *from* the state, as represented by local authorities, *to* the private citizen.

The Secretary of State announced plans to make immediate changes to the existing law and policy on sale, and these were duly incorporated in new consents to sales.

The Secretary of State stated that he hoped local authorities would make rapid use of these new consents to sell, though, of course, he would obviously know that the discretion was unlikely to be used by Labour-controlled councils. Accordingly he went on to unveil plans for imposing a *duty* on authorities to sell their dwellings. The Secretary proposed that local authority tenants should have the legal right to purchase their homes on a generous discount basis, but subject to safe-guards on re-sale. The Minister of State amplified these proposals in his speech.

1) The right to purchase would be enshrined in the law and would be so phrased as to be undeniable.

2) Power would be given to local authorities to grant valid options to purchase.

3) The Government would also continue to give its support to shared-equity schemes.

4) Sales to tenants would continue to be at generous discount rates. The right to purchase would be attached to a tenant's present dwelling-house, *but* the size of the discount would depend on the length of time that the tenant had been a tenant, despite moves between houses.

Even some Conservative controlled authorities were perturbed by the notion of compulsory sales. At the June 1979 Institute of Housing Conference some of the smaller authorities expressed concern that an indiscriminate forced sales policy might seriously deplete their already limited housing stocks. The problems that could result might be:

1) In some attractive rural areas many council houses could simply become second homes for wealthy city dwellers;

2) In popular holiday and tourist areas the municipal housing stock would be so depleted that authorities might find it difficult to meet their obligations under the Housing Acts and the Housing (Homeless Persons) Act 1977;

3) Some authorities might need to plead for exemption from the new legislation in order to preserve any meaningful municipal housing stock.

As will be seen the new law does go some way towards meeting some of these objections. However, there can be no doubt that a compulsory sales policy is unacceptable to many people working in the field of housing — and not just for political reasons. Many are opposed to the element of compulsion in the sales policy and the consequent erosion of local discretion. Others oppose the very idea of a sales policy, arguing that it will lead to sales of only the most desirable municipal houses, leaving local authorities with only a 'rump' of unpopular housing, and thus restricting the range of choice open to remaining, and potential, council tenants. Such an erosion of the municipal housing stock could reduce the social rôle of council house to that of being merely welfare housing provision. This could lead to social segregation and stigmatisation of the remaining municipal stock and its inhabitants. Against this it has been argued, even by some left wing thinkers, that a really effective sales policy would lead to a massive redistribution of wealth in society, that this would be a major direct attack on the cycle of poverty, and that it would increase the total amount of individual freedom from bureaucratic rules and restrictions. The real tragedy is that the sale of council houses issue has become a political football which is kicked from one legal extreme to the other with each change of government. This is one area of law and practice that can safely be predicted as likely to be subject to regular change.

The 'right to buy' under the Housing Act 1980

'The right to buy' is enshrined in Part I, Chapter I of the 1980 Act, and unless otherwise stated all subsequent references are to that legislation.

Section 1 grants a secure tenant (see Chapter 3 for the definition of 'secure tenant') the right to acquire the freehold of his dwelling where it is a house, or, where his dwelling is a flat, to take a long lease of it. Dwelling-houses and flats are defined by section 3 so that:

(a) where a building is divided horizontally the units into which it is divided are *not* houses;

(b) where a building is not structurally detached from its neighbours it is *not* a house if a material part of it lies above or below the remainder of the structure (this covers maisonettes and flats built over municipal shop developments);

(c) where a building is divided vertically the units may be houses so a dwelling in a terrace is a house, provided it is otherwise a structure reasonably so called.

Any dwelling which is not a house must be treated as a flat for sale purposes. Any land used for the purposes of the dwelling may be included in the disposal by agreement between the parties (section 3(4)) and any land let with a dwelling is to be treated as part of the dwelling unless it is agricultural land exceeding two acres (section 50(2)(b)).

This right to buy only arises after the secure tenant has enjoyed that status for a period of not less than three years, or for a number of shorter periods amounting together to three years. During that period neither the landlord nor the dwelling-house need have been the same throughout so a secure tenant can build up his entitlement to buy, for example, during a time in which he moves from one secure tenancy with a local authority to another.

In support of a claim to have complied with the qualification period a tenant may have to make a statutory declaration, particularly where he has moved around the country from one local authority dwelling to another and has no other proof of residence. Such declarations may be accepted as sufficient evidence of the matters contained in them by virtue of section 25.

However, any time spent as a tenant of a housing trust or a housing association having a certain charitable status will not be accounted as reckoning towards the three year qualification period. On the other hand where a secure tenant occupied a dwelling-house as his only or principal home by virtue of a joint tenancy such a period of occupation does count towards the three year period. Likewise where a tenant became a secure tenant on the death of spouse, and where, at the time of death, they occupied the same dwelling as their only or principal home, any period during which the deceased spouse was a secure tenant is also to count towards the qualification period. References in Chapter I of the Housing Act 1980 to 'secure tenancy' or 'secure tenant' are, under section 27(3), in relation to any time before the commencement of Part I of the Act, i.e. 3 October 1980, references to a tenancy which would have been a secure tenancy, or to a person who would have been a secure tenant if the Act of 1980 had then been in force. Thus a retrospective secure tenant status is conferred on most municipal tenants, which enables the 'right to buy' provisions to take immediate effect.

Section 2 lays down certain exceptions where the right to buy does not apply. These are as follows:

1) Where the landlord is a charity which is a housing trust within the meaning of the Charities Act 1960;

2) Where the landlord is a housing association which either —
   (a) is a charity within the Act of 1960; or
   (b) is registered under the Industrial and Provident Societies Act 1965 (that is it has a restricted membership such as a co-owner-ship scheme);
   (c) has never received a grant from public funds;

3) Where the landlord does not own the freehold;

4) Where Schedule 1, Part I applies, i.e.:
   (a) the landlord is a local authority and they hold the dwelling-house otherwise than under Part V of the Housing Act 1957; (Though the Secretary of State may by order extend the right to buy provisions to cover such properties)
   (b) the landlord is a development corporation, the Commission for the New Towns or the Development Board for Rural Wales and
       (i) the dwelling-house is held by them for purposes not corres-ponding to those for which dwelling-houses are held by local authorities under Part V of the Housing Act 1957; and
       (ii) the landlord, or on an appeal the Secretary of State, is of opinion that the right to buy ought not to be capable of being exercised with respect to the dwelling-house;
   (c) the dwelling-house has features which are substantially different from those of ordinary dwelling-houses and which are designed to make it suitable for occupation by physically disabled persons;
   (d) the dwelling is one of a group which it is the practice of the land-lord to let to pensioners, and social services or other special

facilities are provided in close proximity to help such persons, and where the landlord has within six weeks of being served with a notice claiming the right to buy applied to the Secretary of State for a determination whether the right is capable of being exercised. The Secretary of State must make a determination *against* the exercise of the right if he is satisfied:

(i) that the house is designed or specially adapted for occupation by persons of pensionable age, and

(ii) that it is the practice of the landlord to let it only for occupation by such persons.

Neither can the right to buy be exercised where either:

1) the tenant is, or will be, obliged to give up possession of the house in pursuance of a court order, or

2) where a bankruptcy petition is pending against the person to whom the right to buy belongs, or where he is an undischarged bankrupt, or has made a composition with his creditors, see section 2(4)(b).

Where a secure tenancy is a joint tenancy section 4 states that the right to buy belongs to all the joint tenants or to such of them as they may agree between them (provided at least one of them occupies the house as his only or principal home). In any case a secure tenant may, under section 4(2), join up to three members of his family in the right to buy even if they are not joint tenants with him provided that the landlord consents, or provided those members of the family joined in the right to buy, occupy the dwelling as their only or principal home, and are either:

1) the tenant's spouse, or

2) have been residing with the tenant throughout the period of twelve months preceding the notice claiming the right to buy.

The claim to join members of a family in the purchase must be made in the notice claiming to exercise the right to buy.

By virtue of sections 27(1) and 50(3) a person is a member of a tenant's family if he is his spouse, parent, grandparent, child, grandchild, brother, sister, uncle, aunt, nephew or niece: relationships by marriage count as relationships by blood; half-blood counts as whole blood, and step-children count as ordinary children, with illegitimate children being treated as legitimate, and also treating persons living together as man and wife as being members of a family.

Under section 15 where a secure tenant dies or ceases to be the secure tenant and thereupon a child of his who occupies the dwelling as his only or principal home becomes the new secure tenant, the landlord may count towards the three year qualification for the right to buy any period during which the new tenant, since reaching the age of sixteen, occupied as his only or principal home a dwelling-house of which a parent of his was a sole or joint secure tenant, and either

1) that period was one at the end of which the new tenant became the secure tenant, or

2) it was a period ending *not* earlier than two years before another period qualifying under section 15.

The price to be paid for the house or flat

By section 6 the price to be paid is the 'value at the relevant time' which is the price the dwelling would fetch on the open market at that time, that is the date on which the tenant's notice claiming to exercise the right to buy was served on a willing vendor basis but subject to certain assumptions:

1) the vendor was selling for an estate in fee simple, or was granting a lease for 125 years, *with vacant possession* (i.e. the existence of a sitting tenant is not to depress the value of the house);

2) neither the tenant nor a member of his family residing with him wished to acquire the property (i.e. the desire of the tenant to buy is not to increase the price in any way);

3) any improvements made by the tenant or his predecessors in title, or by a member of his family who immediately before the present secure tenancy was granted was the secure tenant of the dwelling together with any failure by them to keep the property in good internal repair are to be disregarded;

4) that the conveyance, or grant of the lease as the case may be, is on the terms laid down in the Housing Act 1980.

But this price must be discounted according to section 7. A person exercising the right to buy is entitled to a discount off the purchase price of his house of 33 per cent, plus 1 per cent for each *complete* year by which his period as a secure tenant exceeds three years up to a maximum of 50 per cent. Neither may the discount reduce the price below the amount which, having been fixed in accordance with determinations made by the Secretary of State, represents that part of the cost incurred after 31 March 1974 in respect of the dwelling. If the price before discount is below that amount, then no discount is allowable. In any case discount may not reduce the price of any dwelling by more than such a sum as is prescribed by the Secretary of State.

Discount entitlement can be built up either as a continuous period spent as a secure tenant, or by aggregating together the various periods during which:

1) the secure tenant or his spouse or deceased spouse was either a secure tenant or the spouse of a secure tenant; or

2) the secure tenant occupied accommodation provided for him as a member of the armed forces of the Crown, or the secure tenant's spouse occupied accommodation so provided for the secure tenant's spouse, and where the secure tenant or his spouse as the case may be was a member of the armed forces on or after 21 December 1979.

However, it should be noted that:

1) a period is to be taken into account whether or not the dwelling-house or the landlord was the same as at the time of the service of the notice claiming to exercise the right to buy;

2) no period during which the tenant's spouse was a secure tenant or the spouse of a secure tenant is to be taken into account unless both the secure tenant and his spouse occupied the dwelling-house as their only or principal home at the time they served notice of their wish to buy that dwelling;

3) a period during which either the tenant or his spouse or deceased spouse was the spouse of a secure tenant shall be taken into account only if during that period the spouses occupied the same dwelling-house as their only or principal home;

4) no period during which the tenant's deceased spouse was a secure tenant or the spouse of a secure tenant shall be taken into account *unless* the tenant became the secure tenant on the death of his spouse and at that time both occupied the dwelling-house as their only or principal home.

5) where the right to buy is being exercised by joint tenants the aggregation of the discount period shall proceed on the basis that whichever of the joint tenants is entitled to the largest discount overall shall be treated, for discount purposes, as a sole tenant so that the largest discount entitlement possible for any joint tenant is to be preserved for the benefit of all. Furthermore where a person occupied a dwelling as his only or principal home under a secure joint tenancy, for discount purposes he is to be treated as having been a secure tenant.

These somewhat tortuous rules are best explained by some examples.

1) Bill is a secure tenant of 20 years' standing — he is presumptively entitled to a 50 per cent discount irrespective, for example, of whether

he has moved from one municipal house to another, or has made moves between local authorities.

2) Ben has been a secure tenant for five years since he married his wife Ada who was the widow of Charles who had been, until the time of his death, a secure tenant for ten years. The period for discount purposes is fifteen years, if Ada lived with Charles for the ten years.

3) Dick has been a secure tenant for five years and is married to Ethel who was the widow of Frank who before his death had been a secure tenant for ten years. However, before Dick served his notice wishing to buy his dwelling Ethel left him. The discount period is only five years.

4) Gus has been a secure tenant for five years, and is now married to Helen who at one time was married to Ivan, also a secure tenant, but whom Helen divorced after five years of marriage during which time they had never lived together. The discount period is only five years.

5) Jack is a secure tenant of eighteen years' standing. He has just married Kay who, before their marriage, was a secure tenant herself of twenty years' standing. After their marriage the local authority granted them a joint tenancy of a house into which they moved from their previous homes. Jack and Kay now wish to buy their house, the discount period will be calculated by reference to Kay and will be 20 years.

No period can be aggregated if it was *prior* to a previous exercise of the right to buy by the tenant, his spouse or deceased spouse whose period of occupation is to be taken into account. But where a secure tenant dies or otherwise ceases to be the secure tenant and thereupon a child of his who occupies the dwelling as his only or principal home becomes the new secure tenant, the landlord may under section 15 count towards discount entitlement any period during which the new tenant, since reaching the age of sixteen, occupied, as his only or principal home, a dwelling-house of which a parent of his was a sole or joint secure tenant, and either:

1) that period was one at the end of which the new tenant became the secure tenant, or

2) it was a period ending *not* earlier than two years before another period qualifying under section 15.

Where the price of a council house is discounted section 8 requires that the purchaser shall covenant to repay on demand to the landlord a specified amount of the discount, if within a period of five years he further conveys, or leases, assigns or sub-leases, as the case may be, the dwelling he has acquired. The amount of discount repayable under this covenant is the discount reduced by 20 per cent for each complete year elapsing after the date of transfer to the purchaser.

Exercising the right to buy

The procedure for initiating the process of transfer is contained in section 5. The tenant must serve on the landlord a written notice claiming to exercise the right to buy. If this notice is not withdrawn the landlord must serve a written counter notice within four weeks which either admits the tenant's right, or denies it, stating the reasons why, in the landlord's opinion, it does not exist. Disputes as to the tenant's right to buy are to be determined by the county court, see section 86. Once the right to buy has been established the landlord must serve, under section 10, 'as soon as practicable', a further notice on the tenant. This will described the dwelling-house and state:

1) the price at which in the opinion of the landlord the tenant is entitled to acquire the property, showing the value as assessed under section 6 and the discount as calculated under section 7 (see above);

2) the tenant's right to have the value of the property determined by the district valuer; and

3) his rights to mortgage facilities together with a form for his use if he wishes to avail himself of them;

4) the provisions which the landlord concludes should be contained in the grant or conveyance.

Two points require comment. First, the local authority in its capacity as a selling landlord is under a duty to serve the notice described above on the tenant 'as soon as practicable'. In a statute as badly drafted as the Housing Act 1980 it is no surprise to find vague expressions such as 'as soon as practicable'. The received understanding of the phrase in town hall and Whitehall is that it places an obligation on an authority to expedite matters with some speed. An authority would not be able to plead lack of staff caused by economy measures, for example, if it were accused of not fulfilling its duty 'as soon as practicable'. The official view is that much of the work of selling-off council houses could be discharged by private firms of solicitors acting as agents for local authorities.

The other point is that where a prospective purchaser is unhappy with the valuation contained in the section 10 notice he may exercise the right, of which he will have been informed in that notice, to have the value determined by the district valuer. He must follow the procedure laid down in section 11 and serve written notice within three months of having received the section 10 notice, requiring the district valuer to determine the value of the property at the 'relevant time', that is the date on which notice claiming to exercise the right to buy was served. The three month period is extended if there are proceedings pending on the determination of any other question arising under Chapter I of Part I of the 1980 Act. In such a case the notice may be served at any time within three months of the final determination of those proceedings. Where such proceedings are begun *after* a determination made by the district valuer, a redetermination may be required under section 11(2)(b) of the 1980 Act by either of the parties within four weeks of the conclusion of the proceedings. The district valuer must consider any representations made to him by either the landlord or the tenant within four weeks from the service of a notice under section 11. It is the duty of the local authority under section 11(5) to inform the tenant of the outcome of any determination or redetermination made by the district valuer. The jurisdiction of the district valuer in such valuations is exclusive.

Completing the transfer

Once all the above steps have been taken, the matters relating to the transfer and the arrangements as to mortgage finance, etc., have been completed, section 16(1) binds the landlord to convey or lease, as the case may be, the dwelling to the tenant. On completion the secure tenancy comes to an end; section 16(11). The landlord is not bound to complete, and the tenant's claim to exercise the right to buy may be deemed to lapse if the tenant is found to be in arrears with his rent or other tenancy outgoings for a period of four weeks after the money due has been lawfully demanded from him (section 16(9)). This provision prevents tenants who are in arrears from proceeding with the purchase of their homes. If there are no impediments to the transfer the landlord must go ahead with it, and the duty is enforceable by way of an injunction (section 16(10)).

The actual transfer to the purchaser takes place according to the registered conveyancing procedure under section 123 of the Land Registration Act 1925. This is so, by virtue of section 20, whether or not the dwelling is in an area subject to registered conveyancing. In those cases where the dwelling is not within a registered conveyancing area, the selling landlord must certify their right to sell.

The right to a mortgage

The 'right to a mortgage' is guaranteed by section 1(1)(c). This phrase, however, is somewhat misleading. It means that the purchasing tenant has the right to leave the whole or part of a sum fixed in accordance with section 9(1) outstanding on the security of the dwelling. Some purchasers will look to the building societies for mortgage assistance.

For those who are not able to rely on building society assistance the 'right to a mortgage' is an essential part of the 'right to buy'. Those sales taking place in reliance on this right will involve little or no capital changing hands at the time of sale for the purchaser will leave the price outstanding secured on the dwelling and will pay it off, with interest, over a period of years.

The amount to be left outstanding

Section 9(1) states that the amount which a secure tenant exercising the right to a mortgage is entitled to leave outstanding on the security of the dwelling is the aggregate of:

1) the purchase price

2) the costs incurred in connection with the exercise of the right to a mortgage (subject to such limit as may be specified by the Secretary of State, section 21(2)).

3) any costs incurred by the tenant and defrayed on his behalf by the landlord.

This aggregate sum is subject, under section 9(2) to a limit; namely that it does not exceed the sum produced by multiplying the amount to be taken into account as the tenant's available annual income by a certain factor. Under section 9(4) the Secretary of State is empowered to make regulations to make provision for calculating in any given case what figure should be taken into account as a tenant's available annual income, and also to specify a multiplying factor appropriate to that amount in order to arrive at the limit for the given individual. The regulations may provide for a person's available annual income to be calculated on the basis that sums related to his needs and commitments are to be excluded from the calculation. They may also specify different amounts and factors in different circumstances. Thus lower multipliers are applied to borrowers nearing or over the normal age of retirement. Where the right to a mortgage belongs to more than one person section 9(3) states that the limit is the aggregate of the amounts for each of them produced by taking their individual available annual incomes and multiplying them by the appropriate multiplyer. Where the appropriate limit in any given case is *less* the aggregate otherwise produced under section 9(1), section 9(5) empowers the landlord, if they think fit, and if the tenant agrees, to allow the tenant to leave all or part of the difference between the limit and aggregate outstanding on the security of the dwelling. (See also S.I. 1980 No. 1423.)

Exercising the right to a mortgage

By section 12 the right to a mortgage must be exercised by serving written notice on the landlord not later than three months after the tenant has himself been served with notice under either section 10 or section 11(5), whichever is appropriate (see above). (Though this period may be extended under section 12(2).) As soon as practicable after the service of the tenant's notice claiming mortgage entitlement the landlord must serve a written counter notice which contains:

1) the amount which, in their opinion, the tenant is entitled to leave outstanding;

2) a statement of how that amount has been arrived at;

3) the provisions which they consider should be contained in the mortgage deed, and

4) a statement of the effect of the provisions of section 16.

Under section 16 where a secure tenant has claimed to exercise the right to buy and that right has been established, the landlord is bound to complete the conveyance or lease, as the case may be, subject to, inter alia, agreement on those matters connected with the right to a mortgage. Conversely, once all the section 16 matters have been agreed the landlord may serve a notice to require the purchasing tenant to complete the transaction in a period of not less than 28 days. The governing provision here are the tortuous and ill-worded sub-sections (3) to (8) of section 16. These must be taken in order.

The landlord's ability to require the tenant to complete the transaction arises in different ways in different circumstances.

1) If the tenant has *not* claimed to exercise the right to a mortgage, notice to complete the transaction may be served three months after the end of the period within which the tenant could have claimed the right to a mortgage.

2) If he has claimed to exercise the right to a mortgage but is not entitled to defer completion, he may be required to complete by a notice served three months after the landlord's notice of the amount and terms of the mortgage under section 12.

3) If he is entitled to defer completion, he may be required to complete by a notice served two years after service of notice claiming the right to buy, or, if later, three months after the service of the notice under section 12(4) (terms and conditions of the mortgage).

A tenant is entitled to defer completion if he has claimed the right of a mortgage and

1) the amount of the mortgage to which he is entitled, or which the landlord agrees to leave outstanding, is *less* than the aggregate cost mentioned in section 9(1), and

2) he has within a period of three months beginning with the service of him of the notice under section 12(4) (amount and terms of mortgage) served a notice claiming entitlement to defer completion and has deposited a sum of £100 with the landlord. (This three month period can be extended on reasonable grounds.)

Thus where the tenant's mortgage entitlement limit is *less* than the amount forming the aggregate cost of the dwelling he may defer completion. The deferment fixes the price of the house at which the tenant can buy while allowing him time to find the purchase money or hope for an improvement in his circumstances to justify a higher mortgage entitlement. During the period of deferment the tenant may, under section 16(8) serve a further notice claiming a mortgage under section 12(1) and this will enable him to have his circumstances reviewed.

Where the £100 deposit is paid, the deposited sum counts towards the purchase price on final completion.

Where the ability to serve a notice to complete has arisen and has been exercised a tenant who fails to comply is deemed to have withdrawn his claim to exercise the right to buy at the end of the stated period. No further notice claiming to exercise the right to buy may be served for twelve months, see section 16(6).

The terms of the mortgage

Where a tenant claims to exercise the right to a mortgage the mortgage deed, unless the parties agree otherwise, must, under section 18:

1) provide for the repayment of the amount secured in equal instalments of principal and interest combined; and

2) provide that the period over which repayment is to be made shall be 25 years (at the option of the mortgagor it can be a shorter period) but this period is capable of being extended by the mortgagee.

Other terms may be included by agreement, or on the order of the Secretary of State. The rate of interest to be charged on a mortgage acquired under the 'right to a mortgage' provisions of the Act is governed by section 110(1)(b) which covers situations where a local authority *has* to allow any sum to be left outstanding on the security of a dwelling. The rate is the same as for normal municipal mortgages, see Chapter 5, below.

No other terms, for example as to the mortgagee's remedies, liability for repairs and insurance, and restrictions on letting, are *required* by section 18, but they would certainly be included by 'agreement' under section 18(c).

Miscellaneous points

Where a former secure tenant has given notice claiming to exercise the right to buy and he is superseded by a new secure tenant under the same secure tenancy, or under a periodic tenancy arising after the end of such a tenancy under section 29, the new tenant is in the same position *as if the notice had been given by him*, see section 13. The new tenant will have the right to a mortgage, and, even if notice of the purchase price and terms of the sale has already been served on the former tenant, another form to enable him to claim a mortgage must be supplied, following which he will have three months in which to claim the mortgage. If the former tenant wished to join members of his family in the right to buy their right to join in will continue *provided* that they are also members of the new tenant's family. For the purposes of entitlement to exercise the right to buy and also discount entitlement it is the new tenant's circumstances that must be considered.

On the other hand where there is a change of landlord, by transfer of the freehold, after the service of notice claiming to exercise the right to buy, section 14 lays down that all parties shall be in the same position as if the acquiring landlord had been landlord before the notice was given and had taken all steps which the former landlord had taken. This deceptively simple formula fails to deal with a major problem — what is the position if the new landlord is a body not subject to the right to buy provisions? The Act is silent on the point, but until amending legislation is passed the better view of the law is that in such cases the right to buy must be lost.

A tenant who has claimed to exercise the right to buy may, in general, withdraw it by serving written notice at any time on his landlord (section 5(1)).

A tenant who exercises the right to buy, but *not* the right to a mortgage, cannot be obliged to bear any part of his landlord's costs in connection with the sale, and any agreement to that effect is void (section 21).

The terms of the freehold sale or long lease

Section 17 and Schedule 2 contain the terms on which the transfer of dwellings takes place. Most reflect common conveyancing practice, but some are deserving of comment.

Leasehold terms

1) The lease must be for a term of not less than 125 years at a ground rent of not more than £10 per annum. But if in a building containing two or more dwellings, for example a block of flats, one has already been sold on a 125 year lease under the 1980 Act, any subsequent long lease granted under the right to buy provisions may be made for a term of less than 125 years so as to expire at the same time as the initial 125 year term.

2) Following the transfer the purchaser will continue to enjoy the common use of any premises, facilities or services enjoyed previously as a secure tenant unless both parties agree otherwise. This ensures not only that the purchaser will retain the use of and access to the common parts of any buildings in which his flat is situated, but also that he will continue to be able to receive the benefit of any services and facilities previously enjoyed in his capacity as a tenant along with other tenants.

3) The landlord is made subject to quite onerous repairing covenants:
   (a) to keep in repair the structure and exterior of the dwelling, and also of the building in which it is situated (including drains, gutters and external pipes) and to make good any defect affecting that structure; 'structure' can include roofing tiles and external wall rendering, see *Granada Theatres Ltd v Freehold Investments (Leytonstone) Ltd* [1959] Ch 592, [1959] 2 All ER 176;
   (b) to keep in repair any other property over or in respect of which the tenant has any rights by virtue of Schedule 2, for example any common parts which the purchaser has the right to use;
   (c) to ensure, so far as practicable, that any services which are to be provided by the landlord and to which the purchaser is entitled (either alone or in common with others) are maintained at a reasonable level, and also to keep in repair any installation connected with the provision of such services;
   (d) to rebuild or reinstate the dwelling and the building in which it is situated in the case of destruction or damage by fire, tempest, flood or any other normally insurable risk.

It will be seen that these covenants go far beyond those implied in short lettings under the Housing Act 1961 (see Chapter 7). But the landlord's liability will not be absolute. They will not be liable for any breach of covenant unless they are given notice of the defect, and the standard of repair required will depend on the age, character and locality of the dwelling, see *Lurcott v Wakely and Wheeler* [1911] 1 KB 905.

The long leases of, so-called, 'luxury' flats sometimes contain covenants binding the builder/freeholder to do certain structural and other repair works if necessary. Almost invariably such covenants also contain a stipulation that the cost of the works is recoverable from the tenants individually and collectively. Under Schedule 2 any such agreement as would enable the landlord to recover from the tenant any part of the costs incurred in discharging or insuring against the obligation to keep the structure and exterior of the dwelling, and the building in which it is situated and the common parts, in repair is void. To this there are two exceptions.

1) There can be an agreement that the purchaser shall bear a reasonable part of the cost of carrying out repairs not amounting to the making good of structural defects.

2) There can be an agreement that the purchaser shall bear a reasonable part of the cost of insuring against or making good structural defects where:

   (a) the landlord notified the tenant of its existence before the long lease was granted (i.e. a sale subject to declared defects), or
   (b) where the landlord does not become aware of the defect earlier than ten years after the lease is granted.

The landlord may insert a term requiring the purchaser to bear a reasonable part of the costs of carrying out repairs *not* concerned with making good structural defects.

The landlord may also require the purchasing tenant to bear a proportionate cost of the maintenance of services.

Schedule 2 also makes void any term of the lease purporting to prohibit or restrict assigning or subletting the dwelling. To make sure that the bargain is not entirely one-sided the schedule imposes an obligation on the tenant, unless the parties agree otherwise, to keep the interior of the dwelling in good repair, including good decorative repair. Even so the purchasers of municipal flats buy on very favourable terms as can easily be seen.

Those who purchase long leasehold interests in flats from local authorities may also rely on the provisions of Schedule 19 to the 1980 Act. In most cases such purchases will arise out of the 'right to buy'. The Schedule only applies to 'flats', that is separate sets of premises, constructed *or* adapted (*and* occupied) as private dwellings, *and* forming part of buildings, *and* divided horizontally from other parts of such buildings. There may be two or more such flats on one floor of a building.

The provisions replace sections 90 to 91A of the Housing Finance Act 1972. They are of significance to local authorities in relation to service charges made under long leases granted under Part I, Chapter I of the

Act (Right to Buy Provisions). The provisions come into effect on a date to be appointed by regulations for the commencement of section 136 but shall not apply to works commenced earlier than six months after the commencement of the section. So far as local authorities are concerned the provisions apply to *long* leases, i.e. of over 21 years.

A 'service charge' is an amount payable by a tenant of a flat (as opposed to a house) in respect of services, repairs, maintenance or insurance or the landlord's costs of management and which amount varies or may vary according to the costs or estimated costs incurred or to be incurred in any period by the landlord in providing the service. These costs are known as 'the relevant costs' and include overheads.

The Schedule controls the extent to which these costs can be recovered as service charges (whatever type of provision is put in the lease) by introducing the test of reasonableness. The tenant will only have to pay where costs can be shown to have been reasonably incurred and where they are for services or works only if the services or works themselves are of reasonable standard.

There is a limitation placed on costs incurred in carrying out works on buildings which can be recovered without getting estimates. This amount is £25 multiplied by the number of flats in the building or £500 whichever is the greaer. The Secretary of State may increase or decrease this figure. Any costs incurred in excess of this sum cannot be regarded as relevant costs unless the following requirements are satisfied:

1) At least two estimates for the work have been obtained, one from a person wholly unconnected with the landlord.

2) A notice with copies of the estimates has been forwarded to the tenant and displayed in the building and, if one exists, forwarded to the relevant Tenants' Association. The notice must describe the works to be carried out and invite comments by a date not earlier than one month after the date of service or posting of the notice.

3) The landlord must consider any comments received and shall not commence the works before the date specified in the notice unless they are required urgently.

In proceedings relating to a service charge, the county court, if satisfied that the landlord has acted reasonably, may allow costs in excess of the prescribed limit to be taken into account in assessing a service charge. The court may also dispense with all or any of the requirements set out above, if it considers the landlord has acted reasonably.

The landlord must supply, on written request by the tenant or secretary of the relevant Tenant's Association, a written summary of costs incurred and from which service charges are determined. In the case of a local authority this information must be provided within six months of the end of the previous accounting period or within one month of the request whichever is the later. In the case of a building with more than four flats or where the relevant costs relate to other buildings, the summary must be signed by a qualified accountant to the effect that it is a genuine summary and in the case of local authorities, this can be by an officer with the appropriate professional qualifications. The landlord must if requested allow the tenant or secretary facilities to conduct his own inspection of the particulars upon which the summary is based.

Any question as to whether costs have been reasonably incurred or whether services or works are of a reasonable standard may only be determined by a county court or by arbitration agreement under section 32 of the Arbitration Act 1950.

Terms common to freehold and leasehold sales

Schedule 2, paragraph 2(1) provides, inter alia, that as regards any rights to support or access of light and air, the passage of water, or sewage or of gas or other piped fuel, smoke and fumes, to the use or maintenance of pipes or other installations for such passage, or to the use or maintenance of cables or other installations for the supply of electricity, the disposal to the purchaser is subject to certain conditions. These are that the purchaser will acquire rights of usage and maintenance equivalent to those enjoyed under the secure tenancy or under any collateral agreement or arrangement on the severance of the dwelling from other property then comprised in the same tenancy, and second that the dwelling will remain subject to all such rights for the benefit of other property *as are capable of existing in law* and are necessary to secure to the person interested in the other property as nearly as may be the same rights against the purchaser as were available when he was a secure tenant, or under any collateral agreement or arrangement made on severance. This provision must be read along with paragraphs 8 and 9 of Schedule 2 (freehold sales only) which state that the conveyance to the purchasing tenant may be subjected to burdens 'in respect of the upkeep or regulation for the benefit of any locality of any land, building, structure, works, ways or water course'.

Restrictions on resale

One of the chief fears of those who oppose an indiscriminate sale of council houses is that the most attractive houses only will be purchased leaving local authorities with the less desirable homes. This argument is also heard in relation to *areas* of houses. It has been argued that there is a danger that houses in rural areas may be purchased by their tenants and then sold to wealthy city dwellers looking for second or holiday homes, thus further eroding the already limited stock of dwellings available to people living and working in rural areas. Section 19 goes some way towards allaying such fears by placing restrictions on the resale of certain council houses.

Where a transfer is made by, inter alia, a district council, the Greater London Council, a London Borough council, the Common Council of the City of London, a county council or the Development Board for Rural Wales, of a dwelling situated in a National Park, an area designated under section 87 of the National Parks and Access to the Countryside Act 1949 (area of outstanding natural beauty) or an area designated by order of the Secretary of State as a rural area, covenants may be imposed limiting the freedom of the purchaser and his successors in title to dispose of the dwelling by way of sale, assignment, lease or sub-lease for a term of more than 21 years otherwise than at a rack rent. Any disposal in breach of such a covenant is void. The grant of an option entitling a person to take a conveyance or long lease, etc., is also classified as a disposal needing consent, but a mortgage term is not so classified, as neither are disposals under section 24 of the Matrimonial Causes Act 1973, or section 2 of the Inheritance (Provision for Family and Dependants) Act 1975, or a vesting in a person entitled under a will or on an intestacy.

The covenant may take either of two forms:

1) A covenant that, until such time (if any) as may be notified to the purchaser, or his successors in writing by the vending authority, that there will be no disposal by sale or long lease without their written consent. That consent, however, shall not be withheld if the proposed disposal is to a person who has, throughout the period of three years immediately preceeding the application for consent either:

   (a) had his place of work in a region designated by order of the Secretary of State and which is wholly or partly situated in an area in which restrictions on resale can apply; or

   (b) has had his only or principal home in such a region, or

   (c) has had the one (for example a place of work) in part or parts of the three year period and the other (for example a home) in the remainder.

It should be noted that the region need not have been the same throughout the whole period, enabling rural works and dwellers to move from one designated region to another over a short period and yet retain the ability to purchase a house that might otherwise be subject to resale restrictions; or

2) *With the consent of the Secretary of State* the covenant may be that until the end of the period of ten years beginning with the initial disposal there will be no further sale or long lease, etc., unless:

   (a) the tenant or his successor in title first offers to re-transfer the dwelling to the original vending authority, and

(b) the authority refuse the offer or fail to accept it within one month of its being made.

The purchase price to be paid by the authority in such cases will be the market value less an appropriate amount of discount should the resale take place within five years of the original transfer.

The powers of the Secretary of State

The sale of council houses to their sitting tenants goes to the very root of the Housing Act 1980 and is also a fundamental plank of government housing policy. The government has shown its determination to pursue that policy by granting in sections 23 and 24 most extensive powers of intervention to the Secretary of State in cases where local authorities, individually or collectively, attempt to resist or hinder the sales policy.

Where it appears to the Secretary of State, presumably on reasonable evidence, that a tenant or tenants of a vending authority or authorities are finding it difficult to exercise the right to buy effectively and expeditiously, he may, by giving written notice of his intention to do so, intervene in the given situation. Once such notice is in force, and it is deemed to be given 72 hours after it has been sent, he may do *all* such things as appear to him necessary or expedient to enable the exercise of the right to buy and the right to a mortgage. The Secretary of State's notice has the effect of preventing further action by a vending authority with regard to the right to buy, and nullifies any previous action they may have taken. The rights and obligations of the authority are vested in the Secretary of State who may exercise and discharge them at the authority's expense, though he is not bound to follow the exact sales procedure required of an authority in the exercise of the right to buy.

For the purpose of making a transfer of a dwelling, section 24 empowers the Secretary of State to make a Vesting Order which has the effect of:

1) vesting the property in question in the tenant on the appropriate tenurial basis; and

2) binding the landlord and the tenant and their successors in title by the covenants it contains.

A vesting order, on presentation to the Chief Land Registrar, requires the registration of the tenant as proprietor of the title concerned.

Where in pursuance of his section 23 powers the Secretary of State receives any sums due to a landlord authority, for example, part of the purchase price of a dwelling, he may retain them, without accounting for interest, during the period in which his powers are in force as against that authority. On the other hand should the Secretary of State incur expense as a consequence of exercising his section 23 powers, it is a debt payable *with interest,* by the authority to the Secretary who may, if he so chooses, recover it by withholding *any* sum due from him.

To help him in the exercise of his section 23 powers the Secretary of State may require an authority or its officers to supply him with information and to produce documents within a specified time.

Other powers of sale

The 'right to buy' is not the only plank in the council house sales policy. Not every tenant will wish to buy the house he occupies, and there will be a number of people who are not existing municipal tenants who may wish to purchase council houses if they are offered for general sale. Part V of the Housing Act 1980 accordingly grants considerable *powers* of sale to local authorities. Sections 91 and 92 repeal section 104 of the Housing Act 1957 and replace it by a series of new provisions, sections 104 to 104C.

The new section 104 of the Housing Act 1957 gives power to local authorities to dispose of land which they have acquired or appropriated for the purposes of Part V of the 1957 Act. In general disposals other than by way of a secure tenancy or under the right to buy provisions require the consent of the Secretary of State. Section 104A makes provision for the giving of either general or individual consents. Sales may also take place at a discount as provided for by section 104A. The provisions in section 104B relating to the payment of discount on an early disposal mirror those of section 8 of the 1980 Act.

The new section 104(5) and (6) allow local authorities limited freedom to impose such covenants or conditions as they think fit on a disposal. But certain covenants and conditions may only be imposed with ministerial consent. These covenants, etc., are:

1) those limiting the price or premium which may be obtained on a further disposal of the dwelling;

2) in the case of a sale those requiring the first purchaser and his successors in title to grant pre-emption rights to the local authority before allowing any other form of sale;

3) in the case of a lease those precluding the lessee and his successors in title from assigning or sub-letting the dwelling.

The new section 104(C) applies similar restrictions on the resale of houses situated in National Parks, areas of outstanding natural beauty and other designated rural areas, to those contained in section 19 of the 1980 Act.

The Secretary of State, in exercise of his powers under sections 104,

104A and 104B of the Housing Act 1957, as substituted by the Housing Act 1980 on 2 September 1980, gave to all local authorities in England the following general consents, coming into operation on 3 September 1980:

1) To sell, or to lease for a term of 99 years or more, any house provided under or appropriated for the purposes of Part V of the Housing Act 1957,

    (a) to a sitting tenant, or

    (b) in the case of a house which is unoccupied or has not been let, to a person who requires a house for his own exclusive use,

subject to the condition that the sale or grant of a lease is effected for a price consideration or rent equal to the current market price, consideration or rent with vacant possession;

2) to sell, or to lease for a term of 99 years or more, such a house as is mentioned in (1), *above,* at *less* than the current market price, consideration or rent

    (a) to a sitting tenant, or

    (b) in the case of a house which is unoccupied or has to been let, to a person who requires a house for his own exclusive use, provided that he is a person who —

        — is a first-time purchaser or has not owned a house within two years prior to indicating to the authority in writing his wish to purchase a house or obtain the grant of a lease; or

        — has a firm offer of regular employment in the area of the local authority in which the house is situated or in the area of any neighbouring authority; or

        — has within six months prior to indicating in writing his wish to purchase a house or obtain the grant of a lease:

            (i) occupied married quarters of the Regular Armed Forces of the Crown; or

            (ii) occupied premises under a contract of employment; or

            (iii) left or been under obligation to leave premises as a result of a programme of slum clearance under Part III of the Housing Act 1957 or as a result of any development (within the meaning of section 22 of the Town and Country Planning Act 1971) carried out by a local authority;

subject to the following conditions:

    (a) in the case of a sale, the price is not to be more than the 'qualifying percentage' *below* the price which would be the current market price for that house with vacant possession and free from any covenant imposed on the sale pursuant to this consent;

    (b) in the case of the grant of a lease, the consideration is not to be more than the 'qualifying percentage' *below* the consideration which would be the market consideration for the grant of a lease with vacant possession on the same terms as the lease granted, but free from any covenant in the lease pursuant to the general consent to sales.

But the price on sale, or the capitalised total consideration for a lease is in no case to be less than the cost incurred by the local authority in providing that house (including the cost of land and site development works, interest charges during construction and any administrative costs, as ascertained by the authority, but in the case of a lease, after deduction of 20 years' purchase of the ground rent thereunder).

The 'qualifying percentage' is defined as:

(a) 30 per cent for a sitting tenant who has been a tenant for a period of less than three years; 33 per cent for a sitting tenant who has been a tenant for a period of three years or more but less than four years, with an additional 1 per cent per annum for every complete year of tenancy thereafter rising to a maximum of 50 per cent for a sitting tenant who has been a tenant for a period of 20 years or more; or

(b) 30 per cent for a person who requires a house for his own exclusive use.

For the purpose of the qualifying percentage, 'period' includes two or more periods which in total amount to the requisite number of years and includes also a tenancy of a development corporation (including the Commission for the New Towns) or one or more local authorities and a tenancy of a housing association. A sitting tenant is to be deemed to have been a tenant at any time when he was not a tenant but was living with a spouse who was a tenant. A further condition of the consent is that in either the case of a sale or the grant of a lease, the local authority is to secure the repayment of the actual percentage by which they have reduced the current market price, consideration or rent with vacant possession by the imposition of a covenant under section 104(B) of the Housing Act 1957 as inserted by the Housing Act 1980.

In calculating the price to be paid for the dwelling a further deduction may be made in respect of the value of any improvements to the house carried out by the purchaser at his own expense.

3) The general consent extends to the sale or grant of a lease to two or more persons jointly, where:

(a) any one or more of them is a tenant of a house provided or appropriated under Part V of the Act of 1957 and the remainder are members of the family of such a tenant occupying the house as their only or principal home, or

(b) in the case of a house which is unoccupied or has not been let, all are members of the same family, and at least one of the purchasers is a first time buyer, or has the offer of work in the area, etc.

This new consent incorporates an important change in the terms for the sale of houses and flats at a discount. Under previous consents such sales were subject to a five or eight year pre-emption condition at a restricted price. Authorities leasing houses or flats at a discount were required to impose an absolute prohibition on assignment for five or eight years. These conditions could cause hardship, particularly for those who were compelled to move before the pre-emption period expired.

The new consent does not provide for the imposition of pre-emption conditions or resale price restrictions (nor do authorities any longer have the power to impose these at their own discretion). Sales and leases at a discount will be subject to a condition requiring the purchaser, if reselling his house within five years, to repay the discount on a sliding scale reducing from 100 per cent in the first year to 20 per cent in the fifth. The new consent replaces previous general consents.

Section 137 of the Housing Act 1980 states that if at any time after July 1980 a local authority dispose of a house or flat in circumstances where, under section 104 of the 1957 Act, ministerial consent is required *but fail to obtain such consent,* the disposition is void. This provision does not apply where the irregular disposition was to an individual or to two or more individuals, and only related to a single dwelling.

The new provisions are the legal tip of the sales policy iceberg. It is government policy to encourage the widest possible spread of low cost home-ownership. That policy includes a whole series of plans to encourage the growth of owner occupation. These are outlined below.

Selling land for starter home schemes

The device of selling housing land with the benefit of planning permission for starter homes, possibly with an arrangement under section 52 of the Town and Country Planning Act 1971 whereby the developer gives some preference to purchasers among an authority's own tenants or those on their waiting list, is one way of meeting the needs of first time buyers. Such 'Starter homes' include: one bedroom houses or flats; extendable homes, and the basic shell of larger houses designed to be fitted out by their occupants. They can be built on cleared sites in inner city and other decaying areas. Section 93 reinforced this policy by declaring that the power of a local authority to acquire land for housing purposes under section 96 of the Housing Act

1957 includes the power to do so for the purpose of disposing of houses erected on the land, *or* of disposing of the land to a house builder.

This power allows local authorities to build starter homes of their own in partnership with private builders. Some authorities have built such houses for sale. Particular arrangements vary, but often the local authority will licence a developer to occupy land owned by them. The developer will design the scheme, finance the building and arrange the sales to purchasers approved by the authority, at prices on a basis that has been agreed in advance. The authority, however, convey the land and the completed dwelling direct to the purchaser. The authority can guarantee to take into their own stock houses that do not sell, though if this happens the full cost will count against their HIP allocation. The general consent of September 1980 allows local authorities to dispose of land acquired or appropriated for the purposes of Part V Housing Act 1957 and not consisting of a house or part of a house, for example the garden of a house. This consent is subject to a condition that the disposal must be made for not less than the best price reasonably obtainable. This does not affect schemes under which authorities permit developers to occupy land under a licence to build dwellings for sale or shared ownership, because such licences are not disposals of the land.

Acquisition and improvement for sale

This is an important new area of activity. It provides a means of improving the older housing stock, bringing empty dwellings back into use, and helping first time buyers by making available a new source of relatively low cost homes. Section 108 empowers the Secretary of State to make schemes to pay contributions to local authorities to aid them in the net cost of disposing of dwellings on which they have carried out works of repair, improvement or conversion. The authorities that may be aided under this provisions include district councils, London Borough councils, the Greater London Council, and the Common Council of the City of London. The disposals that will qualify for aid will be those where:

1) an authority dispose of a house as one dwelling;

2) they divide a house into two or more separate dwellings and dispose of them; or

3) where they combine two houses to form one dwelling for disposal.

The cost to which contributions may be made may not exceed £5,000 for any one dwelling, though this figure may be altered by the Secretary of State. (See Department of the Environment Circular No. 20/80.)

Shared ownership schemes

The idea behind such schemes has been basically one of deferred purchase: for example, the tenant takes a long lease of his home at a premium equal to half its assessed freehold value; he then pays a rent equal to half the assessed reasonable rent of the property until such time as he elects to exercise an option in the lease to acquire the freehold for the payment of half of its then assessed value. The scheme was pioneered by the City of Birmingham in its '50:50' scheme, and was subsequently taken up by the Greater London Council for many of its 'new-build' estates on the fringe of the metropolitan area.

These plans attracted considerable interest in places as widely separated as: Tewkesbury, Blackpool, Eastbourne, Colchester, East Hertfordshire, Chester, Nuneaton and Sunderland, though not all the municipalities mentioned decided to implement such schemes. Government policy is to encourage local authorities to use their sale powers to promote such schemes to allow the less well-off to have access to home ownership, and to offer such schemes as an alternative to outright purchase.

In order more effectively to promote shared ownership the Housing Act 1980 made a number of important changes in the law. At the heart of such schemes is the option to purchase the freehold contained as a term in the lease. There was doubt whether section 104 of the Housing Act 1957 as it stood before 1980 allowed a local authority to grant an option to purchase. Section 94 of the 1980 Act validates all options already granted. For the future the *new* section 104(9) of the Housing Act 1957 allows the granting of options to purchase the freehold of land and houses held for the purposes of Part V of that Act.

Section 140 excludes shared ownership tenancies from the provisions of the Leasehold Reform Act 1967 in so far as they relate to the enfranchisement and extension of long tenancies at low rents.

The local authorities who may create such a shared ownership tenancy include district councils, the Greater London Council, a London Borough council and the Common Council of the City of London, a development corporation, the Commission for the New Towns and the Development Board for Rural Wales. The lease to the tenant must provide that he may acquire the freehold, whether under an option to purchase or otherwise, for a consideration to be calculated in accordance with the terms of the lease and which is reasonable, having regard to the premium or premiums paid under the lease.

Schedule 26 repeals section 113(5) of the Housing Act 1957. This provided for a virtual prohibition on the assignment of local authority leases otherwise than in return for no more than a reasonable rent. It operated as a disincentive to building society finance for house purchase

Local authorities' estimates of the disposals of local authority dwellings 1979/80 – 1983/84 — England

Thousand

England		Local authorities excluding GLC		
		Built for sale	Other	Total
1976/77		0.8	7.6	8.4
1977/78		0.9	17.2	18.1
1978/79		0.6	36.2	36.8
1979/80		2.0	57.0	59.0
1980/81		2.9	63.0	65.9
1981/82		3.0	47.0	50.0
1982/83		2.6	41.0	43.6
1983/84		2.3	40.0	42.3
Total for 5 years 1979/80 to 1983/84		12.8	248.0	260.8
% of all LA stock		0.3	5.3	5.6

Local authorities' estimates of the expected disposals of local authority dwellings 1979/80 – 1983/84 by region

Thousand

DOE Region	1979/80 to 1983/84			
	Built for sale	Other		All disposals
		Number	Per cent of LA dwelling stock	
Northern	1.1	5.9	1.3	7.0
Yorkshire & Humberside ..	0.5	24.9	4.3	25.4
East Midlands	0.5	21.1	5.3	21.6
Eastern	1.9	40.9	8.4	42.8
London excl. GLC	3.2	26.1	4.1	29.3
South East	1.7	42.1	9.0	43.8
South West	1.5	33.1	9.4	34.6
West Midlands	1.6	27.9	4.8	29.5
North West	0.8	26.0	3.9	26.8
England excl. GLC	12.8	248.0	5.3	260.8

(Taken from the First Report of the Environment Committee, July 1980, H.C. 714.)

on a shared ownership basis as a mortgagee wishing to exercise his power of sale might find that course of action blocked.

Those purchasers unable to look to a building society for funds will be within the general powers of local authorities under new section 104(4) of the Housing Act 1957: 'On the disposal of any house under this section . . . the local authority may, if they think fit, agree to the price or premium, or any part thereof, and any expenses incurred by the purchaser being secured by a mortgage of the premises'. (See also the model shared ownership scheme prepared by the Department of the Environment and contained in a letter to Chief Executives on 15 October 1980.)

Further reading

Cullingworth, J.B., *Essays on Housing Policy* (George Allen and Unwin, 1979), Chap. 6.

English, J. and Jones, C., *The Sale of Council Houses* (University of Glasgow, Discussion Papers in Social Research No. 18, 1977).

Field, F., *Do We Need Council Houses?* (Catholic Housing Aid Society, Occasional Paper No. 2, 1975).

Forrest, R. and Murie, A., *Social Segregation, Housing Needs and the Sale of Council Houses* (University of Birmingham Centre for Urban and Regional Studies, Research Memorandum No. 53, 1976).

Murie, A., *The Sale of Council Houses* (University of Birmingham, Centre for Urban and Regional Studies, Occasional Paper No. 35, 1975).

Alternative Forms of Tenure: Preferences and Cost (Southwark Community Development Project and the Joint Docklands Action Group).

An Appraisal of the Financial Effects of Council House Sales (Department of the Environment, the Scottish Development Office and the Welsh Office, January 1980).

Symposium on Council House Sales: Policy and Politics, vol. 8, No. 3, pp. 287 – 340, August 1980.

Hughes, D.J., 'Half and Half Mortgages: What They're About', *Roof,* November 1976, pp. 164 – 167.

Hughes, D.J., 'The Law of Equity Sharing', *Roof,* January 1977, pp. 19 – 21.

Hughes, D.J., 'Mr Shore Tightens the Rules on Equity Sharing Options', *Roof,* September 1978, pp. 132 – 133.

Chapter 3

The management of council housing

The 1970's were a period of increasing dissatisfaction with regard to the management of council housing, and particularly its allocation. The 1969 report *Council Housing: Purposes, Procedures and Priorities* rejected the idea of increased central control over local allocation policies, but following years witnessed a great growth of criticism with regard to many aspects of municipal housing management. In particular complaints were heard about allocation policies, about the tenurial basis of council housing and about the lack of tenant involvement and control over municipal houses.

Allocation policies

Section 111 of the Housing Act 1957 vests the general management, regulation and control of municipal housing in the local authority, and gives them power to pick and choose their tenants at will. It is true that section 113(2), as amended, states that: 'the local authority shall secure that in the selection of their tenants a reasonable preference is given to persons who are occupying insanitary or overcrowded houses, have large families or are living in unsatisfactory housing conditions and to persons towards whom they are subject to a duty under section 4 or 5 of the Housing (Homeless Persons) Act 1977'. But this requirement is far from specific and creates no *duty* towards those mentioned. Apart from specific statutory obligations, such as that under section 39 of the Land Compensation Act 1973, the general selection and allocation powers of local authorities are subject to very little legal supervision. As Lord Porter said in *Shelley v LCC* [1949] AC 56 at 66, [1948] 2 All ER 898 at 900: 'it is to my mind one of the important duties of management that the local body should be able to pick and choose their tenants at their will. It is true that an ordinary private landlord cannot do so, but local authorities who have wider duties laid on them may well be expected to exercise their powers with discretion . . . .'.

From a strictly *legal* point of view local authorities have virtually complete control over the process whereby they select their tenants. They do not have to observe limits as to income, social class or length of residence, though they may not discriminate in the allocation of their houses on either racial or sexual grounds.

In nearly every district there is more demand for housing than the local authority can supply, and so their allocation powers operate as a way of 'metering out' or sharing round a scarce resource amongst an over-large number of potential beneficiaries. Until sufficient resources are allocated to the creation of a *surplus* of good quality municipal housing then the municipal housing system will always be open to two major criticisms:

1) that it is no more than a welfare net designed to 'catch and accommodate' the worst off and most underprivileged section of society;

2) that even within the context of welfare, it fails to take account of, and be responsive to, various forms of housing needs.

On the other hand most local authorities do the best they can with severely limited resources. In any given year the number of persons who can be housed is limited by the number of houses falling vacant, or created by new building or acquisition. Against this authorities receive requests for housing from an increasingly large and diverse number of people such as: those living in houses due for demolition; the homeless; other households wishing to move into municipal accommodation, for example young married couples living with inlaws; existing municipal tenants wishing to transfer houses; persons from outside the district wishing to move into it, for example those in search of work, and a miscellaneous group, consisting mainly of young single people wishing, or having, to leave their parental homes for various reasons. In 1975 some 260,000 households entered municipal housing in England, 18 per cent as a result of slum clearance programmes, 9 per cent in consequence of homelessness, 64 per cent from the waiting lists of other applicants for housing and some 9 per cent made up of migrant workers and others considered to be in some form of priority housing need.

The frequently contradictory and mutually exclusive claims of these various groups have to be met in some way by local authorities and they have evolved various administrative procedures for dealing with the problem. These schemes have been subject to criticism. When a resource is in short supply no system for its rationing out can ever be fully accepted as fair, for any sort of rationing inevitably means disappointment for someone — a disappointment that can easily be viewed as unfair treatment. Furthermore it must be admitted that some authorities have adopted practices and procedures that leave much to be desired from the point of view of equitable fair dealing.

Residence qualifications

To operate allocation procedures local authorities maintain what are officially termed 'housing registers' but which are more colloquially, and correctly, referred to as 'waiting lists'. Some authorities go beyond this and impose conditions for the entry of an applicant's name on the waiting list: for example a condition that an applicant must be living in the district at the time of his application; or that he has lived in the district for the previous two years, and has not lived elsewhere for more than five years; or that he has been working in the district for ten years. Other authorities achieve the same result by operating two waiting lists, the first a 'live' list made up of applicants with a real chance of being housed and the second a 'deferred' list made up of those considered not to be in serious need. Such pre-conditions for inclusion on the housing waiting list have been repeatedly criticised; the Central Housing Advisory Committee attacked them in 1949, 1953 and in 1955. The 1969 report, *Council Housing: Purposes, Procedures and Priorities* said at paragraph 468: '. . . no one should be precluded from applying for, or being considered for, a council tenancy on any ground whatsoever'. This statement was made against a research finding that showed that in 1968 only 17 per cent of the authorities questioned had no residence qualifications.

In 1978 the Housing Services Advisory Group Report 'Housing for People' discovered:

1) The frequent use of residential qualifications for housing or other policies designed to confer advantages on long standing residents in an area;

2) The use of age limits for applicants to the housing waiting list;

3) Restrictions on applications by single persons, and, in some cases, by cohabitees;

4) Restrictions on applications by those owing money in respect of existing or previous accommodation;

5) Few opportunities for reciprocal transfer arrangements between authorities, though transfers are permitted on an ad hoc basis;

6) Restrictions on the number of offers of accommodation an applicant might 'unreasonably' refuse — what is 'unreasonable' being decided by the individual authority concerned.

They made the following recommendations.

1) Allocation systems must be fair, and seen to be fair. While there must be a system of priorities within any allocation scheme, residential

qualifications should be abolished. National mobility can only be secured by the abolition of waiting periods before applications for housing are accepted. Likewise restrictions based on age or marital status cannot be justified.

2) Allocation systems must be easily understood by both applicants and staff. The scheme used should be published, though for general consumption an explanatory booklet would be adequate. Applicants should be given details of the assessment made of their needs and some indication of the length of time they are likely to have to wait for an offer. They should be fully informed of the range of choice of dwellings available

3) The system must be sufficiently flexible to cater for unusual circumstances. Authorities must be prepared to be more liberal on exchanges, and consider the setting up of regional 'transfer pools' for those wishing to move between neighbouring towns. Allocation systems should be so designed as to take into account the special needs of certain groups such as the elderly, families with small children, one parent families, the handicapped and ethnic minorities.

4) The system should always promote the best use of the housing stock, and also ensure that the allocations made fit the needs and preferences of applicants so far as this is practicable. Thus no scheme should ever be based on the making only of single offers of accommodation, and where an applicant is penalised for refusing an offer of accommodation he should be able to defend himself by being able to challenge the initial 'reasonableness' of the offer — preferably by being able to appeal to the council and not just a housing officer. The applicant's reasons for refusing an offer should be noted and kept on file so that similar unacceptable offers are not made in the future.

5) Any selection scheme should attempt to avoid social polarisation and yet should also seek to maintain communities. To ensure this allocation policies must always be considered in relation to other community services.

The response of the then government was to issue two Consultation Papers on 'Mobility' and 'Eligibility', as these were obviously seen as being the most crucial issues in the general selection and allocation problem. That on 'Mobility' proposed that there should be some system whereby workers moving between areas could be housed almost immediately upon moving, and that this scheme should cover the whole of England and Wales. The consultation paper proposed that the Secretary of State should be given power to fix (and subsequently vary) a national 'mobility quota', though this power was only to be used in the event of local authorities failing to develop some voluntary arrangement of their own. The consultation paper stated that 5 per cent of all allocations would be a reasonable figure to devote to the 'mobility quota'.

The paper on 'Eligibility' contained a very tame proposal to reduce the influence of residential qualifications in allocation procedures. The '*easing*' of residential requirements would take the following form:

1) Local authorities should no longer be able to require applicants to have lived in their area for a fixed period of time, or to have been born there before being capable of being *registered* on the housing list;

2) Regular employment in an area should count as residence from the point of view of registration;

3) There should be a prohibition on the setting of any predetermined period of time between the acceptance of an application and the granting of a tenancy.

It can be appreciated that these proposals were considerably less far reaching than those of the Housing Services Advisory Group.

The 1979 Housing Bill contained clauses that would have implemented these proposals on residential qualifications and the creation of a national mobility scheme. The Housing Act 1980, however, did not implement the proposed changes and so residence qualifications may still be imposed — subject to the requirements of the race relations legislation which will be examined subsequently.

So far as mobility is concerned the present government has preferred to create a voluntary scheme between local authorities.

The details of this scheme include the following guidelines:

1) Within the conurbations and within counties there is to be a regional mobility scheme. This will involve district councils all agreeing to accept nominated tenants from other districts in the same county on a reciprocal basis;

2) 1 per cent of all lettings will be made available to people wishing to move to an area outside their immediate county *in addition* to the normal reciprocal arrangement between authorities.

Some central financial assistance may be forthcoming to aid the cost of such arrangements to facilitate moves within the public housing sector under the powers granted to the Secretary of State by section 46 of the Housing Act 1980.

Selection schemes

Even after an applicant's name is on a housing waiting list there is no guarantee of speedy rehousing taking place. Some authorities allocate their houses according to date order on a 'first-come-first-served' basis. According to such schemes housing will be offered, as it becomes available, to those whose names appear at the top of the list. A small number of authorities use merit schemes to allocate houses. Here tenants are selected according to the knowledge of councillors as to individual applicants. Such schemes have been criticised in the past, for example by the Housing Services Advisory Group in *Housing for People* (1978), and in *Council Housing: Purposes Procedures and Priorities*, which stated at paragraphs 122 and 123: 'Without [a clearly defined and publicised selection policy] it is difficult to achieve fairness and even more difficult to demonstrate it: particularly in small authorities and in scattered rural areas members will be subject to pressure from applicants and officers will be subject to pressure from individual members'.

It remains perfectly lawful for a local authority to allocate their houses according to such a 'merit' scheme. Indeed there is a virtual absence of control and supervision over the means whereby municipal housing is allocated. As Murie, Niner and Watson say in *Housing Policy and the Housing System* p. 119:

'Local authorities have devised a multiplicity of schemes for deter-mining allocation priorities among those on the waiting list. Decisions may be delegated to officers; taken jointly by officers and councillors; or made entirely by the Council or Housing Committee. The scheme may be formal or informal; it may be simple or extremely complicated; . . . . Authorities A, B and C each operate a quite different system. In Authority A, allocations are made in date order of application, within groupings determined by the type of house and area requested . . . . Authority B operates a sophisticated points scheme covering measures of overcrowding, size of family, ill health, lack of amenities and length of time on the list. The Housing Manager of Authority C has complete discretion in tenant selection. In practice applicants are divided into three groups — lodgers, households and persons of pensionable age. Lack of amenities, medical needs and application date are taken into account in determining priorities, but the procedures are not formalised'.

Most authorities allocate their houses according to some sort of points system. Once an applicant is registered on the waiting list the speed with which he is housed will depend on the number of points he can amass.

That general statement about points schemes obscures their vast diversity in practice. Their working varies, often quite dramatically, according to the factors selected for 'pointing' and according to the number of points actually allocated under each head of entitlement. An applicant may do well under the points scheme operated by one local authority, whereas he could do badly, on exactly similar facts, according to the scheme operated by the neighbouring district. This possibility of variation has been a cause of considerable concern to the critics of municipal housing practice. Factors frequently selected for 'pointing' include:

1) The date of application;
2) The number of bedrooms needed by an applicant;
3) The size of the family involved;
4) Whether the applicant is living in rooms as opposed to a self-contained house or flat;
5) Whether the applicant has a separate living room;
6) Whether the applicant, having children, occupies only a bed sitting room;
7) The existence of illegal overcrowding;
8) The enforced splitting-up of a family because of accommodation difficulties;
9) Sexual embarrassments arising out of unsatisfactory sleeping arrangements;
10) Ill-health or disability;
11) Lack of amenities;
12) Sharing of kitchen facilities;
13) Being forced to occupy badly located accommodation;
14) The age of the applicant;
15) The length of time the applicant has been registered on the waiting list;
16) The suitability of the applicant for the accommodation sought;
17) Other factors, such as hardship, or the desire of the applicant to be accommodated near to friends or relatives.

Some local authorities retain a discretion to simply 'add on' extra points in individual cases, or otherwise to vary the points awarded so as to promote or retard an applicant's progress up the waiting list. Points schemes have been criticised for giving too much weight to factors which have no real relevance to housing *need*, for example length of residence in a district, or length of time on the list, while other factors, such as disrepair or harassment by a landlord, are not considered 'pointable'.

It is probably impossible to create one national housing allocation scheme because the needs and resources of local authorities vary so much. Likewise some matters, such as cases of severe ill-health, or illegal eviction, or where the social services authority is involved, etc., cannot be dealt with by the routine points system, but must be considered separately under special allocations procedures.

When a person has qualified to be housed by amassing a sufficiently large number of points, or by falling within the rehousing obligations of the local authority, he will not be offered a free choice amongst the available municipal housing. A completely free choice is impossible because factors such as the numbers of bedrooms needed have to be taken into account in the allocation process. Some authorities, however, base their allocations on the reports of housing department officials who pay visits to potential tenants before the offer of a municipal house is made. These reports are frequently used to grade applicants, and, in general, the better the grade the applicant receives the better will be the choice of housing offered to him. As Murie, Niner and Watson say in *Housing Policy and the Housing System* pp. 125 to 126: 'Grading systems are developed to different degrees in different areas, and can range from a very general comment on "housekeeping standards" to a formal classification of applicants (and, of course, property) into three, five or more categories. While an unfavourable visit report might not influence the family's chance of being rehoused, it can often influence the type of property or area offered. If vacancies of a particular grade arise only rarely, a very rigid grading system could, in fact, delay rehousing'.

An example of the way in which gradings may be recorded is given in Merrett's, *State Housing in Britain* p. 224: 'The following remarks . . . reveal the factors considered in assessing households and may be taken as an illustration of the practices in many local authorities: "Excellent tenant, suitable for new property". "Fairly good type — suitable for new or post war re-let". "Poor type, will need supervision — suitable for old property . . . seems to have taken over the tenancy of this house and sat back until rehoused". "Fair only — suitable for pre-war property". "A good type of applicant — this is not a long haired person. Suitable for a post-war re-let"'.

The danger is obvious: a grading report based on the professional and social values of the housing official may work to the detriment of an applicant whose standards and values do not conform. Merrett goes on to say: 'grading may be explained or rationalised in other ways, including: making supervision of unsatisfactory tenants easier; being an incentive to improve (with the promise of a reward in the form of a better dwelling in due course); as a deterrent to other potentially unsatisfactory tenants; as a means of minimising disturbance and protecting other tenants; a way of reducing the level of rent arrears from 'bad-payers' and the subsidy payments to low income households; and a method of maintaining the quality of high status dwellings . . . . At times these views may be held so strongly that the local authority secures low quality accommodation for the purpose of housing unsatisfactory tenants. Short-life properties in clearance areas may be used in this way'.

Thus the discretionary powers conferred on local housing authorities can be used in a wide variety of ways. When Parliament confers discretionary power it intends local authorities to make decisions. It would be wrong to argue that discretion should be entirely replaced by rigid legal rules which would be too inflexible to meet the wide variety of circumstances with which local housing authorities have to cope. Nevertheless there is room for centrally laid down guidelines and/or model allocation schemes designed to iron out the most extreme variations that may be caused as a result of the adoption of differing selection and allocation practices.

The Housing Act 1980 takes a few tentative steps in this direction. Section 44 states:

'(1) Every landlord authority shall publish a summary of its rules —

> (a) for determining priority as between applicants in the allocation of its housing accommodation; and
>
> (b) governing cases where secure tenants wish to move (whether or not by way of an exchange of dwelling-houses) to other dwelling-houses let under secure tenancies by that landlord authority or by any other body.

(2) Every landlord authority shall —

> (a) maintain a set of those rules and of the rules it has laid down governing the procedure to be followed in allocating its housing accommodation; and
>
> (b) . . . make them available at its principal office for inspection at all reasonable hours without charge by members of the public. . . .

(5) A copy of any summary published under sub-section (1) above shall be furnished without charge, and a copy of any set of rules maintained under sub-section (2) above shall be furnished on payment of a reasonable fee, to any member of the public who asks for one'.

The reasoning behind this provision is that 'publicity is control'. As local authorities are democratically elected bodies their electors may reject them at the polls should they disapprove of policies and procedures made public for discussion and comment. That is the theory; whether local elections are conducted quite in that way is open to doubt! It can also be argued that public disquiet over a particular policy or procedure, especially as aired in the local press, *might* lead to a change on the part of the local authority.

So far as an individual applicant for housing is concerned, section 44(6) of the 1980 Act provides:

'At the request of any person who has applied to it for housing accommodation, a landlord authority shall make available to him, at all reasonable times and without charge, details of the particulars which he has given to the authority about himself and his family and which the authority has recorded as being relevant to his application for accommodation'.

This provision enables an applicant to check that the local authority have recorded the relevant details of his application as he has supplied them correctly. It does *not* entitle the applicant to see any other facts, opinions, assessments or gradings recorded about him. Neither does it confer any right to change or challenge any particulars other than those which '*he* has given to the authority'.

Reform

The courts have repeatedly stated their unwillingness to intervene in the exercise of a local housing authority's discretion unless the impossibly heavy burden of proving an act of bad faith or unreasonableness can be discharged (*Bristol District Council v Clark* [1975] 3 All ER 976, [1975] 1 WLR 1443 and *Cannock Chase District Council v Kelly* [1978] 1 All ER 152, [1978] 1 WLR 1). Reform can only come from the legislature. The following principles should be enshrined in housing law and practice.

1) Elected members should concern themselves with the formulation of policy and should, in general, be excluded from day to day housing administration and allocation.

2) There should be *national* guidelines for the creation of local allocation, transfer and exchange schemes.

3) In the processing and consideration of housing applications, etc., wherever possible, anonymity for the applicant should be the rule so as to reduce any possibility of bias.

4) There should be an obligation on local authorities to inform disappointed applicants why their requests have met with no success. This should be coupled with a provision requiring greater disclosure of the contents of an applicant's file to him than the 1980 Act requires.

5) Local authorities should be encouraged to set up systems whereby disappointed applicants may appeal against housing allocations, and the contents of housing files.

Housing allocation is a highly judgmental process. Inevitably some of the judgments reached must give rise to feelings of real or imagined grievance. Where the local authority have committed an act of maladministration there will be a remedy via the offices of the local ombudsman (see Chapter 12, below). The creation of an appeals system would, however, be a useful and speedy supplement to the local ombudsman. In *Housing Allocation Policy and its Effects* Lewis Corina found that an embryonic appeals system can exist. He states at page 17:

'Someone who "knew his way around the system" of housing, might just do a little better than another person because he refused to accept the decision and knew how to appeal against it.

An "appeal" is not a formal procedure, there is no defined mechanism of appeal. What exists as an appeal mechanism, and this can only be detected by observing such activities over a period of several weeks, is a continuing dialogue between various officers and tenants, and between officers and other officers, about the merits of cases and the problems which surround these cases.

The transfer officer, housing visitor and lettings officers, are all involved in this dialogue and its nature is evaluative and comparative. "Look at this case, it has such and such priority features". "Yes, it's a deserving case but I have an application for the only *available* house of *that type* and this case has such and such and such *priority features*".

The Lettings Officers may decided that from the *competing* claims for *scarce* stock that applicant has to be preferred. If the other officers are not satisfied they can turn to the Chief Lettings Officer and ask him to arbitrate. Even then, an appeal need not lapse, any case may be taken to higher authority, although it would have to be exceptional case if it were to be taken to the Housing Committee for resolution.

It was not possible to get evidence on the working of the "higher appeals system" . . . the practice of allocating "Committee Priority" to a case has been abandoned and the records do not show if a case has been subject to appeal. This meant that it was not possible to get evidence about the number of appeals. The Chief Lettings Officer guessed that "we are talking about 5 per cent or 10 per cent of cases" when reference was made to dispute. "The majority of allocations are not disputed", he claimed'.

Something more structured and formal than this is required. It should involve senior officers and elected members and there should be the possibility of legal or other representatives having rights to address the appellate body on behalf of the disappointed applicant.

Racial and sexual discrimination in housing allocation

This is an extremely sensitive area within municipal housing. In *State Housing in Britain* pp. 225 to 228 Stephen Merrett states the issue well.

'The council sector reveals a clear internal spatial patterning of people. The most noted aspect of this tendency is for various minority groups, such as "unsatisfactory tenants", "problem families", black people, single-parent families, the low status, and so on, to inhabit the poorest and lowest status areas and dwellings. In most local authorities areas exist which have been variously termed as "ghetto", "sink", "stigmatised", or "residual" estates . . . . Black people have been observed to be under-represented in the council sector, and if in the tenure group then in generally poorer dwellings than white people. Discrimination on the basis of colour appears to be but one factor contributing to this situation . . . . Black people have tended to enter the council sector as a result of homelessness. Relatively little clearance has occurred of private sector housing occupied by a large proportion of racial minorities. Similarly they tend to be well down waiting lists . . . . Black people not only have an inferior bargaining position than many whites, but in addition their experience and knowledge of the council sector may be slight and their housing conditions prior to entrance to public housing often worse. Both factors, and others, tend to lead to managers offering inferior housing, and to black people accepting what is offered'.

In a multi-racial society, both the law and administration of municipal housing must operate so as to minimise housing disadvantage arising because of a person's colour, race, or sex, etc. Section 71 of the Race Relations Act 1976 makes it the general duty of local authorities to work towards the elimination of discrimination and to promote good race relations and equal opportunities for all. Other provisions are even more relevant to housing. Section 21 of the 1976 Act provides:

'(1) It is unlawful for a person, in relation to premises . . . of which he has power to dispose, to discriminate against another —
  (a) in the terms on which he offers him those premises; or
  (b) by refusing his application for those premises; or
  (c) in his treatment of him in relation to any list of persons in need of premises of that description.
(2) It is also unlawful for a person, in relation to any premises managed by him, to discriminate against a person occupying the premises —
  (a) in the way he affords him access to any benefits or facilities, or by refusing or deliberately omitting to afford him access to them; or
  (b) by evicting him, or subjecting him to any other detriment'.

Such unlawful discrimination can happen in two ways.

Direct discrimination

This is the act of treating another less favourably on grounds of colour, race, nationality or ethnic or national origins, see sections 1(1)(a) and

3(1) of the Race Relations Act 1976. Thus, for example, it is unlawful to refuse an applicant's name for rehousing because he is black, or to affect his priority on the waiting list because of his colour, or to allocate him a house in a particular area solely because of his race.

This can have serious consequences for local authorities. Racial minorities tend to be found in a definite number of localities where they form tightly knit communities. Members of minority groups who have moved into municipal housing have tended to move as close as possible to houses occupied by members of their own race or nationality for mutual support and aid, and because of family ties amongst extended families. The danger is that white families can panic and leave leading to the creation of ghettoes isolated from, and embattled against, the outside world.

Faced with this problem the City of Birmingham operated a policy of 'discrete dispersal' whereby a black/white balance ratio was kept on all estates, within streets and in blocks of flats. In *Housing Policy and the State*, Lambert, Paris and Blackaby relate, at p. 54, that the keys of council dwellings were marked as vacancies occurred to ensure that the racial balance programme could be maintained. The Race Relations Board declared this practice to be discriminatory and it was abandoned. Even where it is operated with the well-motivated desire of preventing the creation of ghettoes a dispersal policy is illegal.

Good race relations can be furthered by the adoption of certain management practices, such as the following:

1) Local authorities should know the racial composition of the various minority groups in their districts and have adequate facilities to communicate with them in their own languages;

2) Housing department staff should know about the cultural and family patterns of minority groups, and equal opportunity programmes should ensure that members of racial minorities are employed;

3) Housing programmes should include the provision of large dwellings of the sort likely to be needed by the extended families in some minority groups;

4) Where racial minorities are moving into public housing the effect this may have on local housing policy should be kept under review, as also must the management of those estates where the minorities are making their new homes. This involves the keeping of racial origin records in relation to applicants for housing. That information must be sympathetically collected by housing department staff. There can be no deliberate dispersal policy and freedom of choice must be retained to the same degree for all families regardless of race.

5) Where racial minorities are concentrated on older estates the physical condition thereof must be maintained at a high level.

Indirect discrimination

This is the act of applying to a person a requirement or condition which applies equally to persons of *other* racial groups but which is:

1) such that the proportion of persons of the *same* racial group as that of the person affected who can comply with the condition is considerably smaller than the proportion of persons not of that group who can comply;

2) not justfiable irrespective of the colour, race, nationality or ethnic or national origins of the person to whom it applies; and

3) is to that person's detriment because he cannot comply with it. See section 1(1)(b) of the 1976 Act.

In 'Indirect Discrimination and the Race Relations Act' (129) New Law Journal 408, Geoffrey Bindman argues that the following are instances of indirect discrimination in housing:

1) A requirement that applicants for local authority housing must have been resident in the authority's area for a specified period because fewer numbers of ethnic minority groups could comply with the residence requirements than could members of the host community, or

2) A requirement that housing points can only be given for children actually living with an applicant, as this works to the detriment of any immigrant, part of whose family has yet to join him.

Those authorities who apply residence qualifications should certainly review them to ensure that they do not result in indirect discrimination.

Similar provisions apply to discrimination on grounds of sex under sections 1 and 30 of the Sex Discrimination Act 1975.

Tenure of council houses

The lack of security of tenure in relation to council housing was for long a source of criticism and concern. This became acute following *Cannock Chase District Council v Kelly* [1978] 1 All ER 152, [1978] 1 WLR 1, as a result of which it became virtually impossible for a council tenant to resist possession proceedings. Central government had already accepted the need for security of tenure in the public sector in *Housing Policy*, Cmnd. 6851, and the Housing Act 1980 has conferred such security on the majority of municipal tenants.

The rights of secure tenants are now contained in Part I, Chapter II of the 1980 Act. Section 28 defines a secure tenancy as being one where the following conditions are satisfied:

1) The dwelling must be let as a separate dwelling-house; there must be no sharing of 'living accommodation' (for example kitchens, but *not* bathrooms or lavatories) with other households, see *Neale v Del Soto* [1945] KB 144 and *Cole v Harris* [1945] KB 474;

2) The landlord must be a local housing authority, (that is a district council, a London Borough council, the Greater London Council, or Common Council of the City of London) or the Commission for the New Towns, or a development corporation or Development Board for Rural Wales, or a county council acting under its reserve powers under section 194 of the Local Government Act 1972;

3) The tenant must be an individual, or in the case of a joint tenancy each joint tenant must be an individual, and he, or in the case of joint tenants at least one of them, must occupy the dwelling as his only or principal home. Possession by a tenant's deserted spouse will count as occupation by the tenant for this purpose, see section 1(5) of the Matrimonial Homes Act 1967 as amended by Schedule 25 to the Housing Act 1980;

4) The tenancy must not fall within the excepted classes as laid down in Schedule 3 to the 1980 Act. These are:
  (a) long tenancies, that is a tenancy granted for a term certain exceeding 21 years;
  (b) premises occupied by a tenant as a requirement of his contract of employment directed to the better performance of his duties;
  (c) where the tenant is an employee of his landlord and —
    (i) the tenancy provides for its own cessation on the termination of such employment, and
    (ii) the landlord holds the dwelling-house under the Education Act 1944, or in pursuance of the statutes specified in Schedule 1 to the Local Authority Social Services Act 1970, and
    (iii) the dwelling forms part of a building held for these purposes or is within the curtilage of such a building, for example, a school caretaker's house;
  (d) where the house stands on land acquired for development and is only being used as temporary housing accommodation;
  (e) where accommodation has been provided temporarily for a homeless person under sections 3(4), 4(3) or 5(6) of the Housing (Homeless Persons) Act 1977, the tenancy cannot become secure before the expiry of a period of twelve months beginning with the date on which he receives notification of the local authority's findings as to his homelessness, unless he is notified otherwise within that period;
  (f) accommodation *specifically* granted by a district council or London Borough Council to a person who was immediately

before the grant not resident in their area and having employment or the offer thereof, within the authority's area, to meet
his need for temporary accommodation, in order to work there
and also to enable him to find permanent housing, cannot be
subject to a secure tenancy before the expiry of one year from the
grant unless the tenant is otherwise notified within that period;

(g) where the local authority has taken only a short term lease from
a body incapable of granting secure tenancies, for example a
private individual, of a dwelling for the purpose of providing
temporary accommodation, on terms including one that the
lessor may obtain vacant possession from the local authority on
the expiry of the specified period or when he requires it, there
is no secure tenancy for *their* lessees;

(h) a tenancy is not secure if it is of a dwelling-house made available
for occupation by the tenant while works are being carried out at
his own former home, *and* provided the tenant was not a secure
tenant of that former home;

(i) where the tenancy is of an agricultural holding under the
Agricultural Holdings Act 1948 and the tenant is a manager;

(j) where the tenancy is of licensed premises;

(k) where the tenancy is one granted specifically to a student to
enable him to attend a designated course at a university or
further education establishment;

(l) where the tenancy is of business premises falling within Part II
Landlord and Tenant Act 1954.

Provided the above conditions are satisfied the tenant is 'secure'. The
Act applies to tenancies granted before, as well as after, the commencement date (see section 47). By section 48 it applies to a licence to occupy
whether or not granted for consideration, provided it was not granted as
a mere temporary expedient to a person who originally entered the
dwelling or any other land as a trespasser.

The rights of secure tenants

Under section 29 of the 1980 Act where a secure tenancy consisting of a
term certain comes to an end, a periodic tenancy arises automatically
unless the tenant is granted another secure tenancy of the dwelling.
Thus a secure tenant at the end of his tenancy enjoys rights equivalent
to those of a statutory tenant under the Rent Act 1977. Most secure
tenancies will, however, be periodic and so more important rights for
secure tenants will be those of succession conferred by sections 30 and 31
of the Act.

Where a secure tenancy is a periodic tenancy, on the death of the
tenant it will vest in one of the following as a successor tenant:

1) the tenant's spouse;

2) any other member of the tenant's family who has resided with him throughout the period of twelve months prior to the tenant's death,

provided, in either case, that the successor occupied the dwelling as his only or principal home at the time of the tenant's death. If more than one person is qualified to succeed, the spouse is to be preferred to all others. If there is no spouse those qualified may agree amongst themselves who is to succeed; if they cannot agree the choice is to be made by the local authority.

Section 30 only provides for a tenancy by succession to arise once. Section 31 classifies the following also as successor tenants for this purpose:

1) a joint tenant who becomes a sole tenant;

2) a tenant holding a periodic tenancy under section 29 of the 1980 Act where the former fixed term tenancy was granted either to another person or to him and another;

3) a tenant who holds by virtue of an assignment, save where the assignment is made under section 24 of the Matrimonial Causes Act 1973, provided the assignor was *not* himself a successor tenant;

4) a tenant who has the tenancy vested in him on the death of a deceased previous secure tenant. The effect of section 31(2) of the 1980 Act should be noted. This provides that where, within six months of the coming to an end of a secure periodic tenancy (Tenancy I), the tenant takes up another secure periodic tenancy (Tenancy II), and

   (a) the tenant was a successor tenant in relation to Tenancy I, and

   (b) under Tenancy II *either* or *both* the dwelling-house and the landlord is or are the same as under Tenancy I, the tenant will be a successor tenant in relation to Tenancy II, unless the tenancy agreement provides otherwise.

Thus, if the widow of a secure tenant succeeds to the dwelling, and then within six months moves, with her children, into a smaller house owned by the same authority, she will continue to have in relation to the new house the status of a successor tenant, so that on her death her children will not be qualified to succeed to that tenancy.

The definition of 'family' under section 50(3) of the 1980 Act should be noted. The term includes spouses, parents, grandparents, children, grandchildren, brothers, sisters, uncles, aunts, nephews and nieces; treating relationships by marriage as by blood, the half-blood as the whole blood, and stepchildren as full children. Illegitimate children are to be treated as the legitimate children of their mothers and reputed fathers, and persons living together as husband and wife are also to be regarded as members of a family.

Security of tenure

Rights of security, the most important of those enjoyed by secure tenants, and the heart of what is colloquially termed 'the Tenants' Charter', are contained in sections 32 to 34 of the 1980 Act.

The basic rule contained in section 32 is that a secure tenancy cannot be brought to an end without an order from the court (that is the county court by virtue of section 86(1) of the 1980 Act). The court may not entertain proceedings for such an order unless the landlord has first served on the tenant a notice in correct form specifying the ground on which the court will be asked to give possession, but the ground may be altered with the leave of the court, see sections 33(2) and 34(1) of the Housing Act 1980. In the case of a periodic tenancy the landlord's notice, which will have a currency of twelve months, must also specify a date after which possession proceedings may be begun. That date must not be earlier than the date on which the tenancy could, apart from the 1980 Act, be brought to an end by notice to quit given on the same day as the landlord's notice.

The grounds on which possession may be given are contained in Schedule 4, Part I to the Housing Act 1980. Their substance, in so far as they are relevant to local authorities, is as follows:

Ground 1

Where any rent lawfully due from the tenant has not been paid, or where any obligation of the tenancy has been broken or not performed.

Ground 2

Where the tenant or any person residing in the dwelling has been guilty of acts of nuisance or annoyance to neighbours, or has been convicted of using the house for illegal or immoral purposes.

Ground 3

Where the condition of the dwelling-house or any common parts of a building comprising the dwelling-house have deteriorated as a result of the tenant's waste, neglect or default, or as a result of the acts of any person residing in the dwelling-house whom the tenant (if that person is a lodger or sub-tenant) has unreasonably failed to remove from the dwelling.

Ground 4

Where the condition of any furniture provided by the landlord for use under the tenancy (or in any common parts of a building as the case may be) has deteriorated as result of ill treatment by the tenant or any person residing in the dwelling.

Ground 5

Where the tenant obtained his tenancy knowingly or recklessly by false statements.

Ground 6

Where the tenant, being a secure tenant of another dwelling which is his home and which is subject to works, has accepted the tenancy of the dwelling of which possession is sought on condition that he would move back to his original home on completion of the works in question, and where the works have been completed.

Ground 7

Where the dwelling-house is illegally overcrowded.

Ground 8

Where the landlord intends within a reasonable time to demolish, or reconstruct or carry out works on the dwelling, etc., and cannot do so without obtaining possession.

Ground 10

Where the dwelling has features which are substantially different from those of ordinary houses so as to make it suitable for occupation by a physically disabled person, and where there is no longer such a disabled person living in the house, while the landlord requires for occupation by such a person.

Ground 12

Where the dwelling is one of a group which it is the practice of the landlord to let for occupation by persons with special needs, and also:

1) a social service or special facility is provided in close proximity to the dwellings in order to assist those with the special needs;

2) there is no longer a person with those needs residing in the house, and

3) the landlord requires the house for someone with those needs.

Ground 13

Where the tenant, being a successor, by virtue of being a member of the deceased previous tenant's family, is underoccupying the dwelling, in that it is too large for his reasonable requirements. But notice of intention to commence possession proceedings must be served *more* than six months but *less* then twelve months after the date of death of the original tenant. (This does not apply to spouse-successors.)
(Ground 9 relates to housing charities and Ground 11 to housing associations and trusts.)

The Court is not to make a possession order on Grounds 1 to 6 unless it considers it reasonable to do so; on Grounds 7 to 9 unless it is satisfied that suitable accommodation will be available for the tenant on the order taking effect, and on Grounds 10 to 13 unless *both* the above conditions are satisfied, see section 34(2) and (3) of the Housing Act 1980. Schedule 4, Part II to that Act defines what is meant by 'suitable accommodation'.

'1.—(1) For the purposes of this Part of this Act, accommodation is suitable if it consists of premises —
   (a) which are to be let as a separate dwelling under a secure tenancy, or
   (b) which are to be let as a separate dwelling under a pro- tected tenancy (other than one of a kind mentioned in sub-paragraph (2) below) within the meaning of the 1977 Act, [The Rent Act 1977]
and in the opinion of the court, the accommodation is reasonably suitable to the needs of the tenant and his family.
(2) The kind of protected tenancy referred to in sub-paragraph (1) above is one under which the landlord might recover possession of the dwelling-house under one of the Cases in Part II of Schedule 15 to the 1977 Act (cases where court must order possession).
2.—In determining whether it is reasonably suitable to those needs regard shall be had to —
   (a) the nature of the accommodation which it is the practice of the landlord to allocate to persons with similar needs;
   (b) the distance of the accommodation available from the place of work or education of the tenant and of any members of his family;
   (c) its distance from the home of any member of the tenant's family

if proximity to it is essential to that member's or the tenant's well-being;
(d) the needs (as regards extent of accommodation) and means of the tenant and his family;
(e) the terms on which the accommodation is available and the terms of the secure tenancy;
(f) if any furniture was provided by the landlord for use under the secure tenancy, whether furniture is to be provided for use in the other accommodation and, if it is, the nature of that furniture;

but where possession is sought on Ground 7 [where the dwelling is overcrowded] accommodation otherwise reasonably suitable to the needs of the tenant and his family shall not be deemed not to be so by reason only that the permitted number of persons, computed under Schedule 6 to the 1957 Act in relation to the number and floor area of the rooms in it, is less than the number of persons living in the dwelling-house of which possession is sought.

3.—Where the landlord is not a local authority for the purposes of Part V of the 1957 Act, [a local housing authority] a certificate of such an authority certifying that the authority will provide suitable accommodation for the tenant by a date specified in the certificate shall be conclusive evidence that suitable accommodation will be available for him by that date, if the dwelling-house of which possession is sought is situated in the district for supplying the needs of which the authority has power under that Part of that Act'.

Under sections 87 and 89 of the Act of 1980 the court is to have extended discretion as to the ordering of possession.

Where possession proceedings are brought under Grounds 1 to 6 and 10 to 13 above, the court may adjourn the proceedings for such periods as it thinks fit. Where a possession order is made under any of the above grounds its execution may be stayed, suspended or postponed for such period as the court thinks fit. Where the court exercises this discretion it must impose conditions with regard to the payment of any arrears of rent, etc., unless it considers that to do so would cause exceptional hardship to the tenant or would be otherwise unreasonable. Other conditions may be imposed. Where these conditions are fulfilled the court may rescind or discharge the order. A tenant's spouse or former spouse having rights of occupation under the Matrimonial Homes Act 1967, and in occupation of a dwelling, the tenancy of which is terminated by possession proceedings, has the same rights with regard to suspensions and adjournments, etc., as if his or her rights of occupation were not affected by the termination.

Where the court makes a possession order on grounds where the reasonableness of the issue is not a deciding factor, discretion is limited by section 89. So far as secure tenancies are concerned this provision is relevant where recovery of possession is sought under Grounds 7 to 8 [cases of overcrowding or where the local authority intends shortly to demolish or reconstruct the dwelling]. In such circumstances the giving up of possession cannot be postponed (where by the order itself, or any variation, suspension or stay) to a date later than fourteen days after the making of the order unless it appears to the court that exceptional hardship would be caused by requiring possession to be given up by that date. In such cases the giving up of possession may be suspended for up to six weeks from the making of the order but for no longer. This provision also applies to non-secure tenancies.

Tenant participation in housing management

Reference has been made in the introduction to the mid 1970's debate as to whether a measure of, if not indeed all, control over municipal housing management should be transferred to tenants. Some local authorities have as a matter of practice set up Joint Estate Management Committees to transfer a measure of power to tenants. The 1979 Housing Bill contained detailed proposals to introduce a real measure of representative but not responsible democracy into housing management. The 1980 Housing Act is even less enterprising than its proposed predecessor. Its provisions can only be described as anodyne — a palpable palliative which by passes the issue of tenant control in municipal housing management.

Section 43 of the 1980 Act requires that certain authorities shall, within twelve months of the commencement of Chapter II of Part I of the Act, make and maintain such arrangements *as they consider appropriate*, to enable secure tenants who are likely to be substantially affected by matters of housing management to be informed of proposed damages and developments, and also to ensure that such persons are able to make their views known to the authority within a specified time. Matters of 'housing management' are defined by section 42 of the Act to include those matters which, *in the opinion of the authority*, relate to the management, maintenance, improvement, or demolition of municipal dwellings, or are connected with the provision of services or amenities to such dwellings, *and* which represent new programmes of maintenance, improvement or demolition, or some change in the practice or policy of the authority, *and* which are likely to affect substantially all an authority's secure tenants or a group of them. A 'group' is defined as tenants forming a distinct social group, or those who occupy dwelling-houses which constitute a distinct class, whether by reference to the kind of dwelling, or the housing estate or larger area in which they are situated.

A matter is *not* one of housing management in so far as it relates to rent payable or to any charge for services or facilities provided by the authority in its capacity as landlord. It is the duty of an authority to *consider* any representations made by secure tenants before making any decisions on a matter of housing management.

Authorities must publish details of their consultation arrangements. A copy of any published material must be made available for free public inspection at their principal offices during reasonable hours. Copies must also be available for sale at reasonable charges. Those authorities made subject to consultation requirements include district councils, London Borough councils, the Greater London Council, the Common Council of the City of London, a development corporation and the Development Board for Rural Wales (though the last two named bodies may be exempted by the Secretary of State). County councils exercising their reserve housing powers and the Commission for the New Towns are not required to consult with their secure tenants.

Other rights of secure tenants

a) Subletting

Section 35(1) of the Housing Act 1980 makes it a term of every secure tenancy that the tenant may allow any persons to reside as lodgers in his dwelling. Section 35(2) goes on to state that tenants must not, without written consent, sublet or part with possession of a part of their dwelling-houses. Such consent is not to be unreasonably withheld. In any dispute over the withholding of consent it is for the local authority to show that its refusal was not unreasonable. The county court has jurisdiction in such matters. Possible overcrowding, and also any proposed carrying out of work on the house in question may be taken into account when determining whether a refusal of consent was unreasonable, see section 36 of the 1980 Act. Consent may not be given conditionally. If the tenant applies for consent in writing the local authority must give their consent within a reasonable time or it is deemed to be withheld. If they withhold consent they must give a written statement of reasons for the refusal.

Secure tenancies cannot be assigned, neither can a secure tenant part with possession of or sublet the whole of a dwelling let on a secure tenancy, without the tenancy ceasing to be secure. See section 37 of the Act of 1980. To this there are three exceptions:

1) where the tenancy is assigned under section 24 of the Matrimonial Causes Act 1973; or

2) where the assignment is to a person in whom the tenancy would or might have vested under section 30 of the Housing Act 1980 had the tenant died immediately before the assignment; or

3) where on the death of a secure tenant the tenancy is vested in or otherwise disposed of, in the course of the administration of the estate, to a person who could have succeeded to it under the terms of the 1980 Act.

Subletting without consent is also a ground for possession for it is a breach of a tenancy obligation.

b) *Improvements*

Section 81 of the 1980 Act replaces section 19(2) of the Landlord and Tenant Act 1927 with regard, inter alia, to secure tenancies. It is to be a term of such tenancies that a tenant may not make any improvement without the landlord's written consent, though such consent is not to be unreasonably withheld. 'Improvement' is defined as any alteration in, or addition to a dwelling and includes additions to or alterations in the landlord's fixtures and fittings, and alterations, etc., to the services to the house; the erection of wireless or television aerials, and the carrying out of *external* decoration. If a dispute arises over the withholding of consent it is for the landlord to show, under section 82 of the 1980 Act, that it was reasonable. The county court may consider any of the following in determining the issue:

1) whether the improvement would make the dwelling or any other premises less safe for the occupier;

2) whether it would be likely to involve the landlord in expenditure which they would otherwise be unlikely to incur; or

3) whether it would be likely to reduce either the price of the house if sold on the open market, or the level of the rent at which it could be let.

Where a tenant applies in writing for the necessary consent the landlord must give it within a reasonable time, otherwise it is deemed to be withheld and must not give it subject to an unreasonable condition, otherwise consent is deemed to be unreasonably withheld. A refusal of consent must be accompanied by a written statement of the reasons for the refusal. Consent that is *unreasonably* withheld is treated as being given.

Consents may be given retrospectively to work already done, and may be given conditionally, though it is for the landlord to show the reasonableness of any condition imposed. Under section 83 a failure to comply with a reasonable condition is to be treated as a breach of a tenancy obligation. This may render the tenant subject to possession proceedings, as also will any carrying out of improvements without consent.

Where a secure tenant begins and makes an improvement to a dwelling after the commencement of Chapter II of Part I of the 1980 Act and this (a) has received the landlord's consent, and, (b) has added materially to the dwelling's sale or rental value, section 38 of the Act gives the landlord power to make such payments to the tenant as they consider appropriate at the end of the tenancy. The amount payable must not exceed the cost or likely cost of the improvement *after* deducting the amount of any grant paid under Part VII of the Housing Act 1974. Under the tortuously worded section 39 of the Housing Act 1980 the rent of a dwelling let on a secure tenancy is not to be increased on account of a tenant's improvements where he has borne the *whole* cost himself, or would have so borne that cost but for a grant paid under the Housing Act 1974. This benefit will enure while the improving tenant, or his spouse as a successor tenant, hold the tenancy. If irrespective of grant aid, only part of the cost is borne by the tenant, a pro rata increase in rent can be made.

Variation of terms and publicity

Under section 40 of the 1980 Act the terms of a secure tenancy, other than those implied by statute, and *other* than with regard to rent etc., may be varied, deleted or added to by agreement between the parties. (For variation of rents see Chapter 4, below.) In the case of a periodic tenancy terms may also be varied by the landlord serving notice on the tenant. Such a notice must specify the variation in question, and the date on which it will take effect. The period between service and the coming into effect of the change must not be shorter than the rental period of the tenancy, nor shorter than four weeks. Before a notice of variation is served, the landlord must serve a preliminary notice on the tenant informing him of the proposed changes and their effects and inviting his comments within a specified time. Any comments received must be considered. When the variation is made it must be explained to the tenant. A variation will not take effect where the tenant gives a valid notice to quit before the arrival of the date specified in the notice of variation. A change in the premises let under a secure tenancy is *not* a variation.

Section 41 of the 1980 Act imposes a duty to publish within two years of the commencement of Chapter II of the Act, and thereafter to update, information about secure tenancies. This must explain in simple terms the effect of the express terms (if any) of secure tenancies, the provision of Parts I and III of the Housing Act 1980, and of sections

32 and 33 of the Housing Act 1961 (implied covenants of repair). Every secure tenant must be supplied with a copy of this information, and also with a written statement of the terms of his tenancy so far as they are not expressed in a lease or tenancy agreement or implied by law. This written statement must be supplied:

1) if the tenancy is granted after the commencement of Chapter II of Part I of the Housing Act 1980, on the grant of the tenancy or as soon as practicable afterwards, or

2) where the tenancy was granted before commencement, within two years of that date. This provision does *not* require local authorities to give their tenants written leases or tenancy agreements, only a written statement of the terms of the tenancy.

Further reading

Cullingworth, J.B., *Housing and Local Government* (George Allen and Unwin, 1960), Chap. 5
Lambert. Paris and Blackaby, *Housing Policy and the State* (Mac-Millan, 1978), Chap. 3
Merrett, S., *State Housing in Britain* (Routledge and Kegan Paul, 1979), Chap. 8
Murie, Niner and Watson, *Housing Policy and the Housing System* (George Allen and Unwin, 1976), Chap. 4
Social Welfare Law (Ed. by D.W. Pollard) (Oyez) paras. B. 453 – B. 744

On racial discrimination

Daniel, W.W., *Racial Discrimination in England* (Penguin, 1968), Part 4
Deakin, N., *Colour, Citizenship and British Society* (Panther, 1970), pp. 148 – 170
Hill, C., *How Colour Prejudiced is Britain?* (Panther, 1967), Chap. 3
Krausz, E., *Ethnic Minorities in Britain* (Paladin, 1971), pp. 88 – 94
Lester and Bindman, *Race and Law* (Penguin, 1972), pp. 57 – 61
Smith, D., *Racial Disadvantage in Britain* (Penguin, 1977), Part 3
Smith and Whalley, *Racial Minorities and Public Housing* (P.E.P., 1975)
Housing in Multi-racial Areas (Community Relations Commission, 1976)
Race Relations and Housing, Cmnd. 6252

On allocation

Corina, L., *Housing Allocation Policy and its Effects* (Department of Social Administration, University of York, 1976)

Vincent, J., *The Housing Needs of Young Single Mothers* (Social Policy Research)

Hughes and Jones, 'Bias in the Allocation and Transfer of Local Authority Housing' (July 1979) Journal of Social Welfare Law 273 to 295

Lewis, N., 'Council Housing Allocation: Problems of Discretion and Control' (1976) Public Administration, Vol. 54, p. 147

On tenant participation

Ward, C., *Tenants Take Over* (Architectural Press, 1974)

Tenants' Participation in Housing Management (Association of London Housing Estates, 1975)

Franey, R., 'Making Tenants' Charters Work' *Roof*, January 1979, pp. 20 – 22

Chapter 4

Rents and rent rebates for municipal houses

At the heart of an individual local authority's rent scheme for its houses lies the Housing Revenue Account (HRA) which local authorities were first required to keep by the Housing Act 1935. Section 12 of the Housing Finance Act 1972 is now the governing provision, and requires the keeping of a HRA in respect of income and expenditure on, inter alia, all houses and buildings provided under Part V of the 1957 Act, unfit houses purchased under that Act, and land acquired or appropriated for the purpose of Part V of the 1957 Act.

'Expenditure' includes the following matters:

1) Supervision of and services to council houses;
    (a) general management costs, i.e. rent collecting, accounting, allocation and operational costs,
    (b) special costs, such as heating supplied to tenants under a common scheme, lighting and cleaning the common parts of flats, the upkeep of estate grounds, roadside verges, etc.,

2) Repair charges;

3) Charges on the capital debt undertaken to provide housing (inevitably the largest single item of expenditure);

4) Other expenditure, such as debt management expenses, revenue contributions to capital outlay, i.e. revenue temporarily treated as capital for building purposes, and a proportionate part of salaries paid and overheads incurred in connection with housing capital works.

'Income' will include:

1) Rents from dwellings;

2) Rents from municipally provided amenities such as common heating schemes;

3) Rents from other properties such as shops on housing estates and garages provided for tenants;

4) Exchequer subsidies;

113

5) Contributions from the General Rate fund;

6) Other miscellaneous income.

Income and expenditure as a general rule should balance, and so a local authority's *total* rent income should in general be equal to its total current expenditure on housing less the amount of subsidies. The general rule for many years has been that local authorities have not been permitted to budget for a surplus on their HRAs, neither have they been allowed to budget for a deficit. Where at the end of a year the HRA is found to be in deficit it must be made to balance by means of a contribution from the local authority's general rate fund under Schedule 1, paragraph 14(2) to the Housing Finance Act 1972. There is no general duty, however, on a local authority to make a *fixed* annual contribution out of the general rate fund to the HRA, though authorities *may* credit their HRAs with such sums as they think fit, see Schedule 1, paragraph 14(3) to the Housing Finance Act 1972 and Schedule 5, paragraph 8(6) to the Housing Rents and Subsidies Act 1975. As we shall subsequently see this discretion has led to wide variations in rent levels across the nation for what are similar houses as some authorities have chosen to make general rate fund contributions to their HRAs while others have not.

Section 134 of the Housing Act 1980, repealing section 1(3) of the Housing Rents and Subsidies Act 1975, now removes restrictions on working balances in HRAs. Furthermore section 135 allows local housing authorities to establish Housing Repairs Accounts beginning in the year 1981 − 82. To such an account are credited the following:

1) contributions from the HRA;

2) income arising from the investment or other use of money credited to the account; and

3) sums received by the authority in connection with the repair and maintenance of any of their housing stock, either from its tenants, or from the sale of scrapped or salvaged materials.

This account, if established, is to be debited with the following:

1) all expenditure (including loan charges) incurred in connection with the repair or maintenance of the local council housing stock, and

2) such expenditure as is incurred in connection with the improvement or replacement of any of the municipal housing stock as is from time to time determined by the Secretary of State.

If an authority decide to establish a Housing Repairs Account they must ensure that sufficient sums are credited to it to prevent it ever going into deficit. If an authority consider that any credit balance in the repairs account at the end of a year will not be needed for the purposes of that account, they may carry some or all of that balance to the credit of the HRA.

Rent pooling

What falls to be paid collectively by municipal tenants is that part of their municipal landlord's costs which have been incurred in providing and maintaining housing and which is not otherwise met by central government subsidies or local contributions from the general rate fund. But an individual tenant does not pay a sum representing those actual costs in relation to the particular house in which he lives. Instead the arrangement is that the gross rents of a local authority's houses are set at such a level that their total sum meets the local authority's costs less subsidies and other contributions. This is known as 'rent pooling'. This is an equitable arrangement. As we have seen, the largest items of expenditure in the provision of housing are the loan charges on the capital debt, and these are much higher on post-war houses than on those built pre-1939. Rent pooling allows the burden of loan charges to be spread across all an authority's housing. So far as an *individual* dwelling is concerned, its gross rent will be based on the concept of 'relative use value', which takes into account factors such as the number of rooms in the dwelling, its total floor area, its age, whether it is a house or a flat, the quality of fixtures and fittings, its location and general condition etc. As a guide many authorities use the gross rateable value of their properties as estimated by the rating valuation officer.

Rents for municipal housing have risen considerably over the years, despite 'rent freezes' imposed by central government from time to time, as, for example, by statute in 1974. The reason for these increases is that housing costs have risen even faster than the general rate of inflation over the last decade because of:

1) the high cost of land and house building costs;

2) the increasing costs of management, maintenance and administrative support services; and

3) the rapid rise in interest rates.

Municipal rents in general have certainly kept pace with inflation, despite increased exchequer subsidies designed to protect local authorities and their tenants against the worst effects of the rising loan charges arising out of capital debts. But they have varied greatly from one part of the country to another. One reason for this variation has been mentioned already, namely policy variations between local authorities as to the exercise of their discretion in making contributions to their HRAs from their general rate funds, but there are other reasons. These include:

1) the age and character of any given authority's housing stock: the newer the stock, the more, in general, it cost to build, and that leads to higher rents;

2) regional variations in construction, maintenance and improvement costs which have been so marked, particularly in the London area, that subsidies have been unable to even them out;

3) the fact that subsidies have been generally related to the historic costs of providing houses, not to any given authority's *current* needs, nor to the needs and/or resources of its tenants.

In *Housing and Public Policy* p. 114 Stewart Lansley wrote: 'In consequence, rent levels vary widely. At April 1976, the average unrebated rent of a post − 1964 three-bedroomed house was as high as £10.80 in the London Borough of Hammersmith, £9.60 in Wokingham, and £8.40 in Brighton, and as low as £3.70 in Chorley (Lancashire), £3.97 in South Derbyshire, and £4.10 in Carlisle, compared with an average in England and Wales of £5.74'.

It is against this background of rising rent levels set against regional and local variations in rent policies that the law relating to municipal rents and rent rebates must be set and examined.

Up till 1972 local discretion as to rent policy was subject to little central direction and control. The law simply required local authorities to charge 'reasonable rents' for their houses, to review those rents from time to time in the light of changing circumstances, and to grant such rent rebates as they thought fit. The Housing Finance Act 1972 substituted new 'fair rents' for 'reasonable rents' in order to bring the public rented sector into line with private lettings. This legislation was bitterly resisted by a number of local authorities, in particular Clay Cross Urban District Council in Derbyshire the members of which, supported by their electors, defied the law and the government. In that case the council's rent policy was investigated by the District Auditor, and ultimately a Housing Commissioner was appointed to administer the municipal housing stock following the resignation of the Council. There were, however, other attempts to avoid the effects of the 1972 Act by legal means. In *Backhouse v Lambeth Borough Council* (1972) 116 Sol Jo 802 a local authority raised the rent of an unoccupied council house from £30.84 *per month* to £18,000 *per week* in order to take advantage of a technicality in section 63(1) of the 1972 Act that if an authority made a *general* rent increase which produced £26 or more per dwelling, they were not to levy any further increase in the same year as part of a move towards 'fair rents'. The council had obviously made the resolution raising the rent on the unoccupied house to £18,000 per week with the intention that their rent total would rise to such a figure as would bar any further 'fair rent' increase that year. It was held that this was an abuse of the local authority's discretion, as it was so unreasonable a decision that no reasonable authority could have reached it, and therefore the resolution was a nullity.

On the change of government in 1974 a 'rent freeze' was quickly introduced and the change to fair rents, which was not in fact far advanced, was halted and then reversed by the Housing Rents and Subsidies Act 1975. This legislation did, however, continue the mandatory rent rebate schemes, introduced by the 1972 Act, which were designed to improve the lot of the worst-off municipal tenants.

Reasonable rents

The principal provision is now section 111(1) of the Housing Act 1957: '. . . the authority may . . . make such reasonable charges for the tenancy or occupation of the houses as they may determine'. This does not give an absolute discretion to local authorities as to the fixing of rents for it was held in *Belcher v Reading Corpn* [1950] Ch 380, [1949] 2 All ER 969 that a local authority must maintain a balance between the interests of their tenants on the one hand and the interests of the ratepayers as a whole on the other. A local authority also are not entitled to indulge in expenditure having no relation to their housing stock for which they propose to pay by increasing the rents paid by their tenants. Apart from those requirements there are few other restrictions on the exercise of their powers. Thus:

1) An authority may spread the cost of their housing over all their properties, and need not take each house or estate separately, they need not limit the rent by reference to the initial cost of providing the house or flat, and may charge different tenants different rents for the same accommodation, see *Summerfield v Hampstead Borough Council* [1957] 1 All ER 221, [1957] 1 WLR 167;

2) Rents may be assessed on the basis of gross rateable values, *Luby v Newcastle-Under-Lyme Corpn* [1965] 1 QB 214, [1964] 3 All ER 169, or by means of comparison with economic rents charged in the private sector, *Evans v Collins* [1964] 1 All ER 808, [1964] 3 WLR 30;

3) Apart from the statutory obligation to grant rent rebates there is no legal requirement that a differential rent scheme be operated, *Luby v Newcastle-Under-Lyme Corpn* though if a local authority wish to operate such a scheme they may do so, and they may take into account the differing means of their tenants, *Leeds Corpn v Jenkinson* [1935]

1 KB 168 and *Smith v Cardiff Corpn (No. 2)* [1955] 1 Ch 159, [1955] 1 All ER 113.

It can thus be appreciated that the courts exercise little effective supervision over the day to day administration of local authority rent policies and will only intervene in extreme circumstances. Moreover in *Smith v Cardiff Corpn* [1954] 1 QB 210, [1954] 2 All ER 1373 great obstacles were placed in the way of a group of tenants wishing to bring a representative action on behalf of themselves and all their fellow tenants. Here the local authority proposed to increase the rents of their houses on a differential basis according to the incomes of the tenants, with the better-off subsidising the less well-off, while the lowest paid tenants were to be subject to no rent increase at all. There were four plaintiffs who sought to bring a representative action on behalf of themselves and all other tenants of the local authority to attack the proposal. It was held by the Court of Appeal that to bring a representative action it must be shown: first, that all the members of the class have a common interest; second, that they all have a common grievance, and third, that the relief sought will in its nature benefit them all. It was held that the plaintiffs in this case did not satisfy the second and third conditions. The very nature of the local authority's scheme was to produce two classes of tenant whose interests, far from being identical, were in conflict, and so the relief sought by way of a declaration to impugn the rent scheme could not benefit *all* the tenants. The plaintiffs were allowed to continue their action as four individuals but, as we have seen from *Smith v Cardiff Corpn (No. 2)*, they were unsuccessful.

Increasing rents

By section 113(1A) of the Housing Act 1957 'a local authority shall from time to time review rents and make such changes, either of rents generally, or of particular rents, as circumstances may require'. The Secretary of State has a reserve power under section 11(1) of the Housing Rents and Subsidies Act 1975 to make orders 'restricting or preventing increases of rent for dwellings which would otherwise take place or for restricting the amount of rent which would otherwise be payable on new lettings'. But the effect of section 15(5) seems to be to restrict this power to 'any specified description of local *authorities*, or new town corporations or to any specified description of buildings', so that an order could not be made in respect of the rents of an individual local authority, nor with regard to the rent of an individual dwelling.

For many years the technical way to increase the rent for a municipal dwelling was to serve a notice to quit and then to create a new tenancy at the increased rent. Where this method was used the notice to quit had to be correct in all respects, see *Bathavon Rural District Council v Carlile* [1958] 1 QB 461, [1958] 1 All ER 801.

With regard to *secure* tenancies section 40 of the Housing Act 1980 allows variations of rent and payments in respect of rates or services to be made either by agreement between landlord and tenant or in accordance with any terms in the lease or the agreement creating the tenancy. In the case of periodic tenancies variations may also be effected by the landlord serving a notice of variation on the tenant. This notice must specify the variation it makes and the date on which it takes effect; and the period between the date on which the notice is served and the date on which it takes effect must not be shorter than the rental period of the tenancy nor in any case shorter than four weeks. Where such a notice is served and, before the arrival of the date specified in it, the tenant gives a valid notice to quit, the notice will not take effect unless the tenant, with the landlord's written consent, withdraws his notice to quit before the relevant date.

Tenancies which are *not* secure tenancies fall to be dealt with under section 12 of the Prices and Incomes Act 1968, as amended by Schedule 25 to the Housing Act 1980. This provision gives local authorities power to increase rents for their houses let on weekly or other periodical tenancies by means of the service of a 'notice of increase' instead of a notice to quit. This notice must inform the tenant that he is entitled to terminate the tenancy by serving his own notice to quit, and the increased rent does not take effect if he serves notice to quit within two weeks of the service of the notice of increase, or such longer time as may be allowed.

Rent arrears

Despite the existence of a statutory rent rebate scheme many local authority tenants still get into arrears with their rents either because of an unforeseen financial problem, such as unemployment, desertion by a spouse, illness, or general poverty, or, much less probably, because of unwillingness or incapacity to manage their financial affairs in a satisfactory way. It is very difficult to assess how many municipal tenants are in rent arrears. The 1976 National Consumer Council Discussion Paper *Behind with the Rent* reported in 1974/75 that about £27,577,224 was owed in rent arrears, or about 3.3 per cent of the collectable rent of £835,159,318. There is evidence that the arrears problem is getting worse, probably as a result of the worsening economic condition of the nation. In mid 1976 arrears of rent in the London area alone were computed as being £12,000,000, and it was estimated that one in every three tenants could have some rent in arrears, though the accuracy of these figures has been doubted by the

National Consumer Council. Nevertheless there is cause for some concern over the problem of rent arrears. In Audrey Harvey, *Remedies for Rent Arrears* (Shelter, 1979), it was said that in 1976 – 77 over £44,000,000 was owing to local housing authorities, an increase from almost £35,000,000 in the previous year. Of course it must be remembered that as rent levels increase annually the important figure is the percentage figure of rent unpaid for any given year. This seems to remain fairly constant at about 3 per cent of the total rent annually collectable. Nevertheless this meant, for example, that in 1978 some 13,000 tenants of the London Borough of Camden owed back rent.

Rent arrears are not primarily caused by a deliberate and wilful refusal on the part of tenants to pay rent simply because they do not want to meet their obligations. As Audrey Harvey says in *Remedies for Rent Arrears* at p. 48: 'Rent arrears often start at a time of crisis such as illness or loss of earnings. People already on low incomes who face such a crisis are forced to choose which bill not to pay. As with other recent studies of rent arrears, this one produced no evidence of bad financial management by the tenants. On contrary tenants frequently practised stringent economies, especially in heating their homes, and had managed much better than might be expected on inadequate incomes . . . . Rent arrears are mainly due to inadequate incomes which are themselves often due to unawareness of financial rights and available state benefits and allowances. Although allowances are available to meet many contingencies most people — and by no means only the poorly educated — have no idea what these cover and who qualifies. Unfortunately this lack of awareness extends to most local authority housing and legal officers'.

The 1976 National Consumer Council Discussion Paper called for much greater counselling and supportive work on behalf of tenants experiencing rent problems. In particular they recommended:

1) Increased pre-tenancy advice, whereby prospective council tenants should be given clear advice as to the likely costs and weekly outgoings of a municipal tenancy, together with advice as to fuel costs, the paying of bills and the perils of becoming over committed on hire-purchase transactions;

2) the giving of clearly understandable statements about rent, methods of payment and the importance of regular payment;

3) the taking of prompt action as soon as arrears begin to occur on the part of an individual tenant, this action should include home visits by housing department staff;

4) the giving of advice as to the financial assistance available for helping tenants to pay their rents or suggesting a voluntary transfer to cheaper accommodation;

5) the involvement of the social services authority in relevant cases;

6) the creation of an arrears committee within each local authority to scrutinise arrears records regularly. 'Committee meetings should be attended by the housing officers responsible for the cases under consideration, and by a social worker, ideally with specialist knowledge of the welfare benefits field; he or she should advise about tenants who are already being seen by the social services department or who should be referred to it. The tenant should have the right to attend particularly if eviction is to be considered'.

Local authorities should remember that they may be able to rely on the provision of section 1 of the Children and Young Persons Act 1963, under which a rent guarantee from the social services authority may be available.

The taking of the administrative steps outlined above may well help prevent arrears problems from arising in a number of cases. If such problems do arise, however, local authorities have a number of powers to deal with them.

An action for the rent ('rent action')

This can be brought in the county court under r.17, County Court (New Procedure) Rules 1971 (S.I. 1971 No. 2152). Where the tenant or former tenant is still in occupation application is made to the county court for the district in which the house in question is situated and a summons for the arrears will issue. The hearing then follows and judgment is given whether or not the tenant appears, unless he files some substantial defence. After judgment has been entered the defendant can pay money into court either on account of the claim or in satisfaction of it. Should he fail to pay the local authority may take enforcement proceedings. Satisfaction of the debt can be achieved by an attachment of earnings order under the Attachment of Earnings Act 1971. Department of the Environment Circular No. 83/72 counsels the use of this method of dealing with arrears.

An attachment of earnings order can only apply to 'earnings', i.e. wages, salaries, fees, bonuses, commission payments, overtime payments, and pensions. The following are not 'earnings': the pay of HM Forces, social security and disablement pensions or allowances. The order once made is directed to the debtor's employer and instructs the employer to make deductions from the debtor's earnings and to pay them to the clerk of the court as specified in the order. The order must also specify:

1) the normal deduction rate, that is to say, the rate at which the court thinks it reasonable for the debtor's earnings to be applied to meeting his debt, and

2) the protected earnings rate, that is the rate below which, having regard to the debtor's resources and needs, the court thinks it reasonable that the earnings actually paid to him should not be reduced.

See generally section 6 of the Attachment of Earnings Act 1971.

By virtue of section 15 of the 1971 Act while an attachment of earnings order is in force the debtor must notify the court in writing of every occasion on which he leaves any employment or becomes employed or re-employed within seven days of the happening of such an event. This notification must include particulars of his earnings. Moreover, any person who becomes the debtor's employer knowing that an attachment of earnings order is in force is required also to inform the court that he is employing the debtor and to give details of earnings. It is an offence for a person to fail to comply with these provisions.

Some authorities remain wary of using the attachment of earnings procedure. An objection frequently voiced by local authorities to this means of proceeding is that it is likely to be effective only where the tenant concerned is in regular employment. Of course many tenants who do fall behind with their rent are in irregular employment or are unemployed.

Distress

In *Abingdon Rural District Council v O'Gorman* [1968] 2 QB 811, at 819, [1968] 3 All ER 79 at 82. Lord Denning MR said: 'It is very rarely that we have a case about distress for rent. It is an archaic remedy which has largely fallen into disuse. Very few landlords have resort to it'. Indeed within the private rented sector section 147 of the Rent Act 1977 provides: 'No distress for the rent of any dwelling-house let on a protected tenancy or subject to a statutory tenancy shall be levied except with the leave of the county court'. But in the public sector no such restriction applies and there is evidence that an increasing number of local authorities do levy distress as a means of recouping rent arrears. The modern use of distress as a way of recovering unpaid rent was first examined in the journal *New Society* on 16 February 1978. Shortly thereafter Shelter published Steve Schifferes' *In Distress over Rent* which contained a list of 106 housing authorities who in March 1978 stated they used distress in rent arrears cases. Eleven of these authorities had only recently introduced the practice. But what is distress?

Distress is a common law remedy enabling the landlord to secure the payment of rent by the seizure of goods and chattels found upon premises in respect of which the rent is due. It need not be expressly created by the lease or tenancy agreement. The basic common law rules have been much modified by statutory intervention over the years, and so though at common law the right to levy distress only entitles the landlord to seize and hold goods until his debt is satisfied, section 1 of the Distress for Rent Act 1689 as amended by section 5 of the Law of Distress Amendment Act 1888 allows the sale of the goods seized as a satisfaction of the debt. Before distress can be levied the relationship of landlord and tenant must exist between the parties, both when the rent becomes due and when the distress is levied, and the rent must also be in arrear. Therefore there can be no distress until the day after rent becomes due, and if the landlord allows the tenant 'days of grace' to pay the rent these must also expire before distress can be levied.

Distress may only be levied on certain goods and personal chattels found on the demised premises. So far as municipal tenants are concerned the chief exemptions from distress are the wearing apparel and bedding of a tenant and his family and the tools and implements of his trade. The protection is, however, limited to such goods to a total value of £100 (in the case of wearing apparel and bedding) and £150 (in the case of tools and implements), see the Protection from Execution (Prescribed Value) Order 1980 (S.I. 1980 No. 26). In the case of municipal tenancies furniture other than bedding, i.e. bedsteads and mattresses, is the usual item upon which distress is levied. Distress itself may not be levied at night, which is the period between sunset and sunrise, nor on a Sunday. Furthermore a tender to the landlord, or his agent, by the tenant, or his agent, of the rent in arrear *before* the seizure of goods extinguishes the right to levy distress and the levying of distress is, in general, a bar to the levying of distress a second time for the *same* rent.

The procedure for levying distress

Local authorities, in common with other corporations, levy distress by bailiffs who must be authorised to carry out this function by their employers. This authorisation is normally put into writing when it is known as a distress warrant, but it is not essential that there be an authorisation in writing. Nevertheless before a person may act as a bailiff he must be certificated under the Law of Distress Amendment Act 1888 by the county court, such certification being for periods of twelve months at a time.

Bailiffs employed by local authorities can rely on the general rule that there is no need to issue a prior demand for the rent in arrear before levying distress, but they have to observe a number of rules in the performance of their duties. They may enter the premises in question to levy distress, but they must not break in nor enter by force. They may enter via an outer door that is closed but not fastened, and they may even unlock a door where the key has been left on the outside of the lock. Once inside, however, inner doors may be broken open during the levying process. Bailiffs may enter via *open* windows and may climb over walls and fences from adjoining premises. Once a bailiff has made a legal entry upon the premises he may obtain the assistance of the police and use force to break open outer doors if he is forcibly expelled from the house by violence on the part of the tenant.

The actual process of levying distress is completed by the bailiff making a seizure of goods. A bailiff levying distress must deliver to the tenant, or leave on the premises where the distress is levied, a memorandum setting out the amounts for which the distress is levied and the fees, charges and expenses to which the bailiff is entitled, together with an inventory of the goods seized, see rule 22 of the Distress for Rent Rules 1953 (S.I. 1953 No. 1702). (For a detailed statement of the law of distress the reader is referred to Halsbury's *Laws of England* (4th edn) vol. 13, paras. 105 – 390.)

Various calls have been made over the years for the abolition of distress for rent culminating in Shelter's 1978 report. There can be no doubt that the remedy is archaic, over-technical and cumbersome. There are many other arguments against its use:

1) it is, as we have seen, a remedy effectively available only against municipal tenants because of statutory restrictions in the private sector;

2) its incidence is unevenly geographically situated, and it seems to be most used in rural areas;

3) some authorities refuse to countenance the use of distress, while others use it only to administer a 'sharp shock' where they feel that the tenant is wilfully withholding the rent. It seems odd that tenants' rights should vary so much according to mere geographical locations and the administrative practice of individual authorities;

4) the remedy is medieval and if used can damage the development of good landlord/tenant relationships;

5) the *threat* or actual levying of distress can be, and sometimes is, used against tenants who are in real financial difficulties through no fault of their own, as such it militates against the idea that local housing authorities should attempt to help such people through their difficulties;

6) the bailiffs employed by local authorities are frequently not public employees but are in private practice. On 5 March 1978 *The Sunday Telegraph* claimed that the Lord Chancellor's Office had received upwards of 600 complaints in two years about the practices of such private bailiffs;

7) finally the evidence is that distress does not solve the problem of rent

arrears. As the 1978 Shelter Report states: 'The so-called "poverty-trap" is one that is as well documented as the difficulties which lead to rent arrears in the first place. When people start to fall into debt, their difficulties increase. In the case of distress, this means that property is sold at considerably less than either what it cost or what it is worth. The tenant must ultimately replace the property, paying full price for it. He has lost out in the sale value, he loses out in the replacement and in addition he will have to pay the bailiff's costs'.

Those authorities who do *not* use distress very often refrain from the practice because they find that the value of the property seized will be insufficient to satisfy the debt owed. In such circumstances the only persons who stand to gain from the distress are the bailiff retained by the local authority and the auctioneer employed to sell the goods seized.

The 1979 Labour Housing Bill provided in its Clause 8 that no distress for the rent of any municipal dwelling-house held under a secure tenancy should be levied without the leave of the county court, a provision that paralleled, without quite reproducing, the provisions of the Rent Act 1977. Unfortunately this provision was not included in the Housing Act 1980. It is odd that a legislative measure designed to confer considerable rights on municipal tenants, and also to harmonise many of the rules regulating the relationship of landlord and tenant in both the public and private sectors should so signally have failed to regulate this area of housing practice where the municipal tenant can be so very disadvantaged, especially when compared with his private sector neighbour.

Eviction

The eviction of a tenant for non-payment of rent does not actually solve the problem of arrears remaining unpaid, and indeed leads to another problem, namely that of a homeless person or family needing accommodation (see Chapter 6, below). Nevertheless in the past some local authorities have evicted some tenants for non-payment of rent as a way of 'cutting their losses'. Secure tenants enjoy the protection of the Housing Act 1980 with regard to possession proceedings brought in respect of non-payment of rent (see Chapter 3, above) but persons who are not secure tenants may still be subject to possession proceedings if they get into rent arrears.

Since the repeal of the Small Tenements Recovery Act 1838 in 1972 all local authorities wishing to obtain an order for possession of one of their dwellings have had to apply to the county court. Nevertheless in *Empty Houses,* a report published by the Bradford Housing Action Group, there was evidence to suggest that some tenants do not realise this and vacate their homes on receipt of the local authority's notice to quit. Many authorities, however, have included an explanatory letter with a notice to quit in rent arrears cases, and some have arranged for the notice to be delivered personally by an official who can explain the effect of it to the tenant and also try to work out some means of reducing the arrears as an alternative to possession proceedings.

The granting of secure tenant status to most municipal tenants will change greatly the use made of possession proceedings by local authorities. Non-secure tenants may still need to defend possession actions. Once a local authority begins possession proceedings against a non-secure tenant they will be automatically entitled to an order of possession under their common law rights as a landlord — because the notice to quit determines the tenancy — unless the tenant can establish an abuse of power on the part of the local authority in seeking to evict him, see *Bristol District Council v Clark* [1975] 3 All ER 976, [1975] 1 WLR 1443 and *Cannock Chase District Council v Kelly* [1978] 1 All ER 152, [1978] 1 WLR 1. This latter case is also authority for the proposition that the burden of proving any abuse of power lies on the tenant, who must set out in his claim the basis of his allegation that his landlord has acted in an ultra vires manner. Where such an allegation is made the proper forum for its examination is generally the county court. In *Cleethorpes Borough Council v Clarkson* [1978] LAG Bulletin 166 it was held that the same principles are applicable where the termination of a license to occupy from a local authority is in issue. The problem arose again in the Court of Appeal in *Sevenoaks District Council v Emmott* [1980] LAG Bulletin 92. The common law proposition was restated and endorsed — where an authority act in bad faith or dishonestly, or take into account something which they should not have taken into account (and vice versa), then their decisions will be ultra vires and must be quashed or ignored by the court. In *Emmott* the Court of Appeal went on to make other points:

1) an authority is under no duty to give reasons for their decisions;

2) they have no *general* duty to give the tenant concerned an opportunity to comment or make representations about any matter brought to their attention even where it is a matter which might be regarded as being to the discredit of the tenant;

3) they are under no duty to hold anything corresponding to an enquiry.

The Editor of LAG Bulletin made the following comment on this case:

'On the face of it, this short report seems to undermine an otherwise viable argument — at least where an eviction is based on tenant's default — that the rules of natural justice, or administrative fairness, require that the tenant be given an opportunity to comment or to meet any "charge" or complaints made against him/her. The implications of the decision are, however, not so sweeping. It is clear from the facts, and was so held by the court, that the tenant had had ample opportunity to comment, but that he had refused to avail himself of it. Moreover, Megaw LJ stressed that he was stating his view "as at present advised", which reflected the fact that the tenant was not legally represented (he was in fact represented, with the permission of the court, by his son). The decision is highly qualified in other ways as can be seen from the following extract: "It is not for this court to tell a housing authority what it ought to do in relation to the making of its decision, *provided that the local authority stays within the limits of fair dealing. It is not a requirement in general — I do not say that there may not be particular circumstances where a different decision might arise — of a* housing authority when it gives notice to a tenant to quit to give its reasons why it has arrived at that decision. Nor, if its reasons are based upon some matter which has been brought to its attention — whether by a complaint from outside or otherwise which might be regarded as being to the discredit of the tenant — is it in general a duty of the local authority to give the tenant concerned the opportunity to make representation about that matter. It certainly is not the duty of a local authority to do anything in the nature of holding a formal inquiry or holding anything that would correspond to the inquiry by a court into the question of who was right and who was wrong . . . . In any event, the highest at which the duty upon a local authority can be put when it is considering the question of complaints made against a tenant is to deal with matter in such a way as to comply with the requirements of fairness . . .". It would seem, therefore, that the court was aware of the limitations of the presentation of the tenant's case and was also aware that, in any case, the authority had behaved fairly. No reference was made to such authorities as *Cooper v Wandsworth Board of Works* (1863) CB NS 180 or *Hopkins v Smethwick Local Board of Health* (1890) 24 QBD 712, CA, in which it was held that where a case concerns the deprivation of property (and, of course, a tenancy is an interest in property), an authority must abide by the rules of natural justice'.

It seems clear that a local authority are not in general bound to hold an inquiry. Equally what amounts to fair administrative action will vary from case to case. The nature of the action the authority proposes to take will affect the nature of the procedural steps it must go through. No hard and fast rules can be laid down. *Emmott* reinforces the proposition that the burden of proof lies on the tenant to show how an authority have behaved in an ultra vires manner, but it does not preclude the possibility of pursuing the argument that, by failing to afford the tenant a reasonable opportunity to be heard, an authority have not acted fairly.

In any case local authorities should remember that central policy for many years, for example as contained in Department of the Environment Circular No. 83/72, has turned its face against the use of eviction in rent arrear cases.

Administrative practices for dealing with rent arrears

Some authorities have in the past published lists of the names of those of their tenants who have been in rent arrears. This is an offence under section 40 of the Administration of Justice Act 1970 which makes it an offence for any person 'who with the object of coercing another person to pay money claimed from the other as a debt due under a contract . . . harasses the other with demands for payment which, in respect of their frequency or the manner or making of such demand, or of any threat or publicity by which any demand is accompanied, are calculated to subject him or members of his family or household to alarm, distress or humiliation'.

A much more laudable practice is the creation of some sort of 'early warning system' whereby by keeping a close watch on their accounts authorities can be prompt to note the first sight of rental default and so initiate supportative action in relation to affected tenants of the sorts already discussed above in relation to the problem of arrears generally. It should also be remembered that section 14(3) of the Supplementary Benefits Act 1976 allows supplementary benefits officers where it appears to them to be necessary for protecting the interests of a claimant that the whole or part of supplementary benefit should be paid to some other person, or where the claimant so requests, to determine that the benefit shall be used to pay the claimant's rent directly to the landlord. The officers are also willing to include in such direct payments up to 50 pence per week of a claimant's benefit entitlement to reduce any rent arrears if they consider this can be done without causing hardship or where the claimant requests it.

In this context, however, the effect of section 119 of the Housing Act 1980 with regard to rent rebates must be noted:

'(1) Except in accordance with directions of the Secretary of State, no rebate or allowance shall be paid by an authority under or by virtue of Part II of the 1972 Act [Housing Finance Act] to any person if, to the authority's knowledge —

  (a) he is receiving supplementary benefit; or
  (b) his income or resources fall to be aggregated under the 1972 Act or the Supplementary Benefits Act 1976 with those of another person who is receiving that benefit'.

Rent rebates

The mention of the relationship between supplementary benefit and rent rebates leads naturally to a discussion of this most useful scheme to help the less well-off council tenant. Before 1972 there had been an attempt to introduce rent rebates contained in section 113(3) of the Housing Act 1957: 'the local authority may grant to any tenants such rebates from rent, subject to such terms and conditions, as they may think fit'. But this scheme was discretionary and was replaced by a mandatory national scheme under section 18 of the Housing Finance Act 1972, as amended by Schedule 15 to the Housing Act 1980. This scheme applies to persons (whether the original tenant or a successor of the original tenant) occupying as their homes dwellings (i.e. *any* residential accommodation provided by an authority, whether or not comprising separate and self contained premises) let to them by the local housing authority other than those cases where:

1) the tenant occupies the dwelling under a license which was granted to him or some other person as a temporary expedient following an entry on the land in question (or any other land) which constituted a trespass (this, for example, would prevent any rebate being given to a licensed squatter); or

2) the tenant occupies the dwelling in pursuance of a contract of service with the authority the terms of which require that he shall be provided with a dwelling at a rent specified in the contract; or

3) Part II of the Landlord and Tenant Act 1954 (security of business tenants) applies to the tenancy.

Licensees other than those mentioned in 1) above are within the terms of the rent rebate scheme by virtue of section 18(4) of the 1972 Act (as amended) provided they have given consideration for their licenses. But note that tenants of *county councils* are classified as 'private tenants' and so fall to be dealt with under the rent allowance system. The sum to be regarded as 'rent' for the purpose of rebates is defined by section 25 of the Act. 'Rent' for this purpose means the 'occupational element', which is a sum *exclusive* of rates and charges for furniture, services or board.

Section 20 of the 1972 Act requires local authorities to comply with the model rent rebate scheme and administrative procedure contained in Schedules 3 and 4 to the Act, though by virtue of section 21 a local authority may make limited departures from the model scheme so as to grant *higher* rebates than normal to persons in exceptional personal or domestic circumstances. Section 24 of the Act of 1972 requires a local authority to deposit a copy of their rebate scheme at their principal office, to make copies available for free public inspection at that office at all reasonable hours, and to furnish a copy to any person on payment of a reasonable sum. Furthermore they must make certain 'statutory particulars' of their scheme known to their tenants; these 'particulars' are:

1) the procedure for making an application for a rent rebate;

2) the information to be included in such an application;

3) the circumstances in which a rebate is likely to be granted.

This duty includes an obligation to give examples of cases in which a rebate is likely to be granted and of the amount of rebate likely to be granted in different cases. It is also the duty of every authority to take such further steps as appear to them best designed to secure that the provisions of their rebate scheme come to the notice of any persons who may be entitled to a rebate under the scheme. Section 24(6) of the Act requires authorities to furnish the 'statutory particulars' to any person who becomes their tenant on or before the date on which the tenancy commences.

The model rent rebate scheme

The basic object of the scheme is to calculate rebate according to a tenant's needs and resources and the detailed rules are to be found in Schedule 3 to the 1972 Act. The basic 'planks' of the scheme are the various allowances and resources to be taken into account in the calculation of rebate.

The first considerations are the so called 'needs allowances'. These are allowed for by paragraph 8 of Schedule 3 to the Act. Different weekly allowances are specified according to the tenant's marital status and whether he has dependent children living with him. The actual sums allowed change with a degree of regularity and to calculate rebate in any given case it is necessary to consult the regulations in force at any given times. It is not appropriate to give that amount of detail in the present work which will instead concentrate on the basic workings of the rent rebate system.

Next the income of the tenant and his spouse, if any, must be determined. The local authority will begin by calculating, according to the terms of Schedule 3 to the 1972 Act, the tenant's gross income which is to include, according to Department of the Environment Circular No. 74/72, child benefit, and family income supplement, national insurance benefits, interest received from a building society, payments from a sub-tenant for the use of services or furniture provided and also, under Schedule 3 to the 1972 Act, as amended, any maintenance payment made to a dependent child aged under sixteen. But from this sum certain 'disregards' have to be made under paragraph 9 of Schedule 3. These 'disregards' include:

1) any rent received from a sub-tenant of part of the dwelling (other than money paid in respect of furniture and services provided);

2) any payment made to the tenant or his spouse by a dependent child, or by a non-dependant;

3) a specified sum of the earnings of the tenant and also of the earnings of the tenant's spouse;

4) any financial assistance for education paid under regulations made under section 81 of the Education Act 1944;

5) any attendance allowance;

6) any sums payable to any person as the holder of either the Victoria Cross or George Cross;

7) any supplementary benefit (though see now section 119 of the Housing Act 1980);

8) a specified sum of any of the following:
    (a) war disablement pension;
    (b) industrial disablement benefit;
    (c) an old cases allowance paid under the Industrial Injuries and Diseases (Old Cases) Act 1975;
    (d) any payment classified by the Secretary of State as being analogous to (a) to (c) above;

9) a specified sum of:
    (a) a widow's pension (by way of industrial death benefit);
    (b) a special widow's pension;
    (c) a payment classified by the Secretary of State as analogous to either of the above;

10) a specified sum of any charitable payment or any voluntary payment made by a person who is not a non-dependant for the maintenance of his spouse (including a spouse with whom he is not living) or his former spouse or children;

11) where the tenant is a qualifying student, an amount equal to any amount prescribed as a deduction for that week under section 25(3) of the 1972 Act (the very detailed rules applicable to students are outside the scope of this work. The reader is referred also to the regulations made under section 25(3)(c) of the Housing Finance Act 1972, see *Social Welfare Law* (Ed. by D.W. Pollard) paras. B. 1269 to B. 1274);

12) where the tenant is a qualifying student, any amount by which his grant is increased on account of his maintaining a home at a place other than that at which he resides during his course;

13) any maintenance payment made by the tenant or his spouse to his or her former spouse or to his or her children (other than dependent children);

14) a specified sum of a lodging allowance paid in connection with the Training Opportunities Scheme.

In addition to the above 'disregards', section 37A(8) of the Social Security Act 1975 states that a mobility allowance is also to be disregarded.

However, the total sum of the various applicable 'disregards' is subject to a specified maximum under paragraph 9(3) of Schedule 3 to the Housing Finance Act 1972.

The calculation of rebate

The method of calculating rebate is contained in paragraphs 10 and 11 of Schedule 3 to the Housing Finance Act 1972. The tenant *must* in general pay some rent and in any given case this is referred to as the 'minimum weekly rent'. This sum will be based initially on a figure of £1 or 40 per cent of the actual charged rent, whichever is the greater, though it may finally be increased or decreased according to the circumstances of the case.

Thus:

1) In any case where the weekly income of the tenant and his spouse is *less* than the calculated needs allowance, 'minimum weekly rent' will be an amount equal to 40 per cent of actual rent or £1 (whichever is the greater) less an amount equal to 25 per cent of the difference between the needs allowance and the weekly income. Should this latter part of the calculation result in a reduction equal to or greater than £1 or 40 per cent of weekly rent, whichever is the greater, then the 'minimum weekly rent' is zero.

2) If the weekly income of the tenant and his spouse is *equal* to the calculated needs allowance, the rebate is to be equal to the amount by which the charged weekly rent exceeds the minimum weekly rent, in other words, the rent payable will be 40 per cent of the charged rent or £1, whichever is greater, and the rebate will make up the difference.

3) If the weekly income of the tenant and his spouse is greater than the calculated needs allowance the rebate is calculated by adding together

(a) an amount equal to the minimum weekly rent and

(b) an amount equal to 17 per cent of the difference between the weekly income and the needs allowance.

In other words the rent actually payable will be 40 per cent of the actual rent or £1, whichever is greater, plus 17p for every £1 of income over the level of the needs allowance, and the rebate will be the difference between the sum so produced and the charged rent for the dwelling.

But it should be noted that under paragraph 12 of Schedule 3 to the Housing Finance Act 1972 that certain deductions have to be made from any rebate once calculated to take account of any 'non-dependants' living with the tenant. Such non-dependants are defined as 'any person who resides in the dwelling occupied by the tenant other than the tenant himself, except a spouse of the tenant and a dependent child of the tenant or his spouse', paragraph 2 of Schedule 3 to the 1972 Act.

Rebate examples

N.B. in this section of this chapter *notional* figures have been used in the examples simply to show how rebates are calculated. The calculation involves the following steps:

1) Take the tenant's weekly rent (WR);

2) Take his weekly income (WI);

3) Calculate his needs allowance (NA);

4) Take a figure of 40 per cent of WR or £1 whichever is greater.

Thus to calculate Minimum Weekly Rent (MWR):

1) Where WI *equals* NA, MWR equals 40 per cent of WR or £1 as the case may be;

2) Where WI is *less* than NA, MWR equals 40 per cent of WR or £1 *less* a sum equal to 25 per cent of the difference between WI and NA;

3) If WI is *greater* than NA, then MWR will be 40 per cent of WR or £1 *plus* 17 per cent of the difference between WI and NA.

Having thus calculated MWR in any given case:

1) Subtract MWR from WR.

2) Further subtract from the resulting figure any deductions for non-dependants living with the tenant,

the resulting sum will be the amount of rebate due to the tenant. Thus:

a) Household of tenant, wife and one child

i)	Weekly Rent (WR)	£10.00
ii)	Weekly Income (WI)	£50.25
iii)	Needs Allowance (in total) (NA)	£53.25
iv)	£1 or 40 per cent of WR whichever is greater	£ 4.00

WI is not equal to NA but is less, therefore subtract from iv) 25 per cent of the difference between ii) and iii), i.e. 25 per cent of £3.00, which is 75p, producing MWR of £3.25. The rebate is therefore £10.00 minus £3.25, which is £6.75.

b) Household of tenant, wife, one child and tenant's non-dependant mother

i)	WR	£10.00
ii)	WI	£55.25
iii)	NA	£53.25
iv)	£1 or 40 per cent of WR	£ 4.00

WI is not equal to NA but is more, therefore add to iv) 17 per cent of the difference between ii) and iii), i.e. 17 per cent of £2.00 which is 34p, producing MWR of £4.34. The rebate is therefore £10.00 minus £4.34 which is £5.26, minus a further deduction on behalf of the non-dependant mother of £1.10, which results in a total rebate of £4.16.

A rebate is thus a sum equal to the difference between the rent actually payable and the charged rent for the premises. But there are statutory minima and maxima for rebates. Paragraphs 13 and 14 of Schedule 3 of the Housing Finance Act 1972, as amended, state these specified amounts; presently the minimum grantable rebate is 20p and the maximum is £25.00 for a dwelling in the area of the Greater London Council or £23.00 for any other dwelling.

Administrative procedures concerning rebates

These are contained in Schedule 4, as amended, to the 1972 Act. The following provisions should be noted:

'An authority may [in general] pay a rebate at any time and in any manner that they think fit; . . .

4(1) Where a rebate . . . is first granted, the rebate period . . . shall commence [in general] at the commencement of the rental period in which the application for a rebate . . . was received; . . .

(2) A rebate period . . . shall end . . .

   (a) if the tenant is of pensionable age, not later than twelve months after the date on which he was notified that his application for a rebate . . . was granted; and

   (b) if the tenant is not of pensionable age —

      (i) where the date of notification falls during the months of

March or April in any year, not later than nine months after that date; and

(ii) in any other case; not later than seven months after that date; . . .

10(1) A tenant to whom a rebate . . . has been granted may apply to the authority for a further rebate . . . commencing with the first rental period after the end of the current rebate period'.

In circumstances where a dwelling has been let to one of two spouses and the tenant spouse is not occupying the dwelling while the other spouse and remained in occupation and has paid the rent, paragraph 1(3) of Schedule 4 to the Housing Finance Act 1972 allows the authority, if in their opinion it is reasonable to do so, to treat the spouse who has paid the rent as the tenant for rebate purposes. An authority may also treat as spouses for such purposes a man and a woman who formerly lived with him in the dwelling as his wife.

If at any time between the making of an application for a rebate and the making of the determination thereon there is a change of circumstances such that the applicant may be reasonably expected to know that it may *reduce* the amount to which he is entitled, it is the duty of the applicant to notify the authority of that change in circumstances. A similar obligation exists in the case of a change in the tenant's circumstances during the currency of a rebate period. In such circumstances the local authority may determine according to the circumstances either to terminate the rebate period on a date earlier than it would otherwise terminate, or to alter the amount of the rebate. It is the duty of the local authority to notify a tenant, in writing, of their determination in relation to any rebate application he may make. Where they determine to grant a rebate their letter to the tenant must state the amount of the rebate and the rebate period. They must also inform the tenant of his obligation to notify them of any change in his circumstances. See paragraphs 2 and 15 of Schedule 4 to the Housing Finance Act 1972. Department of the Environment Circular No. 17/78 contains further advice on the sort of information local authorities should give to their tenants about the events that could be regarded as amounting to a change in circumstances.

Where some person who resides in the dwelling occupied by the tenant appears to the local authority to have a higher income than the tenant, and the authority have grounds for considering that in the special circumstances of the case it would be reasonable to make their calculations as to rebate entitlement by reference to the income of that other person they may, under paragraph 5 of Schedule 3 to the 1972 Act, treat that other person as the tenant and make such payments of rebate as ought to be made on that basis. Department of the Environment Circular No. 74/72 gives as an example of when it would be proper to use this power: 'where . . . a non-dependant with very high earnings has made his home, possibly with other earners also, in the tenant's dwelling and where the responsibility for meeting the rent has in all but name been assumed by the non-dependant'. Likewise under paragraph 4 of the Schedule for the purposes of calculating rebate entitlement, 'an authority may treat as a sole tenant . . . one of two or more joint tenants'. However, in the circumstances outlined above paragraph 15 of Schedule 4 to the Act requires the local authority to notify the person who will fall to be treated as the tenant for rebate purposes of their determination.

We have already seen that local authorities are under a duty to notify tenants in writing of their determinations in relation to rent rebate decisions affecting those tenants, also of any decision to treat some person other than the tenant as a tenant, and also of any decision to treat one of two or more joint tenants as a sole tenant for rebate purposes. In such circumstances paragraph 15 of Schedule 4 of the Housing Finance Act 1972 enables the tenant or other affected person to make representations to the authority concerning such determinations. If any such representations are received within one month of the notification of the authority's determination, the authority must consider them, and they may then alter or confirm the determination according to the circumstances. Whether they alter or confirm the determination they must notify the person affected in writing of their reasons for having acted as they have done.

The details of the rent allowance scheme which local authorities administer for the benefit of tenants in the private sector are very similar to those of the rent rebate scheme. It should also be remembered that under section 117(2) of the Housing Act 1980 the amount of modified rent rebate subsidy payable to a local authority or new town corporation for the credit of their general rate fund is to be 90 per cent of the authority's standard amount of rent rebates for any given year. This leaves an authority to make a rate fund contribution for each year of 10 per cent of the standard amount of rebate.

Further reading

Grant, M., *Local Authority Housing: Law Policy and Practice in Hampshire* (Hampshire Legal Action Group, 1976) in particular see Chap. 4

Harvey, A., *Remedies for Rent Arrears* (Shelter, 1979)

Legg, C., and Brion, M., *The Administration of the Rent Rebate and Rent Allowance Schemes* (Department of the Environment, 1976)

Schifferes, S., *In Distress over Rent* (Shelter, 1979)

Behind with the Rent (National Consumer Council Discussion Paper, 1976)

Empty Houses (Bradford Housing Action Group Report, 1976)
Social Welfare Law (Ed. by D.W. Pollard) (Oyez) paras. B. 1081 –
B. 1390
Franey, R., 'Punishment for Rent Arrears' *Roof*, May/June 1980,
pp. 80 – 84

Chapter 5

Municipal housing, matrimony and mortgages

This chapter covers a miscellany of matters loosely connected by the theme of rights of occupation and access thereto, in so far as they touch upon and are affected by municipal housing powers. The 'mortgages' section of the chapter is devoted to local authority general powers to grant mortgages to those seeking such finance, to act as guarantors for mortgagors and their general relations with the building societies.

The council house as the matrimonial home

Conveyancing practice has for many years tended, in the private sector, to treat joint ownership of the house as the norm where property is to be occupied as the matrimonial home. In municipal housing historic practice was to assume that where a married couple occupied a council house the husband would be the tenant. The 1976 National Consumer Council discussion paper *Tenancy Agreements* stated: 'In preparing our model agreement we have taken note of the Sex Discrimination Act 1975 since in future it cannot be assumed in all cases that the male partner of a marriage or couple living together may automatically be designated the tenant'. In 1977 the Housing Services Advisory Group (HSAG) in its report on tenancy agreements said: 'There are as many arguments in favour of, as there are against, tenancies in joint names and we think that prospective tenants should be given the opportunity to choose between a joint tenancy and a sole tenancy'. By 1978 the HSAG in its report on the housing of one parent families actually recommenced the use of joint tenancies in municipal lettings: 'In council tenancies too there are strong advantages to joint tenancies . . . . For common-law wives there is a great advantage in having a joint tenancy. Unfortunately many authorities refuse to give tenancies to unmarried couples. Some even refuse to house them at all. We believe that such policies should be reconsidered'.

There are obvious advantages for a woman if she has a joint tenancy of a council house with her husband:

138

1) In the event of his death or desertion there is no need for her to apply for a transfer of the tenancy to herself;

2) In proceedings for divorce, nullity or judicial separation the court may make an order with regard to the transfer of the property under section 24 of the Matrimonial Causes Act 1973;

3) If the marriage breaks up she will be entitled to remain in occupation of the home by virtue of her legal estate and she can apply to the court for orders under section 1 of the Matrimonial Homes Act 1967, as amended by section 4 of the Domestic Violence and Matrimonial Proceedings Act 1976, which enables one of two joint tenants to apply to the court, with respect to the exercise during the subsistence of the marriage of the right to occupy the dwelling-house, for an order prohibiting, suspending, or restricting its exercise by the other spouse, or requiring that other to permit its exercise by the applicant. She will also have rights under section 7 of the Matrimonial Homes Act 1967, as amended by the Housing Act 1980. (See below.)

The disadvantage of a joint tenancy to a wife is that she can be held liable for any rent arrears accrued by her husband before his death or desertion, etc.

The Housing Act 1980 recognises in a number of its provisions that local authorities may grant joint tenancies but goes no further in encouraging them to do so. One practice that will be impossible under the new law is that of issuing notice to quit to a deserted joint tenant before granting a new sole tenancy, unless, of course, the local authority can show one of the grounds for possession. For the future it may be hoped that local authorities will use joint tenancies when letting to couples. Administrative practice should reflect the legal situation and communications from the local authority should be sent to tenants jointly in both names. It should also be made clear in the tenancy agreement that the authorisation of either partner will be sufficient to authorise or agree to the doing of works and repairs by the landlord. Where joint tenancies are not possible and a single tenant is required, a couple being allocated a house should be given a choice as to which of them will be named as tenant. Before a choice is made between different kinds of tenancy it is obviously a matter of good housing management for a local authority to explain the implications of each to intending tenants.

The rights of a non-tenant wife

A wife who is not a tenant has the right to occupy and use the matrimonial home because at common law she is entitled to maintenance by her husband. Legislation goes further than this. Under section 1 of the Matrimonial Homes Act 1967:

'(1) Where one spouse is entitled to occupy a dwelling by virtue of any estate or interest or contract or by virtue of any enactment giving him or her the right to remain in occupation, and the other spouse is not so entitled, then, subject to the provisions of this Act, the spouse not so entitled shall have the following rights . . .

(a) If in occupation, a right not to be evicted or excluded from the dwelling or any part thereof by the other spouse except with the leave of the court . . .

(b) If not in occupation, a right with the leave of the court . . . to enter into and occupy the dwelling house'.

The jurisdiction of the court to make orders declaring, enforcing, restricting or terminating the rights of occupation of spouses, or to prohibit, suspend or restrict the exercise of those rights of occupation exists so long as one spouse has rights of occupation. The court has wide discretion in the making of orders and is to take into account the conduct of the parties, their needs and resources, the needs of any children and all other circumstances of the case. Thus a non-tenant wife has protection against eviction or exclusion from her matrimonial home.

The Matrimonial Homes Act 1967 was amended by the Domestic Violence and Matrimonial Proceedings Act 1976 to make it clear that either spouse may apply to the court for an order prohibiting, suspending or restricting the exercise by the other of the right to occupy, or to require that other to permit the applicant spouse to exercise the right. The above rights only apply within marriage, not outside it. This is a very good reason why 'common law' wives should seek to obtain joint tenancies wherever possible as a way of obtaining at least some legal interest in the property.

Domestic violence

'Domestic violence' is the euphemism for the social phenomenon of wife-battering. The Select Committee on Violence in Marriage Report (H.C. 553, 1974 – 5) recognised the extent of this problem and recommended that special refuges be set up where women could go to get away from violent men, and that the initial target provision should be one family place per 10,000 of the population. Local authorities should assist in making this provision and the HSAG report *The Housing of One Parent Families* stated at pp. 15 – 16: 'The refuge need not be in the form of a hostel. In fact in rural areas and small towns it will probably be more appropriate to have mutual arrangements between the police, probation services, social services and housing departments for the provision of emergency accommodation and social work support where and when the need arises. In cities, there may be a strong case for hostel-type provision, but this should be only for short stay emergency accommodation and more satisfactory family accommodation should be provided as quickly as possible, even if this is an intermediate step before permanent rehousing . . . . The local authority should undertake to rehouse, if needed, women who leave these refuges having separated from their partners. Some authorities are now giving a general undertaking to rehouse all women who go through these hostels within six months of their arrival, whether or not they have any legal separation or custody order and whether or not they have previous arrears'.

Unfortunately these hopes have not always been realised in practice. *The Times* 9 August 1980 reported that many refuges in towns consist of ill maintained pre-1919 housing. These properties are often overcrowded, accommodating on average five women and nine children at any given time, and lack many of the amenities needed to allow children to play in safety.

To protect the woman in the home the Domestic Violence and Matrimonial Proceedings Act 1976 was enacted. This legislation was necessary because the existing law was inadequate. Previously a wife could commence assault proceedings against her husband, and this might result in the husband being bound over with, perhaps, some supervision by a probation officer. Likewise where a wife had commenced divorce or judicial separation proceedings she could also apply for an injunction to prohibit molestation, or even a mandatory injunction excluding the husband from the home. But faster and simpler legal machinery was needed. The 1976 Act therefore provides:

'1(1) Without prejudice to the jurisdiction of the High Court, on an application by a party to a marriage a court shall have jurisdiction to grant an injunction containing one or more of the following provisions, namely,

    (a) a provision restraining the other party to the marriage from molesting the applicant;

    (b) a provision restraining the other party from molesting a child living with the applicant;

    (c) a provision excluding the other party from the matrimonial home or a part of the matrimonial home or from a specified area in which the matrimonial home is included;

    (d) a provision requiring the other party to permit the applicant to enter and remain in the matrimonial home or a part of the matrimonial home; whether or not any other relief is sought in the proceedings.

(2) Sub-section (1) above shall apply to a man and a woman who are living with each other in the same household as man and wife as it applies to the parties to a marriage and any reference to the matrimonial home shall be construed accordingly'.

This provision was tested in *Davis v Johnson* [1979] AC 264, [1978] 1 All ER 1132. A young unmarried mother held a joint tenancy of a council flat with the father of her child. She left the flat with her child because of the father's violent behaviour towards her and applied to the county court under the 1976 Act for an injunction to restrain him from molesting her or the child and also excluding him from the flat. The House of Lords held that the county court has jurisdiction under section 1 of the Act to grant an injunction excluding a violent person from a home where he has lived, with a woman, irrespective of their marital status, and irrespective of any right of property vested in the person excluded, whether as owner, tenant or joint tenant. A further illustrative case is *Adeoso v Adeoso* [1981] 1 All ER 107. The parties began living together in a council flat in January 1975, and were subsequently moved into another flat consisting of one bedroom, a sitting-room, kitchen and bathroom. They did not marry, but Mrs Adeoso adopted her partner's name. By July 1979 the relationship had become unhappy and Mr Adeoso had begun to resort to violence. The parties slept in different rooms, and Mrs Adeoso ceased to cook or wash for Mr Adeoso. Their only communication was by notes. They locked the rooms they occupied individually. Mrs Adeoso applied for an order under the domestic violence legislation requiring Mr Adeoso to stop molesting her and also to leave the flat. Mr Adeoso argued that the 1976 Act did not apply as the parties were not in fact living together, and also because they occupied separate accommodation. The Court of Appeal rejected both contentions. Ormrod LJ said that looking at the Adeoso household from the outside it would be assumed that the parties were living together, and that the case fell within the rule in *Davis v Johnson*. Also it was impossible to say that the parties were living separately in a flat with only two rooms.

In practical terms exclusions are not permanent, but should be for such a period of time as will enable the applicant to make other arrangements for accommodation, or effect a reconciliation, or commence separation proceedings, as the case may be. As a general rule following a *Practice Direction* [1978] 1 WLR 1123, an injunction excluding a person from his former home is likely to last for up to three months, subject to discharge or extension.

Section 2 of the 1976 Act provides extra enforcement proceedings for breach of injunctions.

'(1) Where on an application by a party to a marriage, a judge grants an injunction containing a provision . . .

   (a) restraining the other party to the marriage from using violence
      against the applicant, or
   (b) restraining the other party from using violence against a child
      living with the applicant, or
   (c) excluding the other party from the matrimonial home or from a
      specified area in which the matrimonial home is included,

The judge may, if he is satisfied that the other party has caused actual
bodily harm to the applicant, or, as the case may be, to the child
concerned and considers that he is likely to do so again, attach a power
of arrest to the injunction'.

Where such a power of arrest is attached to an injunction, a police
constable may arrest without a warrant any person whom he reasonably
suspects of being in breach of the provisions detailed above included in
the injunction. Again, this section applies both to married couples and
to a man and a woman living together as man and wife.

Section 16 of the Domestic Proceedings and Magistrates' Courts Act
1978 empowers a magistrates' court to make a personal protection order
prohibiting a spouse from threatening, or using violence against, the
other spouse, or any child of the family:

'(2) Either party to a marriage may . . . apply to a magistrates' court
for an order under this section . . . .

(3) Where on an application for an order under this section the court is
satisfied;

   (a) that the respondent has used violence against the person of the
      applicant or a child of the family, or
   (b) that the respondent has threatened to use violence against the
      person of the applicant or a child of the family and has used
      violence against some other person, or
   (c) that the respondent has in contravention of an order [made
      previously under section 16(2) requiring the respondent to
      refrain from violence] threatened to use violence against the
      person of the applicant or a child of the family,

and that the applicant or a child of the family is in danger of being
physically injured by the respondent (or would be in such danger if the
applicant or child were to enter the matrimonial home) the court may
make one or both of the following orders, that is to say —

   (i) an order requiring the respondent to leave the matrimonial
      home;
   (ii) an order prohibiting the respondent from entering the matri-
      monial home.

(4) Where the court makes an order under sub-section (3) above, the
court may, if it thinks fit, make a further order requiring the respondent
to permit the applicant to enter and remain in the matrimonial home'.

Provision is made for extremely rapid hearings in such situations. Section 18 of this Act allows the magistrates to annex a power of arrest to an exclusion order where they are satisfied that the respondent has physically injured the applicant or a child of the family, and consider him likely to do so again.

Thus the magistrates in the exercise of their domestic jurisdiction now have powers approximating to those of the county court, but it must be remembered that their powers apply only within the context of marriage.

The rights of the parties on the break-up of a marriage

Section 24(1)(a) of the Matrimonial Causes Act 1973 provides:

'On granting a decree of divorce, a decree of nullity of marriage, or a decree of judicial separation or at any time thereafter . . . the court may make any one or more of the following orders, that is to say — an order that a party to the marriage shall transfer to the other party, to any child of the family or to such person as may be specified in the order for the benefit of such a child such property as may be so specified, being property to which the first-mentioned party is entitled, either in possession or reversion'.

After some initial judicial hesitation it is settled that this provision applies to municipal tenancies. Nevertheless its application in practice was difficult because section 113(5) of the Housing Act 1957 required that there should be a term in every municipal tenancy that the consent of the local authority in writing be obtained before any assignment could take place. Where local authorities were prepared to consent to assignments no problems arose, but where they were opposed the courts found their powers effectively blocked. As Sir George Baker P said in *Regan v Regan* [1977] 1 All ER 428, [1977] 1 WLR 84 at 85: 'The problem has been debated whether [there can be an order under the 1973 Act] when there is a covenant or condition in the lease against assigning or subletting without the consent of the landlord, and if there is, the question will then arise whether the landlord is prepared to consent. If there is such a provision and the landlord is not prepared to consent, then that seems to me to be the end of the matter and the court should not make a transfer of property order'.

Section 113(5) of the Housing Act 1957 has been repealed, and the position is governed by section 37 of the Housing Act 1980. The 'penalty' for assigning a secure tenancy is that it ceases to be secure, but special provision is made by section 37(1)(a) that secure tenancies *can* be assigned in pursuance of orders made under section 24 of the Matrimonial Causes Act 1973. Thus in the case of secure tenancies the court has wide powers to order their transfer between the parties to a divorce, a decree of nullity, or a judicial separation.

The Housing Act 1980, Schedule 25 further amends section 7 of the Matrimonial Homes Act 1967 (as amended by Schedule 8 to the Rent (Agriculture) Act 1976). This now provides, inter alia:

'(1) Where one spouse is entitled, either in his or her own right or jointly with the other spouse to occupy a dwelling-house by virtue of . . .

    (c) a secure tenancy within the meaning of section 28 of the Housing Act 1980

and the marriage is terminated by the grant of a decree of divorce or nullity of marriage, the court by which the decree is granted may make an order under sub-section (2) . . . below according to the circumstances.

(2) Where a spouse is entitled as aforesaid to occupy the dwelling-house by virtue of a . . . secure tenancy within the meaning of section 28 of the Housing Act 1980 the court may be order direct that, as from the date on which the decree is made absolute, there shall, by virtue of the order and without further assurance, be transferred to and vested in his, or her, former spouse —

    (a) the estate or interest which the spouse so entitled had in the dwelling-house immediately before that date by virtue of the lease or agreement creating the tenancy, and any assignment of that lease or agreement, with all rights, privileges and appurtenances attaching to that estate or interest but subject to all covenants, obligations, liabilities and incumbrances to which it is subject, . . .'.

The court has power to *transfer by its own order* municipal tenancies between spouses *where marriage is terminated by divorce or a decree of nullity*, if the order is applied for before the decree absolute.

The modification to the Acts of 1967 and 1973 will lead to an increase in legal protection for wives living in council houses when they find their marriages are breaking down and divorce, or separation at least, becomes inevitable. But what of husbands who lose their homes as a result of court orders? A single man is unlikely to fall within the priority classes of homeless persons, but the husband may have formed another liaison, and children, other than those of the marriage may be involved. In this connection the findings and recommendations of the HSAG in *The Housing of One-Parent Families* should be remembered.

1) Local authorities should remember that on the break-up of a marriage two tenancies may be needed rather than one. This 'two for one' element should be remembered in computing the future housing needs of an area.

2) Where a man is living in the former matrimonial home with a woman who is not his wife, following the break-down of marriage, and the court makes an order against him in respect of that home, simple eviction merely leads to an increase in the number of homeless persons. An increasing number of authorities try to offer the displaced husband suitable alternative housing.

3) Where the husband has developed no new relationship and is alone following marital break-down, the local authority should attempt to *rehouse* him bearing in mind the following factors:

    (a) will the man be living near enough his children to be able to see them?

    (b) will he need to be able to have them to stay?

    (c) is he expecting to remarry?

    (d) is he emotionally upset and unable to cope with eviction on top of losing his wife and children?

The general tenor of the HSAG's findings is that, while local authorities have no desire to encourage marital break-ups by the premature allocation of separate tenancies to husband and wife, wherever possible housing should be provided for parties to a marriage leaving the matrimonial home. The group added (at p. 10 of their report): 'Though this may appear to be a far-reaching decision, we consider it essential if the local authority is to develop a routine policy towards marital break-ups rather than a policy of intervening when a crisis occurs. It is worth recalling the very large proportions of the homeless who are lone parent families and the very great cost to the authority of providing emergency accommodation for the homeless'.

Other housing problems arising after marital break-up

After marital break-ups where there are children the parent having custody of them will face other problems, in particular those of a financial nature. The HSAG have made recommendations with regard to local authority housing practice in relation to such one-parent families.

1) It is the best policy to house one-parent families in ordinary family housing in a mixed development, as such accommodation accords with their needs and helps prevent social stigmatisation.

2) Even where both former partners have been responsible for a build-up of rent arrears, it should be remembered that these may have arisen during a period of stress. Local authorities should make arrangements for the gradual repayment of arrears, but should not otherwise penalise the parties.

3) Liaison between housing and social service departments is essential in order to provide all-round support for the one-parent family. Though this is difficult where the services are administered by different tiers of the local government system, such co-operation is essential if financial and emotional distress amongst one-parent families is to be reduced.

4) A wife who retains, or is granted possession of, the former matrimonial home may not wish to stay there. Requests for transfers to housing closer to relatives, schools, places of work or nursery facilities, or to the area of another authority, should be treated sympathetically. A transfer request should not be made conditional on a woman paying off arrears of rent on the former matrimonial home for which her husband was solely responsible. Local authorities should also be prepared to make rapid housing exchanges in the case of any woman who fears violence from her former husband. Similar conclusions were reached in the Finer Report, Cmnd. 5629. Other general advice to local authorities can be found in *Housing for One-Parent Families*, Department of the Environment Circular No. 78/77, paragraph 28 of which states that, as part of an overall scheme of helping families to manage their affairs more satisfactorily, local authorities should consider making more use of the power granted to social services authorities by section 1 of the Children and Young Persons Act 1963 to give rent guarantees.

Progressive authorities operate wherever possible, within the constraints of finance and the available housing stock, liberal policies with regard to the marital problems of their tenants. Unfortunately there are pockets of resistance to the introduction of such policies. Some authorities have adopted harsh, and indeed even illegal, practices with regard to lone parents. In such circumstances the best remedy is an investigation for maladministration by the local ombudsman.

Mortgages

Local authorities are providers of and channels for mortgage finance for would-be home owners other than those wishing to purchase municipal houses. This portion of the chapter will discuss the miscellaneous powers possessed by local authorities to provide such assistance.

The Small Dwellings Acquisition Act 1899 as amended grants very limited powers to local authorities to finance owner occupation. Section 1 of this Act allows local authorities to advance money to a resident in any house within their area for the purpose of enabling him to acquire the ownership of *that* house. But this power only applies where the local authority conclude that the value of the house does *not* exceed £5,000. This restriction obviously makes this power of very little use.

The vast majority of local authority mortgage lending, apart from monies secured on a charge on a former council house, is now conducted under section 43 of the Housing (Financial Provisions) Act 1958, as amended. Local housing authorities for the purposes of Part V of the Housing Act 1957, together with county councils, may advance mortgage finance 'to any persons' for the purposes of acquiring or constructing houses, or converting buildings into houses, or altering, enlarging, repairing or improving houses. They may make advances to enable the mortgagor to discharge a previous loan made in order to facilitate house purchase or improvement provided they conclude that the primary effect of the advance will be to meet the housing needs of the mortgagor by enabling him to retain his interest in the house in question, or will enable him to carry out proper works of conversion, improvement or repair on the house. The power to make an advance to pay off a previous loan on a house enables a local authority to allow re-mortgaging of property. This power is very useful where houses have been purchased jointly by husband and wife and the wife has given up or lost her job making repayment of the mortgage difficult. The new mortgage will provide for a longer mortgage period and lower monthly outgoings.

These powers exist in respect of houses both inside and outside the local authority's area, though some authorities are reluctant to lend on houses outside their areas. The range of property capable of forming the subject of a local authority mortgage is also wide, and includes freehold and leasehold property, though in such a case authorities *must* require that the unexpired portion of the term should be at least ten years more than the period of the mortgage. Premises comprising accommodation for residential and other purposes may form the subject of an advance, provided that the principal object to be secured in their purchase is the housing needs of the person seeking mortgage assistance.

The range of potential borrowers is also great. The Act says money may be advanced 'to any persons' but authorities tend to give preferential treatment to various categories of people such as their own tenants, or persons on, or eligible for, the housing waiting list, first time buyers living or working within their areas, those who are homeless and those who wish to convert or improve older large properties with a view to relieving overcrowding.

In the allocation of mortgage finance, local authorities should not discriminate on racial or sexual grounds (see Department of the Environment Circular No. 1/78). Before advancing money the local authority must be satisfied that the house in question is or will be made fit for human habitation. They must then proceed to have the property duly valued to ascertain its *market* value. Thereafter they may proceed to advance the money and secure both capital and interest on the house by way of mortgage. Where the money is advanced for purposes of construction, conversion, repair or improvement, etc., it may be paid by way of instalments as the work progresses. By virtue of section 3 of the House Purchase and Housing Act 1959 local authorities may advance a sum up to the full value of the property in question.

Local authority mortgage interest rates

In the past local authorities had considerable freedom to fix their interest rates. Some adopted a variable rate fixed by reference to the Consolidated Loan Fund Rate, others had a rate fixed by reference to the yearly borrowing charges of the authority. Section 110 of the Housing Act 1980 takes away this discretion and substitutes a most complex formula. *For the future* people looking to local authorities for mortgage finance in connection with house purchase, improvement or conversion, etc. (whether or not they acquire their houses from the local authority) will currently pay as their rate of interest *whichever is the highest* of:

1) The standard national rate, i.e. the rate declared from time to time by the Secretary of State after taking into account rates of interest charged by United Kingdom building societies, or

2) The applicable local average rate, i.e. a rate to be determined and declared by each local authority on a six monthly basis and tied to the amount the authority has itself to pay to service its loan charges plus ¼ per cent. These rates apply to all local authority mortgages, including those in connection with the 'right to buy' provisions of the 1980 Act.

3) A rate specified by the Secretary of State in a written notice to an authority.

The notice will direct the authority to treat the specified rate as the highest, and therefore the one to be applied. Where a variation in the interest rate occurs a local authority may allow a variation of the mortgage repayments, and must do so if the period over which the repayment of the principal sum is to be made would otherwise be reduced below the period fixed when the mortgage was effected. When an interest rate is varied the local authority must serve on the person liable to pay the interest written notice of the variation not later than two months after the change. Thereafter the variation will take effect in relation to his liability on the first payment of interest due after a date specified in the notice, which

1) if the variation is a reduction, must be not later than one month *after* the change, or

2) if it is an increase, must be not *earlier* than one month nor *later* than three months *after the service of the written notice*.

Where certain conditions are satisfied section 110(11) and (12) of the Housing Act 1980 allow local authorities to waive or reduce the interest payable on a mortgage, and also to dispense with the repayment of any of the principal sum, for a period of five years. The conditions are:

1) The loan must be made to a person acquiring a house in need of repair or improvement, whether from them or some other person;

2) The person acquiring the house must enter into an agreement with the local authority to carry out within a specified period specified works of repair or improvement;

3) The mortgage assistance must be given in accordance with a scheme conforming with the requirements of, or approved by the Secretary of State.

Section 43 of the 1958 Act was amended by section 37 of the Local Government Act 1974 to provide for the repayment of the principal of the mortgage either by way of instalments — as is the usual practice — or by way of a single payment at the end of a fixed period or on the happening of some specified event before the end of that period. This latter provision enables local authorities to grant maturity loans. Maturity loans are a useful form of advancing money which is, in effect, only to be repaid on the death of the mortgagor, usually from the proceeds of sale of the property in question. Such loans are most helpful as a means of assisting elderly owner occupiers to meet the cost of major repairs on their homes. Generally maturity loans are offered to applicants who are in receipt of supplementary benefits, subject to an assurance from the local offices of the Department of Health and Social Security that they are prepared to meet the interest payments on the loan. The mortgagor is then assured of sufficient capital to repair his house while not having to make any payments himself during his life. After death the mortgage will be a debt on the estate to be settled during administration, but the value of the house as repaired will be able to meet this burden. The use of maturity loans in this way can obviate any need for the permanent rehousing of elderly house owners.

Local authority lending in practice

Local authorities cannot surplant the building societies as the main source of mortgage finance for house purchase. The Building Societies Association Bulletin for April 1980 showed that the net sources of loans for house purchase were as follows:

Period	Local Authorities	Other Public Sector	Banks	Building Societies	Other
	£M	£M	£M	£M	£M
1977	4	27	130	4,000	23
1978	− 62	− 56	270	5,112	77
1979	312	47	600	4,912	N/A

The share of the mortgage market taken by each source varies from year to year but the overwhelming dominance of building society lending is easily apparent. It is established government policy, as expressed in Department of the Environment Circular No. 22/71, that local authorities are to concentrate their lending for the benefit of younger borrowers and the lower income groups. Their lending is on cheaper and older properties capable of improvement.

To obtain money to lend to mortgagors local authorities must them-selves borrow it. Section 54 of the Housing (Financial Provisions) Act 1958 grants a power to borrow and/or to issue housing bonds for the purposes of subsequent re-lending. As we have seen very strict central controls exist over local authority powers to raise capital. These powers can be used to restrict the lending role of local authorities. In 1976 in *Public Expenditure to 1979−80*, Cmnd. 6393 the Government announced: 'local authorities will in future be acting as lenders of the last resort; and their individual allocations for 1976 − 77 are designed to concentrate their lending in areas of greatest need and to assist in preserving the stock of older houses'.

The new system of block capital allocations technically allows local authorities a measure of freedom in deciding how much to devote to mortgage lending. Nevertheless it remains government policy that authorities should act only as lenders of last resort, and, in a time of scarce resources, should concentrate their lending on those who are unable to get a mortgage elsewhere. Central guidance has been issued from time to time as to the 'priority categories' of those who ought to receive local authority mortgage assistance. See, for example, Depart-ment of the Environment Circular No. 38/78 where the categories included:

1) Existing tenants of local and new town corporations, people high on a housing waiting list, people displaced by slum clearance to whom the rehousing duty is owed;

2) Applicants who are homeless or threatened with homelessness or

living in conditions that are overcrowded or otherwise detrimental to health;

3) Individual members of self-build groups;

4) Applicants wishing to buy older property suitable for one family occupation and unlikely to attract a commercial mortgage advance.

It has also been central policy to restrict the maximum advance limit on mortgages advanced by local authorities. Since 1974 there have been *administrative* limits set on local authority mortgage advances. These figures were £15,000 in Greater London and £13,000 elsewhere. These limits were introduced to tie local authority lending into the Special Advance Limits which regulate building society lending and have been used to control the direction of local authority lending. The figures are not statutory but are arrived at by consultation. Recently it has been recognised that the limits are too low because of rises in house prices. The limit has now been set at £25,000.

Co-operation between local authorities and the building societies

Because of the financial and other constraints upon local authority mortgage lending it has for many years been apparent that they cannot satisfy the aspirations of all those who look to them for house purchase assistance. It also became clear by the mid-1970's that inner city areas were suffering from a lack of mortgage finance, that houses in such areas were becoming unsaleable because purchasers with mortgage finance were becoming harder to find, and that young people who might otherwise revitalise old and decaying areas were finding it increasingly hard to borrow sufficient money to enable them to become home owners in such areas. Allegations have been made that the building societies' practice of 'redlining' has been largely responsible for these problems. Redlining is a practice, it is alleged, whereby whole areas of certain towns and cities are categorised as being places where mortgage lending by a particular building society or societies will seldom, if ever, take place. The evidence for the existence of such a practice in Leicester, Birmingham, Leeds, Newcastle and Huddersfield was gathered together by Stuart Weir in 'Red Line Districts', *Roof*, May 1976, p. 109 – 114. Questions were asked and ministerial assurances given in the House of Commons at the time, see H.C. Debs., 29 July 1976, Vol. 916, col. 355, H.C. Debs., 13 October 1976, Vol. 917, col. 412 and H.C. Debs., 4 March 1977, Vol. 927, cols. 786 – 880.

Against this the building societies have argued with absolute and correct logic that their first duty is to protect their investors' money, and that they have a second duty of vital importance, namely to dissuade potential house buyers from taking on commitments to house purchase in unsuitable areas. As Harry Brompton puts it in 'Mortgage Lending in the Inner Urban Areas', published in *Co-operation between Building Societies and Local Authorities*: 'In my view, a building society, acting responsibly will neither hazard the funds with which it is entrusted, nor encourage a purchaser of modest means to acquire a house out of income, if it may not maintain its relative value. Indeed, a borrowing member will not appreciate the help of the society at the time of purchase, committing him to repayment, if when he attempts to sell possibly seven years hence he finds the society is then unable to repeat the facility to his purchaser. It is essential for a society to take a relatively long term view'.

Because of public disquiet and debate the building societies have examined their lending policies so as to reduce or eliminate any direct bias against lending for house purchase in given areas taken as a whole. Nevertheless they classify both properties and potential borrowers and are prepared to lend less on certain types of property. In *The Building Societies*, Martin Boddy states at pp. 70 – 71: 'It must . . . be recognised that societies policies vary, that it is not claimed that there are necessarily *no* loans in these areas . . . . The significant point to be made is that societies' lending policies, aiming at what they consider adequate mortgage security, create areas of older, mainly inner-city housing where they will only rarely lend'.

Most inner city property falls into building society classes C and D, i.e. pre-1918 housing, particularly terraced houses lacking garage space and in a secondary location, but otherwise structurally sound and modernised, also unmodernised properties subject to an assurance of modernisation. Loans for the purchase of such properties are generally given over a 20 year period for Class C and 15 years for Class D, and the loan maxima are in the region of 70 per cent (basic) to 90 per cent (with insurance cover) of a society's valuation for a Class C house and 60 per cent to 80 per cent for one in Class D. So far as borrowers are concerned societies have been prepared to lend *up to* two and a half times gross annual salary on a 20 year term, and two and a quarter times that salary on a fifteen year term. The result is that on older properties less will be offered as mortgage finance, and for a shorter term. It can be argued that this amounts to consequential redlining as most Class C and D properties are likely to be found concentrated in particular areas.

It might be asked whether there is any room for co-operation between local authorities and building societies. In fact they have been working together for some while, though it has taken time and effort on both sides to work out the implications of the relationship.

The first co-operative venture was the Local Authority Replacement Lending Scheme of 1975. This was designed to cushion local authority mortgage lending against a reduction in public spending which cut the amount of money available for lending schemes. The building societies agreed to make £100 million available to aid house buyers who would otherwise have looked to local authorities for assistance. The scheme was at first beset by problems of communication and ignorance of aims and objectives on both sides. Even in the late 1970's it was clear that both had much to learn about each others' philosophies and principles. Nevertheless the Building Societies Support Lending Scheme, as it is now known, has continued and local authorities have been able to refer potential house buyers to a building society when their own mortgage funds have been insufficient. In 1980 £400 million was allocated to the support lending scheme and it was estimated that this would be enough to produce about 35,000 mortgages on properties which might not otherwise have been mortgageable.

Loans for house purchase 1975/76 to 1978/79 — England

England excl. GLC	Applications in priority categories	Applications granted loans	Applications referred to building society	Referrals resulting in building society loans
	thousand	thousand	thousand	thousand
1975/76	63	51	13	5
1976/77	60	26	32	13
1977/78	41	15	31	14
1978/79	64	23	45	27
Total for four years 1975/76 to 1978/79	228	115	121	59

But it remains true that the basic philosophies, aims and objectives of building societies and local authorities do not always coincide. A building society is at heart a club, and its directors' prime responsibility is to the members who are likely to be vigilant as to the safety of their money, and to make their views known at general meetings. A building society must retain the confidence, and funds, of its members. Consequently societies are concerned to lend only on irreproachable securities and are unwilling to encourage any member to make what they consider would be a 'bad buy'. Local authorities on the other hand do not raise their mortgage funds from a large number of small investors but simply as part of their general borrowing. They do not look at a house as security, but rather as a unit of accommodation.

Bringing these disparate philosophies together will take a long time. The law can help.

Local authority mortgage guarantee powers

Section 45 of the Housing (Financial Provisions) Act 1958 gave local authorities power to guarantee the repayment of mortgage advances made by building societies. These powers were used for some time but less use was made of them as the years progressed. A lack of mortgage finance has undoubtedly impeded improvement policies and accelerated urban decay. The lack of an effective mortgage guarantee system would seem to have been an important contributory factor in making the building societies wary of inner city lending. Following the Housing Policy Green Paper, Cmnd. 6851, the government examined the possibility of revitalising local authority mortgage guarantee powers as a way of encouraging a wider spread of lending by building societies. The powers in the 1958 Act have been replaced by provisions in the Housing Act 1980.

Section 111 of this Act allows a local authority, with the approval of the Secretary of State, to enter into an agreement with a building society whereby, in the event of the mortgagor's default, and subject to the terms of the initial agreement, the authority will be bound to indemnify the society in respect of:

1) The whole or part of the outstanding mortgage debt, and

2) Any loss consequent on the default falling on the society.

This power is exercisable by county and district councils, the Greater London Council, the London Boroughs, and the Common Council of the City of London.

The form of the agreement may provide for the authority to take a transfer of the mortgage, together with the benefit and burden of all proceeding acts, omissions and events, so that the building society is entirely discharged of its obligations, provided the mortgagor is a party to the agreement.

It remains to be seen how these new powers will work in practice. Clearly they are not to be used to encourage a lender to risk either the funds entrusted to it, or those of a potential house buyer, on a property that is likely to decline in value. Neither should they be used to assist a person who is unlikely to be able to meet his mortgage obligations. They should be used within the context of strategic housing renewal strategies especially those taking place in inner city neighbourhoods where property values are likely to rise as a result of repair and improvement.

These new powers are likely to make only a modest contribution towards the widening of access to home ownership.

Other local authority mortgage powers

Section 100 of the Housing Act 1974 places local authorities under a duty to offer home loans to persons made subject to compulsory improvement notices, or who have entered into improvement undertakings, under Part VIII of that Act. Before making such an offer a local authority must be satisfied:

1) that an applicant for a loan is capable of repaying it;

2) that an applicant's interest in the dwelling concerned consists either of the fee simple, or is a leasehold term which will not expire before the date of the final repayment of the loan; and

3) that the amount of the principal of the loan does not exceed the value which it is estimated the mortgaged security will bear after the requisite works of improvement have been carried out.

No loan is to be made for any part of the necessary expenditure that can be met by a grant payable under Part VII of the 1974 Act. Applications for loans under this provision must be made in writing within a period of three months beginning with the date when the compulsory improvement notice becomes operative, or the improvement undertaking is accepted, as the case may be. A local authority may, in writing, allow a longer period for applications.

The local authority's powers as a mortgagee

A mortgagee's power of sale as it applies to a local authority is modified by section 112 of the Housing Act 1980. In *Williams v Wellingborough Borough Council* [1975] 3 All ER 462, [1975] 1 WLR 327 a local authority sold a council house to a sitting tenant, and the purchase price was secured by a legal charge on the property. The mortgage conferred the power of sale contained in section 101(1) of the Law of Property Act 1925 on the local authority in case of a default on repayment. The mortgagor defaulted and the local authority purported to 'sell' the house to themselves. It was held that the local authority had no power to do this. There was no power to re-take the property in a case of default. This decision will now for certain purposes be set aside. Section 112 of the 1980 Act provides that where an authority has sold a council house under the *old* sale powers contained in the former section 104 of the Housing Act 1957, *and* in the conveyance or lease they have included a right of pre-emption for themselves, *and* where that pre-emption period is still current, *and*, if the right to exercise the power of sale as conferred by the mortgage deed or by the Law of Property Act 1925 arises, then, with the leave of the county court, they may vest the property in themselves free of the mortgage, subject to the payment of compensation to affected parties under section 113.

Local authority home purchase assistance powers

Section 1 of the Home Purchase Assistance and Housing Corporation Guarantee Act 1978 enables the Secretary of State to make advances to 'recognised lending institutions' to enable them to provide assistance to first time house buyers. County and district councils, London Borough councils, the Greater London Council, the Common Council of the City of London, and new town development corporations are among the recognised institutions. The assistance is only available where mortgage finance for house purchase is obtained by way of a secured loan from the lending institution, subject to the purchase price of the property being within the limits specified from time to time by the Secretary of State.

In addition the recipient of the assistance must satisfy certain conditions before being aided.

1) He must be a 'first time buyer'. Paragraph 24(2) of the Home Purchase Assistance Directions 1978, states: 'A person is not to be treated as a first-time purchaser if he has previously been the beneficial owner (whether individually or jointly with others) of [the freehold or the interest of the tenant under a lease granted for a term of more than 21 years] in a house in the United Kingdom in which he made his home'.

2) He must intend to make the property he is purchasing his home.

3) He must have been saving with a recognised savings institution for at least two years proceeding the date of his application for assistance, and also throughout the twelve months proceeding the date of his application he must have had at least £300 worth of such savings. Also by the date of his application he must have accumulated at least £600 worth of such savings, though the Secretary of State has power to relax or modify this requirement in particular cases. Recognised savings institutions include building societies, local authorities, Trustee Savings Banks, certain banking companies, Friendly Societies, the Director of Savings and the Post Office.

Assistance under the Act may take the following forms.

1) The secured loan may be financed by the Secretary of State to the extent of £600, that amount being normally additional to that which

the lending institution would have lent, but the totality of the loan is not to exceed the loan value of the property, which is stated by paragraph 37(1) of the Home Purchase Assistance Directions 1978 to be the purchase price of the property, or its estimated value, whichever is lower.

2) £600 of the total loan may be made free of interest and of any obligation to repay that sum of the principal, for up to five years from the date of purchase.

3) The lending institution may provide the purchaser with a tax free bonus on his savings up to a maximum of £110, payable towards the purchase or expenses arising in connection with it.

Exactly *what* assistance is available to any individual applicant is determined by section 1(5) of the 1978 Act, a complex provision whose effect is:

1) the £600 assistance is available to an applicant who has accumulated £600 of savings, has saved for two years, and has maintained a minimum balance of £300 in his savings for the year before his application. Such a borrower can also qualify for the bonus.

2) the bonus *only* is available to an applicant who has satisfied all the above conditions, save that he has not managed to accumulate savings worth £600.

3) No one qualifies for assistance unless he is borrowing at least £1,600, and the sum that he is borrowing amounts to at least a quarter of the purchase price. This means that the lowest purchase price qualifying for assistance is £6,400, a sum which is still, despite high house prices, sufficiently great to exclude from the ambit of the Act smaller older inner city properties.

4) the amount of bonus payable in any case is determined by paragraph 35 of the Home Purchase Directions 1978. A sliding scale is established whereby the greater the amount saved, the greater is the bonus payment. To qualify for the full £110 bonus the minimum amount of savings held in the twelve months proceeding the date of application for assistance must be not less than £1,000.

Miscellaneous points

The various figures in the Act can be varied by the Secretary of State, subject to Treasury approval, by Statutory Instrument subject to annulment by resolution in the House of Commons. Section 2(4) of the 1978 Act enables the Secretary of State to indemnify a lending institution against losses suffered in cases where assistance has been given under the Act. The Home Purchase Assistance Directions 1978, para. 34(5) require a person who is intending to save with a view to obtaining assistance under the Act to give notice of his intention to the savings institution before beginning to save.

In 'Inner City Obstacle Course', *Roof*, March 1978, pp. 48 – 49, Jim Wintour argued that the legislation would be of little value in the inner city areas, and within those areas of little help to the ethnic minorities. In such areas racial minority house buying tends to be financed by loans from relatives and friends, or by bank loans *not* secured on the property to be purchased. Such mortgage finance is outside the terms of the 1978 Act and so fails to qualify for assistance under it.

The object of the Act is to encourage saving as a means of access to home ownership, and is especially designed to help first time buyers. It may help only some by failing to take account of the special problems of inner city dwellers. The restrictive wording of the Act with regard to the sources of mortgage finance to be favoured with special assistance, and also as to the *lower* price limit below which assistance is not available discriminates against inner city areas and their inhabitants.

Option mortgages

The object of the option mortgage scheme is to give certain borrowers (whether they are borrowing for house purchase or home improvements) from certain qualifying lenders, the choice of receiving an Exchequer subsidy towards the cost of repaying their mortgages in return for foregoing income tax relief in respect of mortgage interest. The purpose of this arrangement is to enable less well off people to receive a benefit equivalent to that enjoyed by the more affluent to whom mortgage interest relief is a considerable hidden subsidy. The scheme was introduced by the Housing Subsidies Act 1967. Though its basic principles remain unaltered, there have been major changes introduced over the years by the Housing Acts 1974 and 1980. The option mortgage scheme, as it now stands, exists in three separate Acts, all of which have to be read together and 'married up' if the complex legalities of the system are to be understood. The law relating to option mortgages is a very good example of a very bad legislative practice of preferring piecemeal change to wholesale repeal and replacement by clear and coherent statutory provisions.

But what of the law itself? Local authorities are 'qualifying lenders' for the purposes of the scheme by virtue of section 27(1)(a) of the Housing Subsidies Act 1967, and in this context 'local authorities' means county and district councils, the Greater London Council, and the Common Council of the City of London. Development corporations and the Commission for the New Towns are also included.

The right to opt for subsidy

Under section 24 of the Act of 1967, as amended by the Housing Acts 1974 and 1980, a borrower from a qualifying lender making an application for a loan after 1 April 1968, on the security of a freehold or leasehold estate in land in Great Britain, may opt by giving notice in writing for the loan to be subsidised by central government, in return for giving up the right to claim mortgage interest relief against income tax. On receipt of the notice the lender must treat the borrower as having paid certain instalments of his mortgage. *The lender is able to recoup himself from the Secretary of State.* Certain conditions apply before this right can be exercised.

1) The loan must be made with a view to enable the borrower to;
   (a) repay a previous home purchase loan; or
   (b) acquire a dwelling; or
   (c) acquire a site for constructing a dwelling; or
   (d) provide a dwelling by the conversion of a building; or
   (e) alter, enlarge, repair or improve a dwelling.

2) The contract for repayment of the loan must include provision for repayment by means of periodical payments of capital and interest or just interest.

3) The loan must *not* be one to which a direction under section 24(3A) of the 1967 Act applies, i.e. a loan where the contract of repayment (as originally entered into or subsequently varied) allows the amount of interest to be paid in respect of a period to be less than the interest that should be payable so that part of the interest is in fact treated as an addition to the capital debt and carried forward as such.

4) The borrower must comply with any conditions prescribed by the Secretary of State under section 24(2A) of the Act particularly as to;
   (a) a borrower's personal circumstances;
   (b) the amount of the loan and the terms of repayment;
   (c) the use and occupation of the property in question, and
   (d) any other outstanding loans taken by the borrower.

5) The borrower must give written notice to the lender of his intention to exercise his option at the same time as applying for the loan, or at such later time as the lender may allow.

6) The option notice itself must be signed not later than the date when a repayment contract in respect of the loan is first entered into.

7) The borrower must sign and deliver to the lender a declaration with respect to his personal circumstances and also his fulfilment of subsidy conditions.

Option mortgage loans may be made either to single borrowers or to two or more persons borrowing jointly.

Extending the right to opt

Section 26 of the Act of 1967 provides that where a borrower's rights and obligations under a repayment contract become vested in some other person beneficially entitled to the interest in the land in question, the right to opt for subsidy is extended to such persons. Section 114 of the Housing Act 1980 goes even further. This provides:

'(1) If an option notice . . . is given —
    (a) with the qualifying lender's agreement and in such circumstances or in such cases or descriptions of case as may be specified in directions given by the Secretary of State; or
    (b) *not earlier* than twelve months after the date of the repayment contract;
it shall have effect notwithstanding that the conditions specified in section 24(3)(a) and (b) of the Act [of 1967] are not satisfied'.

Thus a person can decide in certain circumstances to 'opt in' to the scheme even though he did not take advantage of it when he first applied for mortgage assistance. Section 114(3) of the 1980 Act also allows a person to leave the option mortgage scheme by cancelling his option notice as from any end of March falling *not less* than twelve months after the date of the repayment contract. Three months written notice of intention to cancel *must* be given to the lender. To prevent borrowers from opting in and out of the scheme section 114(4) provides that, *in general*, where a person opts *in* to the scheme *after* he has begun to repay his mortgage, he cannot subsequently cancel his option, and where a person opts *out* of the scheme by giving a cancellation notice, he will not be allowed to come back into the scheme in respect of the same repayment contract.

Section 115 of the Housing Act 1980 extends the option mortgage system to cover home income plans, that is schemes whereby a home-owner raises a loan against the security of his house and uses the money to buy an annuity to increase his income. Income tax relief is available on the loan interest, but only to a person who pays tax. It is elderly house owning non-taxpayers who will benefit from section 115. This applies to schemes where not less than nine-tenths of the proceeds of a loan are applied to the purchase of qualifying annuities by persons who are aged 65 at the time the loan is made, and brings them within the scope of the 1967 Act. Such persons can now choose to take an option mortgage and pay the reduced rate of interest appropriate to such a loan.

The end of the option

Section 24A(1) of the 1967 Act provides:

'An option notice shall have effect for the period beginning with the date on which it is signed and ending with whichever of the following events first occurs, namely —

  (a) the satisfaction of the borrower's debt to the lender;
  (b) the realisation of the security on the interest in land in question, whether or not the borrower's debt is fully satisfied thereby;
  (c) that interest's ceasing to be security for the loan;
  (d) the vesting of the rights and obligations under the repayment contract of the borrower [or borrowers] in some other person who has become beneficially entitled to the interest;
  (e) . . . the vesting of the lender's rights under the repayment contract in some other person; [save where that other person is another qualifying lender, in which case the option continues in force];
  (f) [where the number of periodical repayments of the loan is not fixed or ascertainable, at the end of 30 years from the beginning of the option period];
  (g) the taking effect of a direction under section 24(3A) with respect to the loan;
  (h) any event which by regulation made under section 24(2A) is made to terminate subsidy entitlement, in consequence of the subsidy conditions having ceased to be fulfilled or otherwise'.

Guarantees for large mortgage advances

Section 30 of the 1967 Act allows ministers, subject to treasury approval, to make arrangements with insurance companies whereby a subsidised loan larger than that which would otherwise have been advanced, may be guaranteed by such a company.

Further reading

The council house as the matrimonial home

Social Welfare Law (Ed. by D.W. Pollard) (Oyez) paras. B. 1392 – B. 1505.

The Housing of One Parent Families (Housing Services Advisory Group Report) (Department of the Environment, 1978)

Tenancy Agreements (Housing Services Advisory Group Report) (Department of the Environment, 1977)

Tenancy Agreements (National Consumer Council, 1976)

Mortgages

Boddy. M., *The Building Societies* (MacMillan, 1980)
Tyler, E.L.G., *Fisher and Lightwood's Law of Mortgage* (9th edn, Butterworths, 1977) Chap. 37, 'The Option Mortgage Scheme'
Co-operation between Building Societies and Local Authorities (a series of papers by various authors) (Building Societies Association, 1978)
Clark. S., 'The Last Resort?', *Roof*, October 1976, pp. 138 – 140
McIntosh, N., 'Mortgage Support Scheme Holds the Lending Lines', *Roof*, March 1978, pp. 44 – 47
Weir, S., 'Red Line Districts', *Roof*, July 1976, pp. 109 – 114
Wintour, J., 'Inner City Obstacle Course', *Roof*, March 1978, pp. 48 – 49

Chapter 6

Homelessness

Causes and numbers

Homelessness is one of the most pernicious social problems. If it could be solved many other problems, for example alcoholism, crime and domestic violence, would undoubtedly decline. Unfortunately, homelessness is a complex phenomenon and, as a complex problem, can only be cured by the concerted application of a whole range of determined, *and expensive*, remedial measures. It is not enough simply to say that it is caused by a lack of housing; it is rather caused by a lack of housing in those areas where there is most housing demand. It is no use telling a homeless family in the middle of Newcastle that there are some acceptable empty cottages somewhere in the wilds of Shropshire — people need homes close to their friends, families and in areas where there is some chance of work.

The issue is also complicated in that there is no nationally acceptable definition of homelessness. That provided in the Housing (Homeless Persons) Act 1977 is a minimum standard based on the notions of a person having no accommodation (or being threatened with that condition in a short time) and being able to appeal to a local authority for help. This excludes many who have roofs over their heads but whose living conditions are very poor. These unfortunates include men and women occupying hostels, common lodging houses and resettlement units. Such people have no privacy or security of tenure. In 1972 some 23,400 men and 2,200 women were found to be living in such accommodation, see Peter Wingfield-Digby, *Hostels and Lodgings for Single People*.

The issue is even more complex in that there is no one single cause of homelessness. People lose their accommodation for many reasons. Among single people the causes range from migration in search of work through the loss of family ties and support to being unable to live in society without constant social and medical support. This last group includes those with severe alcoholic problems and others who find it hard to adjust to a pattern of living outside a rigid organisational framework such as hospital, prison or the armed forces. Homeless families find themselves in that position for a variety of reasons. One common factor in nearly all such cases is poverty. Where a family is dependent for most of its income on a wage earner who has a low paid job in an uncertain industry, sudden illness, unemployment or marital break-up can precipitate homelessness. Another common circumstance is that many such families have never had a real home of their own but have frequently been illegal sub-tenants, or service tenants, or living with in-laws. In *Roof*, March/April 1980 it was stated that the most common cause of homelessness in England in the first six months of 1979 was relatives or friends being no longer willing or able to accommodate (39 per cent of cases) followed by inter-spouse disputes which accounted for 15 per cent of instances of homelessness. In Wales the homelessness statistics for 1 April to 31 December 1978 show that some 47 per cent of households became homeless as a result of disputes with spouse/cohabitee/parents/relatives/friends; 22 per cent became homeless because of action by their landlords; action by the local authority caused the homelessness in 6 per cent of the cases. Action by a mortgagee accounted for a further 10 per cent, while only 3 per cent were accounted for by fire, floods and/or storms. Within the various household types the causes of homelessness revealed by the Welsh figures show that two thirds of *lone* parent households with children became homeless as a result of disputes, mainly with a spouse or cohabitee.

The English figures show the same pattern of reasons for homelessness: in the second half of 1979 68 per cent of those accepted under the 1977 Act were households with dependent children. 12 per cent of households were accepted on the ground of pregnancy. Some 43 per cent of the households accepted had been living with parents, relatives or friends immediately before becoming homeless. Only 4 per cent of the accepted households fell outside of the priority need categories laid down by the Housing (Homeless Persons) Act 1977.

Homelessness strikes those families most at risk through poverty and/or unstable living or other family conditions. It is increasing within our society. *New Society* for 3 January 1980 reported a sharp rise in cases of homelessness. During the first six months of 1979 local authorities accommodated 27,620 homeless households compared with 24,460 in the first half of 1978, a rise of 4.4 per cent. The reason for this increase was a sharp rise in homelessness in Greater London and the other metropolitan areas. These areas showed an increase in homelessness of 13.3 per cent over 1978 figures. Inner London, with 4.5 homeless households per 1000 showed a 9 per cent increase, while in Outer London the increase was 18.6 per cent. These figures should be studied in the light of those of previous years. Despite the changes in the methods used to gather the figures these tables taken together show an alarming increase in the recorded instances of homelessness over the last fifteen years. Yet the problem is not a new one.

Table A	Numbers of homeless Families/Persons at given date	
Year	Families in Temporary Accommodation on 31 December	Number of persons in temporary accommodation on 31 December
1966	2,558	13,031
1968	3,624	18,849
1970	4,926	24,283
1971	5,630	26,879

Table B	Households accepted as homeless in a year		
Year	London	Rest of England	Circumstances
1971	3,918	4,015	
1972	5,894	4,195	
1973	7,829	5,588	New statistics system (London)
1974	11,360	8,491	
1975	12,800	21,920	New statistics system (England)
1976	12,440	21,280	
1977	10,840	20,970	
1978	14,430	38,680	New statistics system
1979	7,920	56,750	(London figures: (Half year)

The old Elizabethan poor law, which was in force until 1948, attempted to curb homelessness by treating homeless persons as 'the undeserving poor' worthy only of the harsh 'comforts' of the workhouse. The National Assistance Act 1948 abolished the poor law. Unfortunately it continued much of the muddled thinking that had characterised the old law in failing to see homelessness as a problem in its own right, and also in that it did not create a single comprehensive institutional framework to deal with the issue. Section 2(1) of the 1948 Act created the National Assistance Board among whose functions was, under section 17 of the Act, the provision of reception centres 'whereby persons without a settled way of living may be influenced to lead a more settled life' and to provide 'temporary board and lodging for such persons'. Responsibility for the wandering homeless was thus entrusted to a *national* authority (now the Secretary of State for Health and Social Security under Schedule 5 to the Social Security Act 1980) while the rest of the homeless came within the care of local authority welfare departments under section 21(1)(a) and (b) of the 1948 Act. The problem was compounded by the division of powers and responsibilities between counties, county boroughs and the various district councils. Responsibility for housing and social service functions, particularly in the case of the counties and urban and rural districts, was also separated. The result was that local *housing* authorities had no real responsibility for the homeless at all.

Administrative confusion was made worse by a general lack of resources and a continued use of out of date hostel accommodation, and the law entrusting responsibility for the homeless to social services departments gave rise to difficulties. Section 21(1)(b) of the 1948 Act created a statutory duty to provide: 'temporary accommodation for persons who are in urgent need thereof, being need arising in circumstances which could not reasonably have been foreseen or in such other circumstances as the authority may in any particular case determine'. The wording was vague, and was certain to give rise to action in the courts at some time.

In *Southwark London Borough Council v Williams* [1971] Ch 734, [1971] 2 All ER 175, some homeless persons in dire need of accommodation squatted in empty houses owned by the local authority. That authority took proceedings for possession and succeeded on the grounds that:

1) even if the local authority was in breach of its duty under section 21 of the 1948 Act the only way to enforce that duty was by approaching the Minister under section 36(1) of the Act;

2) the defendants' homelessness was not a sufficient circumstance to ground a defence of necessity for their acts.

The legal and administrative difficulties of the situation became 'confusion worse confounded' following the reorganisation of local government under the Local Government Act 1972. Section 195 and Schedule 23 of that Act converted the duty under section 21(1) of the 1948 Act into a power, though reserving a power to the Secretary of State to re-impose the duty. The Act of 1972 came into force in 1974 and the Department of the Environment issued joint circular No. 18/74 *Homelessness* (Department of Health and Social Security Circular No. 4/74, Welsh Office Circular No. 34/74). This stated that: 'suitable accommodation for the homeless should in future be undertaken as an integral part of the statutory responsibility of housing authorities . . . in accordance with Part V of the Housing Act 1957'. The statutory responsibility still lay with the social services authorities under the 1948 Act as amended by the 1972 Act. Worse was to follow because on 1 February 1974 the Secretary of State for Social Services issued Department of Health and Social Security Local Authority Circular No. 13/74. This re-imposed the duty on social services authorities to provide temporary accommodation.

The results of this mis-government by circular were chaotic. The existence of some sort of duty on *social services* authorities encouraged some *housing* authorities to ignore the exhortations of Department of the Environment Circular No. 18/74. By the end of 1975 only 28 per cent of housing authorities had accepted responsibility for the homeless while 31 per cent had accepted the main part of the responsibility. Of the remainder 11 per cent left the task to the social services authority, 19 per cent gave some support to those bodies, and 7 per cent divided the responsibility with them.

It was obvious that urgent changes in the law were necessary. The government had expressed dissatisfaction with the law in 1974, but said in May 1975 that the time was inappropriate for change. By November 1975 a further change of mind occurred and legislation was promised. In November 1976 the commitment to introduce legislation was withdrawn when the government discovered it had not sufficient parliamentary time to debate the measure. It was left to a private member, Mr Stephen Ross, to introduce legislation. His Bill was based on a draft already prepared by the Department of the Environment and it achieved a measure of all party support in Parliament.

Even so the Bill was drastically amended in Parliament, largely as a result of fears of large numbers of homeless people moving themselves around the country with the object of jumping local authority housing queues. Such fears are, and were, totally illusory. The 1979 figures on homelessness from the Welsh Office show that:

1) some 88 per cent of homeless households were living in the same district one month previous to becoming homeless, and

2) over 90 per cent of those households were also resident in the same district six months before.

The 1979 English figures also show that 90 per cent of households aided had been living in the area of the same authority one month before becoming homeless, while 78 per cent had been living in the same area one year previously. There is no evidence to suggest that a body of 'scroungers and scrimshankers' (to repeat terms used in Parliament) exists, nor any to show that there are numbers of deviously minded persons setting out to make themselves homeless so as to leapfrog the housing waiting list.

The marks of its passage through Parliament are still borne by the Housing (Homeless Persons) Act 1977 which emerged from the legislature as a somewhat vague, and indeed woolly, piece of social engineering. This has, predictably, led to the Act becoming a 'happy hunting ground' for the litigious, and even more so for lawyers and the appellate courts. Equally unfortunately the Government refused to allocate any new resources to housing authorities to implement the Act, despite repeated requests for aid. The Act is one more step in the progression that has become too familiar over the last 30 years whereby local government has been loaded with more and more responsibilities without being given a commensurate increase in resources to enable the proper and efficient discharge of those duties.

The defects of the homelessness law and practice today reflect centuries during which the official attitude towards the homeless was that they were at worst a threat to domestic peace and at best undeserving and feckless. More recently, though more liberal attitudes have been in evidence, there is still confusion of thought about homelessness and what to do about it. The result is that there are three types of organisation charged with dealing with the problem:

1) *The Secretary of State for Health and Social Security* is under a duty to provide resettlement units;

2) *Social service departments* have a duty to provide some residential accommodation even though their responsibilities under section 21(1)(b) of the 1948 Act have been repealed by the 1977 Act;

3) *Local housing authorities* are under certain obligations to certain classes of persons under the Act of 1977.

The new law

In this section of the book all references, unless otherwise stated, are to the Housing (Homeless Persons) Act 1977.

Who are 'the homeless'?

Those persons falling within the Act are defined by section 1:

'(1) A person is homeless for the purposes of this Act if he has no accommodation, and a person is to be treated as having no accommodation for those purposes if there is no accommodation —
    (a) which he, together with any other person who normally resides with him as a member of his family or in circumstances in which the housing authority consider it reasonable for that person to reside with him —

> (i) is entitled to occupy by virtue of an interest in it or of an order of a court, or
>
> (ii) has, in England or Wales, an express or implied licence to occupy, . . .
>
> (b) which he (together with any such person) is occupying as a residence by virtue of any enactment or rule of law giving him the right to remain in occupation or restricting the right of any other person to recover possession of it.
>
> (2) A person is also homeless for the purposes of this Act if he has accommodation but —
>
> (a) he cannot secure entry to it, or
>
> (b) it is probable that occupation of it will lead to violence from some other person residing in it or to threats of violence from some other person residing in it and likely to carry out the threats, or
>
> (c) it consists of a movable structure, vehicle or vessel designed or adapted for human habitation and there is no place where he is entitled or permitted both to place it and to reside in it.
>
> (3) For the purposes of this Act a person is threatened with homelessness if it is likely that he will become homeless within 28 days'.

This defines the class of persons to whom the *various* obligations under the Act can be owed. The persons covered are those having no accommodation, or who will shortly be in that position, in other words those without a roof over their heads. A person will be homeless if he has no accommodation which he has the *right* to occupy (for example as an owner) or is allowed to occupy under some rule of law (for example a statutory tenant), or which he is allowed to occupy by some express or implied licence (for example a person living with relatives). This works injustice on many single persons having a licence to occupy a room, or part of a room, in a hostel, resettlement unit, or common lodging house. They are not classified as 'homeless' though it is clear they have no *home*. Much here, as elsewhere under the Act, depends on the attitude of individual local authorities. Some follow a liberal interpretation of the Act and classify such people as threatened with homelessness as they have no security of tenure. A person is also homeless if, though he has accommodation, he is unable to use it because, for example, he has been evicted by squatters, or because he will probably be subject to violence from some other person living there if he stays, or if, in the case of a mobile home he has no place in which to site it.

The Act covers those who 'normally reside' with the homeless person either as members of his family 'or in circumstances in which the local authority consider it reasonable for that person to reside with him'. This definition was an amendment, made as the Bill went through Parliament. In other places the Act refers simply to persons who 'might reasonably be expected to reside' with the homeless person. According to the Code of Guidance issued under the Act, paragraph 2.8., the amended definition covers: 'not only established households where there is a blood or marriage relationship but also other circumstances where people are living together as if they were members of a family, e.g. cohabiting couples, or adults with foster children. Other circumstances in which people might reasonably live together include those where elderly or disabled people are accompanied by housekeepers or other companions. The Secretaries of State consider that authorities should regard as homeless any households who are separated for no other reason than that they have no accommodation in which they can live together'.

Local authorities are also under certain obligations to those who are *threatened* with homelessness which is *likely* to arise within 28 days. Obviously the '28 day rule' should not be rigidly interpreted. If an instance of potential homelessness comes to the attention of the local housing authority they should deal with it as soon as possible. Prompt early action may prevent actual homelessness.

Initial contact with the local authority

When a homeless or potentially homeless person makes contact with the local authority they come under certain duties under section 3 to make 'appropriate inquiries'.

'(1) If —
    (a) a person applies to a housing authority for accommodation or for assistance in obtaining accommodation, and
    (b) the authority have reason to believe that he may be homeless or threatened with homelessness,
the authority shall make appropriate inquiries.
(2) In sub-section (1) above "appropriate inquiries" means —
    (a) such inquiries as are necessary to satisfy the authority whether the person who applied to them is homeless or threatened with homelessness'.

Local housing authorities should have some officer responsible for dealing with these matters. The Act does not lay down any rules for the conduct of inquiries. The Code of Guidance urges that they be speedy, but sympathetic. There is no requirement to operate a 24 hours a day, seven days a week service. The Code of Guidance counsels that there should be clearly worked out and well-known arrangements for dealing with people who become homeless outside office hours. Co-operation with the social services authority is useful in such circumstances, and progressive authorities have '24 hour-a-day' arrangements.

Once these initial inquiries are made section 3(2)(b) places the authority under a further duty to make inquiries, thus:

'if the authority are satisfied that he is homeless or threatened with homelessness, any further inquiries necessary to satisfy them —
   (i) whether he has a priority need, and
  (ii) whether he became homeless or threatened with homelessness intentionally'.

To aid them in this task they have powers under section 3(3), but section 3(4) makes it clear that the use of these cannot prevent the authority from being under an obligation to a person whom they believe may be homeless having priority need:

'(3) If the authority think fit, they may also make inquiries as to whether the person who applied to them has a local connection with the area of another housing authority.
(4) If the authority have reason to believe that the person who applied to them may be homeless and have a priority need, they shall secure that accommodation is made available for his occupation pending any decision which they may make as a result of their inquiries (irrespective of any local connection he may have with the area of another housing authority)'.

The duty in section 3(4) means that no-one who appears to be homeless and also in priority need should ever be left without accommodation pending the completion of inquiries. This accommodation must be continued until inquiries are completed and the authority able to make a final decision.

Whether the section 3(4) duty is owed depends on whether the applicant is in 'priority need', and many other provisions of the Act also depend on this circumstance. 'Priority need' is defined in section 2.

'(1) For the purposes of this Act a homeless person or a person threatened with homelessness has a priority need for accommodation when the housing authority are satisfied that he is within one of the following categories: —
  (a) he has dependent children who are residing with him or who might reasonably be expected to reside with him;
  (b) he is homeless or threatened with homelessness as a result of any emergency such as flood, fire or any other disaster;
  (c) he or any person who resides or might reasonably be expected to reside with him is vulnerable as a result of old age, mental illness or handicap or physical disability or other special reason.
(2) for the purposes of this Act a homeless person or a person threatened with homelessness who is a pregnant woman or resides or

might reasonably be expected to reside with a pregnant woman has a priority need for accommodation'.

This definition is far from clear. Though the Code gives amplifying guidance, there is too much room for uncertainty and differing interpretation. There is little problem with the categories in section 2(1)(a) and (b). The Code states: 'The Secretaries of State consider that authorities should treat [as dependent children] all those under the age of sixteen and others under the age of nineteen who are either receiving full-time education or training or are otherwise unable to support themselves'. The Code also states that where appropriate grandchildren, foster and adopted children may all be regarded as dependent. Problems arise with section 2(1)(c). The Code suggests that a person has priority need if he is, or his household contains one or more persons, vulnerable for any of the following reasons:

1) Old age, that is being over or nearing normal retiring age;

2) Mental illness or handicap or physical disability, including being deaf, dumb or blind or otherwise substantially disabled;

3) Any other special reason such as being a battered woman *without* a dependent child, or a homeless young person at risk of sexual and/or financial exploitation.

But the advice given in the Code is not legally binding being only a matter for consideration, nor does it go far enough. A man who has just been released from prison or some other sort of institution is undoubtedly vulnerable, yet some local authorities argue that he would not fall within the terms of section 2(1)(c). Neither is the definition of vulnerability by reason of age sufficiently clear. Some authorities operate policies of not considering persons under the normal retiring age, while there are recorded instances of people over 65 being denied aid as not being vulnerable by reason of age. There is no proper definition given to vulnerability by virtue of mental illness; for example, would this cover a homeless alcoholic?

Section 2(2) is also most curiously worded. It gives priority need status to pregnant women and also those who reside or might reasonably be expected to reside with a pregnant woman. Who falls within that category? It is reasonable to include a husband or cohabitee who is the father of the child-to-be. Is it also reasonable to include some other man, such as a parent, brother or boyfriend having no connection with the pregnancy? Much is left to local discretion. Where a girl aged under eighteen is accommodated under this provision she cannot hold a legal tenancy, and so it will be necessary to obtain a sponsor who will take the tenancy on her behalf. This will usually be the local social services authority.

The duties owed to the homeless

These are contained in section 4:

'(1) If a housing authority are satisfied, as a result of inquiries under section 3 above, that a person who has applied to them for accommodation or for assistance in obtaining accommodation is homeless or threatened with homelessness, they shall be subject to a duty towards him under this section.

(2) Where —

> (a) they are not satisfied that he has a priority need, or
>
> (b) they are satisfied that he has a priority need but are also satisfied that he became homeless or threatened with homelessness intentionally,

their duty is to furnish him with advice and appropriate assistance.

(3) Where —

> (a) they are satisfied that he is homeless, and
>
> (b) they are subject to a duty towards him by virtue of sub-section (2)(b) above,

they shall secure that accommodation is made available for his occupation for such period as they consider will give him a reasonable opportunity of himself securing accommodation for his occupation.

(4) Where —

> (a) they are satisfied —
>
> > (i) that he is threatened with homelessness, and
> >
> > (ii) that he has a priority need, but
>
> (b) they are not satisfied that he became threatened with homelessness intentionally,

their duty, subject to sub-section (6) below, is to take reasonable steps to secure that accommodation does not cease to be available for his occupation.

(5) Where —

> (a) they are satisfied —
>
> > (i) that he is homeless, and
> >
> > (ii) that he has a priority need, but
>
> (b) they are not satisfied that he became homeless intentionally,

their duty, subject to section 5 below, is to secure that accommodation becomes available for his occupation'.

This cumbersome section creates several classes of persons to whom differing duties are owed.

1) A person who is homeless unintentionally and in priority need, to whom the full duty is owed.

2) A person who is threatened with homelessness, and is in priority need, and who has not become so threatened intentionally, to whom a

duty is owed to secure that accommodation does not cease to be available.

3) A person who is homeless, and who has priority need, but who is homeless because of his own intentional act, to whom a duty is owed to make available accommodation for such period as the local authority considers will give him a reasonable opportunity of finding his own accommodation.

4) A person who is homeless but who has no priority need, to whom the only duty owed is to give advice and appropriate assistance. 'Advice' is not further defined in the Act, but section 19(1) defines 'appropriate assistance' as 'such assistance as a housing authority consider it appropriate in the circumstances to give him' — a definition that leaves much to the discretion of individual authorities.

Much depends on whether the applicant for aid has committed an act of intentional homelessness. Such acts are defined by section 17.

'(1) Subject to sub-section (3) below, for the purposes of this Act a person becomes homeless intentionally if he deliberately does or fails to do anything in consequence of which he ceases to occupy accommodation which is available for his occupation and which it would have been reasonable for him to continue to occupy.

(2) Subject to sub-section (3) below, for the purposes of this Act a person becomes threatened with homelessness intentionally if he deliberately does or fails to do anything the likely result of which is that he will be forced to leave accommodation which is available for his occupation and which it would have been reasonable for him to continue to occupy.

(3) An act or omission in good faith on the part of a person who was unaware of any relevant fact is not to be treated as deliberate for the purposes of sub-section (1) or (2) above.

(4) Regard may be had, in determining for the purposes of sub-sections (1) and (2) above whether it would have been reasonable for a person to continue to occupy accommodation, to the general circumstances prevailing in relation to housing in the area of the housing authority to whom he applied for accommodation or for assistance in obtaining accommodation'.

This section has been subject to much debate in and out of court. It is another example of bad legislative drafting for 'intentionally' is not properly defined. The word 'deliberately' in section 17(2) implies that 'intentionally' is at least to be given a meaning equivalent to acting on a well weighed, considered and carefully thought out purpose. Unfortunately it is not clear from the cases that the courts have followed that line of reasoning. It is still a matter for debate whether a tenant who failed to defend possession proceedings could be regarded as intentionally homeless.

Before a person can be treated as 'intentionally' homeless the local authority should be satisfied as to certain matters:

1) did the person have accommodation;

2) was it, under section 16, accommodation available for him and also for any other person who might reasonably be expected to reside with him'

3) was it reasonable for him to continue in occupation;

4) is his present condition the result of something he did or failed to do;

5) was that act or omission 'deliberate';

6) was the person aware of all the relevant facts or did he act in good faith and ignorance?

The Code of Guidance gives examples of actions that should not be regarded as intentional homelessness. For example:

1) failing to keep up mortgage payments, or getting into rent arrears because of real personal financial difficulties, or incapacity to manage financial affairs because of age or illness;

2) fleeing a marital home because of domestic violence;

3) quitting accommodation so overcrowded or defective that a reasonable man could not have been expected to stay there; though in such cases regard must be had to the general housing conditions of the area and whether there are many other people there living in worse conditions than those of the applicant for aid.

See Code of Guidance, paras. 2.13 to 2.19.

Despite the Code of Guidance much has had to be worked out by individual local authorities whose practices have, inevitably, varied with some following a more liberal interpretation of the Act than others. Attitudes vary as to how to deal with the problem of rent arrears. Some authorities regard homelessness as a result of rent arrears as intentional homelessness, yet as has been shown in Chapter 4 rent arrears are rarely run up *wilfully*.

Section 17 was considered in *De Falco v Crawley Borough Council* [1980] QB 460, [1980] 1 All ER 913. Some Italian families came to England and obtained work here, living with relatives until they were asked to leave. The plaintiffs applied to Crawley BC who found them to be homeless and in priority need. As they were EEC nationals they were to be treated in the same way as United Kingdom citizens and so they were accommodated, while inquiries were made, in guest houses for some five or six weeks. The local authority concluded they were intentionally homeless as they had come to this country without ensuring permanent accommodation for themselves, and so they required the plaintiffs to leave the accommodation provided within four days. The plaintiffs brought actions against the local authority, and lost. In a somewhat emotive judgment Lord Denning MR made a number of most important points.

1) The local authority's decision complied with section 17 in that the plaintiffs had come to England without ensuring proper accommodation for themselves. Furthermore section 17(4) entitles a local authority to consider the reasonableness of an applicant's leaving his home (*wherever it was*) in relation to the general housing circumstances prevailing in *their* area. It is proper for a local authority to say: 'You should not have left your former home without finding some other permanent accommodation first, especially as we have a severe housing shortage in this district. We cannot house you before all our other people'.

This enables a local authority to set up a lack of housing in its area as a defence against having to fulfil its obligations under the 1977 Act.

2) The Code of Guidance is not binding upon local authorities. Section 12, under which it is issued, says it is only a matter to which local authorities must 'have regard'. Local authorities may depart from the code if they think fit. Accordingly, paragraph 2.18 which states that only the *most immediate* cause of homelessness should be considered can be disregarded.

3) In deciding whether the local authority has allowed persons held to be intentionally homeless a reasonable time to find their own accommodation, regard may be had to the length of time spent in accommodation before notice of the council's findings is served, though this point is open to question.

De Falco was followed by a spate of other litigation. *In Youngs v Thanet District Council*, Chancery Division (1980) *Times*, 26 February. Mr Youngs and his family were evicted from their council house in 1978 for arrears of rent. They found a private rented flat for which the Department of Health and Social Security paid the rent, and which was let only on a short term basis as it fell within the 'holiday let' exception of the Rent Acts. A possession order was obtained in due course against Mr Youngs. The Council at first said they would try to find him bed and breakfast somewhere in the private sector, but subsequently decided only to give 'advice and assistance' as they treated the family's homeless as being merely a continuation of their situation in 1978. In other words the council argued that the initial act of intentional homelessness continued to taint Mr Youngs' application for aid. The Court found that this was an unjustified finding. Mr Youngs had found accommodation by himself after his eviction and so had broken the connection with the earlier act of intentional homelessness. Homelessness is a matter of fact — an act of intentional homelessness does not endure for ever to put the homeless person beyond the law. The Council were ordered to accommodate.

In *Miller v Wandsworth London Borough Council,* Chancery Division (1980) *Times,* 19 March. Mr Miller and his pregnant wife lived in a flat in Ealing until 4 August 1979. There was then a fire in the kitchen. The water heater was burnt out, there was minor decorative damages, the flat required cleaning and there was no hot water. The landlady asked them to move out while repairs were done and she was unable to say when these would be completed. The Millers went to stay with in-laws and told the landlady they wanted to give up the flat and to receive back the money paid as rent in advance. They then made a first application on 9 August 1979 to Wandsworth LB as homeless persons. The Council advised them not to give up their flat and told them that if they did they would make themselves intentionally homeless. On 20 December 1979 the Millers again went to the Council and said their in-laws could no longer house them. The Council informed them that they were still regarded as intentionally homeless and so they qualified only for 28 days bed and breakfast accommodation. The Millers then sought a mandatory injunction requiring the Council to accommodate them until the hearing of the action brought under the 1977 Act.

Walton J stated that the courts are not appellate bodies from the decisions of local authorities made under the 1977 Act. The courts may only review the legality of decisions, particularly their reasonableness. Was the Council's decision reasonable? The Millers' principal contention was that the Council had not made sufficient inquiries before coming to their decision in August, but the Court rejected this on the facts. The Council had come to a perfectly proper decision and the Millers had inflicted homelessness on themselves.

The distinction between *Miller* and *Youngs* is that in *Youngs* Mr Youngs had made a real effort after his first act of intentional homelessness to put a roof over his head. Mr Miller had acted somewhat foolishly and had done little to aid himself, his wife and child. If a man commits an act of intentional homelessness and then simply moves in with relatives this is not sufficient of itself to break the continued effect of the initial intentional act.

In *Lally v Kensington and Chelsea Royal Borough,* Chancery Division (1980) *Times,* 27 March, on the rather complicated facts, Mr Lally was found to be intentionally homeless. The inquiries which the local authority had made into his condition were found to have been perfectly reasonable. Browne-Wilkinson J stressed that while a local authority must pursue their duties rigorously and fairly, they are under no duty to carry out detailed 'CID type' inquiries. Moreover, the Court will only intervene if they are found to have acted unreasonably. However, after Mr Lally had been found intentionally homeless he was given only fourteen days temporary accommodation, then the police were called in to remove him and his pregnant wife until an interim injunction prevented their ejection. The Court found this period far too short to be a fulfilling of the duty under section 4(3). The local authority had also adopted a policy of granting only fourteen days accommodation to persons found intentionally homeless. The Court did not specifically condemn this policy but seemed to indicate that, again, it did not amount to a fulfilling of the duties under the Act. The Council conceded that it would not be able to evict the Lallys and the Court also awarded £30 damages.

Two points emerge:

1) The length of time that is 'reasonable' for a local authority to allow an intentionally homeless person temporary accommodation while he searches for accommodation varies from place to place, and also depends on the general shortage of accommodation in a given area. In London where accommodation is in short supply fourteen days is quite inadequate — *three to four months or even more is reasonable.*

2) It is wrong for a local authority to adopt a policy of *only* granting a specific period of such temporary accommodation in all cases — the needs of each applicant must be considered and what is 'reasonable' will vary from case to case.

But it was still not clear as to how the 'reasonableness' of the period allowed was to be computed. In *De Falco* Lord Denning MR favoured beginning with the time the applicant was first accommodated, while Bridge LJ took the better view of the law that the period begins when the local authority's adverse decision on intentional homelessness is first communicated to the applicant.

In *Tickner v Mole Valley District Council* [1980] LAG Bulletin 187 the applicants had been living in caravans in unacceptable conditions and under an agreement designed to evade the Rent Acts. They refused to pay increased rents and possession orders were made against them. Though Lord Denning MR considered that the local authority had made inadequate inquiries, he nevertheless considered that the applicants were intentionally homeless because they had refused to pay a rent they could afford. The site was going to be improved and so it would have been reasonable for them to stay. Lord Denning repeated his views in *De Falco* on the use a local authority may make of section 17(4) entitling them to have regard to their waiting lists in deciding whether or not an applicant is intentionally homeless. He also stated that local authorities must decide each case honestly in good faith, and are only challengeable in court on points of law such as an allegation of unreasonableness.

The *Youngs* case was followed in *R v Penwith District Council ex parte Hughes* [1980] LAG Bulletin 188, but in *Dyson v Kerrier District Council* [1980] 3 All ER 313, [1980] 1 WLR 1205 the Court of Appeal reinforced the distinction between the decisions in *Youngs* and *Miller*, and also weakened the effect of *Youngs*. The facts were that the applicant, who was pregnant, moved in with her sister, a council house tenant. The sister left, and the council transferred the tenancy into the name of the applicant. Notwithstanding this, she left soon after and moved into an out-of-season holiday letting. While this still had some time to run, she applied to another authority, saying that she was homeless on account of her sister's departure. Once the authority had investigated and established what had really happened, they decided to treat her as intentionally homeless. She was told this in a letter received shortly before the holiday letting expired. She remained in occupation pending a court order, and shortly before the time allowed by the court expired, the authority again wrote to her, stating that they would assist her with one month's hotel accommodation from the date she actually became homeless. In fact she was allowed to stay for longer. A few days before the expiry of her time in this temporary accommodation, they wrote a formal letter informing her that the housing committee had adopted the decision. The applicant sued for breach of statutory duty in the county court and appealed against the dismissal of that action.

The Court of Appeal made three points in their judgment:

1) the authority could look at past events, and they were not confined to considering a present, or the last, home occupied by the applicant;

2) although when the applicant applied she was threatened with homelessness, a duty under section 4(3) to secure short term accommodation did arise at the time when she *actually* became homeless; and

3) time could begin to run under section 4(3) from the date of the officer's decision, and not necessarily the date of the committee decision, notwithstanding that it required ratification by the committee.

In *Delahaye v Oswestry Borough Council* (1980) *Times*, 29 July 1980 Mr Delahaye, his wife and four children, left their home in Merton, Surrey, because of unpleasant conduct in the neighbourhood. They travelled around the countryside and arrived in Oswestry in January 1978. Temporary accommodation was provided by the council until their fifth child was born. They then moved to Omega Point in Oswestry where they stayed until they were illegally evicted in June 1978.

Mr Delahaye then applied for accommodation under the 1977 Act but the application was rejected on the grounds that he was homeless intentionally and that his local connection lay with Merton. After living in tents for three weeks, the family were given accommodation by the council in caravans. A referee then determined that the local connection lay with Merton and the council served a notice to quit to expire in November 1978.

On 12 October a second application was made for temporary accommodation. On 16 October a possession order was made and the council informed Mr Delahaye that it had fulfilled its obligations under the Act and would not be offering him further accommodation when the possession order was enforced.

Mr Delahaye applied for an order of mandamus requiring Oswestry Borough Council to make enquiries with regard to his homelessness.

It was held that when a person is granted temporary accommodation, he cannot, when that accommodation is terminated, or threatened with termination, rely solely on the same matters as he relied on in his earlier application. It could not have been the intention of Parliament that the Act be used by someone who was not entitled to permanent accommodation to obtain the continuous use of temporary accommodation by means of successive applications. That is not to say, however, that a new application cannot be made where there is a change of circumstances, see *Wyness v Poole District Council* [1980] LAG Bulletin 16. The important finding there was that a person is entitled to make a new application for housing under the Act, after an earlier one has been properly dealt with, where there is a change in material circumstances.

The consequences of this protracted litigation are as follows.

1) The courts will only intervene if a local authority makes a clear error of law or use their powers in an unreasonable way.

2) The effectiveness of the Code of Guidance has been enormously reduced.

3) A local authority may look back through an applicant's housing history to find that an act of intentional homelessness still taints his application for aid, but there must be a direct relationship between the present homelessness and the initial intentional act, and it must also have been apparent to the applicant after his initial act that an intervening period spent in accommodation could only be temporary. Where there is a direct relationship between the applicant's initial acts and his present homeless condition and no intervening change of circumstances, the applicant cannot make repeated applications.

4) The issue that divided Lord Denning and Bridge LJ in *De Falco*, namely as to proper method of computing a reasonable period during which an intentionally homeless person must be accommodated is somewhat clearer. In *Dyson* the Court of Appeal held that the time should be computed as from the date when the local authority *first* wrote to say

she would be given only one month's accommodation. This issue must now be decided on the facts of each case and the reasonableness of a period must be computed as from the *real and effective* time that the applicant is informed as to the decision on intentional homelessness, whether that point of time is a formal housing committee decision, or some earlier clear statement by an officer. The test must be 'when did the applicant truly know he was regarded as intentionally homeless?'.

5) An authority is entitled to measure the reasonableness of an applicant's acts against the general housing conditions in their area, including any shortages and the length of the waiting list. People who become homeless in areas where pressure on housing is relatively light will be in a better position to argue that their actions in leaving accommodation were reasonable. (See also addendum in Preface.)

Once a person is found to be unintentionally homeless (and in priority need) he is owed a duty by the local authority unless he has a 'local connection' with the area of some other authority. Section 5(1) provides:

'A housing authority are not subject to a duty under section 4(5) above —

   (a) if they are of the opinion —

     (i)   that neither the person who applied to them for accommodation or for assistance in obtaining accommodation nor any person who might reasonably be expected to reside with him has a local connection with their area, and

     (ii) that the person who so applied or a person who might reasonably be expected to reside with him has a local connection with another housing authority's area, and

     (iii) that neither the person who so applied nor any person who might reasonably be expected to reside with him will run the risk of domestic violence in that housing authority's area, and

   (b) if they notify that authority —

     (i)   that the application has been made, and

     (ii) that they are of the opinion specified in paragraph (a) above'.

The requirements of this provision must be noted carefully.

1) The first question is whether the applicant or any other person who may reasonably be expected to reside with him has a local connection *with the area to whom the application for aid is being made.* 'Local connection' is defined by section 18.

'(1) Any reference in this Act to a person having a local connection with an area is a reference to his having a connection with that area —

    (a) because he is or in the past was normally resident in it and his
        residence in it is or was of his own choice; or
    (b) because he is employed in it, or
    (c) because of family associations, or
    (d) because of any special circumstances.
(2) Residence in an area is not of a person's own choice for the purposes
of sub-section (1) above if he became resident in it —
    (a) because he or any person who might reasonably be expected
        to reside with him —
        (i) was serving in the regular armed forces of the Crown, or
        (ii) was detained under the authority of any Act of Parlia-
            ment, or
    (b) in such other circumstances as the Secretary of State may by
        order specify.
(3) A person is not employed in an area for the purposes of sub-section
(1) above —
    (a) if he is serving in the regular armed forces of the Crown, or
    (b) in such other circumstances as the Secretary of State may by
        order specify'.

2) Satisfying any one of the four criteria in section 18(1)(a) – (d)
qualifies the applicant as having a 'local connection'. If no such connection is found the authority applied to may ask whether there is a 'local
connection' with another authority's area. If the answer to that question
is 'no' the responsibility remains with the authority applied to.

In *R v Hillingdon London Borough Council ex parte Streeting* [1980]
3 All ER 413, Mrs Streeting was an Ethiopian woman who lived in
Ethiopia all her life until 1975 when she bigamously (but innocently)
married A, and subsequently bore his child. They lived abroad, from
time to time visiting the United Kingdom on leave. In 1979 A died and
Mrs Streeting was then living in Athens. She came to the United
Kingdom for A's funeral and was given limited permission to stay until
November 1979. She was then refused permission to return to Greece,
and was frightened to return to Ethiopia. The Home Office classified
her as a refugee in November 1979 and Hillingdon LBC gave her
temporary accommodation pending inquiries under the 1977 Act. The
Council concluded that they owed her no duty because, they argued, no
duty under the Act was owed to an applicant who has or had no local
connection with the area of any housing authority in Great Britain.

    This argument was rejected both at first instance and in the Court of
Appeal. Lord Denning MR made the point that it is up to the
immigration authorities to ensure that large numbers of homeless
persons from abroad do not enter this country. Once a person is in this
country, and is homeless unintentionally, and has priority need, the
duties under the Act are owed to him.

Two riders must be added:

(a) If a person from abroad *deliberately* gives up his accommodation in his own country for no good reason so that he is homeless there, and then comes to this country, then he is to be treated as being intentionally homeless in this country. Merely coming to this country to look for work is not a good reason for giving up a home in another country;

(b) The obligation to the homeless person can be discharged by arranging for accommodation to be provided in the country from which the homeless person has come.

3) The next step in the 'local connection' procedure is to ascertain under section 5(1)(a)(iii) whether the applicant, or any member of his household, would be at risk of domestic violence if returned to another area with which he has a local connection. If the answer is 'yes' then responsibility remains with the authority first applied to. In this connection section 5(11) should be noted.

'For the purposes of this section a person runs the risk of domestic violence —

(a) if he runs the risk of violence from any person with whom, but for the risk of violence, he might reasonably be expected to reside or from any person with whom he formerly resided, or

(b) if he runs the risk of threats of violence from any such person which are likely to be carried out'.

But it follows from the decision in *R v Bristol City Council ex parte Browne* [1979] 3 All ER 344, [1979] WLR 1437 that the fact that an applicant has suffered domestic violence in the past does not *necessarily* mean that the person runs the risk of such violence in the future. Each case must be carefully decided on its own facts.

4) If an applicant is found not to have a local connection with the authority first applied to ('the notifying authority') while having such a connection with another authority ('the notified authority') the procedure laid down in section 5(3) − (8) must be followed.

'(3) If shall be the duty of the notified authority to secure that accommodation becomes available for occupation by the person to whom the notification relates if neither he nor any person who might reasonably be expected to reside with him has a local connection with the area of the notifying authority but the conditions specified in sub-section (4) below are satisfied.

(4) The conditions mentioned in sub-section (3) above are —

(a) that the person to whom the notification relates or some person who might reasonably be expected to reside with him has a local connection with the area of the notified authority, and

(b) that neither he nor any such person will run the risk of domestic violence in that area.

(5) In any other case it shall be the duty of the notifying authority to secure that accommodation becomes available for occupation by the person to whom the notification relates.

(6) It shall also be the duty of the notifying authority to secure that accommodation is available for occupation by the person to whom notification relates until it is determined whether sub-section (3) or (5) above applies to him.

(7) Any question which falls to be determined under this section shall be determined by agreement between the notifying authority and the notified authority or, in default of such agreement in accordance with the appropriate arrangements.

(8) The appropriate arrangements for the purposes of this section are any such arrangements as the Secretary of State may by order direct'. (For the code of agreement between local authorities and the Secretary of State's arrangements, see *The Agreement on Procedures for Referral of the Homeless*, obtainable from the Association of District Councils, the Association of Metropolitan Authorities and the London Boroughs Association, and the Housing (Homeless Persons) (Appropriate Arrangements) Order (S.I. 1978 No. 69).) The important point about section 5 is that it ensures that one authority must finally accept responsibility for the applicant and that during the period of investigation temporary accommodation must be provided. Section 5 was considered in *R v London Borough of Hillingdon, ex parte Slough Borough Council* (1980) 130 NLJ 881, DC. certain homeless persons applied to a local authority for aid. They were found to be unintentionally homeless, and in priority need, but were considered to have a local connection with another authority. The second authority refused to accept this. Arbitrators were appointed under section 5(7) of the 1977 Act, and the second authority contended that the arbitrators should consider the issue of intentional homelessness. It was held that an arbitrator should only consider the question of local connection, and not the prior issue of entitlement to accommodation. During the second half of 1979 English local authorities referred 870 households (about 3 per cent of the total) to other authorities under the local connection provisions but only 500 households were finally recorded as being transferred.

Section 9(1) allows bodies other than local housing authorities to co-operate in the provision of accommodation for the homeless.

'Where a housing authority —
  (a) request —
    (i)   another housing authority;
    (ii) the Greater London Council;
    (iii) a development corporation;
    (iv) the Commission for the New Towns;

(v) a registered housing association; or

(vi) the Scottish Special Housing Association

to assist them in the discharge of their functions under sections 3, 4 or 5 above, or

(b) request a social services authority or a social work authority to exercise any of their functions in relation to a case with which the housing authority are dealing under sections 3, 4 or 5 above,

they shall co-operate with the housing authority in rendering such assistance in the discharge of the functions to which the request relates as is reasonable in the circumstances'.

The wording of this provision is so vague as to make it of little value. (See also addendum in Preface.)

The duty to accommodate

The actual duty to accommodate a person who has successfully cleared all the hurdles in the Act is contained in section 6.

'(1) A housing authority may perform any duty under section 4 or 5 above to secure that accommodation becomes available for the occupation of a person —

(a) by making available accommodation held by them under Part V of the Housing Act 1957 . . . or under any other anactment, or

(b) by securing that he obtains accommodation from some other person, or

(c) by giving him such advice and assistance as will secure that he obtains accommodation from some other person'.

Again it will be seen that this grants a very wide discretion. The Code of Guidance, paras. A2.1 to A2.15 suggests other ways in which this duty can be discharged such as:

1) granting mortgage assistance to aid house purchase;

2) helping the applicant to obtain a tenancy in the private sector;

3) obtaining accommodation for the applicant from a housing association.

The use of caravans and other interim accommodation such as hostels is recognised reluctantly by the code. There is evidence that authorities, particularly in areas where there is a great deal of housing stress, are using interm accommodation, especially bed and breakfast hotels and other poor quality housing in order to satisfy their obligations under the Act.

Households accepted as homeless and then placed in bed and breakfast accommodation rose from 1,260 at the end of 1978 to 2,030 at the end of 1979, an increase of 61 per cent. During the same period the number of households in hostels rose from 2,440 to 3,560. 43 per cent of homeless households were, however, placed in local authority dwellings during this period.

In *R v Bristol City Council ex parte Browne* [1979] 3 All ER 344 the Queens Bench Divisional Court showed just how wide a discretion is conferred on local authorities by section 6. The applicant and her seven children left the matrimonial home in Tralee, Eire, on medical advice because of the husband's violence. At first the applicant went to a women's hostel in Limerick but when the husband discovered she was there, the hostel arranged for her and the children to go to Bristol. They spent the first night in Bristol in a local hostel but, being unable to stay there any longer, the applicant applied the following day to the Bristol District Council for accommodation as a homeless person. The housing authority commenced inquiries and telephoned the community welfare officer in Tralee who was aware of the husband's violence. He gave an assurance to the housing authority that if the applicant and her children were to return to Tralee he would secure suitable accommodation for them on their arrival. From their inquiries the housing authority concluded that the applicant had become homeless unintentionally and had a priority need and, though she had no connection with Bristol and responsibility for her could not be transferred to any other authority under the 1977 Act (because she came from Eire) that the authority had a duty under section 4(5) to secure accommodation for her. Under section 6(1)(c) the authority could fulfil that duty by giving the applicant 'such advice and assistance' as would secure that she obtained 'accommodation from some other person'. Since the Tralee welfare officer was willing to secure accommodation for the applicant, the authority considered that they could properly carry out their statutory duty by advising the applicant to return to Tralee and contact the welfare officer there, and by offering to arrange and pay for her journey. The applicant, who did not wish to return to Tralee, applied for judicial review by way of mandamus requiring the authority to provide accommodation for her and the children in Bristol. It was, inter alia, held that:

1) When giving an applicant advice and assistance for the purpose of carrying out their duty within the terms of section 6(1)(c) a housing authority were not confined to securing that accommodation was obtained from 'some other person' within the authority's area. Accordingly, the housing authority were entitled to carry out and thereby fulfil their duty by advising and assisting the applicant to obtain accommodation from the welfare officer in Tralee;

2) Even though the welfare officer in Tralee had not specified to the Bristol authority a particular house as being available for the applicant, his offer of accommodation in Tralee was 'accommodation available for occupation' within section 16 since it was sufficient for the housing authority to be satisfied that accommodation would be available if the applicant returned to Tralee.

The accommodation secured for a person under section 6 must comply with section 16 and be available not only for occupation by the applicant but also by any other person who might reasonably be expected to reside with him. But where a person or body, as in *Browne*, promises an authority to find accommodation for a homeless person, then the authority need not be told the exact identity of the proposed accommodation.

The Act is silent as to the character, location, and condition of the accommodation a local authority may secure for a homeless person. Such accommodation should not be prejudicial to health or a nuisance, it should be fit for human habitation and it should not be statutorily overcrowded. An authority that does not comply with these general requirements is open to legal proceedings and could not raise the 1977 Act in any way as a defence. This should be borne in mind by local authorities, especially where they use their powers under section 10 to charge for accommodation made available in consequnce of the performance of their statutory duties. In any case such charges must be 'reasonable'.

Duties of notification

Various duties of notification are imposed by section 8. When certain determinations are made they, and the reasons for them, must be given to the applicant.

These determinations are:

1) whether the person is homeless or threatened with homelessness;

2) whether he has priority need;

3) whether he has become homeless or threatened with homeless intentionally;

4) whether he has a 'local connection' with another housing authority.

Any such notification of a decision and/or reasons must be made available for a reasonable period by the authority at their office for collection by or on behalf of the applicant. Obviously such decisions, etc., must be in writing, and the reasons given for a decision must be such as to enable the applicant to discern what influenced it.

In *R v Beverley Borough Council ex parte McPhee* (1978) 122 Sol Jo 760, it was held that the obligation to accommodate under section 4 arises *before* the section 8 duty to notify, and as soon as the local authority decide that the applicant is homeless, etc.

Offences

Various offences are created by section 11.

'(1) If *any* person, *with intent* to induce a housing authority, in connection with the exercise of their functions under this Act, to believe that he or any other person —

    (a) is homeless or threatened with homelessness, or

    (b) has a priority need, or

    (c) did not become homeless or threatened with homelessness intentionally,

knowingly or recklessly makes a statement which is false in a material particular *or knowingly withholds information* which the authority have reasonably required him to give in connection with the exercise of their functions under this Act, he shall be guilty of an offence.

(2) A person who has applied to a housing authority for accommodation or for assistance in obtaining accommodation *shall* notify to the authority as soon as possible any change of facts material to his case which occurs before he receives notification under section 8 above of the authority's decision on it.

(3) The authority shall explain to any such person in ordinary language —

    (a) the duty imposed by sub-section (2) above, and

    (b) the effect of sub-section (4) below.

(4) A person who fails to comply with sub-section (2) above shall be guilty of an offence unless he shows —

    (a) that he was not given the explanation required by sub-section (3) above, or

    (b) that he was given it but nevertheless had a reasonable excuse for his non-compliance.

(5) A person guilty of an offence under this section shall be liable on summary conviction to a fine not exceeding £500'.

Section 11(2) and (4) are most controversial as they virtually amount to a case of 'anything you do *not* say may be used in evidence against you'. It should be a matter of good local authority practice for the explanation required by section 11(3) to be given in a sensitive and non-intimidating fashion. Anything approaching a crude warning of possible criminal sanctions should be avoided. A homeless person will be distraught enough without being put in fear of penal sanctions.

Protecting the property of the homeless

By virtue of section 7(1) where a housing authority are under a duty under sections 3(4), 4(3) − (5) and 5 and have reason to believe that there is:

1) a danger of loss or damage to the property of a homeless person by reason of his inability to deal with or protect it; and

2) that no other suitable arrangements have been made, they are under a duty to take reasonable steps to prevent such loss or damage. Even where they have no duty under the above provisions they have *power* to protect the property of homeless persons. An authority may decide to exercise these powers and duties subject to conditions, which may include conditions relating to charges and the disposal of goods. If they decide to exercise their powers and duties under section 7 they have power at all reasonable times to enter any premises which are the usual place of residence of the homeless person, or which were his last residence, and deal with the relevant personal property in any way which is reasonably necessary. The provisions of this section cease to be applicable when the local authority consider there is reason to believe that the danger of loss or damage has passed. In such circumstances they must, under section 8(6), notify the homeless person of their decision and the reasons for it. This notification may be given:

    (a) by delivering it to the person; or

    (b) by leaving it at his proper address, or

    (c) sending it by post to him at that address.

Challenging decisions made under the Act and enforcing the duties

When a person feels that the local authority have wrongly determined his application he may follow certain avenues of 'appeal':

1) to a senior officer of the authority who may be able to review the initial decision;

2) to his local councillor;

3) to his MP;

4) to the Commission for Local Administration (see Chapter 12, below). This course of action can only be followed where there is maladministration which arises out of failure to fulfil obligations, or unreasonable delay or inefficiency, etc., causing injustice. A failure to follow the provisions of the Code of Guidance could also be a prima facie instance of maladministration.

Recourse to the courts will be rarely available as a remedy since they have shown they wish to leave the day to day administration of the Act to local authorities, and will only involve themselves on points of law. Four courses of action are available where such a point is involved.

1) Mandamus. This will lie to compel the performance of a public duty, but it is necessary to spell out exactly which duty an authority is required to perform. No order will be granted to make an authority perform its duties under the Act generally, see *R v Beverley Borough Council ex parte McPhee* (1978) 122 Sol Jo 760. To obtain mandamus the applicant would have to commence proceedings for judicial review under RSC Ord. 53. In those proceedings he could get a declaration and an injunction as well as interim relief.

2) An action for breach of statutory duty. This would normally be commenced in the county court. In *Thornton v Kirklees Metropolitan Borough Council* [1979] QB 626, [1979] 2 All ER 349 the plaintiff brought an action against the defendant council in the county court claiming a mandatory injunction ordering the council, as housing authority, to provide him with accommodation, and damages for distress and inconvenience as a consequence of the council's breach of statutory duty. By his particulars of claim the plaintiff claimed to be a homeless person with a priority need; that the council was under a statutory duty to make inquiries into his situation and make accommodation available for his occupation pending their decision; that he had applied to the council for accommodation and no accommodation had been provided and that therefore the council were in breach of their statutory duty under section 3(4) of the Act. On an application for an interim order directing the council to provide the plaintiff with accommodation forthwith, the county court judge held that he had no jurisdiction to entertain the action. He refused to make the order, struck out the particulars of claim as disclosing no reasonable cause of action and dismissed the action.

The Court of Appeal held that in the absence of any provision for the enforcement of the duty in the Act itself and on the true construction of section 3(4) in the context in which it appeared, if a housing authority failed, pending their decision as a result of their inquiries, to carry out their duty by securing that accommodation was made available to an applicant whom they had reason to believe was homeless with a priority need, a civil action for damages would lie against the housing authority for any loss or damage which the applicant could prove he had suffered as a result of the authority's breach of duty.

The problem lies in proving the loss or damage flowing from the alleged breach of duty.

3) An application for a mandatory injunction, as in *Thornton's* case, with or without an action for damages.

4) An application for an interim injunction to enforce the duty under section 3(4) (the duty to accommodate pending inquiries). Here the applicant needs *interim* relief immediately in the form of an injunction requiring the LA to secure accommodation for him pending the making of a valid decision. Such an interim or *interlocutory* injunction cannot carry with it a declaration to the effect that a local authority's decision on intentional homelessness was invalidly made. BUT if the court has before it evidence showing the local authority have clearly erred in a way that invalidates their decision adverse to the applicant, it may in its discretion, for an injunction is discretionary, require the local authority to perform its interim housing duty pending the making of a valid decision. This discretion is not to be lightly used, and will only be used where the applicant can make out a strong prima facie case that the initial finding of intentional homelessness was invalid. Lord Denning in *De Falco* went even further than this and said that the discretion should not be exercised unless certiorari and mandamus would have granted had the application been for judicial review. This, of course, places a heavy burden of proof on an applicant.

The principles laid down in *American Cynamid Co v Ethnicon Ltd* [1975] AC 396, [1975] 1 All ER 504, that in relation to interim injunctions the plaintiff need only satisfy the court that there is a serious question to be tried and that whether such relief is granted depends on a 'balance of convenience', do not apply in homelessness cases, see *De Falco v Crawley Borough Council* [1980] 1 All ER 913.

Other provisions to aid the homeless

One criticism of the 1977 Act is that it does nothing to bring together the various provisions relating to, and authorities having responsibility for, the homeless. These can only be briefly mentioned here but they should not be forgotten.

1) Schedule 5 to the Social Security Act 1980 making it the duty of the Social Services Secretary to provide resettlement units for those without a settled way of life.

2) Section 21(1)(a) of the National Assistance Act 1948 as amended by section 195 of and Schedule 23 to the Local Government Act 1972 and reimposed by Department of Health and Social Security Local Authority Circular No. 13/74. This makes it the duty of social services

authorities to provide residential accommodation for persons who are ordinarily resident in their areas or for other persons who are in urgent need thereof and who by reason of age, infirmity or any other circumstances are in need of care and attention which is not otherwise available to them.

3) Section 1 of the Children and Young Persons Act 1963. This makes it the duty of social services authorities to 'make available such advice, guidance and assistance as may promote the welfare of children by diminishing the need to receive children into care'. This provision is used by some local authorities to pay for hostel or hotel accommodation, particularly where a family has been found intentionally homeless. A policy of *refusing* to use the provisions of this Act where applicants are intentionally homeless was held to be unlawful in *A-G (exrel Tilley) v Wandsworth London Borough Council* (1980) Times, 21st March.

Further reading

General

Bailey, R., *The Homeless and the Family Houses* (Penguin, 1977)
Bailey, R., *The Squatters* (Penguin, 1973)
Richardson, P., *The Homeless in London* (SHAC, 1980)
Wingfield Digby, P., *Hostels and Lodging for Single People* (HMSO, 1976)
Blunt Powers — Sharp Practices (Shelter, 1976)
The Grief Report (Shelter, 1972)
Report of the Working Group on Single Young People (Department of Health and Social Security, 1976)
Vagrancy (Ed. by Tim Cook) (Academic Press, 1979)
Who are the Homeless? Face the Facts (Shelter, 1969)
James, D.C., 'Homelessness: Can the Courts Help?' Vol. 1 British Journal of Law and Society, p. 195

On the 1977 Act

Carnworth, R., *A Guide to the Housing (Homeless Persons) Act 1977* (Charles Knight, 1978)
Partington, M., *The Housing (Homeless Persons) Act 1977 and Code of Guidance* (Sweet & Maxwell, 1978)
A Guide to the Housing (Homeless Persons) Act 1977 (Joint Charities Group)

Social Welfare Law (Ed. by D.W. Pollard) (Oyez), paras. B. 801 – B. 911

Brown, A.J. and Harvey, A., 'Housing (Homeless Persons) Act 1977: Two Views' (1978) 128 NLJ 971

De Friend, R., 'The Housing (Homeless Persons) Act 1977' (1978) 41 MLR 173

Lewis, N. and Birkenshawe, P.J., 'Housing (Homeless Persons) Act 1977' (in two parts) (1978) JPEL 437 and 524

Woodward, P., 'Housing (Homeless Persons) Act 1977: A Paper Tiger?' (1978) JPEL 445

On the working in practice of the 1977 Act

Cairns, M., *Inspection Report re: Bed and Breakfast Accommodation* (Wandsworth Housing Project, 1980)

Homelessness Statistics: 1 April – 31 December 1978 (Welsh Office, 1979)

The Implementation of the Housing (Homeless Persons) Act 1977: An Appraisal after Four Months (Joint Housing Charities, 1978)

Where Homelessness means Helplessness (Shelter, 1978)

Arden, A., 'Enforcing the Homeless Persons Act' (in two parts) LAG Bulletin, December 1979, p. 283 and January 1980, p. 14

Bamford, T., 'The Housing (Homeless Persons) Act One Year On: Is it really Working?' Vol. 10 Social Work Today, No. 11 (7 November 1978), p. 9

Billcliffe, S., 'Dumped in the Interim', *Roof*, July 1979, pp. 118 – 121

Culley, L., 'Council Referral Procedures', *Roof*, November 1978, pp. 188 – 191

Franey, R., 'Apart from the Law', *Roof*, November/December 1980, pp. 172 – 174

'The Lobby against the Homeless Persons Act', *Roof*, May/June 1980, pp. 85 – 86

Part II
Repairs, housing standards and remedies

Chapter 7

The landlord's obligation to repair and maintain

(Except where expressly stated it may be assumed that the remedies referred to in this chapter apply to both private and municipal tenancies.)

Until recently neither in contract nor tort did the common law give any protection to tenants. The whole attitude of the law was encapsulated in the maxim caveat emptor, or as Erle CJ said in *Robbins v Jones* (1863) 15 CBNS 221 at 239: '. . . fraud apart, there is no law against letting a tumbledown house: and the tenant's remedy is upon his contract, if any'. This view of the law was endorsed by Lord Atkinson in *Cavalier v Pope* [1906] AC 428 at 432: '. . . it is well established that no duty is, at law, cast upon a landlord not to let a house in a dangerous or dilapidated condition . . .'. There was no liability in tort whether the damage arose from the landlord's mere neglect or from his careless doing of works of maintenance or installation. Scrutton LJ held in *Bottomley v Bannister* [1932] 1 KB 458 at 468 that: '. . . in the absence of express contract, a landlord of an unfurnished house is not liable to his tenant . . . for defects in the house or land rendering it dangerous or unfit for occupation, even if he has constructed the defects himself or is aware of their existence'. In *Otto v Bolton and Norris* [1936] 2 KB 46, [1936] 1 All ER 960 that principle was held to be good law despite *Donoghue v Stevenson*, and it was again applied in *Davis v Foots* [1940] 1 KB 116, [1939] 4 All ER 4 and *Travers v Gloucester Corpn* [1947] KB 71, [1946] 2 All ER 506. Here a local authority let a house with the vent pipe of a gas geyser terminating under the eaves of the house. This dangerous installation led to a build-up of toxic exhaust fumes and as a consequence the tenant's lodger was gassed in the bathroom. The corporation was held not liable in tort.

A growing body of opinion viewed the exemption of lessors from liability in negligence with growing distaste and various attempts were made to end it. For example it was said in *Ball v LCC* [1949] 2 KB 159, [1949] 1 All ER 1056 that a landlord could be liable in *contract* to his tenant for negligent installation work carried out *after* the start of the lease, through non-contracting parties could not sue under this rule.

197

Great changes have now been made in the law, both by statute and by
the action of the courts, and it is to these that we must now turn.

Landlord's obligations in tort

a) *At common law*

Following the decisions in *Cunard v Antifyre Ltd* [1933] 1 KB 551 and
Taylor v Liverpool Corpn [1939] 3 All ER 329 there is no difficulty in
holding a landlord liable in negligence for damage caused *by buildings
retained in his occupation* to persons or to buildings let to a tenant.
In the *Taylor* case the corporation acquired a house with view to
demolishing it. Because there was no other available accommodation
for the tenant he was allowed to stay in the three rooms of the house he
occupied. A brick fell from the chimney stack of the house and hit the
tenant's daughter who was in the back yard of the house at the time.
The Corporation had previously been warned of the defective condition
of the chimney. It was held, as the yard did not comprise part of the
demised premises, that the Corporation were liable for the injury. In
A.C. Billings & Son v Riden [1958] AC 240, [1957] 3 All ER 1 the
House of Lords stated that, irrespective of the lack of a contractual
relationship, any person who executes work on premises is under a
general duty to use reasonable care for the safety of those whom he
knows, or ought reasonably to know, may be affected by or lawfully in
the vicinity of the work. Thus a landlord can be liable in tort for
dangers he creates *after* the commencement of the lease. But what of
the long established exemption from tortious liability in respect of
dangers existing at the time of the demise? There are dicta in *Anns v
London Borough of Merton* [1977] 2 All ER 492 that a careless *owner-
builder* should be liable in negligence to those who acquire houses from
him, and it may be that this applies to a landowner who builds new
houses or flats for letting. Indeed in *Batty v Metropolitan Property
Realisations Ltd* [1978] QB 554, [1978] 2 All ER 445 both the builders
and the vendors of a house sold on a very long lease were held liable in
negligence when the property was found to be dangerously defective
because it was built on unsure ground, a fact of which they should
have known. At the moment the builder-lessor of new premises may be
liable for defects constituting a present or future threat to the health or
safety of the first occupants of the premises in question. This liability
could well also extend to their successors in title. Any action in tort
must be commenced when the defects become patent to reasonable
inspection. Some light was shed on what is meant by 'reasonable
inspection' by the vendor/purchaser decision in *Sutherland v C.R.*

Maton & Son Ltd (1976) 240 Estates Gazette 135, (1976) JPL 753. Here a house had been built on land that had been incorrectly levelled with the result that, some years later, serious cracks appeared in the wall. The plaintiffs had purchased from the original occupier who had bought the house from the builders who were now sued in negligence. The defendants alleged that the plaintiff's failure to have a full independent survey of the house carried out before purchase (they had relied on their building society's inspection report) broke the chain of causation because the plaintiffs had failed to carry out a reasonable inspection of the property. Cobb J held that it was a perfectly ordinary and reasonable practice for an intending purchaser to rely on the inspection report by a building society. A reasonable man will therefore only be put on his guard if there are patent defects, if his own survey (assuming he has one) shows up defects, or, if as a result of its inspection, the building society itself raises serious queries about the property.

Can lessor of older premises now be liable for letting them in a defective condition? Lord Salmon said in *Anns* at page 512 of the report: 'The immunity of a landlord who sells or lets his house which is dangerous or unfit for habitation is deeply entrenched in our law'. Indeed it goes back as far as *Arden v Pullen* (1842) 10 M & W 322 and *Hart v Windsor* (1844) 12 M & W 68. It would be unwise at the moment to assert that a landlord who buys up older properties and refurbishes them with a view to letting them out will be liable *at common law* for any negligent work he does. Nor can we be certain what the common law position would be in relation to negligent omissions or other defects. However, the categories of negligence are truly never closed, and caveat emptor is largely defunct with regard to *sales* of houses. The common law may in the future impose liability on a landlord for the negligent doing of maintenance works, or even, in a proper case, for the failure to do them. In *Sharpe v Manchester Metropolitan District Council* (1977) 5 April (unreported) (CA) a local authority were held to be negligent in that they did not carry out a proper and thorough disinfection of premises infested with cockroaches. The plaintiff took a tenancy of a council flat in 1972 and found it infested with cockroaches. For two years the local authority tried to eliminate the insects in the flat by using emulsified DDT. They failed in their attempts. It was held that they had been negligent because they had failed to treat the service ducts and other spaces in the walls and floors, and also because they had used a discredited insecticide.

b) *Under statute*

What the common law has not yet done statute has gone some way to doing by the Defective Premises Act 1972. Section 1 provides (inter alia):

'(1) A person taking on work for or in connection with the provision of a dwelling (whether the dwelling is provided by the erection or by the conversion or enlargement of a building) owes a duty —

(a) if the building is provided to the order of any person to that person; and

(b) without prejudice to paragraph (a) above to every person who acquires an interest (whether legal or equitable) in the dwelling; to see that the work which he takes on is done in a workmanlike or, as the case may be, professional manner, with proper materials and so that as regards that work the dwelling will be fit for habitation when completed . . .

(4) A person who —

(a) in the course of a business which consists of or includes providing or arranging for the provision of dwellings or installation in dwellings; or

(b) in the exercise of a power of making such provision or arrangements conferred by or by virtue of any enactment; arranges for another to take on work for or in connection with the provision of a dwelling shall be treated for the purposes of this section as included among the persons who have taken on the work'.

So far as municipal dwellings are concerned this provision imposes liability on local authorities, their builders, sub-contractors and architects if they fail to build in a professional or workmanlike manner (as the case may be) with proper materials, or fail to ensure that the dwelling is fit for human habitation, a phrase which may be capable of covering such matters as defective design or lay-out. (See Law Com. No. 40, para. 34.) The duty, *which is strict*, is owed to, inter alia, those persons having legal or equitable interests in the dwelling, for example tenants, but *not* their children or visitors. Moreover the duty will only arise in connection with the provision, whether by new construction, conversion or enlargement, of a *dwelling*. The mere enlargement of an existing single dwelling unit would not attract the operation of the law. The provision is limited in other ways. First, it only applies to dwellings constructed after 1 January 1974, by virtue of section 7(2) of the Act. Second, it is far from clear whether a person wishing to sue under section 1 must show that he has suffered either personal injury and/or property damage, or whether simple economic loss alone is recoverable. Finally, section 1(5) lays down in general that the appropriate period of limitation for the bringing of an action under the provision begins to run as from the time when the building was completed. This period will generally be six years, but only three years in the case of personal injuries. It is not possible to exclude or restrict the operation of section 1 by agreement, see section 6(3) of the Act.

The effect and content of section 1 of the 1972 Act were considered by the Court of Appeal in *Alexander v Mercouris* [1979] 3 All ER 305, [1979] 1 WLR 1270. On 20 November 1972 the defendants entered into an agreement with the plaintiff to purchase a property for him and arrange for its modernisation and conversion into flats. Pursuant to this agreement the defendants contracted in August 1973 with a firm of builders to do the work, which was completed on 27 February 1974, just after the 1972 Act came into force on 1 January. The plaintiff subsequently alleged that the defendants were in breach of the statutory duty to ensure that the work was done in a professional manner with proper materials and had failed to ensure that the property would be fit for habitation on completion. The Court of Appeal dismissed the claim on the basis that the Act is not retroactive in effect and so only applies to work *commenced*, or contracts entered into, after its coming into operation. The work in the instant case was commenced before the Act came into force and was only completed after it had come into effect and so fell outside the terms of the statute.

The decision in this case together with statements made by the court support the following propositions.

1) The Defective Premises Act, s. 1, only applies to contracts entered into or work commenced after the commencement of the provision, i.e. 1 January 1974.

2) The duty is broken as soon as bad workmanship or the use of faulty materials takes place because the duty is a continuing one which arises as soon as the work is commenced and carries on until completion. The plaintiff need not wait until the work is finished before he can sue. Thus for example installation of faulty foundations at the start of building operations would be a breach of the duty.

3) The reference in the provision to the dwelling being 'fit for habitation when completed' merely indicates the intended consequence of the proper performance of the duty and provides a measure of the standard of the requisite work and materials; it does not mean that the duty is such that no relief can be obtained until completion.

4) The fact that a breach is actionable as from the date when it occurs would not seem to affect the running of time under section 1(5) of the Act. As we have seen under this provision time is *deemed* to run for limitation purposes as from the date of the completion of the building. The effect of this is that there is a *terminus* beyond which action cannot be taken — generally a period of six or three years, as the case may be, running from the date of completion. The effect of *Alexander* is to extend that period for the taking of action *backwards* to the date of the

breach. Time does *not* begin to run in these circumstances from the date of the breach which may seem to be a somewhat odd legal phenomenon but it is the consequence of the wording of section 1(5).

Section 3(1) of the Defective Premises Act 1972 provides:

'Where work of construction, repair, maintenance or demolition or any other work is done on or in relation to premises, any duty of care owed, because of the doing of the work, to persons who might reasonably be expected to be affected by the defects in the state of the premises created by the doing of the work shall not be abated by the subsequent disposal of the premises by the person who owed the duty'.

But this statutory displacement of a landlord's immunity in negligence is not without its own problems. First, it only applies, by virtue of section 3(2)(a), to those lettings of premises entered into after the commencement of the Act, 1 January 1974. Second, liability can only arise where there has been a defect created by a positive act classifiable as 'work of construction, repair maintenance or demolition or any other work done on or in relation to premises'. Thus it seems not *all* 'work' can give rise to liability but only that of the specified kinds, or other 'work' which can be said to be 'done on or in relation to premises' such as, for example, installation of central heating. Nor does this section impose any liability for negligent omissions to do repairs.

Liability for an omission may, however, arise along with other forms of liability under section 4 of the 1972 Act. Section 4(1) provides:

'Where premises are let under a tenancy which puts on the landlord an obligation to the tenant for the maintenance or repair of the premises, the landlord owes to all persons who might reasonably be expected to be affected by defects in the state of the premises a duty to take such care as is reasonable in all the circumstances to see that they are reasonably safe from personal injury or from damage to the property caused by a relevant defect'.

This imposes tortious liability on a landlord towards his tenants, their families and those other persons foreseeably likely to be in the premises, and, by section 6(3) of the Act, he cannot exclude or restrict this duty.

As with section 3, this section also poses problems of interpretation. Liability can only arise in respect of a 'relevant defect'. Such is defined by sub-section (3) as '. . . a defect in the state of the premises existing at or after the material time and arising from, or continuing because of, an act or omission by the landlord which constitutes or would if he had notice of the defect, have constituted a failure by him to carry out his obligation to the tenant for the maintenance or repair of the premises . . .'. Such defects must arise 'at or after the material time', which is further defined by the sub-section as being, in general terms, for tenancies commencing before the Act, the commencement date of the Act (1 January 1974), and in other cases the earliest date on which the tenancy commenced or the tenancy agreement was entered into. Liability arises out of those defects which constitute a breach of the landlord's obligations to repair and maintain. These obligations will include any express covenant to repair given by the landlord and, by virtue of sub-section (5), those implied by statute, such as section 32 of the Housing Act 1961. An even more extended meaning is given to 'obligation' by sub-section (4) which deems for the purposes of the section any *power* a landlord has to repair actually to be an *obligation* to repair. Such powers can arise in many situations. A landlord may have power to enter and do repairs simply because the tenant has defaulted on his own repairing covenants. In such circumstances the Act provides that the landlord, while remaining liable to third parties, shall not actually be liable to the tenant himself. The effect of the decision in *Mint v Good* [1951] 1 KB 517, [1950] 2 All ER 1159 should also be remembered for here Somervell LJ said (at page 522): '. . . in the case of a weekly tenancy, business efficacy will not be effected if the house is allowed to fall into disrepair and no one keeps it in reasonable condition; and it seems to me, therefore, necessary . . . that the . . . landlord should at any rate have the power to keep the place in proper repair . . .'.

Thus an implied power to enter and do repairs would seem to arise in relation to any *weekly* tenancy of a dwelling-house and this will be deemed to the an obligation to repair under sub-section (4).

There are a number of subsidiary points to note about this provision. Sub-section (2) provides:

'The said duty is owed if the landlord knows (whether as the result of being notified by the tenant or otherwise) or if he ought in all the circumstances to have known of the relevant defect'.

Thus there is no need for a tenant to give his landlord notice of a defect provided it would be patent on reasonable inspection.

In *Clarke v Taff Ely Borough Council* (1980) *Daily Telegraph*, 1 April 1980, Mrs Clarke visited her sister's council house and was injured when the rotten floorboards gave way beneath a table on which she was standing. The house was one of a number of pre-war council houses known to have a potentially dangerous floor construction. The local authority admitted it had never heard of the Defective Premises Act 1972, and their chief housing surveyor agreed that in view of the age of the house, its type and the presence of damp it was foreseeable that rot would occur. Damages of £5,100 were awarded. This, admittedly brief, report seems to be the first relating to an action brought against a local authority under the 1972 Act. It is unwise to place too much reliance on it, but it would seem that local authorities should inspect their older properties, and that they can be liable if they negligently fail to discover defects a reasonable man would suspect from facts already known to him.

Second, a very extended meaning is given to the word 'tenancy' by section 6 of the 1972 Act. The term includes leases and underleases, tenancies at will and sufferance and statutory tenancies. Furthermore section 4(6) itself states:

'This section applies to a right of occupation given by contract or any enactment and not amounting to a tenancy as if the right were a tenancy'.

Thus contractual licenses and restricted contracts under the Rent Act 1977 will both attract the operation of this provision.

Liability under the Occupiers' Liability Act 1957

The common law, as we have already seen in *Taylor v Liverpool Corpn* imposes liability on a landlord for defects on his premises which cause injury to his tenants. Thus if a local authority let the flats in a tower block and retain the common parts, such as the staircases, in their own occupation they will be responsible in tort to persons injured by the defective condition of any of those parts. The Occupiers' Liability Act 1957 adds to the landlord's obligation by stating in section 3(1):

'Where an occupier of premises is bound by contract to permit persons who are strangers to the contract to enter or use the premises, the duty of care which he owes to them as his visitors cannot be restricted or excluded by that contract, but (subject to any provision of the contract to the contrary) shall include the duty to perform his obligations under the contract, whether undertaken for their protection or not, in so far as those obligations go beyond the obligations otherwise involved in that duty'.

The effect of this sub-section is that the landlord cannot by virtue of his contract with his tenants reduce his obligations to their visitors below the standard required by the Act, the 'common duty of care'. Furthermore the tenant's visitors are enabled to claim the benefit of any more onerous obligations inserted in the lease, unless the lease itself specifically excludes this. Whether the landlord can simply exclude the common duty to tenants' visitors simply by posting exclusionary notices, as is allowed generally by section 2(1) of the 1957 Act, is an open question, but the better view of the law is that such an exclusion would not be lawful. The interested reader is referred to the current editions of the standard works on torts such as Winfield, Street and Clerk and Lindsell for further details.

Liability for breach of the Building Regulations

The Building Regulations 1976 are a body of rules designed to secure a uniform system of building control throughout the nation. They are principally concerned with matters such as building works and fittings, and are made generally under the Public Health Acts 1936 – 61. Considerable changes were introduced by Part III of the Health and Safety at Work etc. Act 1974. This legislation provided for extensions in the scope and coverage of the Building Regulations, and also the purposes for which they can be made. Provision was also made to enable the Building Regulations to be applied to all types of buildings and erected structures and a general supervisory control over the regulations was entrusted to the Secretary of State. So far as the present work is concerned section 71 was the most important provision of the 1974 Act as it makes breaches of the regulations actionable at common law except where the regulations themselves provide otherwise, or create any other defence to a civil action. 'Damage' is defined so as to include death and personal injury, including disease and mental or physical impairment. This provision was brought into effect in 1977, but so far no regulations imposing civil liability have been made. Interested readers are referred to any of the standard works on the Building Regulations such as Whyte and Powell-Smith, *The Building Regulations Explained and Illustrated.*

Landlord's obligations in contract

a) At common law

Before discussing the contractual position it should be stated that contractual remedies will only apply as between contracting parties. Any third party injured by the defective state of a dwelling-house must find his remedy in tort. It should also be noted that it is established by *Batty's* case, as well as by other recent decisions of the Court of Appeal not in the sphere of housing, that the existence of a contractual remedy will not prevent concurrent liability from arising in tort. Indeed it may be preferable for an injured tenant to sue in tort rather than contract because of the periods of limitation. In contract, time begins to run from the moment the breach occurs, in tort it runs as from the time when the damage is sustained by the plaintiff. It seems clear from the decisions in *Anns* and *Batty* mentioned above, and also in *Sparham-Souter v Town and Country Developments (Essex) Ltd* [1976] QB 858, [1976] 2 All ER 65, that this means, in relation to premises, that time begins to run as from the moment when the defect becomes patent to reasonable inspection. That said, a landlord may be liable to his tenant for a breach of an express covenant to repair and maintain a dwelling-house. In such a case the extent of the landlord's liability will depend upon the wording of the covenant. Such express covenants are rare, particularly as many, if not indeed most, leases of small dwelling-houses are created orally on a weekly basis under section 54(2) of the Law of Property Act 1925. The common law has also been unwilling to imply terms into leases. In *Smith v Marrable* (1843) 11 M & W 5, Parke B implied a term into a letting of *furnished* premises that, at the start of the lease, they would be in a habitable condition. The nature of the obligation should be noted: it exists at the start of the lease, and, according to *Sarson v Roberts* [1895] 2 QB 395, it will not arise if the premises become uninhabitable during the course of the lease. The cases show that what is likely to make a house unfit for habitation in this context are matters likely to affect the health of the incoming tenant, such as infestation by bugs, or defects in the drains, or recent occupation by a person suffering from an easily communicable disease. The meaning given by the common law to 'unfit for human habitation' is therefore different from the meaning the phrase has under the unfitness provisions of the Housing Act 1957, which are discussed in the next chapter and the two concepts should not be confused. If furnished premises are 'unfit' at common law the tenant is entitled to quit them by repudiating the tenancy. He may also sue for any loss he has suffered, see: *Wilson v Finch-Hatton* (1877) 2 Ex D 336, and *Charsley v Jones* (1889) 53 JP 280. This implied condition is limited to lettings of furnished dwellings. In *Sleafer v Lambeth Metropolitan Borough Council* [1960] 1 QB 43, [1959] 3 All ER 378 it was said that where a landlord lets unfurnished dwellings there will generally be no implied term that they are free of defects.

The law has on occasions implied certain terms into contracts of letting. In *Liverpool City Council v Irwin* [1977] AC 239 the House of Lords implied a term into a letting of a flat in a high rise block. The facts were that the local authority owned a tower block of flats, access to which was provided by a common staircase and two electrically operated lifts. The tenants also had the use of internal chutes into which to discharge rubbish. Over the years the condition of the block deteriorated, partly as a result of vandalism. Continual defects included: failed lifts; a lack of lighting on the staircases, and blocked rubbish chutes. The tenants refused to pay rent and so the landlords applied for possession orders on the flats, to which the tenants replied with a counter-claim that (inter alia) the landlords were in breach of the covenant of quiet enjoyment. The House of Lords said that as this was a contract in which the parties had not themselves fully expressed the terms then the court could imply certain terms solely to prevent the contract of letting from becoming inefficacious and absurdly futile. The reasoning that followed was:

1) The tenants had in their leases an implied right or easement to use the stairs, lifts and rubbish chutes as these were necessarily incidental to their occupation of high-rise flats;

2) The landlords must therefore be placed under an implied obligation to take reasonable care to maintain those common areas and facilities;

3) Such an obligation is not, however, absolute because tenants of high-rise blocks must themselves resist vandalism and co-operate in maintaining the common areas in reasonable condition, and

4) The courts have no power to imply such terms in municipal tenancy agreements as they think 'reasonable'. They may only supply such terms as are truly necessary for the functioning of the contract.

It should also be noted that the fact that the landlord is in breach of *his* covenant to repair does not automatically entitle the tenant to treat the lease as at an end, see *Surplice v Farnsworth* (1884) 13 LJ CP 215.

Before leaving the common law some comment must be made on what can be termed the 'self-help' remedy created by the decision in *Lee-Parker v Izzet* [1971] 3 All ER 1099, [1971] 1 WLR 1688. Here it was held that, irrespective of the common law rules as to set off, the occupiers of property had a right to recoup themselves out of *future* rent for the cost of repairs to the property, in so far as the repairs fell within the landlord's express or implied covenants, provided that he was in fact in breach of them, and only after due notice had been given to him. The exact limits of this remedy should be noted. A tenant has no right to *withhold* payment of rent to compel his landlord to carry out repairs, and if he does so he will be in breach of his own obligation under the lease. The rule only authorises the deducting of the *proper* cost of repairs from future rent: a tenant is not entitled to expend vast sums on his home and then present his landlord with the bill. The authorities agree that the following steps should be taken before reliance is placed on the rule:

1) The tenant *must* notify the landlord of the disrepair which itself must arise from a breach of the landlord's covenants;

2) At the same time he should obtain at least two builders' estimates as to the likely cost of the repairs and send them to the landlord, warning him at the same time that if repairs are not effected then the tenant will carry out the work and will deduct the cost from future rent;

3) To be absolutely safe, a county court declaration should be obtained authorising this course of action, and

4) having given his landlord time to execute the repairs, the tenant may then proceed to do them himself.

It can be seen that this procedure is neither simple nor rapid. It does, however, have the advantage in that the principle constitutes a defence to a claim for rent, and monies paid on repairs are treated as payments of the rent itself. Some local authorities phrase their tenancy agreements in such a way as to attempt to exclude the operation of the *Lee-Parker* principle, for example: 'The council will not accept responsibility for orders which are given by the tenant direct to statutory undertakings or any other bodies or persons, and any charges arising from such orders will be the tenant's responsibility.' The effect of such wording would not yet seem to have been elucidated in court.

In *Asco Developments Ltd v Lowes* [1978] LAG Bulletin 293 the landlords sought summary judgment for arrears of rent under RSC Ord. 14 alleging that there was no defence to the action. The tenants sought to defend on the grounds that the landlords were in breach of their repairing obligations. Megarry V-C held that in certain special circumstances the *Lee-Parker* principle could be applied to monies accrued in rent arrears, and that in the present case the tenants could defend the action. However, the court stated that nothing in the decision should be taken to encourage rent strikes as a means of forcing action on the part of a landlord. It was made quite clear in *Camden Nominees v Forcey* [1940] Ch 352, [1940] 2 All ER 1 that it is no answer to a claim for rent by a landlord for the tenant to say that the landlord has failed to perform his obligations. That case is also authority for the proposition that it is an actionable interference with the contract between a landlord and his tenant for another tenant of that landlord to persuade his fellow tenant not to pay rent in an attempt to force the landlord to perform his obligations. If a tenant is to use the *Lee-Parker* principle in respect of rent arrears, he must specify to the court the sums and costs in question, and must particularise the issues. A judge faced with such issues should act with considerable discretion before allowing the tenant to defend the claim for rent. It would also seem that the fact that the landlords were in voluntary liquidation in the *Asco Developments* case was a factor of great importance to the mind of the judge, and therefore it would be unwise to regard the decision as a major extension of the law. It is, moreover, uncertain whether the *Lee-Parker* principle applies only to the cost of repairs or whether it can be extended to cover other heads of damage. The *common law* only allows the recovery of liquidated damages. In *British Anzani (Felixstowe) Ltd v International Marine Management (UK) Ltd* [1979] 2 All ER 1063, [1979] 3 WLR 451 Forbes J indicated that *in equity* unliquidated damages, for example claims for inconvenience and loss of enjoyment, might be recoverable against rent under a tenancy agreement. The tenant must prove, if he wishes to rely on this principle, that it would be inequitable in view of the condition of the property for the landlord to be allowed to recover the amount of rent he wishes to claim. This will not be an easy burden to discharge as damages for breach of a repairing covenant relating to a dwelling-house are not often substantial. It is unlikely that a court would find it equitable to deny a landlord the *entire* amount of rent claimed.

The facts and the judgment in the *British Anzani* case are worth considering at some length because of the light they shed on the limitations of the remedies available to tenants.

The litigation arose out of a commercial building lease. The tenants of certain warehouses counter claimed for damages in respect of the defective floors of the premises when they were sued by the landlords for arrears of rent. The question was whether the defendants were in any way entitled to set off the damages against the liability to pay rent. Forbes J reviewed all the previous law and came to the following conclusions.

1) At common law there can be a set off against rent where a tenant expends money on repairs to the demised premises which the landlord has covenanted to carry out, but, in breach of which agreement, he has failed to do. The breach must probably significantly affect the use of the premises, and the remedy is not available unless the tenant has previously notified the landlord of the want of repair so as to activate the covenant. This is the principle in *Lee-Parker*.

2) At common law there can also be a set off where the tenant has expended money at the landlord's request in respect of some obligation of the landlord connected with the land demised.

3) The common factor in both these situations is that the set off is a known and fixed, i.e. liquidated, sum which has actually been paid by the tenant, and that payment can be regarded as payment pro-tanto of the rent.

4) Historically equity has granted relief against ejectment for non payment of rent where there has been a counter-claim for unliquidated damages against the landlord for breach of a covenant in the lease, provided that the tenant has no other common law remedy, and provided that the cross claim arises out of the same contract as the claim and is so directly connected with it that it would be manifestly unjust to allow the landlord to recover without taking into account the cross claim.

5) *Hart v Rogers* [1916] 1 KB 646 where Scrutton J held that a counter-claim for damages based on a breach of an implied covenant to repair could not be a defence to an action for rent was incorrectly decided.

6) Nowadays it is not *absolutely* necessary that the claim and counter-claim should arise out of the same contract, provided both arise out of

very closely connected transactions. What is required is that equity must recognise that the defendant's counter-claim goes right to the very root of the plaintiff's claim.

7) The principles of equity thus apply to counter-claims for unliquidated damages.

A set off of unliquidated damages is a defence to as much of the plaintiff's claim as is represented by the eventual amount of the award made. If the defendant limits *his* damages to a sum less than that claimed from him then he must pay the balance over and above his counter-claim. But where the defendant's damages are claimed at large and are to be finally to be decided by the court, and where it is bona fide claimed that they over top the plaintiff's claim, even though they are not yet quantified, then the defendant's set off amounts to a complete defence to the whole of the plaintiff's claim.

As has been said previously it is most unlikely that a court would allow such a measure of equitable relief as would entitle a tenant counter-claiming for unliquidated damages to escape the payment of the whole of a claim for unpaid rent. Any house would have to be in quite awful condition and any rent payable would have to be quite high before these principles could really begin to bring a great deal of relief to tenants. In relation to low rented houses they could hardly operate at all. Furthermore this equitable relief is discretionary, and as, 'he who comes to equity must come with clean hands', it is unlikely to be available to a tenant who has been guilty of wrongdoing in relation to the transaction in question. The *British Anzani* case is not likely to be of assistance to rent strikers.

b) Under statute

We have seen how, with some few exceptions, the common law has failed to impose repairing obligations on landlords. Parliament has on a number of occasions attempted to remedy the omission of the common law, but, sadly, the courts have adopted a somewhat restrictive interpretation of the legislation.

As J.I. Reynolds has shown in 'Statutory Covenants of Fitness and Repair: Social Legislation and the Judges' (1974) 37 MLR 377, the restrictive attitude of the common law in relation to landlords' repairing obligations dates from the 1840's — the very period when much evidence was coming to light as to the appalling housing conditions suffered by large numbers of people. Parliament was not slow to act, and the Nuisances Removal, etc (1846) began the great march of public health legislation that was to culminate in the Public Health Act 1875. However, it was not until the 1880's that tenants were given the right to recover damages for a landlord's 'neglect or default in sanitary matters'. Section 12 of the Housing of the Working Classes Act 1885 was designed to remove the anomaly whereby the common law gave protection under *Smith v Marrable* only to tenants of furnished dwellings. The provision was opposed in the House of Lords by Lord Bramwell as an unwarranted interference with the principles of freedom of contract and caveat emptor. That was an ill omen. Though the provision has been retained and refined in subsequent legislation and is presently section 6 of the Housing Act 1957, the attitude of the courts has remained restrictive. Section 6 of the Housing Act 1957 (as amended) provides (inter alia):

'(2) Subject to the provisions of this Act, in any contract to which this section applies there shall, notwithstanding any stipulation to the contrary, be implied a condition and undertaking that the house will be kept by the landlord during the tenancy, fit for human habitation. Provided that the condition and undertaking aforesaid shall not be implied when a house is let for a term of less than three years upon the terms that it shall be put by the lessee into a condition reasonably fit for human habitation, and the lease is not determinable at the option of either party before the expiration of three years'.

The principal difficulty with section 6 is that sub-section (1) limits its applicability to contracts of letting where the rent is not more than £80 in relation to Inner London Boroughs or £52 elsewhere in the country, and thus the range of properties covered is very small indeed. The courts have 'discovered' other difficulties in the wording of this provision and its ancestors and these have hardened into rules of interpretation which apply not only to section 6 but also to section 32 of the Housing Act 1961. The first point to note is that *Middleton v Hall* (1913) 108 LT 804 and *Ryall v Kidwell* [1914] 3 KB 135 stated that only the tenant can sue. While these decisions have been effectively overruled in tort by section 4 of the Defective Premises Act 1972 (see above) the technical rule remains that privity of contract limits the possibility of suing on the implied covenant only to the contracting parties. Next it should be noted that the landlord cannot be liable under the implied covenant unless the tenant has previously given him notice of the defect. This was decided, in the case of patent defects, by *McCarrick v Liverpool Corpn* [1947] AC 219, [1946] 2 All ER 646, and was applied to latent defects by *O'Brien v Robinson* [1973] AC 912. It should again be remembered that the tortious remedy under section 4 of the Defective Premises Act 1972 is not made so dependent upon the giving of actual notice. In the case of local authority dwellings, it was held in *Sheldon v West Bromwich Corpn* (1973) 25 P & CR 360 that where a local authority employee knows that premises are defective then his knowledge will be treated as giving the authority notice. Here plumbers employed by a local authority had discovered that the water tank in a council house was old and defective. No action was taken to replace the tank which subsequently burst causing damage, and the local authority were held liable for this to their tenant.

The most serious limitation on section 6 was imposed by the Court of Appeal in *Buswell v Goodwin* [1971] 1 All ER 418, [1971] 1 WLR 92. Here a cottage was statutorily unfit and, as the local authority had made a closing order on it, the landlord had commenced possession proceedings against the tenant. He in turn argued that the house was only unfit because the landlord was in breach of his implied contractual obligation under section 6. It can be argued that the standard of repair imported by the implied covenant is absolute, but the Court of Appeal rejected this. Instead they restricted the ambit of operation of the implied covenant to those cases where a house is capable of being made fit at reasonable expense. The result is that where a house has fallen into an extreme state of disrepair the tenant can no longer rely on the implied covenant. The paradox thus emerges of the tenants of the worst housing receiving the lowest level of legal protection.

We shall now discover that a very similar process of judicial reasoning has emptied much of the meaning from the other statutorily implied covenant, that found under section 32 of the Housing Act 1961. This provides:

'(1) In any lease of a dwelling-house, being a lease to which this section applies, there shall be implied a covenant by the lessor —
    (a) to keep in repair the structure and exterior of the dwelling-house (including drains, gutters and external pipes); and
    (b) to keep in repair and proper working order the installations in the dwelling-house —
        (i) for the supply of water, gas and electricity, and for sanitation (including basins, sinks, baths and sanitary conveniences but not, except as aforesaid, fixtures and fittings and appliances for making use of the supply of water, gas or electricity), and
        (ii) for space heating or heating water,
and any other covenant by the lessee for the repair of the premises (including any covenant to put in repair to deliver up in repair, to paint, point or render or to pay money in lieu of repairs by the lessee or on account of repairs by the lessor) shall be of no effect so far as it relates to the matters mentioned in paragraphs (a) and (b) of this subsection . . .
(3) In determining the standard of repair required by the lessor's repairing covenant, regard shall be had to the age, character and prospective life of the dwelling-house and the locality in which it is situated'.

The provision goes on to grant a power to enter and view to the land-lord; to make it clear that 'lease' includes 'underlease' and also agreements for leases, and 'any other tenancy', and also that the covenant is implied in relation to flats as well as houses. Section 33 applies section 32 to any lease of a dwelling-house granted after the passing of the Act, where the lease is for less than seven years, subject to certain restrictions in section 33(3)(a) or (b)(i) or (ii), and section 33(4). It also forbids 'contracting out' of the implied covenant or making any agreements limiting its operation or forbidding reliance upon it, see section 33(7).

The policy of Parliament in creating the implied covenant was to prevent unscrupulous landlords from imposing unreasonable repairing obligations on their tenants. It cannot be said, however, that the law has been as successful as it might have been in preventing the occurrence of disrepair and bad housing conditions. Tenants are generally ignorant of their rights, which should be remedied so far as municipal tenants are concerned by the information provisions of 'the Tenants' Charter' (see below). Many tenants do not complain about disrepair until it becomes exceptional and intolerable. Alongside this general ignorance and unwillingness to act on the part of tenants there exists the same restrictive judicial attitude as we have seen in relation to the covenant implied under the 1957 Act.

This can be seen in decisions as to which matters fall within the scope of the implied covenant. In *Brown v Liverpool Corpn* [1969] 3 All ER 1345, paving flagstones and shallow steps leading to a house were held to be part of its 'exterior', though not its structure. They were necessary for the purpose of gaining access to the house and so fell within the scope of the implied covenant. In *Hopwood v Cannock Chase District Council* [1975] 1 All ER 796, [1975] 1 WLR 373 the slabs in a back yard were held not to fall within the scope of the covenant as the back yard was not the essential means of access to the house. Thus it may be argued that, essential means of access apart, 'exterior' in section 32(1)(a) simply means the outer part of the 'structure' of the dwelling-house and not the contiguous land also included in the lease. So far as the application of the implied covenant to flats is concerned, dicta of the Court of Appeal in *Campden Hill Towers v Gardner* [1977] QB 823, [1977] 1 All ER 739 are most important. The obligation implied by section 32(1)(a), which deals with structural matters, must be taken separately from that implied by section 32(1)(b), which deals with installations. Where the structure is concerned the landlord's obligation extends to anything which can ordinarily be regarded as part of the structure or exterior of the dwelling in question. Thus section 32(1)(a) applies, irrespective of the words of the lease, to the outside walls of a flat, (even though they may have been excluded from the demise), the outer sides of horizontal divisions between flats, the outside of the inner party walls of the flat and the structural framework and beams directly supporting the floors, ceilings and walls of a flat. The test to be used in determining the scope of the implied covenant is whether the particular item of disrepair affects the stability or usability of the particular flat in question. So far as section 32(1)(b) is concerned, however, the obligation is merely one to keep in repair and sound working order those relevant installations actually within the physical confines of the flat itself.

The covenant is one to repair, so what is the meaning of the word 'repair'? There is very little recent guidance to be found in the law relating to domestic lettings, but recourse can be had to the quite considerable body of judicial dicta arising out of covenants to repair in commercial lettings. In *Ravenseft Properties v Davstone (Holdings) Ltd* [1980] QB 12, [1979] 1 All ER 929 a distinction was made between the process of repair and a completely different process which is replacement. Replacement is a process of reconstruction so drastic that at the end of the lease the landlord receives back a wholly different property from that which he demised. 'Repair' on the other hand, according to the decision in *Greg v Planque* [1936] 1 KB 669, simply means making good defects, including renewal where necessary. In other words, simply keeping the property in a condition suitable for the purpose for which it was let. The distinction between these two processes is the scale and degree of the work involved. The fact that work, because of modern statutory requirements or building practices, has to be done to a higher standard than that of the original does not necessarily mean that it cannot be classed as 'repair'. Work will not be classifiable as 'repair' if it results in a reconstruction of the whole, or substantially the whole, of a building. The balance of authority indicates that where new walls resting on new foundations are required the work will be outside the meaning of the word 'repair'.

Thus if the landlord can show that the work required on any given house is so drastic that it would amount to his getting back, at the end of the term, a substantially different house from that which he let, then that work is outside his obligation to repair. This would seem to be so whether the condition of the property has arisen from either a want of maintenance or faulty design or construction. In *Pembery v Lamdin* [1940] 2 All ER 434 a landlord let certain old premises not constructed with a dampcourse or with waterproofing for the external walls, and covenanted to keep the external part of the let premises in good repair and condition. The tenant claimed that this put the landlord under an obligation to waterproof the outside walls and so render the premises dry. This would have required major construction work both inside and outside the premises. It was held that the obligation on the landlord was only to keep the premises in repair in the condition in which they were demised. In this case he would be required only to point the external brickwork. This, of course, limits the operation of the implied repairing covenant and again produces the paradox that the worse the condition of the property the less is the legal protection enjoyed by the tenant.

It is possible to come to exactly the same conclusion by a different argument, as was shown in *Newham London Borough v Patel* [1979] JPL 303. Here there was general agreement between the parties that Mr Patel's house was in a severely sub-standard condition. The local authority wished to move him to other accommodation and commenced possession proceedings which he resisted, and replied to with a counterclaim for breach of the implied covenant. The Court of Appeal needed little time to dispose of Mr Patel's argument. They looked to section 32(3) which, as we have seen, states that the standard of repair required by the covenant is to be determined by having regard to the 'age, character and prospective life of the dwelling-house and the locality in which it is situated'. Mr Patel's house was a poor, old dwelling in bad condition shortly destined for redevelopment. On this basis the court concluded that the prospective life of the dwelling affected the content of the section 32 duty. The local authority could not be required to carry out repairs which the court categorised as 'wholly useless'. The standard of repair thus required under section 32 is far from absolute and will vary according to the factors which the section says have to be taken into account. It would seem that only the stated factors can be considered. The result is that poor, old property, for example that acquired compulsorily and then used on a 'short life' basis, perhaps to accommodate otherwise homeless persons, is effectively outside the protection of the implied covenant.

Even if a tenant is able to prove that his landlord is in breach of the implied covenant it will not always be easy for him to quantify his loss as damages. The brief report of *Devereux v Liverpool City Council*, a county court decision, in [1978] LAG Bulletin 266 indicates that, where a house is in an apparently reasonable condition on the tenant's initial inspection, and on that basis the tenant takes it at the rent offered, but subsequently it turns out to be subject to defects within the scope of the implied covenant, then the tenant is entitled to damages. The fact that the initial rent offered was below market values because of housing subsidies does not mean that the damages must only be nominal. Furthermore the fact that a municipal landlord owns many houses and so has many calls on its resources is no defence to a claim under the implied covenant. But how are the damages to be quantified? Damages for injury to health or possessions are not too difficult to quantify, but what about those for the distress and inconvenience of having to live in a sub-standard house? In *Patel* £300 was claimed under these latter heads of damage. The Court of Appeal found no difficulty in rejecting this claim, partly because it had not been properly itemised in the counterclaim and argued before the county court, and partly because the local authority had charged a very low rent on the property in consequence of its poor condition. It was pointed out that a tenant cannot have the benefit of both a low rent and an award of damages for the poor condition of the property. It is thus possible for a local authority to resist a claim for damages arising out of disrepair if that disrepair is taken into account when the rent is fixed. If there is no reduction in rent then the claim must be properly itemised and the exact inconveniences, hardships and difficulties particularised and quantified at the commencement of the action. In any case in *Hewitt v Rowlands* (1924) 131 LT 757 it was held that the general rule for assessing the tenant's damages in respect of the landlord's breach of covenant to repair is to take the difference in value to the tenant, from the date when the landlord has notice of the breach, between the premises in repair and out of repair, and to add to this any damage to the tenant's property during that period caused by the landlord's default. The tenant cannot claim the cost of occupation of alternative premises as part of his damages even if the condition of his house is uninhabitable by reason of disrepair, see *Green v Eales* (1841) 2 QB 225, 11 LJQB 63.

It should be remembered that the onus of proof in relation to these matters is on the tenant, see: *Foster v Day* (1968) 208 Estates Gazette 495.

Of course a tenant is not entitled to treat his home in a cavalier and wilful fashion. It was made clear in *Warren v Keen* [1954] 1 QB 15, [1953] 2 All ER 1118 that a tenant is always under some sort of obligation to look after the property he inhabits. In the case of a long lease, say 99 years, the tenant is usually made subject to full repairing covenants which normally are:

1) to keep the premises in good repair both internally and externally;

2) to do certain specific works of repair at stated intervals;

3) to permit the landlord from time to time to enter and view the state of repair;

4) to make good any defects on notice given by the landlord, and

5) to deliver up the premises in good repair at the expiration of the term.

It should not be forgotten that a long residential leaseholder is in virtually the same beneficial position as a freeholder who would, of course, be responsible for the entire maintenance of his property. The aggregate liability under these covenants is really no different from that which falls on a freehold owner occupier.

On the other hand weekly tenants, and that includes the vast majority of municipal tenants, are usually only bound to use the premises in a tenant-like manner. This means taking proper care of the premises, for example cleaning chimneys and windows, replacing electric light bulbs, mending fuses, and unstopping blocked sinks. Neither does it seem from *Warren v Keen* that a weekly tenant can be liable under the doctrine of waste.

Subject to any legal prohibition, such as that forbidding contracting out of the section 32 implied covenant, implied obligations are always superseded by any express terms in the lease. It is still the case that the law leaves the form and content of municipal tenancy agreements very much to the discretion of individual authorities. In 1977 the Housing Services Advisory Group in their report *Tenancy Agreements* (Department of the Environment, 1977) argued that all municipal tenants should be given a summary tenancy agreement giving the details of the respective obligations of landlord and tenant in a brief form, and, as *a separate document*, a full agreement describing the rights, remedies and duties of the parties in detail, and also stating the way in which they should be interpreted and carried out. One of the proposed clauses of this 'full' agreement would have laid down specific times for the doing of various classes of repairs and maintenance by the landlord. This recommendation was not given full legal effect in the recent housing legislation.

Section 41 of the Housing Act 1980 requires local authority landlords to publish, within two years of the commencement of the Act (and thereafter to revise and republish) information, in simple terms, about its secure tenancies. This information must explain inter alia the effect of the implied covenant to repair under the Housing Act 1961. All secure tenants must be supplied with a copy of this information.

Before concluding this chapter three matters have to be mentioned. The first is to say that it was held in *Proudfoot v Hart* (1890) 25 QBD 42 that where a covenant is one '*to keep in repair*' this imports an initial obligation to put *into* repair, though the standard of repair will vary according to the age, character and locality of the property and the social class of the tenant. Second, something must be said about the remedy of specific performance in relation to repairing covenants. In many cases an award of damages will not be a sufficient remedy for a tenant whose home is in a state of disrepair. He will be more concerned to see the defective premises put into repair. It was thought the remedy of specific performance was not available to a tenant to enable him to force his landlord to perform his repairing obligations. In *Jeune v Queen's Cross Properties Ltd* [1974] Ch 97, [1973] 3 All ER 97 it was, however, held that the remedy was available. The law is now contained in section 125 of the Housing Act 1974 which provides:

'(1) In any proceedings in which a tenant of a dwelling alleges a breach on the part of his landlord of a repairing covenant relating to any part of the premises in which the dwelling is comprised, the court may, in its

discretion, order specific performance of that covenant, whether or not the breach relates to a part of the premises let to the tenant and notwithstanding any equitable rule restricting the scope of that remedy, whether on the basis of a lack of mutuality or otherwise.
(2) In this section . . .
repairing covenant means a covenant to repair, maintain, renew, construct, or replace any property . . .'.

This section came into force on 21 July 1974 and applies both to express and implied covenants, so long as the landlord has been given notice of the defect in question. The apparently wide wording of the section should not deceive the reader into believing that any tenant may apply for specific performance of repairing covenants relating to premises demised to other tenants of the same landlord where their dwellings are in the same building. The section is designed to enable tenants to claim specific performance not only of covenants relating to their dwellings, but also of those relating to the common parts of a building containing a number of dwellings. In *Francis v Cowcliffe Ltd* (1977) 33 P & CR 368 the plaintiff's flat on the third floor of a block owned by the defendants was served by a lift. This became inoperable with consequent inconvenience to the plaintiff. The defendants could not install a new life because they lacked the necessary finance. The provision of lift services was a specific provision of the plaintiff's lease and she applied for specific performance of it. It was held that she was entitled to a decree of specific performance despite the financial difficulties of the defendants, which were of their own making.

Where a covenant to repair relates to the structure of a flat specific performance is available and, it is submitted, would extend, as in *Campden Hill Towers*, to cover the supporting structure, etc., even where that is not comprised in the lease. It must be remembered that the remedy is discretionary. Thus it is unlikely, in the light of the decisions reached on section 6 of the Housing Act 1957 and section 32 of the Housing Act 1961, that a court would order specific performance of a repairing covenant in relation to a dwelling in an extreme state of disrepair with a foreseeably brief life.

Finally it should be noted that by virtue of section 80 of the Housing Act 1980 the implied covenant to repair contained in the Housing Act 1961, s. 32 does not apply to any lease granted after the commencement of the section, inter alia, *to* a local authority. Of course that authority will remain liable under the 1961 Act to persons to whom it sublets such property.

Further reading

Social Welfare Law (Ed. by D.W. Pollard) (Oyez) paras. A. 412 – A. 415 and B. 588 – B. 608

Hughes, D.J., 'The Saga of Campdem Hill Towers' (1979) NLJ 691

Reynolds, J.I., 'Statutory Covenants of Fitness and Repair' (1974) 37 MLR 377

Smith, P.F., 'Remedies of Tenant for Breach of Landlord's Covenant to Repair' (1980) 130 NLJ 330

Spencer, J.R., 'The Defective Premises Act 1972 — Defective Law and Defective Law Reform' (1974) 33 CLJ 307 and (1975) 34 CLJ 48

Wilkinson, H.W., 'The Lessons of Ravenseft' (1979) 129 NLJ 839

Chapter 8

The individual sub-standard house:
problems and remedies

The previous chapter dealt with the repairing obligations imposed by
the law on both public and private landlords. However, despite legislative attempts to create minimum standards of housing maintenance, the
problem of sub-standard accommodation is still with us. The English
House Condition Survey Part I, published in 1978 revealed that in
England alone in 1976 there were 794,000 dwellings unfit for human
habitation, or some 4.6 per cent of the stock of dwellings. Most of these
properties were built before 1919, and most were either owner occupied
or privately rented, though some 46,000 were owned by local
authorities. The same survey also revealed that the majority of these
houses could be dealt with on an individual basis, though some 44 per
cent of the total were situated in potential clearance areas. The survey
claimed that hardly any post war dwellings can be regarded as unfit for
human habitation, but the evidence of the media, of various pressure
groups and charities such as Shelter, and from independent commentators suggests that the legal standard of unfitness is far too lax
and that a great deal of poorly constructed housing has been erected
since 1945. Though this housing is, perhaps, just *within* the legal
standards, nevertheless it is the cause of considerable distress to its
occupants. As Mr P.J. Dixon, Chief Executive Officer of the North
Eastern Housing Association Ltd, and North Housing Ltd, said at the
1975 Royal Society of Health Congress at Eastbourne: 'The fight to
provide decent housing for every household in the land has been going
on for something like 80 years, and it is somewhat sobering to realise
that most of the worst housing of that period has been built during the
last twenty years — some of it very recently indeed'.

To deal with these sub-standard dwellings the law has developed a
number of different techniques. Area action, be it by way of clearance
or improvement, forms the subject matter of the following chapters: our
concern here is to examine the means available for dealing with
individual properties. Sadly, the law has never quite been able to decide
whether housing standards are primarily matters of construction and
stability or of health with the result that we have two 'codes' which can
both apply to housing, and which can occasionally conflict. Further-

more should any given property fall within the ambit of both codes compliance with the requirements of one will not necessarily satisfy the terms of the other. One of these codes is found in the Housing Act 1957, and the other in the Public Health Act 1936.

The requirements of the Housing Act 1957

In this portion of this chapter all references are, unless otherwise indicated, to the Housing Act 1957.

The standard of fitness

The object of this legislation is to eradicate unfit housing, and in this context the word 'house' (which is not actually defined in the Act) includes the yard, gardens and outhouses, etc., belonging to any house, and also any part of a building which is occupied or intended to be occupied as a separate dwelling: see section 189(1). Thus purpose-built dwelling-houses, flats and converted premises are covered. The standard of fitness is laid down in section 4 as amended by section 71 of the Housing Act 1969. By this provision a dwelling is unfit for human habitation only if it is so far defective in relation to certain listed particulars that its condition renders it unsuitable for reasonable occupation. The list of matters to which regard must be had in determining the issue of unfitness is: repair; stability; freedom from damp; internal arrangement; natural lighting; ventilation; water supply; drainage and sanitary conveniences, and the facilities for preparation and cooking of food and for the disposal of waste water. There is *no* legal requirement for a dwelling to have a bathroom, an inside lavatory, a hot water supply, or even an up-to-date system of electrical wiring. Nor does the ministerial guidance on 'unfitness' contained in Ministry of Housing and Local Government Circular No. 69/67 require particularly high standards for any dwelling to be classified as 'fit'. Disrepair in a dwelling must either prevent it functioning in the manner in which it was intended, or be a danger or serious inconvenience to the occupants before action can be taken. A mere lack of internal decoration is not enough, though a lack of exterior painting may lead to such serious disrepair of woodwork as to justify action. Likewise the Circular lays down that evidence of instability is only 'significant if it indicates the probability of further movement which would constitute a threat to the occupants of the house'. Dampness only justifies action where it amounts to a health hazard, and dampness caused by merely temporary condensation or by some small item of disrepair is not of itself a justification for unfitness proceedings.

The Circular does suggest that there must be sufficient natural lighting in all living rooms to enable domestic work to be done without artificial light, and that windows should be capable of being opened so that fresh air can circulate readily in the rooms. However, one tap regularly supplying wholesome water is all that the law requires, and it is also satisfied if the occupants of a dwelling have the exclusive use of a readily accessible water closet which is both properly lit and ventilated.

The duties of local authorities

It is for local housing authorities (district councils and London Boroughs) to decide whether any given house does or does not comply with the statutory standard, though in *Hall v Manchester Corpn* (1915) 84 LJ Ch 732, it was stated that in coming to such a decision they must act in a judicial spirit. Further guidance was given by Atkin LJ in *Morgan v Liverpool Corpn* [1927] 2 KB 131 at 145 where he said the test was: 'If the state of repair of a house is such that by ordinary user damage may naturally be caused to the occupier, either in respect of personal injury to life or limb or injury to health, then the house is not in all respects reasonably fit for human habitation'. By applying that test the House of Lords concluded in *Summers v Salford Corpn* [1943] AC 283, [1943] 1 All ER 68 that a defective sash cord may, in proper circumstances, be enough to render a house unfit. Here the jamming of a bedroom window so that it could 'not be moved without danger so impaired the ventilation of a bedroom that it constituted an unacceptable interference with ordinary reasonable use.

However, it is obvious that before a local authority can come to any decision as to fitness they must know of the existence of the property in question. Section 70 of the Housing Act 1969 states: 'It shall be the duty of every local authority . . . to cause an inspection of their district to be made from time to time with a view to determining what action to take in the performance of their functions under Part II or III of the [Housing Act 1957] . . .'. Thus local authorities are under a duty to carry out a periodical review of the housing conditions in their areas to discover, inter alia, whether there are any unfit houses. The language of this section is mandatory and so a local authority who refused to carry out a period of review might find themselves subject to an order of mandamus. However, a more effective way of bringing the facts in relation to any given house before the local authority exists in section 157(2) of the Housing Act 1957. This reads, as amended:

'If any Justice of the Peace having jurisdiction in any part of the area of a local authority . . . complains to the medical officer of health in writing that any house is unfit for human habitation . . . it shall be his duty forthwith to inspect that house . . . and to make a report to the local authority, stating the facts of the case and whether, in his opinion, the house is unfit for human habitation . . .'.

Thus it is a condition precedent to any form of action by a private citizen under the provision to gain the ear of a sympathetic local magistrate. The procedure is also complicated by virtue of section 112 of the Local Government Act 1972 which no longer requires local authorities to appoint medical officers of health. However, complaints under the 1957 provision should be addressed via the district community physician, a health service employee, or, by virtue of Schedule 29, paragraph 4(a) to the Local Government Act 1972, to that officer of the local authority appointed for the proper discharge of its housing functions.

Once a local authority possess information either from a review of their area, or from their officers following complaints from the local justices, or indeed from any other source, they come under a duty to consider it. This consideration of the information activates the specific duties laid on them in respect of unfit housing.

The duty where the house can be made fit at reasonable expense

The duty contained in section 9(1) relates to those houses capable of being made fit at reasonable expense. It reads:

'Where a local authority upon consideration of an official representation, or a report from any of their officers, or any other information in their possession, are satisfied that any house is unfit for human habitation, they shall, unless they are satisfied that it is not capable at a reasonable expense of being rendered so fit, serve upon the person having control of the house a notice

  (a) requiring him within such reasonable time, not being less than twenty days, as may be specified in the notice, to execute the works specified in the notice, and

  (b) stating that, in the opinion of the authority, these works will render the house fit for human habitation'.

Thus if the authority possess information about a house and consideration of this leads them to conclude that it is presently unfit but could be made fit at reasonable expense then they are under a duty to proceed according to section 9(1). The notice, usually known as a 'repair notice', has to be served on the person 'having control of the house' who is defined by section 39(2) as 'the person who receives the rack rent', and a rack rent is any rent which is *not* less than two-thirds of the net annual value of the house. This rent, according to *Rawlence v Croydon Corpn*

[1952] 2 QB 803, [1952] 2 All ER 535, is now effectively the maximum rent recoverable at law; for example a 'fair rent' fixed under the Rent Acts. An estate agent who collects rents on behalf of a landlord would be the relevant person within this definition. In addition section 9(2) gives the local authority a discretion to serve copies of the notice on any other person having an interest in the house, which clearly covers tenants and mortgagees, etc. The repair notice can be challenged under section 11(1)(a) in the county court within 21 days of service by 'any person aggrieved', a character of notoriously indeterminate legal identity, but here presumably meaning any person whose legal interests in the house in question are affected by the notice. Section 11(3) further allows the judge at that hearing to confirm, quash or vary the notice as he thinks fit, though if he does allow an appeal against a repair notice he must, at the local authority's request, actually make a finding as to whether the house can or cannot be rendered fit at reasonable expense. Section 12 gives power to local authorities to buy, either by agreement or compulsorily, any house found on appeal to the court not to be capable of repair at reasonable cost, but only where: 'the judge in allowing the appeal has found that the house cannot be rendered fit for human habitation at reasonable expense'. Should the Local Authority proceed by way of compulsory purchase they must submit their order to the Secretary of State for the Environment within six months of the determination of the appeal, and he cannot confirm it if the owner or a mortgagee, if any, gives a satisfactory undertaking to carry out the works specified in the repair notice. However, on confirmation of the order the local authority may proceed to acquire the house paying the owner its cleared site value. They must then execute all the works specified in the notice and thereafter the house may enter their normal stock of dwellings.

Should the repair notice be ignored the authority *may* themselves carry out the specified works (once it has expired) under section 10(1). They may recover their necessary costs from the person having control of the house either summarily as a civil debt or in instalments: see section 10(3) and (5). Furthermore under section 10(7) they may register their costs as a charge on the property in the Local Land Charges Register. A person aggrieved by the service of a demand for the recovery of such expenses may appeal to the county court under section 11(1)(b). In *Elliott v Brighton Borough Council* [1979] 9 CLY 1384 (Brighton County Court) the appellants were the freehold owners of a large early-Victorian terraced property. In February 1978 the council, being satisfied that the tenanted basement flat at the premises was unfit for human habitation, served a notice on the appellants under section 9(1) requiring them to execute works recited in the schedule to the notice. The appellants did not carry out the works within the time limit and in October the Council instructed a building contractor to execute the works in default. A demand for the recovery of expenses incurred was rendered to the appellants in December; the appellants then appealed under section 11(1)(b). The grounds of appeal included, inter alia, that the respondent had a discretion under section 10(1) as to whether or not they should themselves do the work required to be done by the notice and that this discretion had not been exercised properly. The council argued that the word 'may' in section 10(1) conferred an enabling power which the local authority were bound to exercise as their power was coupled with a duty under section 9(1). Consequently the council had no discretion in the matter and were not obliged to consult further before undertaking the default works. It was held: (1) on appeal under section 11(1)(a), the court in considering the validity and reasonableness of a notice served under section 9(1), has jurisdiction to consider all relevant surrounding circumstances including, for example, the personal circumstances of the owner or the person having control of the premises. On the other hand, on an appeal under section 11(1)(b), the court cannot consider such matters; (2) the word 'may' in section 10(1) does not confer a discretion which must be exercised: it is an enabling provision giving an absolute discretion. The council was therefore not subject to a duty to investigate further or to consult with the recipient of the statutory notice. The council was under a duty to ensure that a house unfit for human habitation was rendered fit.

The duty where the house cannot be made fit at reasonable expense

The principal provision here is section 16 which reads:

'(1) Where a local authority, on consideration of an official representation, or a report from any of their officers, or other information in their possession, are satisfied that any house

(a) is unfit for human habitation, and

(b) is not capable at a reasonable expense of being rendered so fit, they shall serve upon the person having control of the house, upon any other person who is an owner thereof, and, so far as it is reasonably practicable to ascertain such persons, upon every mortgagee thereof, notice of the time (being some time not less than 21 days after the service of the notice) and place at which the condition of the house and any offer with respect to the carrying out of works, or the future user of the house, which he may wish to submit will be considered by them'.

Thus a 'time and place' notice calls together the local authority and the persons interested in the house to discuss its future. Section 16(3) allows any person served with such a notice to make an offer to the local authority to carry out works on the house. These proposed works together with any other proposals or undertakings as to the future of the house will then be considered at the meeting convened by the notice. For example: an owner may undertake that he will cease to use the property as a dwelling-house, and if this is accepted by the local authority any tenants will, by virtue of section 16(5), lose any Rent Act protection they may have.

An undertaking may take many other forms, such as a proposal to convert two unfit houses into one fit one, as in *Johnson v Leicester Corpn* [1934] 1 KB 638, or to spend a very large sum of money on a house to bring it up to standard as in *Stidworthy and Stidworthy v Brixham UDC* (1935) 2 LJCCR 41. No matter what proposals are put forward at the meeting, by virtue of section 16(2), every person on whom a 'time and place' notice has been served is entitled to be heard, and it was held in *Broadbent v Rotherham Corpn* [1917] 2 Ch 31 that such persons must be given a fair and adequate chance to air their views, for example, furnishing specifications of proposed works. If an undertaking is accepted that premises will not be used as a dwelling-house under section 16(4) then they may become dangerous if they are not made secure against children or vandals, etc. Section 8(1) of the Local Government (Miscellaneous Provisions) Act 1976 enables a local authority to do such works as they think fit to keep out unauthorised persons and/or to prevent the premises from being a danger to public health. Such action can be taken rapidly as the authority can proceed after giving not less than 48 hours' notice to the owner. The need for such a power is illustrated by the situation that arose in *Harris v Birkenhead Corpn* [1976] 1 All ER 341, [1976] 1 WLR 279, CA. Here a local authority made a compulsory purchase order in pursuance of their slum clearance powers in consequence of which an area of houses became vacant and vandalised. An infant wandered into one of the houses and was injured as a result of its condition. It was held that the local authority were the occupiers of the property and were liable for breach of duty to the plaintiff under the rule in *British Railways Board v Herrington* [1972] AC 877, [1972] 1 All ER 749. A prudent local authority should use their powers to protect the children and other residents in their area against such injury.

A local authority are under no obligation to accept any offer made. If they do not accept an undertaking they have a number of alternatives one of which they must choose. Normally they will make a demolition order. Section 19 requires them to serve a copy of this order on every person on whom a 'time and place' notice was served. The order *must* require the premises to be vacated within a specified period, not being less than 28 days from the date on which the order becomes operative. *R v Epsom and Ewell Corpn, ex parte R.B. Property Investments (Eastern)* [1964] 2 All ER 832, [1964] 1 WLR 1060 states that it is mandatory under section 22(1) that the occupier of the house must be informed of the effect of the order and the date by which it requires the building to be vacated. He must be required to quit the building before that date, or before the expiration of 28 days from the service of the notice, whichever is the later. A demolition order removes any Rent Act protection enjoyed by tenants. It is also an offence under section 22(4) for anyone knowingly to occupy or to allow occupation of any premises subject to such an order. Summary conviction leads to a fine of up to £20 and a further £5 a day for every day the offence continues after conviction. The demolition order must also under section 21(b) require the premises to be demolished within six weeks of the expiration of the period allowed for vacation, or from the actual date of vacation, which-ever is the later. The local authority may extend this period either under section 21(b), or under section 24 (as amended by section 25 of the Housing Act 1961) where an owner puts forward proposals to improve and/or reconstruct the house so as to provide one or more fit houses. Such extensions may not be for unreasonable lengths of time, and a seven year extension was held unreasonable in *Pocklington v Melksham UDC* [1964] 2 QB 673, [1964] 2 All ER 862. If there is a failure to comply with a demolition order the local authority are empowered by section 23 to carry out the demolition themselves and to recover their outstanding expenses as a simple contract debt in the local county court from the owner. A person aggrieved by the making of a demolition order may appeal against it to the county court. Appeals will be considered more fully below.

Other powers for dealing with houses which cannot be made fit

Demolition may not be a suitable way of dealing with an unfit house which may, for example, be necessary for the support of other houses, or which may have special historical or architectural importance. In such a case the local authority may decide to serve a closing order. The general power to make closing orders is contained in section 17(1) and (3) and is limited to situations where:

1) The authority consider it inexpedient to make a demolition order having regard to the effect of the demolition of that house upon any other house or building, or

2) the house has been listed, or has been stated to be of historic or architectural interest by the minister. Indeed in this latter situation the *only* order that can be made is a closing order; though in the *former* situation the authority *may* subsequently change their minds and make a demolition order by virtue of section 28. Further provision with respect to such orders is to be found in section 27 which permits the

local authority to allow the premises to be used for purposes other than as a dwelling-house, and they are not permitted under section 27(1) to withhold their approval unreasonably to such other uses. It is a fineable offence to use the premises knowingly for any purpose other than one approved by the local authority. Under section 27(5) the making of a closing order takes away any Rent Act security of tenure enjoyed by tenants. Closing orders may also be made by virtue of section 18 in respect of parts of buildings actually used or suitable for use as dwellings and any underground room which is unfit for human habitation. (Such 'underground rooms' are unfit if their floor surfaces are more than three feet below the adjacent ground surface level, and the average height of the room is not at least seven feet, or the room fails to comply with other local regulations.) In general the procedure for the making of a closing order is similar to that for making a demolition order and there are the same rights of appeal to the county court under section 20.

Another choice is allowed by section 17(2): 'Where a local authority would under the foregoing sub-section be required to make a demolition or closing order in respect of a house they may, if it appears to them that the house is or can be rendered capable of providing accommodation which is adequate for the time being, purchase the house instead of making a demolition or closing order'. This provision only applies to properties that can be 'patched up' to provide temporary shelter on a very short term basis. It was held in *Victoria Square Property Co Ltd v Southwark London Borough Council* [1978] 2 All ER 281, [1978] 1 WLR 463 that this does not permit an authority to acquire old, unfit houses with a view to bringing them up to standard so that they can be added to the normal municipal housing stock. Before the power to purchase can be used a copy of the determination to purchase must, by virtue of section 19(b), be served on all persons on whom a 'time and place' notice was served. This again activates the rights of appeal given by section 20. However, in most cases the local authority will be able to proceed to purchase according to section 29 either by agreement, or, with ministerial approval, compulsorily. If a compulsory purchase is made then the compensation to be paid according to section 29(2) is: 'the value, at the time when the valuation is made, of the site as a cleared site available for development in accordance with the requirements of the building byelaws [or building regulations]'. It should be remembered that the cleared site value may be greater than that of the land encumbered with an unfit house and in such cases the Second Schedule to the Land Compensation Act 1961 provides that the amount of compensation payable is not to exceed the value of the site *plus* the house. This problem is considered at greater length in Chapter 9, below, in relation to clearance procedures.

The appeals procedure

Mention has been made of the procedure available under section 20, which provides:

'(1) Any person aggrieved by —
    (a) a demolition or closing order made under this Part of this Act, or
    (b) a notice of the determination of a local authority to purchase a house served under the last foregoing section,

may, within 21 days after the date of the service of the order or notice, appeal to the county court within the jurisdiction of which the premises to which the order or notices relates are situate, and no proceedings shall be taken by the local authority to enforce any order or notice in relation to which an appeal is brought before the appeal has been finally determined.

(3) On appeal to the county court . . . the judge may make such order either confirming or quashing or varying the order or notice as he thinks fit, and may, if he thinks fit accept from an appellant any such undertaking as might have been accepted by the local authority, and any undertaking so accepted by the judge shall have the like effect as if it had been given to and accepted by the local authority . . .'.

It should, however, be noted that section 20(2) excludes from the definition of 'person aggrieved' any person 'who is in occupation of the premises . . . under a lease or agreement of which the unexpired term does not exceed three years'. Statutory tenants are also probably excluded. Thus in the case of a small dwelling-house only the landlord will normally be able to appeal. Such an appeal, according to *Fletcher v Ilkeston Corpn* (1931) 96 JP 7, may be either or both on questions of law or fact. From the county court an appeal lies to the Court of Appeal. In *Victoria Square Property Co Ltd v Southwark London Borough Council* [1978] 2 All ER 281, [1978] 1 WLR 463 the Court of Appeal made it clear that they will only upset the decision of the county court if it can be shown to be wrong in point of law, or if irrelevant considerations have been taken into account, or the relevant ones left unconsidered, or if the decision is totally unreasonable. The considerations which should be considered would seem to include: (i) any need to prevent a loss of residential accommodation in an area; (ii) the desire of a local authority to secure accommodation for persons on their housing waiting list; (iii) the need to prevent over great strain on the general rate fund consequent on the purchase of too much old property, and (iv) the financial implications for the land owner of any decision made. Not all of these considerations will be of equal weight in any given case, and where an owner has deliberately allowed his house to go to rack and ruin the financial implications of subjecting him to a forced sale at site value only may be almost discounted. A prudent local authority should also bear these factors in mind when they are considering any undertaking put forward under section 16(4).

Subject to this appeal procedure once a demolition or closing order or notice has become operative (which is according to section 37 on the expiration of 21 days from its service) no further proceedings can be taken as to any of the matters which could have been raised on an appeal. Professor Garner has, however, argued in *Slum Clearance and Compensation* pp. 28 to 30, that this would not prevent the High Court from issuing an order of certiorari to quash a demolition or closing order if there has been an error of law on the face of the record or some other ultra vires act by the local authority, such as a breach of the rules of natural justice or some improper motive on the part of the members of the authority.

Well-maintained payments

Following the service of a demolition order or of a notice of determination to purchase a house 'any person' has a three month period under section 30(1) to make representations to the authority that the house has been well maintained as a result of work wholly or partly carried out by him or at his expense. Any 'well-maintained payment' made to such a person in consequence of his application is now calculated by reference to Schedule 2, Part 1 to the 1957 Act as substituted by section 66 of and Schedule 4 to the Housing Act 1969 and amended by the Housing (Payment for Well-Maintained Houses) Order 1973 (S.I. 1973 No. 753). The amount may be as much as $3\frac{1}{8}$ times the rateable value of the house, but it may not exceed the amount by which the full market value exceeds the site value, which may lead to a nil payment as the cleared site value may be quite substantial. Thus if the full market value of a house is £1,000, its cleared site value is £500 and its rateable value is £50 *per annum*, then the difference between cleared site and full value is £500, and £50 $\times$ $3\frac{1}{8}$ = £156.25, and that will be the amount of the well-maintained payment. But if the full value is £900 and the cleared site value is £800 so that their difference is only £100 and the property is still rated as being worth £50 per annum, then the maximum amount payable by way of a well-maintained payment will be only £100, for that payment cannot exceed the difference in price between the two stated values for the property.

The mandatory character of the requirements of the legislation

It should now be quite obvious that a local authority faced with evidence of unfitness in respect of an individual house have a number of possible courses of action open to them. What is, however, beyond question is that possession of such evidence activates their statutory duties, and that they come under an obligation to take action. This follows from the decision of the Court of Appeal in *R v Kerrier District Council ex parte Guppy's (Bridport) Ltd* (1976) 32 P & CR 411 that the word 'shall', which occurs in both sections 9 and 16, is imperative. But which duty are the authority to fulfil, that based on repair under section 9 or that based on demolition under section 16? The answer will depend upon whether the house is capable of being made fit at 'reasonable expense', and it is to the definition of this term that we must now turn.

The question falls to be decided according to section 39(1) which provides:

'In determining for the purposes of this Part of this Act whether a house can be rendered fit for human habitation at a reasonable expense, regard shall be had to the estimated cost of the works necessary to render it so fit and the value which it is estimated that the house will have when the works are completed'.

The sub-section therefore requires that those two factors must be considered. But this leaves many questions unanswered such as: are these the only factors to be taken into account, and what is the meaning of the word 'value'? For many years the approach adopted was that suggested by Denning LJ in *Bacon v Grimsby Corpn* [1950] 1 KB 272, [1949] 2 All ER 875 which was simply to ask 'is the house worth the cost of the repairs?' Subsequent litigation has given us rather more detailed tests to apply, though sadly the principles laid down have not been entirely consistent. To take the provisions of the sub-section in order:

a) 'the estimated cost of the works necessary to render it so fit' was considered in *Ellis Copp & Co v Richmond-upon-Thames London Borough Council* (1976) 245 Estates Gazette 931 and would seem to include both the cost of necessary structural works and the cost of making good the decoration of the house after the doing of those works, and

b) 'the value which it is estimated that the house will have' has been considered in *Inworth Property v Southwark London Borough Council* (1977) 34 P & CR 186, and said to mean the open market value.

The problem with this latter definition is whether the presence of a sitting tenant, if any, is to be taken into account. In this context the decision of the Court of Appeal in *Dudlow Estates Ltd v Sefton*

Metropolitan Borough Council (1978) 249 Estates Gazette 1271 is helpful. The test which it seems should be applied is that of a 'willing buyer and a willing seller'. In other words, the assessment of 'open market value' must be based on a consideration of all the facts and future possibilities about the house, including those about a sitting tenant having Rent Act protection. A greater likelihood of obtaining vacant possession at an early date will increase the value of the property, though it will not probably increase the valuation to the level it would be on a purely vacant possession basis.

Provided these factors are taken into account there is no obligation to consider any others. Nor, apparently, according to Browne LJ in the *Dudlow Estates* case, is there any need under section 39 for a county court judge to set out specific mathematical calculations in his judgement. There are other factors which *may* properly from time to time be considered. There include matters such as the cost of demolition and the present unrepaired value of the property. In any given case, however, the first task is to calculate the cost of the necessary repairs and then to compare these with the estimated repaired value of the house. This value will itself depend on a sliding scale measurement linked to the likelihood of the owner being able to obtain vacant possession. It follows that where the estimated cost of repairs is high and the house in question is occupied by a tenant enjoying Rent Act protection, and who shows no early desire of vacating the property, that the question whether the expense is 'reasonable' is likely to be answered in the negative, and so the property will fall to be dealt with according to section 16 of the 1957 Act.

Supplementary powers to prevent houses becoming unfit

In this context it is worth remembering that the 1976 English House Condition Survey found that of the 447,000 individual unfit dwellings comprised in the report some 28 per cent required repairs costing over £4,000 and a further 35 per cent required expenditure of between £2,000 and £4,000 per dwelling, and that was at 1976 prices. Obviously there is a danger that an unscrupulous landlord will let his houses run to rack and ruin so that they are incapable of repair at reasonable expense in the hope that the local authority will take action to demolish them. He will then be freed of his tenants and left with valuable cleared sites. The need to prevent such situations was faced by the legislature when it enacted section 9(1A) which was inserted by section 72 of the Housing Act 1969. It provides:

'Where a local authority, upon consideration of an official representation, or a report from any of their officers or other information in their possession, are satisfied that a house is in such a state of disrepair that, although it is not unfit for human habitation, substantial repairs are required to bring it up to a reasonable standard, having regard to its age, character and locality, they may serve upon the person having control of the house a notice requiring him, within such reasonable time, not being less than 21 days, as may be specified in the notice to execute the works specified in the notice, not being works of internal decorative repair'.

It must be noted that this provision grants only a power to local authorities, it does not put them under any duty to act, though the information upon which they may act can come from the usual wide variety of sources. Next it must be remembered that the provision applies to houses that are *in danger of becoming unfit* through disrepair and that there is no power to require the doing of works of mere internal decoration. The power also applies only in those cases where *substantial* repairs are required, and 'substantial' probably means 'large items of repair, or a considerable collection of smaller items'. Finally in the exercise of their power the local authority must have regard to the 'age, character and locality' of the house when deciding what works are necessary to bring it up to a reasonable standard. The nature of this provision was considered in *Hillbank Properties Ltd v Hackney London Borough Council, Talisman Properties Ltd v The Same* [1978] 3 All ER 343, [1978] 3 WLR 260, litigation involving 'one house' property companies, which gives some guidance as to the meaning of 'age, character and locality'. The Court of Appeal in the *Hillbank Properties* case seem to have held that the considerations imported by the phrase 'age, character and locality' include those mentioned by section 39(1), i.e. the estimated cost of the works and the estimated value of the house made fit. The question to be asked under section 9(1A) is basically the same as that to be asked under section 39(1): 'is the house worth the cost of repairs?' In determining this question the presence of a sitting tenant cannot be ignored, but in this present case rather more consideration was given to the vacant possession value as, according to Lord Denning at p. 268 of the report: 'It seems to me that the policy of Parliament was to make the owners of houses keep them in proper repair. Not only so as to keep up the stock of houses but also to see that protected tenants should be able to have their houses properly kept up. It would be deplorable if there were no means of compelling owners of old houses keeping them in repair: or if the owners could let them fall into disrepair — as a means of evicting the tenants. Of course if the state of a house is so bad that it should be condemned — whoever was occupying it — then let it be demolished or closed or purchased. But if it is worth repairing, then it should be repaired, no matter whether it is occupied by a protected or an unprotected tenant'.

Furthermore if there is an appeal against a section 9(1A) notice under section 11 then the county court judge may take into account the resources of the owner available to pay for the repairs. In this respect much more can be demanded of a property company, whose 'corporate veil' may be torn so as to reveal the real strength of the finances behind it, than of a poor widow. The *Hillbank* case states that there is no need for local authorities to take this wider range of factors into account when they are taking the administrative decision to issue a section 9(1A) notice. All they need to consider is the information they have and then they must be satisfied as to the need for substantial repairs, taking into account the age, character and locality of the property. However, it is submitted that the prudent local authority should pay at least some heed to the other considerations that might arise on an appeal such as the character of the landowner and his past action or inaction in relation to the house in question. It is quite proper for a local authority to serve a section 9(1A) notice where they suspect a property owner of allowing disrepair with a view to reaping an unearned reward from the application of the unfitness provisions. Section 9(1A) is not to be used as a charter for the worst sort of slum landlord.

Section 149 of the Housing Act 1980 further amends section 9 of the 1957 Act by inserting two further sub-sections. Section 9(1B) provides that where a local authority are satisfied, following representations made by an occupying tenant, that a house is in such a state of disrepair that, although it is *not* unfit for human habitation, its condition is such as to interfere materially with the personal comfort of the occupying tenant, they may serve on the person having control a notice requiring the doing of specified works, other than those of internal decorative repair, within a specified reasonable time. Section 9(1C) defines 'occupying tenant' by reference to section 104 of the Housing Act 1974. This defines such a person as someone who is *not* an owner-occupier, but who occupies, or is entitled to occupy, the dwelling as a lessee, or statutory tenant, or as a party to a restricted contract, or in pursuance of agricultural employment.

This new provision will give tenants the right to complain to the local authority in those cases where their homes are falling into disrepair serious enough to be a substantial interference with their comfort. The local authority are, however, under no duty to take action in response to such complaints. Should they take action the same considerations will apply to section 9(1B) and (1C) as apply under section 9(1A). This provision was inserted to overcome the effects of the decision in *National Coal Board v Neath Borough Council* [1976] 2 All ER 478 (see below). Any proceedings in respect of a house that is a source of substantial discomfort to its occupying tenant, but which is not unfit or otherwise a statutory nuisance, should in future be brought under these new powers.

The requirements of the Public Health Act 1936

In this portion of the chapter all section references are, unless otherwise indicated, to the Public Health Act 1936

The definition of 'statutory nuisance'

The general object of this legislation is the protection of the public health and Part III of the Act is specifically designed to do this by the eradication of certain 'statutory nuisances'. By virtue of section 92(1)(a) a dwelling-house may be such a statutory nuisance as the law provides: 'Without prejudice to the exercise by a local authority of any other powers vested in them by or under this Act, the following matters may, subject to the provisions of this Part of this Act be dealt with summarily, and are in this Part of this Act referred to as "statutory nuisances", that is to say: — (a) any premises in such a state as to be prejudicial to health or a nuisance . . .'. 'Premises' are defined by section 343 to include messuages, buildings, lands, and easements.

It is thus clear that a dwelling-house can be a statutory nuisance if it is 'prejudicial to health', a term which is itself defined in section 343(1) as 'injurious, or likely to cause injury to health'. 'Health' itself is not statutorily defined. In *Coventry City Council v Cartwright* [1975] 2 All ER 99, [1975] 1 WLR 845, a case arising out of an alleged nuisance caused by the dumping of rubbish, the Divisional Court gave some consideration to whether mental health could be within the protection of the law but reached no concluded opinion on this point. It can be argued that a breakdown in mental health can be caused as a result of a person having to live in a sub-standard house. However, judicial opinion seems to disagree, and to hold that conditions that are 'prejudicial to health' are those which are likely to cause physical illness or disease or to result in an infestation by vermin.

If premises are to be shown to be a statutory nuisance their condition *as a whole* must be so serious that in consequence they are a real risk to health or are a nuisance; a mere lack of internal decorative repair is not enough: see *Springett v Harold* [1954] 1 All ER 568, [1954] 1 WLR 521. Nor is any matter which merely affects the *comfort* of the occupants, even if it amounts to an act of harassment. The decision in *Betts v Penge UDC* [1942] 2 KB 154, [1942] 2 All ER 61 which held otherwise was said to be wrongly decided by the House of Lords in *Salford City Council v McNally* [1976] AC 379, [1975] 2 All ER 860. It may be enough for conditions to be 'prejudicial to health' if they are such as to cause a person who is already ill to become worse: see the judgment of Kelly CB in *Malton Board of Health v Malton Manure Co* (1879) 4 ExD 302 at 305.

Premises may also come within the statutory definition if they are 'a nuisance'. Does this mean that any common law nuisance is also *ipso facto* a statutory nuisance? The answer is partly 'yes'. For a complainant to prove an allegation based on the 'or a nuisance' limb of the definition he must show that the act or default complained of is either a public or private nuisance, i.e. something causing deleterious affectation to a class of Her Majesty's subjects, *or* a substantial interference with land (or the use and enjoyment thereof) arising outside that land and then proceeding to affect it. So much is clear from the decision in *National Coal Board v Neath Borough Council* [1976] 2 All ER 478 where there were merely minor disrepairs affecting the comfort of the occupiers. However, there is a judicial tradition stretching back to *Malton Board of Health v Malton Manure Co* (1879) 4 ExD 302, *Great Western Rly Co v Bishop* (1872) LR 7 QB 550, and *Bishop Auckland Local Board v Bishop Auckland Iron Co* (1882) 10 QBD 138, that situations contemplated as falling within the 'or a nuisance' limb of the definition must have some relation to health. That relation to health is still a requirement of the law. Thus in a case where it is alleged that premises are 'prejudicial to health' it will not matter that only the occupier is affected by the acts, defaults or state of affairs complained of. Where on the other hand it is alleged that the premises are 'a nuisance' the act or default, etc., *must affect persons other than the occupier of the premises.* Furthermore in this latter situation the informant must be able to prove that the nuisance is one that in some way affects or has relevance to his health. It must also be remembered that *R v Newham East Justices, ex parte Hunt* and *R v Oxted Justices, ex parte Franklin* [1976] 1 All ER 839, [1976] 1 WLR 420 established that proceedings brought in respect of a statutory nuisance are criminal in nature and thus the burden of proof on any informant will be correspondingly high.

The procedures for taking action in respect of a statutory nuisance

Both local authorities and private individuals are empowered to take action in respect of statutory nuisances. It will be convenient to consider the powers and duties of local authorities first.

Section 91 places a general duty on local authorities (effectively the district councils and London Boroughs) to inspect their districts to detect statutory nuisances. Sections 93 to 98 thereafter lay down the procedure which a local authority has to follow in the abatement of statutory nuisances, and it would seem from *Cocker v Cardwell* (1869) LR 5 QB 15 that this procedure is mandatory once a local authority decide to act. Where an authority are satisfied of the existence of a statutory nuisance the Act says they 'shall serve' an abatement notice on the person responsible requiring the abatement of the nuisance, and, according to *Bristol Corpn v Sinnott* [1918] 1 Ch 62, giving him a specified reasonable time in which to comply with the notice. However, it was said in *Nottingham Corpn v Newton* [1974] 2 All ER 760, [1974] 1 WLR 923, the first case where a local authority was successfully prosecuted in respect of unfit property also constituting a statutory nuisance, by Lord Widgery CJ that 'shall' in section 93 is not mandatory. Where a local authority have a choice of remedies between the Public Health Act 1936 and the Housing Act 1957 the courts will not order them to use the former in preference to the latter, though as will subsequently be shown the converse is not necessarily so!

The abatement notice is to be served on the person by whose act, default or sufferance the nuisance arises or continues, or, if he cannot be found, the owner or occupier of the premises concerned, provided that where the nuisance arises from any structural defect the notice is to be served on the owner of the premises. In this context section 343(1) defines the owner as the person who receives the rack rent of the property either on his own account or as an agent or trustee, or who would receive it if the premises were let at a rack rent. Should the abatement notice be disregarded section 94(1) (as amended by section 42 of the Magistrates' Courts Act 1952) enables the local authority to lay an information before a justice of the peace who thereupon must summon the defaulter to appear before the magistrates. The *Newton* case again indicates that the local authority have a discretion whether to proceed under this provision. If at the hearing before the court it is proved that the alleged nuisance still exists, or although abated, it is likely to recur then section 94(2) directs that the court 'shall' make a nuisance order. This order may require the defendant to comply with all or any of the requirements of the abatement notice, or otherwise to abate the nuisance within a time to be specified in the order, and to execute any works necessary for these purposes, and/or prohibit a recurrence of the nuisance and require the defendant to execute, within a specified time, any works necessary to prevent a recurrence. In this context the *Newton* case states clearly that the justices *must* issue a nuisance order if the existence or future recurrence of the nuisance is proved. But, as is clear from the words of the Statute, they have a very considerable discretion as to the *terms* of the order. When deciding the terms of the order the justices should consider all the circumstances of the case including the possible gravity of the danger to the health of the occupants and the imminence of demolition. They may quite properly require work to be done in phases, allowing for absolutely necessary jobs to be done first, while other tasks can be left till later, perhaps to be rendered unnecessary by demolition and thus saving expense.

A recent decision illustrates the ambit of the justices' discretion. In *Lambeth London Borough Council v Stubbs* (1980) *Times*, 14 May, the local authority owned an old house the tenants of which were Mr and

Mrs Stubbs. The condition of the house constituted a statutory nuisance which was admitted by the council before the justices in proceedings commenced against them by the tenants. The justices refused to adjourn the hearing so that the authority could obtain vacant possession, and instead made a nuisance order requiring the remedying of the most serious defects within 21 days of the vacation of the premises and of the others in 42 days. Shortly thereafter Mr and Mrs Stubbs were rehoused and the house was simply left vacant until it was demolished. The question for the court was whether the action of the council in securing vacant possession was sufficient abatement to comply with the nuisance order. It was held that it was not. Where a house is prejudicial to health simply to move the present occupiers out does not cure the problem, for if other occupiers should move in at a future date their health will then be imperilled. Therefore where the justices make a nuisance order requiring the doing of remedial work, that work must be done; moving the sitting tenant is not enough. Of course where the local authority intend to demolish the property in question within a very short time the court should take that into account when drawing up the order. In such circumstances the local authority should ask the justices to exercise their discretion under section 94(2), to be examined below, to order that the house shall not be used for human habitation. Such an order will remove the need for great expenditure.

In these section 94 proceedings the justices may also fine the defendant up to £200 by virtue of section 99 of and Schedule 2, paragraph 11 to the Control of Pollution Act 1974. Section 94(2) also states:

'Where a nuisance proved to exist is such as to render a building, in the opinion of the court, unfit for human habitation, the nuisance order may prohibit the use of the building for that purpose until a court of summary jurisdiction, being satisfied that it has been rendered fit for human habitation withdraws the prohibition'.

'Unfit for human habitation' in this context does *not* bear its Housing Act meaning, nor is a person displaced from his house as a result of such a prohibition within the rehousing obligations of section 39 of the Land Compensation Act 1973, though he might fall to be dealt with under section 1(2)(a) of the Housing (Homeless Persons) Act 1977, as having accommodation to which he cannot secure entry. It should also be noted that by virtue of section 94(6) the nuisance order may be addressed to the local authority 'if it appears to the court that the person by whose act or default the nuisance arises, or the owner or occupier of the premises cannot be found'.

Once the nuisance order is issued the penalty for knowingly contravening it, or for failing without reasonable excuse to comply with its term is, under section 95(1) as amended by section 99 of and Schedule

2, paragraph 12 to the Control of Pollution Act 1974, a fine not exceeding £400 and a further fine of up to £50 a day for each day on which the offence continues after conviction. It should also be noted that local authorities may, under section 96, recover their expenses from the person on whom the nuisance order was served. Section 100 allows an authority who are of the opinion that summary proceedings would afford an inadequate remedy to take proceedings in their own name in the High Court for the abatement or prohibition of the nuisance. Local authorities, but *not* private citizens, also have power to deal with nuisances that are likely to recur. If an authority are satisfied that a nuisance is likely to recur on premises they may under section 1(1) of the Public Health (Recurring Nuisances) Act 1961 serve a prohibition notice on the persons on whom an abatement notice can be served. The notice may prohibit a recurrence of the nuisance and may also specify any works necessary to secure this. A failure to comply with the notice is an offence under section 3(1) of the 1961 Act. Section 26 of the 1961 Act also provides a streamlined procedure for dealing with premises comprising statutory nuisances where an authority consider the normal procedure would be too long and drawn out. They may serve notice on the person on whom an abatement notice could have been served of their intention to remedy specific defects. If the addressee does not signify within nine days of service his own intention to do the necessary work they may then proceed to do the works themselves and recover their expenses from him.

The taking of action in respect of statutory nuisances by private citizens

The majority of statutory nuisances will be dealt with by local authorities under the above procedures, but there will be cases where an individual will wish to take action, either because, for example, the local authority is proving dilatory or because it is itself responsible for the nuisance. In these circumstances he can rely on section 99 which provides: 'Complaint of the existence of a statutory nuisance under this Act may be made to a justice of the peace by any person aggrieved by the nuisance, and thereupon the like proceedings shall be had, with the like incidents and consequences as to the making of orders, penalties for disobedience of orders and otherwise, as in the case of a complaint by the local authority, but any such order made in such proceedings may, if the court after giving the local authority an opportunity of being heard thinks fit, direct the authority to abate the nuisance'. Where an individual uses this provision he 'short circuits' the normal procedure and is able to initiate proceedings under section 94 without having first to issue an abatement notice under section 93, though common sense and good manners dictate that some 'letter of intent' should be sent to the other interested parties before proceedings are commenced.

It was held in *R v Epping (Waltham Abbey) Justices, ex parte Burlinson* [1948] 1 KB 79, [1947] 2 All ER 537 that a private citizen can proceed against a defaulting local authority under section 99, and in *Salford City Council v McNally* it was further held that the fact that the nuisance arose as a result of the authority's exercise of their Housing Act powers was no defence to action taken by one of their tenants deleteriously affected in consequence. In order to use the section 99 procedure an individual must be a 'person aggrieved'. In the present context this includes anyone whose health has actually been injured by the nuisance, or any occupant of the premises or indeed anyone with a legal interest in a house which is permanently affected by the nuisance. In *Gould v Times Square Estates Ltd,* Camberwell Magistrates Court, 1 April 1975, [1975] LAG Bulletin 147, even a squatter in an empty former shop and dwelling accommodation was held able to use section 99 procedure, but the applicability of this provision to trespassers was expressly left undecided in *Coventry City Council v Cartwright.*

In some cases the mere laying of an information by an individual will suffice to bring about remedial action. However, provided the nuisance existed at the date of the laying of the information it seems that the magistrates must order the payment of the reasonable expenses of the 'person aggrieved'. This follows from the fact that the same 'consequences' are required to flow under section 99 proceedings as in the case of proceedings commenced by a local authority, and they, of course, are entitled to their reasonable expenses under section 94(3). The magistrates also have discretion in section 99 proceedings to make a compensation order of up to £1,000 in favour of an occupier under section 35 of the Powers of Criminal Courts Act 1973 as amended by section 60 of the Criminal Law Act 1977. Also under the Litigants in Person (Costs and Expenses) Act 1975 any litigant appearing in person before the county court, Supreme Court, House of Lords or Lands Tribunal, who is awarded costs, can claim not only the cost of appearing in court and the cost of any documents, but also the cost of preparing the case and any other work involved in the proceedings, subject to review by the court.

An individual can also complain under section 322 to the Secretary of State for the Environment that a local authority have not discharged their Public Health Act functions properly. On receipt of such a complaint the Secretary *may* decide to hold a local inquiry to investigate the matter. If he does and finds the complaint justified he may direct the authority to discharge their functions correctly within the time he specifies. If the authority fail to comply the Secretary may apply for an order of mandamus against them or he may transfer their functions to himself.

The relationship between the Housing and Public Health Acts

It cannot be sufficiently stressed that the requirements of the housing and public health 'codes' are separate and equal. Remedial action taken under one will not necessarily satisfy the requirements of the other. Of course action taken to eliminate unfitness in a house will nearly always ensure that it will not be prejudicial to health because in general the standards required by the Housing Act are higher than those under the Public Health Act. This can be illustrated by a simple example: if a house is unfit through dampness caused by the lack of damp-proof course then the Housing Act would require the insertion of such a course to make the house fit and free from damp; if the same house is prejudicial to health because of damp, then the Public Health Act will only require it to be made reasonably free from damp on a periodic basis which may be achieved by lining the walls with damp-proof paper. There are times when the two codes do appear to be in conflict: thus in the *Newton* case the court said local authorities have a discretion as to how best to deal with sub-standard housing: in the *Kerrier* case the unfitness provisions were said to be mandatory, while in the *Salford* case action taken under the Housing Act was said to be no defence to subsequent prosecution under the public health legislation. In fact there is no real conflict between the codes, and the cases can be reconciled. The question always to bear in mind in these situations is: *who* is seeking to do *what* to *whom* by *which* procedure? This question can receive different answers in different circumstances as the following instances will show.

The individual sub-standard house in private ownership

This situation can be illustrated by the facts of the *Kerrier* case. The landlords owned two unfit dwelling-houses, both of which were tenanted. The owners were prepared to make one good house of the two but could not do so without obtaining vacant possession, and had no accommodation for the displaced tenants. The local authority said it had no accommodation either (though it did subsequently rehouse the tenants) and so decided to commence proceedings against the landlords under the Public Health Act in order to require remedial action on the roofs of the houses. The landlords countered this by alleging that the houses were statutorily unfit and that the local authority were therefore in breach of their mandatory duties under the unfitness provisions of the Housing Act 1957 if they failed to proceed under them. The court accepted the landlord's contention. Thus where a *local authority* commence proceedings under the 1936 Act in respect of any house which is a statutory nuisance, the *owner* of the house may allege that they are in dereliction of their duties under the Act of 1957 and may apply for mandamus to compel the performance of whichever of the Housing Act duties is relevant to the house. It is only where it is the local authority seeking to initiate action that the 1957 Act can be used to bar proceedings under the Act of 1936, and even here it must be remembered that mandamus is a discretionary remedy and so a landlord is not guaranteed success if he adopts the style of counter argument developed in the *Kerrier* case. Where the proceedings are between the *tenant* and the *landlord* the local authority's duties have no relevance save insofar as the landlord, having begun separate proceedings against a local authority to compel performances of their duties, might argue that the justices should consider the possible outcome of those proceedings when deciding the content of any nuisance order issued under section 99 of the 1936 Act.

The sub-standard older house in local authority ownership

Such a house is likely to be in the ownership of a local authority because it has already been subject to earlier action under the housing legislation. Thus an individual house or one occupied in an area scheme may have been purchased and retained by an authority as capable of providing 'accommodation which is adequate for the time being' under sections 17, 46, 48 and 54 of the Housing Act 1957. The underlying conception behind these provisions is that such houses should be retained only temporarily and generally only while their occupants are being found newer council-built houses. But there are cases where whole areas of unfit houses have been retained in use for many years. By definition these houses are unfit and so no further action can be taken in relation to them under the Act of 1957. Of course the repairing obligations imported by sections 32 and 33 of the Housing Act 1961 do apply, but as we have seen in our study of these provisions in Chapter 7, above, the 'age, character, prospective life and locality' requirement in section 32 ensures that the courts will hardly ever order a local authority to spend a great sum on any of its old sub-standard houses awaiting ultimate demolition. In these circumstances, provided the existence of a statutory nuisance can be proved, the 1936 Act can be used and the prior action taken under the 1957 Act will be no defence to the local authority.

This was the situation in the *Salford* case. In 1967 Salford Corporation declared certain areas in Lower Broughton, Salford to be clearance areas, and at the same time made compulsory purchase orders on the houses within the areas. However, once the compulsory purchase orders were confirmed the Corporation, realising it could not rehouse all the residents quickly, deferred demolition of the houses under section 48 of the 1957 Act for a *minimum* period of *seven* years. By 1974 Mrs

McNally's house suffered from an accumulation of refuse, dampness, defective sanitary fittings, unsealed drains, rats, defective windows and/or doors, a leaking roof, defective drainage, and defective plaster work. She commenced proceedings in respect of the statutory nuisance comprised by her house under section 99 of the 1936 Act and succeeded. The House of Lords held that the resolution to defer demolition under section 48 was no defence to statutory nuisance proceedings. Thus a local authority may not acquire sub-standard houses and retain them until the occupants can be rehoused without at least ensuring that the houses are not prejudicial to the health of their occupants. It must be remembered that section 99 proceedings are an individual remedy for an individual house and that some local authorities have in the past simply moved the tenant out of any house which formed the basis of statutory nuisance proceedings and into another one which could be in just as bad condition, thus forcing the proceedings to begin all over again. Furthermore it must be remembered that even where an old sub-standard house is made the subject of a nuisance order the justice's discretion should be so used as to prevent the expenditure of unnecessary sums. The best that can be hoped for is a 'make and mend' operation designed to make the house reasonably bearable as a dwelling. It should be remembered that, after *Saddleworth UDC v Aggregate and Sand Ltd* (1970) 114 Sol Jo 931, a lack of finance does not seem to be a reasonable excuse for not complying with a nuisance order. Local authorities cannot plead poverty in the hope of entirely escaping from the requirements of nuisance orders!

The sub-standard modern council-built house

Evidence is not lacking that bad construction, poor design, unproved building techniques and misguided planning policies have led to the erection of many recent council houses and flats whose inhabitants frequently have to endure extremely unpleasant living conditions. In some modern council properties there are severe problems of damp and condensation which can lead to ruined furniture and clothes and illness in the occupants. In such circumstances the housing legislation offers little consolation to the tenant. We have already noted above that the official view as expressed in Ministry of Housing and Local Government Circular No. 69/67 is that dampness caused by temporary condensation does not generally render a house statutorily unfit. In any case even if it were possible to show that such a modern dwelling is unfit within section 4 of the 1957 Act it is unlikely that either section 9 or section 16 would apply as the tenor of their wording is that they apply to houses in private ownership. Moreover local authorities possess specific powers to retain unfit houses in use. Neither are the repairing covenants imposed by sections 32 and 33 of the Housing Act 1961 likely to be of much assistance in dealing with condensation as the ooligation extends only to the structure and exterior of the building and the installations for the supply of water, gas, electricity and for sanitary purposes. In such circumstances statutory nuisance proceedings would seem to be the most effective way for a tenant to take action against his municipal landlord.

There are instances where such action has been initiated successfully. In *Northwood Flat Dwellers and Tenants Association v Knowsley District Council,* (1974) October (unreported) Knowsley Magistrates Court, a local authority were proceeded against in respect of the extremely poor condition of some of their blocks of flats. Numerous defects affected these properties including drinking water smelling of sewage, blocked drains, damp walls and cracked ceiling plaster, and these were in properties not then more than fifteen years old. Summonses were issued under section 99 of the 1936 Act and, though the local authority hurriedly completed remedial works before the date of the hearings, the magistrates nevertheless awarded costs to the tenants. In *Tusting v Royal Borough of Kensington and Chelsea* (1974) 6 July (unreported) Inner London Crown Court, a tenant alleged that her home in a council block of flats suffered from a defective entrance doorway, split floorboards, dampness and a defective sink and draining board. At the hearing before the justices a nuisance order in respect only of some of the defects was made and Mrs Tusting appealed against this to the Crown Court where the whole matter was reheard. The crown court gave a specific judgment on the problem of dampness caused by condensation which was found to be caused by the inherent coldness of the walls. The court ordered the local authority to alleviate the dampness and condensation within nine months bearing in mind a municipal offer to install central heating and to put interior cladding on the cold walls.

Thus when faced with a problem caused by the existence of a sub-standard house it is wise to remember that this is very much an area in which there are 'horses for courses'. As a general rule wherever health is at risk or where only temporary patching-up on a short term basis is required, it is best to proceed under the Act of 1936. However, the basic question must remain that asked earlier: *who* is seeking to do *what* to *whom* by *which* procedure?

Miscellaneous powers to deal with sub-standard housing

Infested dwellings

Under the Prevention of Damage by Pests Act 1949 both local

authorities (London Boroughs and county districts) and private individuals have obligations to secure the eradication of rats and mice. Section 2 of the Act states that, so far as practicable, local authorities are to keep their areas free of such vermin. They must carry out periodic inspection of their areas, destroy rats and mice on their own land and enforce the obligations of private landowners. These obligations are to be found in sections 3 and 4. So far as houses and the land occupied with them are concerned, it is an offence punishable by a fine of up to £5 for the occupier not to give notice to his local authority if he knows that rats and mice are living on or resorting to his land in substantial numbers. Once the local authority know of infestation on private land, whether as a result of the occupier's notice or otherwise, they may serve notice on the occupier, and the owner, of the land requiring, within a specified reasonable time, that the rats and mice on the land should be destroyed and that it should be kept free from such vermin. The local authority may specify reasonable steps to secure this object, including the application of specific treatments to the land and the carrying out of works of structural repair. They may not serve a merely general and unspecific notice; see *Perry v Garner* [1953] 1QB 335, [1953] 1 All ER 285. They may also specify the times at which any treatment required by the notice is to be carried out.

Other verminous premises

Section 83 of the Public Health Act 1936, as amended by section 35 of the Public Health Act 1961 provides:

'(1) Where a local authority, [county districts] upon consideration of a report from any of their officers, or other information in their possession, are satisfied that any premises —

    (a) are in such a filthy or unwholesome condition as to be prejudicial to health or

    (b) are verminous,

the local authority shall give notice to the owner or occupier of the premises requiring him to take such steps as may be specified in the notice to remedy the condition of the premises by cleansing and disinfecting them, and the notice may require among other things the removal of wallpaper or other covering of the walls, or, in the case of verminous premises, the taking of such steps as may be necessary for destroying or removing vermin'.

The notice may also require, by virtue of sub-section (1A), in the case of premises used for human habitation that they be papered, painted or distempered inside at the choice of the person doing the work. It is an offence to fail to comply with such a notice, and failure to comply may also result in the local authority doing the work and recovering their costs from the defaulter. This provision only applies in extreme cases and does not entitle local authorities to demand a high standard of internal decorative repair from householders. In any proceedings under the provision it is open to the defendant to question the reasonableness of the authority's requirements, or their decision to address the notice to him and not some other affected person.

Dangerous and obstructive buildings

A general power to order the demolition not just of dwelling-houses but of any building classified as 'obstructive' is granted to local authorities by section 72 of the Housing Act 1957. The phrase 'obstructive building' is defined as meaning 'a building which, by reason only of its contact with or proximity to, other buildings, is dangerous or injurious to health'. It should also be noted that this provision does *not* apply to any building which is the property of a local authority. The procedure is very similar to that laid down by section 16 of the 1957 Act and involves the service of a 'time and place' notice on the *owner*, i.e. the person entitled to the fee simple, and also any lessee whose unexpired term exceeds three years, giving at least 21 days' notice of the calling of a conference when the future of the property will be considered. If after that conference the authority remain convinced that the property is obstructive they may make a demolition order as to part or the whole of the structure, and require the vacation of the property within two months of the date on which the order becomes operative. Persons aggrieved by the making of the order have 21 days from its date of service to appeal to the county court. In this context 'person aggrieved' does *not* include a tenant with *less* than three years of his term unexpired, and this effectively limits the range of possible appellants to landlords only in the case of most tenanted property. On appeal the court may confirm, quash or vary the order.

The public health legislation also applies to certain buildings classifiable as 'dangerous'. Section 58 of the Public Health Act 1936, as amended by section 24 of the Public Health Act 1961, grants power to local authorities (London Boroughs and district councils) to apply to a court of summary jurisdiction for an order in respect of any building or part of a building that appears to them to be dangerous. If they make out their case the court may make the order requiring the owner (in this context meaning the person receiving the rack rent, or who would receive it if the premises were so let) to execute the works necessary to obviate the danger. The order need not specify how these works are to be done; see *R v Bolton Recorder, ex parte McVittie* [1940] 1 KB 290, [1939] 4 All ER 236. This case was one of a pair, the other being *McVittie v Bolton Corpn* [1945] 1 KB 281, [1945] 1 All ER 379. They both arose out of Mr McVittie's abandonment of two adjoining plots of land following a fire which destroyed the buildings on one of them. It took years of action of various sorts to clear the site. Following these cases local authorities should always be careful to specify exactly the land made subject to their order. The cases also establish that the power to demolish a building necessarily extends to all of it including the basement, cellars and foundation.

Failure to comply with such an order enables the local authority to do the work themselves and to recover their reasonable expenses from the defaulter who also makes himself liable to a fine of up to £10. This power is available whether the building is dangerous either to those in the building itself and adjoining buildings, or to persons in the street outside. Emergency powers to deal with dangerous buildings where immediate action appears necessary to the local authority are conferred by section 24 of the Public Health Act 1961. Under this provision notice of the local authority's intention to take immediate preventive action need only be served on the owner and occupier of a building where it is reasonably practicable to do so. Moreover the local authority may recover their reasonable expenses from the owner in respect of their emergency action.

The position in Greater London

The law is irritatingly complex because some of the above *public health legislation* powers do *not* apply to the *inner* London Boroughs, the City of London and the Temples who still retain an inherited independence in public health matters from the old London County Council. The law relating to these areas is to be found in Part VII of the London Building Acts (Amendment) Act 1939 as amended by the London County Council (General Powers) Act 1958. The powers granted are very similar to those under the general public health legislation and include a power to remove or otherwise eradicate dilapidated and neglected structures. Readers wishing to find out more about this legal geographical anomaly are referred to Halsbury's *Statutes of England* (3rd ed.) Vol. 20, pp. 185 to 191.

Before concluding this review of supplementary housing powers it is necessary to add a cautionary note reminding readers that these powers are specific and do not exist to be used as substitutes for the general housing and public health powers conferred by law.

Further reading

Garner, J.F., *Slum Clearance and Compensation* (Oyez, 1975) pp. 17 – 35

Social Welfare Law (Ed. by D.W. Pollard) (Oyez) paras. C. 101 – C. 3124

Garner, J.F., 'Unfit for Human Habitation' (1954) JPL 833

Garner, J.F., 'Unfit for Human Habitation' (1958) JPL 699

Haddon, T.B., 'Public Health and Housing Legislation' (1976) 27 NILQ 245

Hughes, D.J., 'Housing and Public Health — A Continuing Saga' (1977) 28 NILQ 233

Hughes, D.J., 'Public Health Legislation and the Improvement of Housing Conditions' (1976) NILQ 1

Hughes, D.J., 'What is a Nuisance? — The Public Health Act Revisited' (1976) 27 NILQ 131

McQuillan, J. and Finnis, N., 'Ways of Seeing Dampness: When Houses Can't Cope with being Lived In' *Roof*, May 1979, p. 85

For the prescribed forms for use under the Housing Act 1957 see the Housing (Prescribed Forms) Regulations 1972 (S.I. 1972 No. 228), as amended.

Chapter 9

Clearance procedures, compulsory purchase and rehousing

The development of the law

Clearance procedures have been part of the law for over a hundred years, the first legislation specifically concerned with such matters being the Artizans and Labourers Dwellings (or 'Torrens') Act 1868. The word 'slum' is not a legal term of art and the law refers, as we have seen in the previous chapter, to dwellings which are 'unfit for human habitation'. The public mind has become accustomed to referring to the various procedures evolved to deal with areas of unfit housing as 'slum clearance'. The lawyer should be wary of using such non-technical language as there have been considerable differences in the past between the various types of clearance procedures. These differences can be traced through the history of the various Acts relating to the subject. Under the Torrens Act local authorities were empowered to declare premises 'unfit', but rehousing and demolition were not local government responsibilities. It was not until the Artizans' and Labourers' Dwellings Improvement (or 'Cross') Act 1875 that the law provided for both the clearance of an area and its subsequent rebuilding. This Act also introduced alternative grounds for taking action in respect of sub-standard housing: first the 'unfitness' of the houses and, second, the danger to health resulting from the generally bad conditions in the area. The Cross Act also included the first rehousing obligation to be laid on a demolishing authority.

Little use was made of this or subsequent housing legislation until after the First World War when the Acquisition of Land (Assessment of Compensation) Act 1919 and the introduction of exchequer subsidies laid the legal and financial basis for local authorities to acquire sub-standard houses and provide decent new homes for their inhabitants. Even so the number of houses demolished in the 1920's remained low with only about 2,000 to 5,000 houses each year being made subject to closing and demolition orders, and then usually on an individual basis. Mounting dissatisfaction with the cumbersome and archaic procedures of the law led to radical change in the Housing Act 1930 which introduced many of the procedures still in use today. This legislation introduced a much simpler procedure for area clearance, and also defined 'unfitness' in terms of bad housing conditions. Despite the financial difficulties of the 1930's, a major clearance policy was inaugurated in 1933, and by 1939 houses were being demolished at the rate of about 90,000 a year. Many more were scheduled for demolition.

The Second World War put an end to slum clearance for six years and the desperate shortage of accommodation after the war led to further restriction of demolition until 1953. Another major clearance programme was begun in that year, though it was admitted that in some areas the task of slum clearance could take as long as twenty years. Various changes in the law were also made and these culminated in the Housing Act 1957 which is still the principal legislation in this area. By 1959 some 200,000 people a year were being rehoused from unfit houses, but this was not enough to deal with the sub-standard property, and it was also realised that the official estimates of the number of unfit dwellings were far too low. Not only were there many more unfit houses than had been realised, but also substantial numbers of others were declining into unfitness for lack of repair or maintenance. Other houses while not 'unfit' lacked the modern amenities that rising housing expectations demanded.

Major housing surveys carried out under the 1964 Labour Government revealed the existence of 1.8 million unfit dwellings in 1967, together with a further 4.5 million needing repairs or lacking at least one basic amenity. A major change of policy was announced in 1968 when it was decided to switch public investment from new house building into the improvement of older houses. Since then the emphasis in housing policy has been less and less on demolition and rehousing and more and more on rehabilitation, initially of individual houses but now on whole areas. Nevertheless slum clearance continued throughout this period and reached a peak in 1970 – 71 when some 70,000 houses a year were demolished. Since then there has been a considerable decline in the number of homes demolished. In 1975 the rate of demolition was down to 49,000 a year and over the years 1973 to 1977 the *average* rate fell to about 41,200 *per annum*. In 1977 itself 32,895 unfit houses in clearance areas in England and Wales were demolished, though the number of other demolitions and closures brought the year's total up to 41,755. In 1976 the English House Condition Survey (Department of the Environment Housing Survey Report No. 10, 1978) revealed that there were still 363,000 dwellings in England which might have to be made subject to clearance schemes. The present rate of area clearance would indicate that it will be somewhere in the region of eight to ten years before all the areas of sub-standard housing needing demolition are so treated. It follows that clearance procedures will remain an important aspect of the public law of housing for some time to come.

The old procedure by way of clearance order

The law has been irritatingly complex because there have been two procedures available to local authorities wishing to secure the clearance of an area. The *older* procedure existed under sections 43 and 44 of the Housing Act 1957. These provided that local authorities could bring about the clearance of buildings once a clearance area had been declared by means of a 'clearance order' which required the owner of the affected building(s) to carry out the demolition work. The problem with this procedure was that it left the land in the ownership of the individual owners and this could give rise to problems of tracing owners and acquiring title when an authority subsequently wished to secure the redevelopment of the land. Section 108(1) and (3) of the Housing Act 1974 abolished the power to make clearance orders in respect of clearance areas declared on or after 31 August 1974. In relation to those areas declared before 31 August 1974 the power to make such orders was discontinued with effect from 1 September 1975. Nevertheless as it would take time for all the clearance orders already made to be fully implemented those provisions of the 1957 Housing Act which related to the *enforcement* of clearance orders were left in force until such time as they could be repealed by a Commencement Order made under section 130 of and Schedule 15 to the Housing Act 1974. The Housing Act 1974 (Commencement No. 6) Order 1979 (S.I. 1979 No. 1214) made on 27 September 1979 brought the repeals into effect as from 9 October 1979.

The modern procedure by way of compulsory purchase

a) Declaring the clearance area

Every local housing authority is under a duty imposed by section 70 of the Housing Act 1969 to inspect its district from time to time with a view to determining what action to take in relation to clearance and redevelopment. It is not only the information so derived that can lead to the declaration of a clearance area. Section 42(1) of the Housing Act 1957 makes it clear that an authority can act on the basis of official representations, made under section 157 of the Act, or any other information in their possession. What the authority must look for is areas where the houses are unfit for human habitation (as defined by section 4 of the Act; see Chapter 8, above), or are, by reason of their bad arrangement, or the narrowness or bad arrangement of the streets, dangerous or injurious to the health of the inhabitants of the area. They must also be satisfied that the most satisfactory method of dealing with the conditions in the area is demolition of the buildings in it. Clearance area procedure is designed to deal with the areas of poorest housing where rehabilitation is not a practical possibility. Nevertheless before resorting to this procedure the local authority should consider all their housing powers with relation to the area including the possibility of rehabilitation or dealing with the properties on an individual basis.

In this context 'house' has been given a somewhat extended meaning and includes, yards, gardens and outhouses appurtenant to houses (Housing Act 1957 s. 189). The courts have also held the following to be 'houses': Shops with living rooms over — *Re Bainbridge, South Shields (D'Arcy Street) Compulsory Purchase Order 1937* [1939] 1 KB 500, [1939] 1 All ER 419; Garages and Stores with dwellings over — *Re Butler, Camberwell (Wingfield Mews), No. 2 Clearance Order 1936* [1939] 1 KB 570, [1939] 1 All ER 590; A tenement house, whether with other properties, or comprising by itself a single plot of land made subject to clearance procedure — *Quiltotex Co Ltd v Minister of Housing and Local Government* [1966] 1 QB 704, [1965] 2 All ER 913, and *Annicola Investments Ltd v Minister of Housing and Local Government* [1968] 1 QB 631, [1965] 3 All ER 850.

A clearance area can also be declared in respect of an area where the houses are badly arranged or the streets are narrow or badly arranged. This limb of the provision refers to houses built around central courts and back-to-back dwellings. Back-to-back dwellings provided for working-class people were automatically deemed to be 'unfit' by section 5(1) of the 1957 Act. 'Back-to-back' was not defined by the statute and each case had to be decided on its own facts. In *White v St. Marylebone Borough Council* [1915] 3 KB 249 the existence of an air shaft which occupied one-third of the air space between what were otherwise contiguous back-to-back dwellings did not prevent the dwellings from being statutorily prohibited. *Chorley Borough Council v Barratt Developments (North West) Ltd* [1979] 3 All ER 634 shed further light on the meaning of the term 'back-to-back'. A development company developed a system of housebuilding which consisted of four small houses, each having two common inner walls, forming together a single large square block. It was held that these dwellings did not fall within the prohibition against 'back-to-back' houses. The normal popular use of the term refers to terraces of houses where all the dwellings, except those at the ends, have three shared inner walls and only one outside wall. In any case the prohibition in section 5(1) only related to houses provided 'as dwellings for the working classes'. In the instant case it was found that the intending purchasers of the houses could not be described as 'working class' — a phrase which over the years had come to mean, in legal terms, the lower income groups — and neither could it be proved that the development company had any intention of providing 'back-to-back' houses for such people.

Section 5 of the Housing Act 1957 is now repealed by Schedule 26 to the Housing Act 1980. For the future local authorities will have to rely on their planning control powers to prevent the erection of 'back-to-back' houses.

A clearance area can only be declared by passing a resolution pursuant to section 42(1) of the Housing Act 1957. Before any such resolution is passed the authority must satisfy themselves:

1) in so far as suitable accommodation available for the persons who will be displaced by the clearance of the area does not exist, that they can provide or secure the provision of such accommodation in advance of the displacement of the residents, and

2) that their resources are sufficient to carry their resolution into effect.

The effect of these requirements has been considered in the courts. In *Savoury v Secretary of State for Wales* (1974) 31 P & CR 344 a local authority declared a clearance area under section 42 of the 1957 Act and subsequently made a compulsory purchase order on the houses which they submitted for confirmation to the Secretary of State, who confirmed it in due course. The challenge to the order was based, inter alia, on the argument that the 'suitable accommodation' proviso was not satisfied. It was contended that the area in question was a closely knit community where there were many elderly people who relied on their neighbours for help and support which would be taken from them if they were forced to move and were dispersed. This was rejected by the court which ruled that the section itself recognises the inevitability of disruption. The words 'suitable accommodation' do not mean perfectly alternative or identical accommodation. A local authority must have regard to what the displaced residents can be reasonably asked to accept in their new houses. The desirability of rehousing residents, immediately or eventually, close to the site of their old houses should be considered by the local authority, though this is not a factor of over-riding importance. The preservation of community spirit should be considered, but this also cannot be an overriding principle as it may not be reasonably practicable to achieve.

In *Eckersley v Secretary of State for the Environment and Southwark London Borough Council* (1977) 34 P & CR 124, the local authority declared a clearance area in which Mr Eckersley's house was included. They made a compulsory purchase order on the area which was confirmed by the Secretary of State. The appellant sought to quash this order on a number of grounds which included an allegation that the Secretary of State had failed to consider certain material considerations when coming to his decision. These included:

1) whether the local authority's financial resources were sufficient to carry into effect the clearance and redevelopment of the land in question, and

2) the relative costs of clearance and redevelopment compared with the costs of retention and rehabilitation of the houses.

The Court of Appeal found that the first contention was outside the Secretary of State's jurisdiction. The provisos to section 42(1) of the 1957 Act are solely matters for the local authority alone. An authority must come in good faith and on proper evidence to a decision on these matters before proceeding to declare a clearance area, but that is a matter solely for them and not the Secretary of State. As to allegation (2) the Court held that questions of cost generally are matters for the Secretary of State to consider. There was no evidence that the issue of comparative costs as between demolition and rehabilitation had been considered properly and so the Secretary of State had failed to consider all the issues that should have been considered. The compulsory purchase order was therefore ultra vires and was quashed. In *Ashridge Investments Ltd v Minister of Housing and Local Government* [1965] 3 All ER 371, [1965] 1 WLR 1320 the Court of Appeal stated that a court should only interfere with the process of clearance, so far as the Secretary of State is concerned, where there is evidence that he has gone beyond the powers granted by Act or has not complied with its requirements. Furthermore, the court should limit its consideration to the material which was before the Secretary to see whether there has been some legal error made. Fresh evidence can only be admitted in exceptional circumstances.

The local authority must truly intend to demolish the properties when it decides to declare a clearance area and must not intend to use the procedure as a cloak for other housing operations. In *Wahiwala v Secretary of State for the Environment* (1977) 75 LGR 651 a local authority resolved to make a clearance area and made a compulsory purchase order which was subsequently confirmed. It was alleged that the local authority was seeking to acquire the sites of the houses at site value only, whereas they planned to let a housing association rehabilitate some houses once they were acquired. The Court of Appeal found this allegation unfounded, but said that once the compulsory purchase order was confirmed the council came under a duty to demolish the properties. This duty could only be deferred for a limited time, thus making a rehabilitation agreement automatically of no effect. In *Goddard v Minister of Housing and Local Government* [1958] 3 All ER 482, [1958] 1 WLR 1151 the court pronounced upon the meaning of the requirement that an authority must be satisfied that their resources are sufficient to carry their resolution into effect before declaring a clearance area. It was held that it is competent for a local authority to be satisfied of the sufficiency of their resources if they act properly on the advice of their committees. They do not have to have specific figures before them, and, in any case, 'resources' in this context includes credit as well as actual cash in hand.

So as soon as the authority have determined to declare a clearance area they must cause the area to be defined on a map in such a manner as to exclude from the area buildings which are *not* unfit for humans or dangerous or injurious to health. They must then pass the actual resolution declaring the area to be a clearance area, that is to say an area to be cleared of all buildings in compliance with the Housing Act 1957. A copy of this resolution must be sent to the Secretary of State, together with a statement of the number of persons occupying the buildings comprised in the area. Detailed rules as to the drawing up of the necessary plans of clearance areas are to be found in the Department of Environment Circular No. 77/75, Appendix B. This states that clearance area maps should generally be to a scale of 1/500 or thereabouts. Unfit houses should be coloured pink (or diagonally hatched), while houses included by reason of their bad arrangement should be coloured pink-hatched-yellow (or diagonally cross hatched). One map may cover several clearance areas so long as each is separately identified. Furthermore the council's resolution declaring a clearance area must correspond in every detail with the map. Pursuant to section 29(3) of the Housing Act 1969, a clearance area is not to be so defined as to include any land which is for the time being included in a general improvement area.

b) The method of dealing with a clearance area

Section 43(1)(b) of the Housing Act 1957 provides:

'So soon as may be after a local authority have declared any area to be a clearance area they shall . . . proceed to secure the clearance of the area by purchasing the land comprised in the area, or otherwise securing the demolition of the building on that land'.

Thus a local authority may agree with the affected land owners that they should demolish the buildings. The procedure here is governed by section 50 of the Housing Act 1957 and is dependent upon proper covenants being given that the clearance will be effected. They may themselves decide to acquire the land by agreement and so proceed to clearance. By section 45(2) where a local authority determine to purchase any land comprised in the clearance area they may also purchase any land which is surrounded by the clearance area, the acquisition of which land is reasonably necessary for the purpose of securing a cleared site of convenient shape and dimensions. They may also acquire any adjoining land where this is reasonably necessary for the satisfactory use or development of the cleared area. Such land is known as 'added land'. This does not entitle a local authority to acquire *any* land they desire. This is illustrated by *Coleen Properties v Minister of Housing and Local Government* [1971] 1 All ER 1049, [1971] 1 WLR

433. Here two streets of poor, old houses met at a corner where there was sited a modern block of shops and flats. The local authority declared the streets to be a clearance area and then included the modern building as added land in their compulsory purchase order. The local authority adduced no evidence as to why they needed the added land. The Court of Appeal held that the council's *ipse dixit* was not enough and that they had to prove their real need for the land. What is 'reasonably necessary' is a question of fact in each case and not one of planning policy.

In *Bass Charrington (North) Ltd v Minister of Housing and Local Government* (1971) 22 P & CR 31 it was held that the word 'adjoining' means land which is at least partly contiguous with the land in the clearance area and has continuous boundaries with it. Nor may land be acquired just to create a site of convenient shape and dimensions. Land can only be acquired if it is reasonably necessary, see *Gosling v Secretary of State for the Environment* [1975] JPL 406. The distinction is, of course, somewhat fine and is probably best illustrated by an example: If the clearance area land is merely to be used as a car park the fact that one side is not perfectly straight would not justify acquiring sufficient land to make it so; but if the land is sought for use as a football pitch and the cleared land was *just* insufficient for this purpose, added land might be acquired to enable the development to be carried out.

If a local authority cannot acquire the land by agreement they have compulsory purchase powers in section 43(3) and (5) of the Housing Act 1957. These require that any compulsory purchase order be confirmed by the Secretary of State.

Compulsory purchase procedure

Before describing this procedure it must be once more stressed that compulsory purchase is only available to a local authority wishing to demolish sub-standard houses where the houses within an area are actually unfit for human habitation, etc.; where those conditions are best dealt with by demolition; where the necessary accommodation exists to rehouse displaced residents, and where the authority's resources are sufficient to carry out the scheme.

The general procedure authorising the compulsory purchase of land is contained in Part I, Schedule 3 to the Housing Act 1957. The order must first of all be in the prescribed form, which is contained in the Housing (Prescribed Forms) Regulations 1972 (S.I. 1972 No. 228, as amended by S.I. 1974 No. 1511 and S.I. 1975 No. 500). The order must describe the land to be acquired by reference to a map, which itself will show the land hatched or coloured according to the rules mentioned earlier in connection with the declaration of the clearance area, so that the unfit houses will be shown as pink, the houses and other buildings included by reason of their bad arrangement will be coloured pink-hatched-grey, and any land to be acquired which is *outside* the clearance area will be coloured grey.

Before submitting the order to the Secretary of State for his confirmation the local authority must first publish in one or more newspapers circulating within their district a notice stating the effect of such an order having been made, and describing the area comprised in the order. They must also state a place where a copy of the order and the map may be seen at all reasonable hours. A similar notice must be served on every owner, lessee, mortgagee and occupier (except tenants for periods of a month or less and statutory tenants) of affected land. This must state the time within which objections (which must be made in writing) to the confirmation of the order can be made. This period must be not less than fourteen days from the service of the notice. If no objections are received then the order may be confirmed. If any are received and are not withdrawn the Secretary of State must hold either a public local inquiry, or afford the objectors an opportunity of being heard by a person appointed by him for that purpose. The date and place of this hearing will be advertised in the local newspapers and the objectors informed. The normal course is to hold a public local inquiry, to which, however, the Inquiries Procedure Rules 1976 (S.I. No. 746) do not apply. No inquiry will, however, be held if the only objections received relate solely to matters of monetary compensation for the compulsory purchase. Representation is allowed to objectors who may employ a lawyer and/or a surveyor to appear. The inquiry will generally follow the usual compulsory purchase pattern with the authority commencing the proceedings before the Secretary of State's Inspector. The objectors will reply and both sides will call, examine and cross-examine witnesses. The normal rules of natural justice will apply, see: *Gill & Co v Secretary of State for the Environment* [1978] JPL 373. After the closing speech by the local authority the inspector accompanied by the parties may view the area. It should be noted that it will be the state of the premises at the date of this inspection that will decide whether any given house is finally classified fit or unfit. It is also at this time that the assessment of any well-maintained payments will be made.

Objections are sometimes received based on the ground that given houses are not in fact 'unfit'. In such circumstances the local authority must serve a written notice on the objector stating their reasons for regarding the property as 'unfit'. The objector will then be allowed at least fourteen days to consider the local authority's case before the opening of the inquiry. Such objectors are also entitled to ask the Secretary of State for a written statement of reasons if he ultimately decides that any such house is unfit.

The inspector submits his report to the Secretary of State who, after considering it, may confirm it with or without modifications which can include the exclusion of land from the compulsory purchase order, but which may not authorise the local authority to purchase any more land than was originally included in the order without modification. Once the order is confirmed the local authority must, according to Schedule 4, paragraph 1 to the Housing Act 1957, publish notice in the local press and also serve notice on the objectors. An administrative undertaking was given in Ministry of Housing and Local Government Circular No. 9/58 that the Secretary of State's letter of decision would include, for the future, the inspector's recommendation and the final decision with the reasons therefor. The letter also will also state that a copy of the inspector's report will be available if a request is made within one month of the date of the letter.

Schedule 4, paragraph 2 to the 1957 Act gives a 'person aggrieved' a six week period to challenge the confirmed order on the grounds that, substantively or procedurally, it goes beyond the powers conferred by the Act. The term 'person aggrieved' is nowadays liberally interpreted to include all persons with genuine legal grievances, but the six weeks time period is rigidly enforced. The statement in Schedule 4, paragraph 3 that, apart from the six weeks right of appeal, the order is not to be questioned 'in any legal proceedings whatsoever' is literally construed, see: *Smith v East Elloe RDC* [1956] AC 736, [1956] 1 All ER 855, and *R v Secretary of State for Home Affairs ex parte Ostler* [1977] QB 122. It seems that no reason, be it an allegation of bad faith on the part of the local authority, or ignorance on the part of the objector, will persuade the courts to depart from this interpretation of the law.

The acquisition of the land

A copy of the confirmed order has to be served by the local authority on every person on whom they served notice of their intention to submit the order for confirmation, i.e. owners, lessees, mortgagees and long term tenants. This must be done 'so soon as may be' after the confirmation, Schedule 4, paragraph 5 to the Housing Act 1957. The local authority may then proceed to acquire the title to the land. This process will be governed by the Compulsory Purchase Act 1965. By section 5(1) of that Act:

'When the acquiring authority require to purchase any of the land subject to compulsory purchase, they shall give notice (hereinafter in this Act referred to as a "notice to treat") to all the persons interested in or having power to sell and convey or release the land, so far as known to the acquiring authority after making diligent inquiry'.

It is obvious that there may therefore be a considerable number of persons who have interests in the land all of which will have to be acquired. In addition to freehold and leasehold estates the courts have held the following to be compensatable interests: an option to acquire the freehold of some fields, *Oppenheimer v Minister of Transport* [1942] 1 KB 242, [1941] 3 All ER 485; an option in a will giving the testatrix's son the option to occupy premises for as long as he wished at a specified rent, which was held to create an equitable lease for life, *Blamires v Bradford Corpn* [1964] Ch 585, [1964] 2 All ER 603.

The notice to treat must be served within three years of the compulsory purchase order becoming operative, see section 4 of the Compulsory Purchase Act 1965. Section 5 also requires that the notice should:

1) give particulars of the land to which it relates;

2) demand particulars of its recipient's estate and interest in the land, and

3) state that the acquiring authority are willing to treat for the purchase of the land, and also as to the compensation to be paid for damage which may be sustained by the execution of the works.

A person served with a notice to treat has, under section 6 of the 1965 Act, 21 days from the time of service to inform the acquiring authority of the particulars of his claim, or to treat with them in respect of it. If he does not do this, or if negotiations as to compensation begin but do not produce agreement, then the question must be referred to the Lands Tribunal for their determination. Once the amount of compensation has been fixed the transfer of the land follows the usual conveyancing pattern. There are minor differences from private transfers by virtue of section 23 of the Compulsory Purchase Act 1965 which provides:

'(1) The costs of all conveyances of the land subject to compulsory purchase shall be borne by the acquiring authority.

(2) The costs shall include all charges and expenses, whether incurred on the part of the seller or on the part of the purchaser,

    (a) of all conveyances and assurances of any of the land, and of any outstanding terms or interests in the land, and

    (b) of declaring, evidencing and verifying the title to the land, terms or interests, and

    (c) of making out and furnishing such abstracts and attested copies as the acquiring authority may require . . . .

(6) Conveyances of the land subject to compulsory purchase may be according to the forms in Schedule 5 to this Act, or as near thereto as the circumstances of the case will admit, or by deed in any other form which the acquiring authority may think fit'.

This provision, along with section 9 of the Act, allows the acquiring authority to deal with the reluctant seller who refuses to co-operate in the transaction. In such circumstances the amount of compensation payable has to be paid into court and the transfer of the title to the interest will be achieved by the authority executing a deed poll.

Entering upon the land

An authority wishing to enter upon the land before completion of the conveyancing procedure may do so by virtue of section 1(1) of the Compulsory Purchase Act 1965. The acquiring authority must have served a notice to treat before they can proceed under this provision but thereafter they may, by giving not less than fourteen days' notice to owners, lessees and occupiers, enter and take possession of the land specified in the notice. In such circumstances the compensation payable will bear interest from the date of entry until the date of payment. This rate of interest is subject to very regular changes.

General vesting declaration procedure

This procedure, available by virtue of section 30 of and Schedule 3 to the Town and Country Planning Act 1968, is designed to expedite the acquisition process. Where a compulsory purchase order has come into operation, an acquiring authority may execute a general vesting declaration in respect of all or any of the land they are authorised to acquire. Before making such a declaration the acquiring authority must include in the statutorily required notices of the making or confirmation of the compulsory purchase order certain statements. These are:

1) that required by the Compulsory Purchase of Land Regulations 1976 (S.I. 1976 No. 300), Regulation 5(b), and

2) a notification to persons entitled to compensation inviting them to give information to the acquiring authority with respect to their names, addresses and the land in question.

These particulars together with the notice of the making or confirmation of the compulsory purchase order must also be registered in the local land charges register. A period of at least two months must then elapse from the first date of publication of the notice before the actual general vesting declaration can be executed, unless all the affected occupiers agree otherwise in writing, thereafter the declaration may be executed. This will begin vesting of the land in the authority. To complete the process further notices must be served on occupiers of affected land (other than those with minor interests) and other persons who have given information in pursuance of the authority's request, stating the effect of the general vesting declaration (S.I. 1976 No. 300). In any case the authority must allow 28 days from the end of this last service of notices before the land finally vests in them.

The effect of general vesting declaration procedure is that a notice to treat is deemed to be served, and also, that at the end of the period specified in the declaration, the land in question together with the right to enter and take possession vests in the acquiring authority. The former owners are then left solely with a right to compensation. General vesting declaration procedure only applies to the acquisition in general of freehold or long leasehold or other long-term interests. The so called 'minor interests', e.g. periodic tenancies for a year or less, are excluded. In such circumstances where houses are concerned section 62 of the Housing Act 1957 enables the local authority by giving of at least fourteen days' notice, and subject to the payment of compensation, to enter and take possession of the land.

The assessment of compensation

'Compensation' can mean many things to many people affected in different ways by the declaration of a clearance area. The various elements of the total price which the acquiring authority will ultimately have to pay must be considered separately.

The purchase price of the land

Section 59 of the Housing Act 1957 (as amended) provides:

'(1) Where land is purchased compulsorily by a local authority under this Part of this Act [i.e. the clearance area provisions] the compensation payable in respect thereof shall be assessed in accordance with the Land Compensation Act 1961 subject to the following provisions of this section.

(2) The compensation to be paid for land, including any buildings thereon, purchased as being land comprised in a clearance area shall be the value at the time the valuation is made as a site cleared of buildings and available for development . . . . Provided that this sub-section shall not have effect in the case of the site of a house or other building properly included in a clearance area only on the ground that by reason of its bad arrangement in relation to other buildings or the narrowness or bad arrangement of the streets, it is dangerous or injurious to the health of the inhabitants of the area, unless it is a building constructed or adapted as, or for the purposes of, a dwelling, or partly for those purposes and partly for other purposes, and part thereof (not being a part used for other purposes) is unfit for human habitation . . . .'.

Thus the normal rules for assessing the compensation payable in respect of compulsorily acquired land are modified in the case of clearance areas *but only* in relation to the houses and land included by virtue of unfitness. In this case the *only* sum payable *for the land* will be the cleared site value. This 'cleared site value' is a matter of considerable technicality because of the provisions of section 10 of and Schedule 2 to the Land Compensation Act 1961. However, *briefly* the rule is that where the cleared site value would *exceed* the existing market value of the land with the house on it the payment is to be restricted to the value of the site plus the house. If any unfit house is owner-occupied then, according to paragraph 3 of the Schedule, the *minimum* compensation payable will be the gross rateable value, but, to prevent over-compensation this minimum payment will be made *inclusive* of any well maintained or other owner-occupier payments. In those cases where the land, etc. is included solely because of bad arrangements, etc., or for any other reason, for example because it is 'added land' under section 43(2) of the 1957 Act, the ordinary rules for assessing compensation apply.

These rules are contained in section 5 of the Land Compensation Act 1961, to which certain extra rules are added in special cases by Part III of Schedule 3 to the Housing Act 1957 (as amended). The basic rules are:

1) No allowance may be made on account of the acquisition being compulsory;

2) The basic value of the land must be assessed on the basis of a willing seller and a willing vendor in the open market;

3) The special suitability or adaptability of the land for any purpose must not be taken into account if that purpose is one to which the land could be applied only in pursuance of statutory powers, or for which there is no market apart from the special needs of a particular purchaser or the requirements of any public authority possessing powers of compulsory acquisition.

4) Where the value of the land is increased by reason of the use thereof or any premises thereon in a manner which could be restrained by any court, or is contrary to law, or is detrimental to the health of the occupants of the premises or to the public health [e.g. if the premises are statutorily overcrowded], the amount of that increase must not be taken into account;

5) Where the land is, and but for the compulsory acquisition would continue to be, devoted to a purpose of such a nature that there is no general demand or market for land for that purpose, the compensation may, if the Lands Tribunal is satisfied that reinstatement in some other place is bona fide intended, be assessed on the basis of the reasonable cost of equivalent reinstatement;

6) The provisions of rule (3) above are not to affect the assessment of compensation for disturbance or any other matter not directly based on the value of the land.

To these rules the Housing Act 1957, Sch. 3, Part III adds:

1) If the Lands Tribunal are satisfied with respect to any premises that the rent was enhanced by reason of their being used for illegal purposes, or because they were statutorily overcrowded the compensation shall, so far as it is based on rent, be based on that rent which would have been recoverable had the premises not been so misused;

2) The local authority may tender evidence as to the matters mentioned above even if they have taken no action to remedy the defects or evils disclosed by the evidence, but before tendering evidence as to sanitation or repair, the authority must furnish the tribunal and the claimant with a written statement of the respects in which the premises are alleged to be defective;

3) The tribunal shall have regard to and make an allowance in respect of any increased value which, in their opinion, will be given to other premises of the same owner;

4) The tribunal must embody in their award a statement showing separately whether compensation has been reduced by reference to the use of the premises for illegal purposes or because of overcrowding or because of the matters mentioned in paragraph (3) above, and the amount, if any by which the compensation has been reduced by reference to each of those matters.

The Housing Act 1957, Sch. 3, Part II, para. 8(5) should also be noted:

'The Tribunal shall not take into account any building erected or any improvement or alteration made or any interest in land created after the date on which notice of the order having been made is published . . . if, in the opinion of the tribunal, the erection of the building or the making of the improvement or alteration or the creation of the interest in respect of which a claim is made was not reasonably necessary and was carried out with a view to obtaining or increasing compensation'.

It must also be remembered that section 50 of the Land Compensation Act 1973 provides that compensation for the compulsory acquisition of an interest in land is not to be reduced because alternative residential accommodation is to be provided for the person entitled to receive compensation.

Well maintained payments

We have already encountered well maintained payments in respect of individual unfit houses in Chapter 8, above, and we must now consider them in relation to houses in clearance areas. It must again be noted that procedures have changed considerably over the years and that it is necessary to bear many dates in mind when deciding *what* law applies to which house. Section 60 of the Housing Act 1957 provides:

'(1) Where as respects a house —
  (a) which is made the subject of a compulsory purchase order under this Part of this Act as being unfit for human habitation
  or
  (b) which is made the subject of a clearance order,
the Minister is satisfied, after causing the house to be inspected by an officer of his department that it has been well maintained, the Minister may give directions for the making by the local authority of a payment in respect of the house under this section of such amount, if any, as is authorised by Part 1 of the Second Schedule to this Act . . .'.

Such payments are made to owner-occupiers, or, if the house is not owner-occupied, to the person legally responsible for repair. Alternatively the payment may be made in whole or part to other persons who satisfy the local authority that they have been responsible to a material extent for the good maintenance of the property. If it appears equitable to make a payment to such persons the local authority may do so. This latter provision will cover tenants provided their entitlement can be made out. A claim by a tenant should be notified to the landlord for his comments before the payment is made: see *Hoggard v Worsborough UDC* [1962] 2 QB 93, [1962] 1 All ER 468. Indeed if rival claims for payments are made each claimant must be given a chance to be heard.

The above provisions apply to houses made subject to clearance or compulsory purchase orders *before* 31 August 1974. In relation to action taken after that date section 108(2) of and Schedule 9 to the Housing Act 1974 substituted new provisions in place of section 60(1) of the Housing Act 1957. These new provisions make the law very much more complex than it was before 1974. This is largely because section 67 of the Housing Act 1969 introduced the concept of the 'partially well maintained house' where, despite the overall bad state of the house, *either* the interior or the exterior have been well maintained, and provided in such cases for a payment of one half of the normal well maintained payment to be made. The law therefore now requires the local authority to take the following steps in relation to both full and partial well maintained payments.

1) Where a house is made subject to a compulsory purchase order as being unfit the local authority must serve notice on every owner, lessee, mortgagee and occupier of the house.

2) This notice must be served not later than that notice which is served explaining the effect of the making of the compulsory purchase order.

3) The notice must state the local authority's opinion of the house, for example whether it is fully or partially well maintained (and if the latter in what respects) or not well maintained at all. The notice must also state the authority's reason for their opinion.

Provision is made for a 'person aggrieved' by a refusal to make a payment or by a decision to make only a partial payment to make written representations to the Secretary of State challenging the authority's decision. If the Secretary of State considers it appropriate he may cause the house to be inspected by a member of his department, and may then give directions to the local authority to make such payments or further payments as he thinks the case requires.

The meaning of 'well maintained'

Oddly enough the phrase 'well maintained' itself is not defined in the legislation. In *Slum Clearance and Compensation* Professor Garner says on page 38: 'A good state of decoration, internal and external, would almost certainly entitle a house to be considered under these provisions, and so would the case where money has been spent on (for example) roof repairs and other necessary matters to keep a house weather-tight'. It must be remembered that, by definition, a house which is the subject of a well maintained payment is statutorily unfit and so what is really being looked for is a genuine effort on the part of the person claiming the payment to have kept the property in the best possible state bearing in mind all the problems with which he or she has been faced.

The amount of the payment

Part I of Schedule 2 to the Housing Act 1957 as amended and sub-stituted by section 66 of and Schedule 4 to the Housing Act 1969 states that amount of a well maintained payment is to be an amount equal to the rateable value multiplied by such a figure as is prescribed from time to time by Statutory Instrument. The current multiplier under S.I. 1973 No. 753 is $3\frac{1}{8}$. Where a partially well maintained payment is made the computation method used is exactly the same as for a full payment but only half of the resulting sum is paid.

It must also be noted that:

1) A well maintained payment may not exceed the amount whereby the full market value of the house exceeds the site value (see Chapter 8, above);

2) No well maintained payment can be made where a payment is due under Part II of Schedule 2 to the Housing Act 1957 or Schedule 5 to the Housing Act 1969. These provisions allow the payment of special supplements to owner-occupiers of unfit houses who have been driven by housing shortages to purchase sub-standard dwellings as homes. These payments have to be made in such cases as the following:

    a) Under the 1957 Act (as amended) where:
- (i) the house was purchased at *site* value because of, for example, a compulsory purchase order;
- (ii) the order, etc. was made before 13 December 1965, or the order was made within fifteen years of the owner-occupier acquiring his interest, *provided* he acquired it within the period 13 December 1950 to 13 December 1955;
- (iii) on the 13 December 1955 the house was wholly or partly occupied as a private dwelling by a person (or a member of his family) who acquired an interest in it by purchase for value, between the dates 1 September 1939 *and* 13 December 1955 *or* the date when the compulsory acquisition, etc., proceedings were begun, whichever was the earlier; *and*
- (iv) at the date of the compulsory purchase, etc., that person or a member of his family was entitled to an interest in the house;

    b) Under the 1969 Act where:
- (i) the house has been purchased at site value following proceedings commenced *after* 23 April 1968; and
- (ii) if on that date of commencement of proceedings, and if for two years before that date, the house has been wholly or partly occupied as a private dwelling by a person entitled to an interest in it or a member of his family.

These two entitlements are mutually exclusive. However, the amount of compensation payable is the same in both cases: the full compulsory purchase value (i.e. the market value of site plus house) *less* the compensation payable in respect of the interest in connection with the compulsory purchase of the house at site value, and *also less* a proportion corresponding to any part of the house not used as a private dwelling. In this context the term 'private dwelling' includes occupation as a private dwelling by the claimant's tenant, see: *Hunter v Manchester City Council* [1975] QB 877, [1975] 2 All ER 966.

So far we have been concerned with payments that go, in general terms, to the owners of certain legally recognised interests in land. In the case of most unfit houses this will mean either the owner-occupier or the landlord, though as we have seen there are times when a tenant can receive a well maintained payment in respect of his home. It is now necessary to consider other payments that may have to be made in respect of unfit houses.

Disturbance payments

These must *not* be confused with disturbance as a head of compensation to be assessed separately under section 5 of the Land Compensation Act 1961. Disturbance as *compensation* is payable to a person whose interest in land has been compulsorily acquired: disturbance as a *payment* is payable to a person whose *occupation* of land is disturbed in consequence of acquisition. Disturbance payments are made according to the provisions of section 37 of the Land Compensation Act 1973, and are payable in respect of displacements occuring on or after 17 October 1972 or 31 July 1974 in the case of displacement following improvements under the Housing Act 1974. The following conditions must be satisfied before a payment can be made.

1) The authority must have acted in relation to the land in question either:
    (a) in the exercise of its compulsory purchase powers, or
    (b) by making or accepting a housing order or undertaking, or serving an improvement notice under Part VIII of the Housing Act 1974, or
    (c) by carrying out redevelopment or improvements in respect of land already acquired compulsorily and retained for such purposes, or
    (d) where a duly registered housing association which has already acquired the land carries out the work of improvement or redevelopment.

2) The person receiving the payment must have been in lawful possession of the land. Such 'lawful possession' must exist at the time of displacement and also at the earlier time when the draft compulsory purchase order, or housing order or undertaking, or agreement to purchase were made. Thus a mere lodger could not receive a payment under the Act as he has no 'possession' of land.

3) The person receiving the payment must:
    (a) have *no* interest in the land for the acquisition of which he is otherwise statutorily entitled to compensation *or*

(b) have such an interest as is compensatable only under a site value provision of the Housing Act 1957 and which does not qualify for any owner-occupier supplement.

4) Where a disturbed occupier is entitled to both a disturbance payment and compensation under section 37 of the Landlord and Tenant Act 1954 he may take only one payment and not both.

Where there is no entitlement to a disturbance payment or to any other form of statutory disturbance an ex gratia payment may be made by the authority concerned under section 37(3) of the Land Compensation Act 1973. Payments can thus be made to lodgers and other mere licensees in deserving cases. Department of the Environment Circular 73/73 urges local authorities to make sympathetic use of this power.

The amount of disturbance payments is governed by section 38 of the 1973 Act. Such a payment must cover:

1) the reasonable moving expenses of the claimant;

2) any loss by reason of disturbance to trade or business (in the case of business premises only), and

3) in the case of a dwelling structurally modified for a disabled person, a reasonable sum to cover the cost of making comparable modifications to his new house, *provided* that in the case of his former home a local authority grant was available to cover the cost of the work.

A disturbance payment carries interest at the rate fixed from time to time under section 32 of the Land Compensation Act 1961 from the date of displacement until payment. Any dispute over the amount of a payment is to be settled by the Lands Tribunal.

Other powers to assist displaced occupiers

The Land Compensation Act 1973, s. 43 allows authorities to pay the reasonable expenses of acquisition of a new dwelling (but *not* the purchase price) to a person displaced from a dwelling in consequence of the exercise of compulsory purchase powers, the making of a housing order or undertaking or the service of an improvement notice under Part VIII of the Housing Act 1974, provided that:

1) the dwelling is acquired within one year of the displacement and is comparable with that from which he was reasonably displaced;

2) that the person displaced had no greater interest in his former dwelling than that of a tenant from year to year.

Home loss payments

Department of the Environment Circular No. 73/73, para. 21, states: 'The intention of these special payments is to recognise the personal upset and distress which people suffer when they are compulsorily displaced from their homes . . . either by compulsory purchase, redevelopment or any action under the Housing Acts. The entitlement to a payment is quite separate from and is not dependent on any right to compensation or a disturbance payment'.

Such payments exist under section 29 of the Land Compensation Act 1973, as amended by Schedule 2 to the Land Compensation (Scotland) Act 1973, the Housing Act 1974 s. 130 and Sch. 13, and the Housing Rents and Subsidies Act 1975, s. 17 and Sch. 5. They are payable to persons who have been in occupation of the dwelling in question, or a substantial part thereof, throughout a period of not less than five years ending with the date of displacement, provided that their occupation arose out of their possessing either an interest in the dwelling, or a statutory tenancy of the dwelling, or a Part VI contract under the Rent Act 1968 in respect of the dwelling, or a right to occupy it under a contract of employment. (Strangely enough the 1973 Act has *not* been amended to take note of the fact that the 1968 Rent Act has been repealed and replaced by the Rent Act 1977 under which the old Part VI Contracts are now called 'restricted contracts'. The legislature's omission could lead to a loss of entitlement for persons claiming under restricted contracts arising after the 1977 Act came into force, i.e. 29 August 1977.)

A person who is otherwise qualified for a home loss payment will be entitled to receive one if he is displaced from his home as a consequence of any of the following circumstances:

1) the compulsory acquisition of the dwelling;

2) the making, or acceptance, of a housing order or undertaking in respect of the dwelling;

3) the service of an improvement notice under Part VII of the Housing Act 1974 in respect of the dwelling;

4) the carrying out by the local authority of works of improvement or redevelopment, etc., in respect of land previously acquired by them.

In this last context it should be noted that a local authority tenant who is displaced from a council owned house because his landlords wish to demolish and replace dwellings which are unfit is entitled to a home loss payment because his loss is due to redevelopment, see: *R v Corby District Council, ex parte McClean* [1975] 2 All ER 568, [1975] 1 WLR 735.

A person who claims a home loss payment as a consequence of the compulsory acquisition of his dwelling will lose his entitlement if he gives up his occupation of the premises on a date before the authority were authorised to acquire them, which would seem to mean the date of confirmation of the compulsory purchase order. Furthermore home loss payments are not payable to persons displaced as a result of their having served planning blight notices under, for example, section 192 of the Town and Country Planning Act 1971. However, payments are to be made where an authority possessing compulsory purchase powers acquires, by agreement, an interest in a dwelling from any person, *to* any other person displaced from the dwelling in consequence. This protects the rights of tenants where the landlord sells his house by agreement to the local authority.

A claim for a payment must be made in writing, and supported by such reasonable particulars as the local authority may reasonably require. Once the entitlement to a payment is made out the authority have to make the payment not later than three months after the date of the claim, or, if those three months end before the date of displacement, on the date of displacement, see the Land Compensation Act 1973 s. 32 (as amended by the Local Government, Planning and Land Act 1980 s. 114). The amount of the payment will be a sum equal to the rateable value of the dwelling multiplied by three, subject to a maximum of £1,500 and a minimum of £150, see section 30(1) of the 1973 Act. By section 32(6) of the 1973 Act where there are two or more persons entitled to claim a home loss payment in respect of the same dwelling, for example because of joint occupancy, the payment is to be divided equally between them.

The fate of the land after acquisition

Under section 47 of the Housing Act 1957 the general duty of a local authority who have acquired land for clearance purposes is to see to the vacation and demolition of all buildings as soon as possible. They may do this themselves or they may sell the land subject to a condition that the buildings must be demolished forthwith. This general duty is subject to the power contained in section 48 of the Act which provides for temporary retention of unfit houses in clearance areas, provided the local authority are of the opinion that the houses are or can be rendered capable of providing accommodation which is adequate for the time being. The thinking behind this provision was explained in Ministry of Housing and Local Government Circular No. 55/54: 'In some areas the numbers of unfit houses liable to demolition is so large that it will still be many years before all the houses can be demolished . . . local authorities should be enabled to make those houses which have to be retained for some time more tolerable for the people who will have to live in them until they can be demolished and replaced'.

Accordingly local authorities are given a further power to do such works as are necessary from time to time to keep the houses up to the standard required by the section. This standard is never very high and does not amount to much more than a requirement of 'patching-up'. Ministry of Housing and Local Government Circular No. 55/54 counsels local authorities to make wind-and-weather tight any houses that have a prospective life of five years or more. A local authority is not justified in resolving to postpone demolition and thereafter simply doing nothing to improve the lot of their tenants living in such properties. The passing of such a resolution will not protect an authority should they be found responsible for the existence of a statutory nuisance comprising premises prejudicial to health in the retained houses, see: *Salford City Council v McNally* [1976] AC 379, [1975] 2 All ER 860, and Chapter 8, above.

Rehousing displaced residents

Section 39 of the Land Compensation Act 1973, as amended by the Land Compensation (Scotland) Act 1973 and section 130(1) of and Schedule 13 to the Housing Act 1974 provides:

'(1) Where a person is displaced from residential accommodation on any land in consequence of
  (a) the acquisition of the land by an authority possessing compulsory purchase powers;
  (b) the making . . . or acceptance of a housing order . . . or undertaking in respect of a house or building on the land;
  (c) where the land has been previously acquired by an authority possessing compulsory purchase powers or appropriated by a local authority and is for the time being held by the authority for the purposes for which it was acquired or appropriated, the carrying out of any improvement to a house or building on the land or of redevelopment on the land;
  (d) the service of an improvement notice, within the meaning of Part VIII of the Housing Act 1974, in respect of premises in which that accommodation is situated,
and suitable alternative accommodation is not otherwise available to that person, then, subject to the provisions of this section, it shall be the duty of the relevant authority to secure that he will be provided with such other accommodation'.

Within the context of slum clearance, either on an individual or an area basis, this means that local authorities have an obligation to rehouse persons displaced as a result of the making of demolition, closing or clearance orders or the accepting of undertakings under section 16 of the Housing Act 1957. Some local authorities adopt a wider obligation as a matter of administrative practice, and the strictly limited nature of the section 39 obligation should be noted. It does not apply to squatters nor to persons permitted to reside in a house pending its demolition or improvement, such as under a municipally licensed short-life property scheme where, for example, university students are permitted to occupy houses awaiting demolition on a strictly limited time basis. The duty only applies, in general terms, to persons resident in the dwelling on the date when the order, or undertaking, etc., was made or accepted or when notice of its making was published, as the case may be. Moreover, in the case of displacements arising out of the doing of works of improvements the obligation is only owed to persons who are *permanently* displaced.

The greatest restriction on the scope of the obligations is that it confers no right on persons displaced to have priority over other persons on the housing waiting list. In *R v Bristol Corpn, ex parte Hendy* [1974] 1 All ER 1047, [1974] 1 WLR 498 the applicant lived in a basement flat where he enjoyed Rent Act security of tenure but which was also statutorily unfit. Mr Hendy had a history of rent arrears with another local authority and Bristol Corporation offered him only temporary accommodation, pending an offer of suitable residential accommodation, on the terms usually offered to prospective municipal tenants. He applied for an order of mandamus to compel the local authority to fulfil their rehousing duty, contending that this was an obligation to provide him with permanent accommodation on terms that gave him a security of tenure equivalent to that which he had enjoyed under his former tenancy. The Court of Appeal refused the order. They concluded that the duty is only to act reasonably and to do the best practicable job in providing a displaced person with other accommodation. A local authority does all that is required by providing such a person with temporary accommodation until a council house is available.

The content of the section 39 duty is not great, though, such as it is, it can be enforced by way of mandamus. Alternatively there may be a remedy by way of an action for breach of statutory duty should a local authority fail to take any action with resultant damage to the plaintiff. As with such actions under the terms of the Housing (Homeless Persons) Act 1977, the exact quantification of loss could prove difficult: see Chapter 6, above.

Rehabilitation of houses in clearance areas

As part of the general change in emphasis from demolition to area improvement, and also because of acute housing shortages in some areas, power is now given to rehabilitate and improve houses within clearance areas which are capable of being improved to the full standard of the Housing Act 1974.

Section 114 of the Housing Act 1974, as substituted by Schedule 5 to the Housing Rents and Subsidies Act 1975 and amended by Schedule 25 to the Housing Act 1980 provides:

'(1) This section applies to any house comprised in a clearance area under Part III of the Housing Act 1957

    (a) which has been purchased by agreement or compulsorily at any time before 2 December 1974 under section 43 of the Housing Act 1957, or

    (b) which is subject to a compulsory purchase order —

        (i) which was made under that section at any time before 2 December 1974 and

        (ii) which at any time before 2 March 1975 has been confirmed in accordance with Schedule 3 to the Housing Act 1957;

(1A) In the case of a clearance area comprising houses within subsection (1)(a) or (b) above, this section also applies to houses comprised in the area which have been included in it by virtue of section 49 of the Housing Act 1957.

(2) Where any house to which this section applies —

    (a) was included in the clearance area by reason of its being unfit for human habitation, and

    (b) in the opinion of the local authority is capable of being, and ought to be, improved to the full standard,

the local authority may make and submit to the Secretary of State an order . . . in relation to that house'.

The procedure for making such a 'rehabilitation order' is contained in Schedule 10 to the Housing Act 1974 as substituted by Schedule 5 to the Housing Rents and Subsidies Act 1975. The owner of an unfit house within a clearance area may apply to the local authority requesting them to make a rehabilitation order. Whether or not to make such an order is for the local authority to decide, though they must direct themselves properly in law and consider all and only the relevant considerations. In *Elliott v Southwark London Borough Council* [1976] 2 All ER 781, [1976] 1 WLR 499, a compulsory purchase order was made and confirmed in respect of certain houses. Following the service of notice to treat some of the affected owners applied for rehabilitation orders on their houses. The Council refused the applications, stating that they considered that the land should be cleared and redeveloped for new housing. Local authorities are, of course, under a duty to give their reasons for such a refusal. The owners sought to impugn the decision on the grounds:

1) that the local authority had failed to give an adequate statement of their reasons for refusing the application, and

2) that they had not taken into account the relevant considerations in coming to their decision, in that they had relied solely on the evidence presented at the public local inquiry into the initial compulsory purchase order, and had failed to take account of changes in housing policy and economics since the date of that inquiry.

The Court of Appeal rejected both contentions. The first ground of the appeal was easily dismissed on factual grounds; the statement given contained the salient reason for the authority's decision. As to the second contention the Court held that the local authority were justified in taking the evidence of the inquiry into account, and there was no evidence that they had failed to consider the other relevant issues. The actual factors to be considered in any given situation will vary from case to case, and the courts will not prescribe a list of matters which must be considered. The courts are concerned solely to prevent abuses of discretion and not to substitute their decisions for those of local authorities. Indeed in *A-G ex rel. Rivers-Moore v Portsmouth City Council* (1978) 36 P & CR 416 at 424, Walton J went further and stated that the declaration of a rehabilitation area 'appears to me to be a matter in the discretion of the council. There is no provision made for any challenge to the council's decision in that regard. That being the case I do not see that this court can do anything about it at all, even if it thought the council was being utterly unreasonable in not considering such a solution to the problem'. This should not be read literally, and should be taken rather as authority for the proposition that a court is not there to dispose of municipal decisions merely if it disagrees with them.

Where a local authority resolve to make a rehabilitation order the procedure they must follow is as follows. The order must be made in the prescribed form and must describe the affected properties by reference to a map. Before submitting the order to the Secretary of State for confirmation they must publish notice in one or more local newspapers stating the making and intended application of the order, and giving notice of the time and place where the order and the map can be seen. They must also serve notice on all those persons who were, or who should have been, informed of the making of the original compulsory purchase order, together with any persons having an interest in the property, other than a tenant for a month or less. These notices must state the local authority's reasons for making the order; the effect of the order; that it is to be submitted for confirmation, and the procedure for making objections. If the Secretary of State receives any objections which are not subsequently withdrawn he must hold a public local inquiry, or arrange for the objectors to be heard before his representative. The Secretary may require objectors to state the grounds of their objections in writing, and he may disregard any objection which relates solely to issues of compensation. After considering the report submitted to him following the hearing of objections the Secretary may confirm or amend the order. Following confirmation notice must be published in the local press, and served on objectors. Persons aggrieved by the making of an order have the usual six week right of appeal on a point of law to the High Court. If no such appeal is made the order will come into force and notice of this must be served on all those on whom notice of the original compulsory purchase order was served.

Once the order becomes operative the duty to demolish the properties in question ceases. In its place the local authority come under a duty under section 114A of the Housing Act 1974 to take such steps as are necessary to bring them up to the full standard of section 103A of the Housing Act 1974 (see below, Chapter 10). They must do the work themselves so as to produce one or more full standard dwellings, or, where a house is not vested in them, they must ensure that the houses are so restored. To this end they may accept undertakings from the owner or other persons who have or will have an interest in the houses that the work will be done within an agreed time. Following the coming into effect of a rehabilitation order any affected building previously acquired by the local authority is deemed to have been acquired under either Part V of the Housing Act 1957 or Part VI of the Town and Country Planning Act 1971. Section 115 of the Housing Act 1974 declares that where such a 'deemed acquisition' takes place, the compensation is to be assessed in accordance with either Part V of the 1957 Act or Part VI of the 1971 Act, and this may lead to an increase in the amount of compensation payable. Any affected building *not yet* acquired and in respect of which a notice to treat has *not* been served is freed from the compulsory purchase order, and the clearance area, as from the date when the rehabilitation order becomes effective, see generally Department of the Environment Circular No. 40/75, and Schedule 10 to the Housing Act 1974 as amended.

Further reading

Berry, F., *Housing: The Great British Failure* (Charles Knight, 1974) pp. 158 – 169

English, J., Madigan, R., and Norman P., *Slum Clearance* (Croom Helm, 1976) Chaps. 1, 2, 3, 6, 7, 8 and 9

Garner, J.F., *Slum Clearance and Compensation* (Oyez, 1975) pp. 35 – 41 and 51 – 107

Gee, D., *Slum Clearance* (Shelter)

Jacobs, S., *The Right to a Decent Home* (Routledge and Kegan Paul, 1976)

Social Welfare Law (Ed. by D.W. Pollard) (Oyez) paras. C. 4152 – C. 4444

Chapter 10

Improvement policies

A response to bad housing conditions based on improvement and area rehabilitation has recently been preferred in housing policy. The temptation has been to regard area improvement as a panacea for the ills of decaying inner city areas.

The problem of decaying inner urban areas has been noted for some time. Such localities suffer from multiple deprivation; bad housing is combined with poor educational facilities, a concentration of work opportunities in badly paid unskilled jobs, sickness, a lack of leisure facilities and feelings of social alienation and powerlessness among the inhabitants. The generally bad conditions of housing, education, leisure, employment, social welfare and nourishment in such areas interact to maintain a poor quality of life. Before any real improvement can be expected there has to be a national commitment to raising standards, not just of housing, but of education, employment, health and social welfare for such localities. Housing improvement by itself is not enough. Unfortunately concentration on such individual aspects of the inner urban problem has too often been the hallmark of central policy.

History

By the 1930's it was realised that many houses were unnecessarily declining in condition because their owners lacked the resources to keep them in good condition. The problem was noted by the Moyne Report Cmd. 4397 in 1933 and the Ridley Report Cmd. 6621 in 1945. The Housing Act 1935 gave local authorities powers to acquire houses which could be made suitable for the working class, and also powers to alter, enlarge, repair and improve such properties. No real use was made of these powers. In 1947 the Hobhouse Report recommended that powers of compulsion should be introduced to ensure rehabilitation. The Housing Act 1949 introduced improvement grants but little use was made of the grant aiding powers. Between 1949 and 1953 only 6,000 grants were given. Improving economic prospects and more liberal grant conditions contained in the Housing Repairs and Rents Act 1954 led to more grants being given. The rate of improvements rose to some 30,000 per annum and by the end of 1958 160,000 grants had been made. In 1960 over 130,000 improvement grants were made. By 1964 the number of houses improved passed 800,000. It became apparent that the logical extension of housing improvement was to create a new system of area improvement as opposed to giving grants on individual houses.

Some 86,000 dwellings a year were cleared during the 1960's but by the end of the decade opinion was moving rapidly in favour of rehabilitation, and 'banishing the bulldozer'. The reasons for this change were:

1) general dissatisfaction with clearance policies, in particular;
    (a) repeated postponement of rehousing dates for residents in clearance areas,
    (b) appalling living conditions in such areas during the rehousing process, and
    (c) lack of communication between those waiting to be rehoused and local authorities;

2) the realisation that much new housing built to replace unfit property was highly unpopular with those living in it;

3) the feeling that comprehensive redevelopment led to the destruction of communities;

4) the fact that the very worst slum housing had been demolished;

5) increasing emphasis placed on owner-occupation, a consequent decline in public sector house building, leading to a cut back in clearance programmes;

6) the argument that improvement was cheaper than redevelopment.

The Housing Act 1964 made area improvement part of the housing obligations of local authorities. Unfortunately cumbersome procedures laid down by the legislation ensured that little progress would be achieved. In four years only 136 of the 1,400 local authorities in England and Wales declared improvement areas, and only 3,500 dwellings in such areas were improved. The Housing Act 1969 introduced a freer and more informal approach. The rate of improvement rose from 124,000 in 1969 to 233,000 in 1971. The debate on redevelopment or improvement was not concluded, however, despite the fact that the improvement rate rose to 454,000 in 1973. The figures were misleading for two-fifths of the improved dwellings were council houses, and two-fifths were owner occupied, while only 74,000 were in the privately rented sector where the worst housing conditions were to be found.

Nevertheless the pressure for a change in housing policy was growing. In 1973 the government accepted as official orthodoxy that comprehensive redevelopment was no longer the answer to the problem of bad housing. It was also realised that an indiscriminate improvement grant policy was not enough to improve the condition of the worst housing. Between 1969 and 1974 some 1⅔ million houses were improved, but most of the money was spent where it was less urgently needed. The same years saw 900 general improvement areas declared, but only 75,000 grants approved in such areas. Many improvement grants were taken up by speculators and persons seeking cheap second homes. The consequence was that the original inhabitants of an area could be gradually displaced by more wealthy folk buying improved dwellings, a process known as 'gentrification'.

The policy changes were enshrined in the Housing Act 1974. This was designed to prevent gentrification, and to concentrate resources on the most needy areas. It also introduced a much greater measure of central control over area rehabilitation policies. However, the law and policy of rehabilitation have not been without their critics, and neither has been completely effective in practice. The problems inherent in developing a housing renewal policy are outlined below.

1) The danger that renewal is seen as a cheap alternative to a major national programme of new house building.

2) The fact that grant aid is tied to the concept of the 'eligible expense' on the house, and not to the householder's income. The poor need substantial help to improve their homes yet they do not receive it; for the poorer the quality of the house the more the householder has to meet from his own pocket. Such out of pocket contributions are way beyond the means of poorer people.

3) The expense and inconvenience of improvement are not reflected in a commensurate increase in the sale value of an improved house.

4) Resistance by private landlords, many of whom derive a substantial income from letting out houses in multiple occupation, and who stand to lose income if their properties are improved and converted into a smaller number of acceptable self-contained units of accommodation.

5) Ignorance and fear on the part of tenants, particularly where many are old or where there is a transient population, leading to a lack of demand for improvement.

6) The complexity and bureaucratic nature of the procedures required to bring about improvement.

7) The fact that areas ripe for improvement from a physical point of view are often socially unready for it because of:

(a) local disbelief in continued governmental commitment to improvement policies, especially where the declaration of some form of area improvement has been followed by no action at all, which can happen because of the inadequate staff levels of the local authority;

(b) racial tensions and jealousies;

(c) disinclination on the part of those who stay in such areas to spend any money on their houses, while those who would be prepared to invest are the socially mobile element of the population who are likely to move out to other more favoured localities.

8) The supicion that improvement policy has become too 'area-orientated' and not enough concerned with improving the lot of those houses and households in the greatest need.

9) Insistence by some local authorities on over high standards of improvement which daunt some would be improvers.

10) A reaction from inhabitants in improvement areas that the level of improvement and the associated environmental works are cosmetic improvements and irrelevant diversions from the *real* needs of the areas.

11) The high inflation rates of the last few years which have sent the price of property repairs soaring.

12) The difficulty of finding reputable builders willing to undertake work under an area improvement scheme; a difficulty experienced particularly amongst the immigrant communities.

13) Continued difficulty experienced by local authorities in attracting building society mortgage finance into improvement areas.

14) The lack of a *comprehensive* and effective rehabilitation code; at the moment the law distinguishes unnecessarily between compulsory *repair* under the Public Health Acts 1936 and 1961 and the Housing Act 1957, and compulsory *improvement* under the Housing Act 1974.

15) Above all the realisation that the policy of improvement can only work if sufficient resources are allotted to it.

Many factors militate against a successful improvement policy. Whether the amendment of the 1974 Act by the Housing Act 1980 will go any way towards bringing about a more favourable climate for the working of the policy is debateable. The First Report of the House of Commons Environment Committee, 24 July 1980, H.C. 714 noted the memoranda accompanying the Housing Bill 1980 stating that, once enacted, the new provisions would lead to additional expenditure on improvement of some £20 million per annum. This increased expenditure will have to be met from within local authorities' existing capital allocations; no new resources are to be made specially available.

How many unsatisfactory houses are there?

It is impossible to state with certainty how many houses fail to meet acceptable standards. The law has many different standards by which a house can be judged, and different statistical sampling techniques produce different figures. In 1976 the English House Condition Survey stated there were 794,000 dwellings *unfit for human habitation* under the Housing Act 1957, some 4.6 per cent of the total housing stock; 921,000 dwellings, 5.4 per cent of the housing stock, were *fit* but lacked certain basic amenities, while 1,480,000 dwellings, 8.7 per cent of the stock, were *fit*, had all the basic amenities but required repairs costing over £500. The Survey found some 550,000 dwellings were *unfit*, lacked at least one basic amenity and also required repairs costing more than £500. It was also pointed out that housing disrepair was an increasingly serious problem and that some 792,000 otherwise fit dwellings with all amenities needed 'substantial repairs' within the meaning of section 9(1A) of the Housing Act 1957. Between 1971 and 1976 the Survey estimated some 317,000 houses had declined into unfitness, an annual rate of 70,000.

The Housing Policy Green Paper Cmnd. 6851 reviewing the number of *households* unsatisfactorily housed produced the following figures for England *and* Wales, with the English figures shown separately in brackets.

Multi person households sharing	275,000	(265,000)
One person households sharing	375,000	(365,000)
Overcrowded households	150,000	(125,000)
'Concealed' households	360,000	(330,000)
Occupiers of dwellings that are unfit and/or lacking in one or more basic amenities	1,650,000	(1,520,000)

The National Dwelling and Housing Survey 1977 estimated by the end of 1977 the figures of unsatisfactorily housed households for *England alone* were:

Multi person households sharing	190,000
One person households sharing	330,000
Overcrowded households	75,000
Concealed households	245,000
Occupiers of dwellings that are unfit and/or lacking in one or more basic amenities	1,270,000

(These figures are open to doubt on the basis that the statistical sample on which they are based was small.)

It should be remembered that the figures show only dwellings failing to comply with the *minimum* standards of the law. In drawing up standards of satisfactory housing conditions the law takes no account of matters which any humane and civilised person would consider essential, such as the need for families with children to be housed at, or very near to, ground level, the need for central heating and safe electrical wiring systems and freedom from environmental deficiency.

Even according to the present low standards it must still be many years before all unsatisfactory dwellings are eradicated. Forecasts made for the Housing Policy Green Paper in 1976 expected the total of *households* unsatisfactorily housed to fall from 1,590,000 in 1976 to 720,000 in 1986. The latest predictions drawn up for the House of Commons Environment Committee show that the present numbers of unsatisfactory *houses* are not likely to disappear as quickly as was hoped.

Local authorities' estimates of changes in substandard stock 1979 – 1984 — England

Thousand

England	Public sector		Private sector (LA view)	
	Over 5 years	Annual rate	Over 5 years	Annual rate
Becoming substandard	26	5	150	30
Acquisition for clearance	92	18	− 92	− 18
Closures and demolitions	− 118	− 24	− 39	− 8
Acquisitions for improvement	98	20	− 98	− 20
Improvement to minimum standard ..	− 32	− 6	− 85	− 17
Improvement above minimum standard ..	− 234	− 47	− 295	− 59
Other transfers	− 3	− 1	− 1	—
Net change 1979 − 1984	− 172	− 34	− 461	− 92

Local authorities' estimates of the rate of renovation 1979 – 1984 — England

Thousand

DOE Region	Public sector				Private	Total
	Local authorities	Housing associations	Other public	All public sector		
1979 SUBSTANDARD						
Number	253	29	33	315	1,377	1,692
Per cent of dwelling stock	5.4	10.5	5.3	5.7	11.4	9.6
CHANGE 1979 – 1984						
Becoming substandard ..	21	2	3	26	150	175
Acquisition for clearance	91	1	0	92	—	92	0
Closures and demolitions	− 112	− 1	− 5	− 118	—	39	− 157
Acquisition for improvement	40	66	− 8	98	—	98	0
Improvement to minimum standard ..	− 20	− 11	− 1	− 32	—	85	− 117
Improvement above minimum standard ..	− 162	− 69	− 3	− 234	− 295	− 529
Other transfers	1	1	− 5	− 3	—	1	− 5
Net change 1979 – 1984	− 142	− 12	− 19	− 172	− 461	− 634
1984 SUBSTANDARD						
Number	112	17	13	142	916	1,058
Per cent of dwelling stock	2.4	6.1	2.1	2.6	7.6	6.0

Local authorities' estimates of the rate of renovation 1979 – 1984 by region

Thousand

DOE Region	Substandard dwellings				Change in number 1979 to 1984
	1979		1984		
	Number	Per cent of dwelling stock	Number	Per cent of dwelling stock	
Northern	86	7.3	33	2.6	− 53
Yorkshire & Humberside ..	251	13.6	161	8.3	− 90
East Midlands	147	10.3	79	5.1	− 68
Eastern .. ·	143	7.2	93	4.3	− 50
London	303	11.1	202	7.1	− 101
South East	174	7.0	124	4.7	− 50
South West	127	7.8	91	5.1	− 36
West Midlands	195	10.4	123	6.2	− 72
North West	266	10.9	152	5.9	− 114
England	1,692	9.6	1.058	5.7	− 634

House renovation grants

General conditions as to availability

The pattern of grants established by the Acts of 1969 to 1980 is that they are percentage payments of those costs of improvement, etc., deemed to be eligible. Under Part VII and section 56 of the Housing Act 1974 local authorities (effectively district councils and London Boroughs) are under a duty to provide grants towards the cost of works required for:

1) the provision of dwellings by conversion;

2) the improvement of dwellings;

3) the repair of dwellings; and

4) the improvement of houses in multiple occupation.

For the purposes of the 1974 Act a 'dwelling' is a 'building or part of a building occupied or intended to be occupied as a separate dwelling, together with any yard, garden, outhouses . . . belonging to or usually enjoyed with that building or part'. Houses, flats and other buildings, used as residences, and also 'separate' in that they do not share living accommodation such as kitchens, are grant aidable.

Various sorts of grants are payable.

1) An improvement grant — a grant in respect of works required for the provision of a dwelling by the conversion of existing houses or other buildings, or for the improvement of a dwelling.

2) An intermediate grant — a grant in respect of the installation in a dwelling of standard amenities.

3) A special grant — a grant in respect of works required for the installation of standard amenities or the means of escape from fire in a house in multiple occupation.

4) A repair grant — a grant payable in respect of repairs or replacement not associated with improvement. In the past such grants were only payable in respect of houses subject to area action. This requirement has been repealed by Schedule 26 to the Housing Act 1980. This could raise the number of such grants paid each year from a few hundred to between 50,000 and 100,000.

In general applications for grants may not be entertained where:

1) the application is for an improvement grant in respect of works of conversion on a house or other building erected after 2 October 1961; or

2) the application is for *any* grant in respect of the improvement or repair of a dwelling provided after 2 October 1961.

The Secretary of State has power to give directions as to circumstances in which local authorities may entertain such applications, see Department of the Environment Circular No. 13/76, paragraph 5.

Other general conditions as to the availability of grants have been altered by the Housing Act 1980. Some changes have been made in section 57 of the Housing Act 1974. The amended general conditions are listed below:

1) An application for a grant must:
    (a) specify the premises to which it relates;
    (b) contain particulars of the works in respect of which the grant is sought and give an estimate of their cost, and
    (c) contain such other particulars as are ministerially specified, see Department of the Environment Circular 160/74.

2) An application may not be *approved* unless the applicant satisfies the local authority that he holds the freehold, or an unexpired leasehold term of at least five years, of the land on which the work is to be carried out. In respect of grants under Part VII of the 1974 Act, *other* than an improvement grant in respect of works required for the *provision* of a dwelling, section 106 of the Housing Act 1980 allows applications from protected, statutory and secure tenants, those having tenancies under section 1 of the Landlord and Tenant Act 1954, protected occupants and statutory tenants under the Rent (Agriculture) Act 1976 and other tenants satisfying conditions prescribed by order. Local authorities may refuse to entertain such applications unless they are accompanied by certificates from the landlord (who may be the freeholder or a superior leaseholder with an unexpired term of five years) that:
    (a) the dwelling will be let or available for letting as a residence, and not for a holiday, to a person other than a member of the family of the person giving the certificate; or
    (b) the dwelling will be occupied or available for occupation by a member of the agricultural population in pursuance of a contract of service and otherwise than as a tenant.
The highly discretionary nature of the provision should be noted.

3) An application for an improvement or intermediate grant may not be approved in contravention of directions given by the Secretary of State. See Department of the Environment Circulars Nos. 160/74 and 13/76.

4) Applications may not be approved where the work has already been begun, unless the authority are satisfied that it was begun for good reasons.

5) Applications may not be entertained from a person who has made an earlier application for a grant if:

(a) the earlier application was approved, and
(b) the second application is in respect wholly or partly of the same work.

These restrictions do not apply if the relevant works have not been begun and either:

(a) more than two years has elapsed since the approval of the earlier application, or
(b) the second application is made with a view to taking advantage of an increase in the percentage of grant aid.

See section 57(6) and (6A) of the Housing Act 1974.

If after an application for a grant has been approved the local authority are satisfied that, because of circumstances beyond the control of the applicant, the works cannot be carried out on the basis of the submitted estimate, they may redetermine and adjust the grant, see section 57(7) of the 1974 Act and Department of the Environment Circular No. 160/74, Appendix B.

The percentage of grant payable

Certain expenses of housing improvement and repair work are counted as eligible for aid; the grant payable is a specified percentage of the eligible expense. Section 59 of the Housing Act 1974 defined the appropriate percentages to be used in determing the amount, or maximum amount, of any grant. Generally 75 per cent of eligible expenses could be met by grant for a house in a housing action area (capable of being increased to 90 per cent in cases of hardship); 60 per cent of the expenses could be met for a house in a general improvement area; while 50 per cent of eligible expenses was the limit for houses elsewhere. This provision has been repealed and replaced by paragraph 5 of Schedule 12 to the Housing Act 1980, which gives the Secretary of State power to make orders varying the various appropriate percentages from time to time, subject to the consent of the Treasury and the approval of Parliament. With regard to improvement, special and repair grants, section 80(b) of the Housing Act 1974 gives local authorities power to fix an amount below the appropriate percentage. If they do they must give the applicant a written statement of their reasons. They must, under section 80(a), give a written statement of reasons for disapproving an application for a grant. [New 'appropriate percentages' were introduced in S.I. 1980 No. 1735 with effect from 14 December 1980.]

Certificates of future occupation

Applications for grants, other than special grants, may not be entertained unless the application is accompanied by a specified certificate under section 60 of the Housing Act 1974 as amended by paragraph 5 of Schedule 12 to the Housing Act 1980.

1) A certificate of owner-occupation under section 60(3) and (4) is a certificate stating that the applicant intends that on or before the first anniversary of the 'certified date' and throughout the period of four years following, the dwelling will be the only or main residence of, and will be occupied exclusively by, either:

    (a) the applicant himself and his household; or

    (b) a person who is a member of his family, or his grandparent or grandchild or his spouse together with that person's household.

A similar certificate can be filed by the personal representatives of a deceased person on behalf of beneficiaries.

2) A certificate of availability for letting under section 60(5) is a certificate stating that the applicant intends that throughout the period of five years beginning with the 'certified date':

    (a) the dwelling will be let or available for letting as a residence, and not for a holiday, to a person other than a member of the applicant's family, or

    (b) the dwelling will be occupied or available for occupation by a member of the agricultural population in pursuance of a contract of service and otherwise than as a tenant.

The 'certified date' is defined by section 75(6) of the 1974 Act as: 'the date certified by the local authority by whom the application was approved as the date on which the dwelling first becomes fit for occupation after the completion of the relevant works to the satisfaction of the local authority'.

The payment of grants

The payment of grants, or parts of grants, is conditional on the grant aided work being done to the satisfaction of the local authority. Under section 82(1) of the Housing Act 1974 a local authority may set a time limit of not less than twelve months within which the relevant grant aided works are to be carried out. Section 82(2) empowers them to allow further time for the doing of the work if they are satisfied that the work cannot be, or could not have been, carried out without the doing of additional works. Section 82(3) allows the payment of grants either in whole on the completion of the work or in instalments. Under paragraph 25 of Schedule 12 of the Housing Act 1980 where a grant is paid in instalments, the aggregate of instalments paid before completion must not at any time exceed:

1) in the case of an intermediate grant the appropriate percentage of the total cost of the work so far executed; or

2) in the case of an improvement, special or repair grant an amount bearing to the total cost of works executed the same proportion as the fixed amount of the grant bears to the eligible expense.

Where an instalment of a grant is paid before the completion of the works, and they are not completed within the time specified, the instalment, and any other sums paid as part of the grant, becomes repayable on the demand of the local authority by the applicant, and carries interest from the date of payment till that of repayment, see section 82(6). Under the provisions of Schedule 6 to the Local Government, Planning and Land Act 1980 the rate of interest is to be fixed at a 'reasonable' level by the local authority.

Residence conditions

As part of an attempt to prevent grants being taken up by speculators, sections 73 to 76 of the Housing Act 1974 were designed to reinforce the certificate of future occupation provisions. These provisions created a period of years during which a grant became repayable with compound interest if the improved dwelling ceased to be used in accordance with the stated intention of the applicant as certified to the local authority. It has been argued that these restrictions have proved unduly onerous for would-be improvers. The 1980 Housing Act has introduced measures that make the restrictions imposed on grant aid much less stringent.

Section 73 of the Housing Act 1974, as amended, provides that where an application for an improvement, intermediate or repairs grant is approved, various conditions as to occupation will apply to the dwelling in question during the ensuring five years. In any case where a certificate of owner occupation was given it is a condition of the grant that:

1) throughout the first year of the initial period the dwelling will be occupied exclusively by, or be available for the exclusive occupation of, a 'qualifying person', and

2) if at any time during the subsequent years of the initial period the dwelling is not so occupied, it will at that time be let or available for letting *by* a 'qualifying person' as a residence, and not for a holiday, *to* persons other than members of his family.

'Qualifying persons' are defined by section 73(3) of the 1974 Act as amended by the 1980 Act as follows:

1) the applicant for the grant;

2) any person deriving title to the dwelling through or under the applicant, for example a purchaser from the applicant;

3) a person who is a member of the applicant's family, or a grandparent or grandchild of the applicant or his spouse;

4) where the estate of a deceased 'qualifying person' is held by personal representatives or trustees, any person beneficially entitled to the estate under the will, intestacy or trust is also a 'qualifying person', and

5) the family, grandparents and grandchildren of such a beneficiary or of his spouse are also qualifying persons.

'Family' is defined by section 129(3) of the Housing Act 1974 as including spouses, sons and daughters, sons-in-law and daughters-in-law, parents and parents-in-law.

In any case where a certificate of availability for letting was given it is a condition of the grant that, *throughout* the initial period:

1) the dwelling will be let or available for letting as a residence, and not for a holiday, *by* a qualifying person *to* persons other than members of the family of that qualifying person; or

2) it will be occupied or available for occupation by a member of the agricultural population in pursuance of a contract of service and otherwise than as a tenant.

In this context 'qualifying person' includes the applicant himself, any person deriving title to the dwelling through or under the applicant *otherwise* than by a conveyance for value, together with the applicant's personal representatives, and beneficiaries, etc.

Thus where an owner-occupied house is grant aided the applicant can sell it without breaking the condition of his grant provided it remains a dwelling. A landlord who applies for grant aid is not given the same freedom.

Other grant conditions

Under section 74 of the 1974 Act, as amended by the 1980 Act, where an application for an improvement, intermediate or repairs grant is approved by a local authority they may impose certain conditions. If a house is comprised in a housing action area or general improvement area they must impose the specified conditions, save that in respect of an owner occupied dwelling they may dispense with the conditions if they conclude it would be reasonable to do so in the special circumstances of the case. Neither can conditions be imposed where the grant relates to a dwelling:

1) in which a housing association has an estate or interest; or

2) in respect of which a certificate of owner-occupation has been given *and* which has not at any time during the preceding period of twelve months been wholly or partly let for residential purposes, disregarding for this purpose any letting to the applicant or a member of his family, or a grandparant or grandchild of the applicant or his spouse; or

3) which is occupied or available for occupation by a member of the agricultural population in pursuance of a contract of service and otherwise than as a tenant; or

4) which is occupied by a person who is a protected occupier or statutory tenant under the Rent (Agriculture) Act 1976.

Where conditions can, or must, be imposed, they are as follows:

1) that the dwelling will be let or available for letting on a regulated tenancy or a restricted contract under the Rent Act 1977;

2) that the grant aiding authority may require the owner of the dwelling to certify, within 21 days, that condition (1) above is satisfied;

3) that any tenant if so required will provide the owner with such information as he may reasonably require to furnish the local authority with the above certificate;

4) where there is no rent registered, or no application or reference for one pending, that steps will be taken to register a rent;

5) where an application or reference for a registered rent has been made that it will be diligently proceeded with and not withdrawn;

6) that no premium shall be required as a condition of the grant, renewal or continuance of the lease or restricted contract as the case may be.

By virtue of section 106(4) of the Housing Act 1980 where an application for a grant is made by a tenant the above grant conditions may not be imposed, unless the application is accompanied by a certificate from the freeholder or long leaseholder of continued availability for letting for a period of five years.

Enforcing the grant conditions

So long as a grant condition remains in force (a period of five years or seven years in the case of houses in housing action areas).

1) it binds any person other than a housing authority or registered

housing association, who is for the time being the owner of the grant aided dwelling, and

2) is enforceable against all other persons having any interest in the dwelling, see section 75 of the Housing Act 1974.

Where a grant condition is broken the provisions of section 76 of the 1974 Act apply. This *empowers but does not oblige* a local authority to demand certain repayments in cases of breach. Where the grant was on a single dwelling the repayment is a sum equal to the grant with interest. Where the grant related to two or more buildings the sum payable is an amount equal to such part of the grant as relates to the dwelling where the breach has occurred. This also will bear interest. The repayment is due from the *owner* for the time of the dwelling in question. Local authorities are not obliged to demand repayment in respect of breaches of condition, they also have a discretion to demand less than their full entitlement. Department of the Environment Circular No. 160/74 gives guidance on the exercise of this discretion. Full repayment of a grant should be demanded where:

1) an owner-occupier improves a house and then uses it only as a second home or sells it at a profit; or

2) a landlord improves a tenanted house and then removes the tenants with a view to selling with vacant possession.

Repayment should not be demanded where, for example, an owner-occupier is forced to sell his home because of a change in his circumstances, job prospects or family commitments.

Under section 77 of the 1974 Act where grant conditions are in force the owner or mortgagee of the affected dwelling may pay to the local authority the amount of the grant with interest and obtain the extinction of the conditions.

The individual grants

Improvement grants

The payment of improvement grants is controlled by section 61 of the Housing Act 1974, as amended by the 1980 Act, under which, subject to certain conditions, local authorities may approve applications for such grants in such circumstances as they think fit. In general an application may not be approved unless they are satisfied that on completion of the relevant works the dwelling or dwellings in question will reach the required standard. To reach this standard a dwelling must:

1) have all the standard amenities for the exclusive use of its occupants, that is —
    (a) a fixed bath or shower,
    (b) a hot and cold water supply at a fixed bath or shower,
    (c) a wash hand basin,
    (d) hot and cold water supply at a wash hand basin,
    (e) a sink,
    (f) hot and cold water supply at a sink,
    (g) a water closet,
    (see section 58 of and Schedule 6 to the Housing Act 1974);

2) be in reasonable repair (disregarding internal decoration) having regard to its age, character and locality;

3) conform with such requirements as are specified by the Secretary of State, these are that the dwelling must —
    (i)   be substantially free from damp,
    (ii)   have adequate natural lighting and ventilation,
    (iii) have adequate provision for artificial lighting and sufficient provision of electrical sockets,
    (iv) have adequate drainage facilities,
    (v)   be structurally stable,
    (vi) have satisfactory internal arrangements,
    (vii) have satisfactory facilities for preparing food,
    (viii) have adequate heating facilities,
    (ix) have proper provision for the storage of fuel and refuse,
    (x)   conform with thermal insulation standards.
(This is known as 'the ten point standard,' see Department of the Environment Circular No. 160/74 Appendix A, paragraph 11.)

4) be likely to provide satisfactory housing for a period of thirty years.

Rigid enforcement of the conditions precludes any improvement of property in very poor condition as the maximum grant aid would not meet the expense. Local authorities have discretion under section 61(4) (4A) and (5) of the 1974 Act to reduce requirements as to the standard amenities, the requisite standard of repair, the ten point standard and the life expectancy of the building, particularly where they are satisfied that an applicant could not, without undue hardship, finance the cost of the works without the assistance of a grant.

In general under section 62 of the Housing Act 1974 improvement grants may only be approved on dwellings *below* a specified rateable value where the application is accompanied by a certificate of owner occupation. The specified rateable values are fixed from time to time by the Secretary of State. Paragraph 7 of Schedule 12 to the Housing Act 1980 lays down that the rateable value restrictions are not to apply to dwellings in housing action areas, nor to applications in respect of a dwelling to be occupied by a disabled person where the relevant works are necessary to meet his particular needs.

An improvement grant may only be used to improve a house, not to repair it. Replacement of electrical wiring, for example, is repair unless carried out as a necessary part of a programme of improvement. Improvement is not renewal but a process of alteration and enlargement, such as providing extensions to give a house a bathroom or an adequate kitchen. Local authorities have a duty under section 63 of the 1974 Act to determine an amount of expense (the 'estimated expense') proper to the carrying out of improvement. Where part of the work is repair and replacement only 50 per cent of its estimated cost can be met by the local authority. The amount of grant payable following this calculation is determined under section 64 of the 1974 Act. It will be the *'appropriate percentage'* (fixed from time to time) of the *'eligible expense'*, which is so much of the *'estimated expense'* as does not exceed the *'relevant limit'*. This limit is fixed from time to time by the Secretary of State. The current limits depend on the geographical location of the dwelling, whether or not it is a listed building and whether or not it is provided by the conversion of a building of three or more storeys. See the Grants by Local Authorities (Eligible Expense Limits) Order (S.I. 1980 No. 1736).

In the past special rules applied under section 64(7) of the Housing Act 1974 to reduce the availability of grants in respect of houses previously grant aided under the Housing Act 1969. These are removed by paragraph 8 of Schedule 12 to the Housing Act 1980.

Intermediate grants

Intermediate grants are paid to secure the provision of standard amenities. Local authorities are required under sections 65 and 67 of the 1974 Act to pay such grants if an application is made in due form. An application must:

1) specify the amenity or amenities to be provided;

2) where only some amenities are to be provided, state whether the dwelling is already provided with the remainder;

3) state, with respect to each amenity to be provided, whether, to the best knowledge of the applicant, the dwelling has been lacking that amenity for a preceding period of not less than twelve months. An application cannot be approved unless the dwelling has been without the amenity in question for a period of not less than twelve months, *or* unless, though the amenity is present, other relevant works involve unavoidable interference with, or the replacement of, the amenity.

An application for an intermediate grant may not be approved unless the local authority are satisfied that the dwelling will comply with the standards laid down by section 66 of the Housing Act 1974 after the work has been done. In the past the requisite standards were quite high, but paragraph 9 of Schedule 12 to the Housing Act 1980 substitutes lower standards. Local authorities will not be able to approve applications for intermediate grants unless:

1) they are satisfied that on completion of the relevant works the dwelling or dwellings in question will be fit for human habitation under section 4 of the Housing Act 1957; or

2) it seems reasonable in the circumstances to approve the application even though the dwelling or dwellings will not reach the section 4 standard on completion of the works.

Under section 67(3) of the 1974 Act as substituted by paragraph 10(2) of Schedule 12 to the Housing Act 1980 where the relevant works in an application for an intermediate grant include works of repair or replacement which, in the opinion of the local authority, go beyond those needed to put the dwelling into reasonable repair, having regard to its age, character, locality and life expectancy, the authority may, with the consent of the applicant, vary the application so that the relevant works:

1) are confined to works *other* than those of repair or replacement, or

2) include only those works of repair and replacement as are necessary for the reasonable repair of the dwelling.

The amount of grant payable is determined by section 68 of the 1974 Act as amended by the 1980 Act. The local authority must first determine the cost of installing the relevant amenity or amenities and also the proper cost of repairs and replacements. The eligible expense for an intermediate grant will then be:

1) so much of the amount determined in relation to repair or replacement as does not exceed a specified limit — which will be either —
   (a) £3,500 (Greater London) £2,500 (elsewhere) where the completion of the relevant works will put the house into reasonable repair, or in cases of financial hardship, or
   (b) *in any other case* the amount obtained by multiplying £350 (Greater London) £250 (elsewhere) by the number of amenities to be provided, up to a maximum of £1,400 (Greater London) £1,000 (elsewhere) (S.I. 1980 No. 1736) — *plus*

2) so much of the amount determined as relating to the provision of amenities as does not exceed the total of the sums allowed under Part 1 of Schedule 6 to the Housing Act 1974, as amended by the Grants by Local Authorities (Eligible Expense Limits) Order (S.I. 1980 No. 1736).

The actual amount of the grant will then be the appropriate percentage of the eligible expense, notification of which must be sent to the applicant.

Special grants

Special grants are payable in respect of a house in multiple occupation, which is defined by section 129 of the 1974 Act as 'a house which is occupied by persons who do not form a single household, *exclusive* of any part thereof which is occupied as a separate dwelling by persons who do form a single household'. Where, for example, a family occupy part of a house and do not share any 'living accommodation' with the other inhabitants of the house, their home should be distinguished as a separate entity, and, on the basis of being a separate dwelling, qualifies for an intermediate grant in its own right.

Section 69 of the 1974 Act makes the payment of special grants discretionary, save that section 69A, as inserted by the 1980 Act, will make mandatory grants for:

1) complying with a notice under section 15 of the Housing Act 1961 in so far as it relates to standard amenities, or

2) complying with a notice served under Schedule 24 to the Housing Act 1980 (means of escape from fire).

Under section 69(2) of the Act of 1974 (as amended) an application for a special grant must state:

1) the number of households and individuals occupying the house in question;

2) the standard amenities already provided;

3) the existing means of escape from fire.

Save in the cases of mandatory grants, an application cannot be approved unless the local authority are satisfied that the completion of the works will bring the house up to a reasonable standard of repair having regard to its age, character and locality. Any proposed works that would exceed that standard may be struck out of the application by the local authority with the consent of the applicant.

The amount of a special grant is determined by sections 70 and 70A of the 1974 Act as substituted by the 1980 Act. The local authority must first determine the proper expense of:

1) providing standard amenities;

2) providing means of escape from fire; and

3) any works of repair and replacement.

In relation to a mandatory special grant the amount will be the appropriate percentage of the eligible expense determined by aggregating:

1) so much of the cost of providing standard amenities as does not exceed the sum of the amounts specified under Schedule 6 to the 1974 Act, allowing for the installation of more than one of any of the standard amenities;
2) the cost of providing means of escape from fire up to £9,000 (Greater London) £6,750 (elsewhere);
3) the cost of works of repair and replacement up to £3,500 (Greater London) £2,500 (elsewhere).

In the case of a discretionary special grant the amount is left to be fixed by the local authority (see S.I. 1980 No. 1736).

Repair grants

These were, until the Housing Act 1980, payable only in respect of dwellings subject to area action. Sections 71 and 71A of the 1974 Act as amended by the Act of 1980 give local authorities discretion to make repair grants, but a mandatory repair grant is payable in respect of an application made by a person subject to an order under section 9 of the Housing Act 1957 (e.g. a house capable of being made fit at reasonable expense). Nor in such cases need any certificate of future occupation be given. Before exercising their discretion a local authority must be satisfied:

1) that the relevant works are of a substantial and structural character, or that they satisfy other centrally prescribed requirements;
2) that the dwelling is 'old' as defined by the Secretary of State, that is erected before 1 January 1919 (S.I. 1980 No. 1737);
3) that in the case of an owner-occupied dwelling situated *outside* a housing action area that it falls within prescribed rateable value limits;
4) that on completion of the relevant works the dwelling will attain a reasonable standard of repair having regard to its age, character and locality.

Section 71(4) gives local authorities power to pay repair grants only in respect of those works necessary in their opinion to bring the dwelling up to a reasonable standard.

The amount of a repair grant is determined under section 72 of the Housing Act 1974 as amended. The local authority must first determine the proper cost of the relevant work. The eligible expense for the purpose of a repair grant must not exceed the sums contained in S.I. 1980 No. 1736, para. 6(2). The actual amount of the grant will be:

1) in the case of a mandatory repairs grant the appropriate percentage, as fixed, of the eligible expense, or

2) in other cases a sum to be fixed by the local authority.

The Secretary of State has power under section 78 of the 1974 Act to make contributions to grants. The sum, payable annually for twenty years, is equal to the 'relevant percentage' of annual loan charges attributable to the amount of the grant. The 'relevant percentage' may now be found specified in the Grants by Local Authorities (Appropriate Percentage and Exchequer Contributions) Order (S.I. 1980 No. 1735).

Area improvement

The Housing Act 1964 allowed the declaration of 'improvement areas', a concept developed by the 1969 Act as 'general improvement areas'. The 1974 Act created housing action areas, general improvement areas and priority neighbourhoods. The 1980 Act abolishes the last named group, though without prejudice to the status of any such area actually declared.

Housing action areas

Housing action areas (HAAs) are areas unsuitable for slum clearance, but where overcrowding and housing stress are acute. The object is that improving action should be fast and concentrated.

Under section 36 of the 1974 Act where a report on an area of housing is submitted to a local authority (that is a district council, a London Borough, and the Common Council of the City of London) by a suitably qualified person (whether or not employed by them) upon their considering it, together with other information, having regard to the physical condition of the housing in and the social conditions of the area, they may resolve to declare the area a HAA and so define it on a map. Such an area can only be declared where the authority are satisfied that within five years their resolution will lead to the improvement of and the proper and effective management and use of housing in the area, and the well being of the residents.

Local authorities are required to have regard to guidance given by the Secretary of State. Such guidance is contained in Department of the Environment Circular No. 14/75. This is especially relevant in relation to the content of the report preceding the resolution. Information should be given about the number of houses in multiple occupation, and hostels in the area, categorised by age, unfitness, lack of amenities, state of repair, rateable value and tenure; the number of households in the area, categorised as above; the presence in an area of significant numbers of persons suffering from social problems such as age, unemployment, ethnic disadvantage, being a single parent, or having a large family; any other special problem of the area, such as harassment, eviction and the numbers of children taken into care; recent changes in housing conditions, improvement grants taken up, planning permission applications and registered rent levels.

The circular also contains guidance on how a local authority should consider the accommodation and social conditions within a potential HAA. Consideration of both is important because the conjunction of bad housing conditions with other social problems and stresses is the indication of the need to declare a HAA. Local authorities should consider the proportion of houses lacking the standard amenities, those that are statutorily unfit or badly laid out, the number of households sharing living and other accommodation, the numbers of households living at a density of more than one and a half persons to a room, the proportion of households in privately rented accommodation, together with the level of 'social problem' households, such as the ill or old, the unemployed or low paid, and the single parent or large families.

Circular No. 14/75 counsels local authorities to consider whether there are sufficient resources to carry through their plan before declaring a HAA. 'Sufficient resources' means the authority's own resources in financial and manpower terms, the resources of local housing associations and the local building industry together with accommodation outside the HAA available to rehouse any persons who may have to be temporarily or permanently displaced. Consideration should be paid to the size of the proposed HAA. There is no 'right' size for a HAA. Much depends upon physical conditions in different localities. The circular suggests an upper limit of 200 – 300 houses, only to be exceeded for good reason. Circular No. 14/75 states that it is not appropriate to declare a HAA which contains estates or a significant number of houses owned by the local authority.

The procedure for declaring a housing action area

After resolving to declare a HAA the local authority must:

1) publish in two or more local newspapers notice of the resolution identifying the area and naming a place where a copy of the resolution and the map and report can be inspected during reasonable hours;

2) take such further steps as will secure that the resolution is brought to the notice of affected owners and residents, and ensuring that such persons know where any inquiry or representation regarding the proposed action may be made;

3) send the Secretary of State a copy of the resolution, map and report, together with their proposals to deal with the area;

4) register the declaration as a local land charge.

See section 36(4) of the Housing Act 1974, and Circular No. 14/75, Memorandum A, paragraph 24.

Under section 37 the Secretary of State may, within 28 days of acknowledging receipt of the proposals, cancel or confirm the resolution, or state that he requires more time to consider it or he may exclude land from the area. Once the Secretary makes his decision the local authority must publish it in at least two local newspapers and notify affected owners and residents. Once declared and confirmed an HAA lasts for five years, with the possibility of a further extension of two years, though it may be determined at any time during its currency by a resolution made and published in due form, see section 39 of the Housing Act 1974.

The consequences of the declaration

Once the HAA is in being the local authority is given a number of powers and duties to enable it to secure its objects.

1) Under section 41 of the Housing Act 1974 they have a duty to bring to the attention of owners and residents details of their proposed action, and information as to the assistance available for the improvement of housing in the area.

2) They may be authorised to acquire land on which is situated living accommodation within the HAA, compulsorily or by agreement, for the purpose of improving the housing and social conditions in the area as a whole, see section 43.

3) Section 44 applies to land acquired under section 43 and allows the local authority, subject to the consent of the Secretary of State under section 105, to provide housing accommodation by construction, conversion or improvement, and also to improve or repair houses, to manage houses and to provide furniture, fittings and services in relation to housing accommodation. Strict control over the conversion and improvement of dwellings by housing authorities can be maintained by the Secretary of State under section 105 of the 1974 Act which gives him power to prohibit the incurring of expense on conversion and improvement except in accordance with plans he has approved.

4) Section 45, as amended by Schedule 13 to the Housing Act 1980 empowers local authorities, in order to improve the amenities of a HAA, to carry out on land belonging to them works other than those to

the interior of housing accommodation, or to give assistance to others to carry out such environmental works. Section 46, as substituted by the 1980 Act, allows the Secretary of State to make contributions to the carrying out of such works of sums equal to one half of the annual loan charges referable to expenditure on the works for a period of twenty years subject to an upper limit for any given HAA of £400 × the number of dwelling-houses, houses in multiple occupation and hostels in the area.

5) Under section 47 landlords of houses in HAAs are under a duty to inform the local authority, within seven days, of any notice to quit. In the case of a tenancy due to expire by efluxion time a similar notice must be served at least four weeks before the tenancy expires. Owners of land intending to dispose of such property must given notice to the local authority not less than four weeks nor more than six months before the disposal is carried out. The authority must acknowledge receipt of the notification and state, within four weeks, what action they propose to take. The object of this provision is to enable the local authority to keep a constant check on vacant premises so that, if necessary, they can obtain the property and use it for the benefit of the HAA.

A failure to comply with section 47 is an offence punishable with a fine of up to £400. In *Fawcett v Newcastle-Upon-Tyne City Council* (1977) 34 P & CR 83 it was claimed that where a notice to quit was invalid there was no necessity for notification. This was rejected: invalidity is no defence to a prosecution under this provision.

General improvement areas

General improvement areas (GIAs) are declared under the Housing Act 1969 as amended by the Acts of 1974 and 1980. (Schedule 13 to the latter enactment restores the law to its 1969 condition.) The procedure under the restored section 28 of the 1969 Act is very similar to that for declaring an HAA, save that the ministerial controls introduced by the 1974 Act are removed. No central approval is required for the declaration of a GIA. A local authority must publish notice of their resolution to declare a GIA in local newspapers, take steps to inform property owners and residents and forward a copy of the resolution to the minister. The difference between the types of improvement areas is that GIAs are restricted to 'predominantly residential areas'. An area including a few shops, offices or factories is not excluded, but the declaration of a GIA is not appropriate within a badly run down area. Neither may a GIA include any land in a clearance area unless it has already been cleared of buildings, nor any land comprised in a HAA, though a GIA may surround either a clearance area or a HAA, see sections 29 and 29A of the Housing Act 1969. The general characteristics of a GIA should be those laid down in *Better Homes: The Next Priorities*, Cmnd. 5339. The area should be one of older residential property, free from housing stress, where the physical condition of the property is fundamentally sound and where the houses are capable of providing good living conditions for many years. A GIA should also be an area where house owners are likely to take the initiative in leading the improvement drive. Once declared the GIA is operative until the local authority cancel it, see the Housing Act 1969, s. 30

The effect of a general improvement area

Local authorities have a number of powers and duties in relation to such areas.

1) Section 31 of the Housing Act 1969 places a duty on local authorities to inform owners and occupiers in the GIA of their proposals to secure the improvement of the amenities of the area and of the assistance available towards the improvement of dwellings.

2) Under section 32 they may acquire land compulsorily or by agreement, and may carry out works on the land or let it or otherwise dispose of it. They may also assist, by making grants or loans or otherwise, in the carrying out of works on land they do not own. They may not use these powers to improve dwellings acquired or provided under other statutory provisions, for example Part V of the Housing Act 1957.

3) Section 33 enables them to improve the amenities of a GIA by closing a highway to traffic and carrying out improvements to it such as landscaping.

4) Section 37, as substituted by Schedule 13 to the Housing Act 1980, allows the Secretary of State to make contributions towards the costs of works carried out by local authorities in GIAs. The sums payable are calculated in a similar way to contributions towards costs incurred in a HAA.

Priority neighbourhoods

Priority neighbourhoods were introduced by Part VI of the 1974 Act in an attempt to safeguard areas adjoining HAAs and GIAs against any worsening of housing conditions due to improvements being carried out in the neighbouring area. It is well known that any attempt to control a particular housing evil in one area may lead to an increase in its incidence in nearby areas. Little use was made of the Part VI powers and they have been repealed by section 109 of the Housing Act 1980.

Compulsory improvement

Compulsory improvement of houses was introduced by the Housing Act 1964, but the cumbersome procedure proved unworkable. The 1969 Act placed emphasis on persuasive improvement with compulsion as a last resort. Persuasive policies failed to secure the improvement of all houses within improvement areas. The continued existence of groups of unimproved dwellings jeopardised the future of some improvement schemes. The 1974 Act revived the policy of compulsory improvement. This is continued, with some modifications, by the 1980 Act. The compulsory improvement powers exist in HAAs and GIAs, and tenants have power to initiate the process in relation to dwellings outside such areas.

Section 85 of the 1974 Act gives local authorities power to serve a 'provisional notice' on the person having control (that is the owner-occupier, or owner or long lessee) of a dwelling within an HAA or GIA if the dwelling:

1) is without one or more of the standard amenities, whether or not it is also in a state of disrepair;

2) was provided before 3 October 1961, and

3) is capable of attaining the standard laid down by section 103A of the Housing Act 1974, as inserted by Schedule 25 to the Housing Act 1980.

'(1) For the purposes of this Part of this Act, a dwelling shall be taken to attain the full standard if the following conditions are fulfilled with respect to it, namely —

    (a) that it is provided with all the standard amenities for the exclusive use of its occupants; and

    (b) that it is in reasonable repair (disregarding the state of internal decorative repair) having regard to its age and character and the locality in which it is situated; and

    (c) that it conforms with such requirements with respect to thermal insulation as may for the time being be specified by the Secretary of State for the purposes of this section; and

    (d) that it is in all other respects fit for human habitation (to be determined in accordance with section 4 of the Housing Act 1957); and

    (e) that it is likely to be available for use as a dwelling for a period of fifteen years or such other period as may for the time being be specified by the Secretary of State for the purposes of this sub-section.

(2) Subject to sub-section (3) below, a local authority may, if they consider it reasonable to do so, dispense wholly or in part with any of the conditions in sub-section (1), and a dwelling shall be taken to attain the reduced standard if the conditions not dispensed with are fulfilled.

(3) A local authority shall not dispense with the conditions in paragraph (a) of sub-section (1) in a case where they are satisfied that the dwelling is, or forms part of, a house or building in respect of which they could by notice under section 15 of the Housing Act 1961 (power to require execution of works) require the execution of such works as are referred to in sub-section (1) of that section'.

(That is a house in multiple occupation.)

No notice can be served in respect of a house owned by a local authority, the Commission for the New Towns, the Housing Corporation, a registered housing association, a development corporation, a housing charity trust, nor in respect of a house owned by the Crown or Duchies of Lancaster and Cornwall, except with the consent of those three authorities, see section 99 of the Housing Act 1974. There are further restrictions on the service of notices in respect of *owner-occupied* dwellings. They may not be made subject to notices unless their improvement is necessary for the improvement of an adjacent dwelling which is not owner-occupied, or for which a grant is being given under Part VII of the 1974 Act, see section 85(3).

The provisional notice must specify the works which the local authority consider necessary to bring the house up to standard, and must also state a date, not less than 21 days after service of the notice, time and place at which their proposals, any alternative proposals, temporary or permanent rehousing arrangements, and the views of the occupying tenant (if any) may be discussed. A copy of the notice must be served on any occupying tenant and every other person having an interest in the dwelling. All are entitled to be heard when the proposals are discussed, and their views taken into account. Any rehousing arrangements must be formally agreed by the parties in writing. A permanently displaced occupier has rehousing rights under section 39(1)(d) of the Land Compensation Act 1973.

Under section 87 of the 1974 Act the local authority may accept an undertaking from the person having control of the dwelling to bring it up to standard. The undertaking must specify the necessary works and a period, generally nine months, within which they must be done. The local authority must be satisfied as to the housing arrangements for any occupying tenant, who must also consent to the work in writing. Where no such undertaking is accepted or where an undertaking is not fulfilled an improvement notice may be served, under section 88 of the Housing Act 1974, within nine months of the service of the provisional notice where no undertaking has been accepted, or within six months of a failure to fulfil an undertaking. Such a notice cannot be served unless the local authority are satisfied that the dwelling is still subject to area action, that it still lacks one or more standard amenities, and is capable of being brought up to standard at reasonable expense, that it is not owner-occupied, that there are satisfactory housing arrangements for the occupying tenant, and that the occupying tenant has not unreasonably refused to enter into any such arrangements.

The improvement notice must, under section 90 of the 1974 Act, specify the required works, give an estimate of the cost and require execution within a period of twelve months. In *Harrington v Croydon Corpn* [1968] 1 QB 656, [1967] 3 All ER 929 it was held that the works required may include an extension to the dwelling. Section 91 gives a six weeks right of appeal to the county court to the person having control of the dwelling, an occupying tenant or any other person with an interest in the dwelling. There are various grounds of appeal.

1) That the requirements of the notice cannot be met at reasonable expense. What constitutes 'reasonable expense' is not defined in the Act. In *F.F.F. Estates Ltd v Hackney London Borough Council* [1981] 1 All ER 32, the Court of Appeal held that a realistic approach to the value of dwelling-houses as saleable assets in the hands of landlords had to be taken when considering the reasonableness of the expense required to improve them. Regard must be had to the presence of tenants and their rights of continued occupation, and the effect this has on market value. The Court also held that where the occupants of a dwelling shared the use of one or more standard amenities with the occupants of another dwelling, that dwelling was 'without one or more of the standard amenities' within the meaning of section 89 of the 1974 Act. This entitles the local authority to serve an improvement notice, though it may be contested on the issue of 'reasonable expense'.

2) That the local authority has unreasonably refused to agree to the execution of alternative works.

3) That the dwelling is in a clearance area.

4) That the dwelling no longer lacks standard amenities.

5) That the works specified will not bring the dwelling up to standard.

6) That some other person will derive a benefit from the work, and so ought to pay all or part of the cost.

7) That the improvement notice is invalid for want of formality, though in this case the notice may only be quashed if it has resulted in substantial prejudice to the appellant. In *De Rothschild v Wing RDC* [1967] 1 All ER 597, [1967] 1 WLR 420 it was held that an owner who

was ordered to do work he was not legally bound to do was 'substantially prejudiced'.

If the period stipulated in the improvement notices elapses without the work being carried out, or if the person on whom the notice was served notifies the local authority that he is unwilling or unable to do the work, or if they are not satisfied following due inquiry that the work will be completed in the specified time, the local authority may, under section 93 of the Housing Act 1974, do the work themselves, and may, under section 94, recover their reasonable expenses from the person having control of the dwelling.

Section 100 of the 1974 Act enables a person who is under an obligation to carry out improvements by reason of an improvement notice or undertaking to apply for a loan from the local authority to pay for the works. If they are satisfied he is able to repay the loan, that his interest in the dwelling will last for as long as the loan is made, and that the dwelling is adequate security for the loan, they must make it. No loan can be made for any part of the expenditure to be met by an improvement or intermediate grant. Alternatively under section 101 a person having control of a dwelling, who has been served with an improvement notice, may require the local authority, within six months of the notice becoming operative, to purchase his interest. The dwelling will be treated as having been acquired compulsorily under Part V of the Housing Act 1957.

Compulsory improvement outside improvement areas

An occupying tenant of a dwelling which:

1) is not in a GIA or HAA; and

2) is without one or more standard amenities, whether or not it is also in a state of disrepair, and

3) was provided before 3 October 1961,

may write to the local authority requesting them to take action under section 89 of the Housing Act 1974. They must notify the person having control of the dwelling of any representation made. They must take the representations of the tenant into account and decide:

1) whether the representations come from an occupying tenant;

2) whether the dwelling is outside any form of area action, is lacking any standard amenities, and was provided before 3 October 1961;

3) whether the dwelling is capable at reasonable expense of improvement;

4) whether, having regard to all the circumstances, the dwelling ought to be improved, and whether it is unlikely to be improved unless they use their compulsory powers.

They must then decide either:

1) to serve on the person having control of the dwelling a provisional notice, in which case the compulsory improvement procedure described above begins, or

2) to notify the occupying tenant that they do not intend to serve such a notice, giving him their written reasons for the decision.

The phrase 'occupying tenant' for this and other purposes of the 1974 Act is defined by section 104(1) as meaning a person who is *not* an owner occupier, but who occupies a dwelling by virtue of a short lease, statutory tenancy, restricted contract or because of agricultural employment. (See generally *F.F.F. Estates Ltd v Hackney London Borough Council*, p. 303 above.)

An assessment of improvement policies

The Housing Act 1980 makes improvement grants more widely available, but it does so at the cost of compromising improvement standards by reducing the level of what is required from 'good' to merely 'reasonable'. Other criticisms can be levelled against the new Act in that it does not create a single comprehensive repair and rehabilitation code, and also in that it continues the fragmented approach of the law to the inner city areas. It was argued earlier that housing is only one amongst many problems affecting the 'twilight zones' and that the cycle of urban deprivation can only be broken by an approach on a broad front embracing housing, education, employment, health and welfare, and social amenities. Presently the legal provisions relating to such issues are scattered across the statute book.

The Inner Urban Areas Act 1978 was designed to counter economic decline, physical decay, dereliction and adverse social conditions in the worst affected towns and cities. The main thrust of the Act is to give selected local authorities extended powers to assist industry by making loans of up to 90 per cent for the acquisition and development of sites, by giving assistance to co-operative and co-ownership enterprises, and to declare 'improvement areas', either industrial or commercial in character, in which loans or grants may be made for the conversion or improvement of industrial and commercial buildings and for carrying out environmental improvements. The Local Government, Planning and Land Act 1980 goes even further. Part XVI provides for the creation of new corporations to regenerate decayed urban areas such as the docklands of London and Liverpool. These corporations are modelled on the new town development corporations and will have powers of land assembly, planning, housing and industrial promotion. Part XVIII and Schedule 32 grant powers to create 'enterprise zones' within which planning controls will be relaxed and where most *non domestic* property will be exempt from rates. This is a further attempt to promote urban industrial growth.

Even if there were to be one comprehensive code designed to deal with all the problems of the inner city areas it would be of no avail unless it were to carry with it human and financial resources. At this point the lawyer is forced to admit that social legislation not reinforced by a commitment to give resources is just so many black marks on pieces of paper. (It should be noted that in connection with the need to conserve energy the Secretary of State must reimburse local authorities for the grants they have to pay towards the cost of improving the thermal insulation of dwellings. Such grants are payable under schemes made under section 1 of the Homes Insulation Act 1980. See also 'The Homes Insulation Scheme 1980' contained in Department of the Environment Circular No. 12/80.)

Further reading

Cullingworth, J.B., *Essays on Housing Policy* (Allen and Unwin, 1979) Chap. 5

Cullingworth, J.B., *Housing and Local Government* (Allen and Unwin, 1st edn., 1966) Chap. 9

Hadden, T., *Compulsory Repair and Improvement* (Centre for Socio-Legal Studies, Wolfson College, Oxford, 1978)

Macey, J., *The Housing Act 1974* (Butterworths, 1975)

Monck, E., and Lomas, G., *Housing Action Areas: Success and Failure* (Centre for Environment Studies, 1980)

Paris, C., and Blackaby, B., *Not Much Improvement* (Heinneman, 1979)

Rowland, J., *Community Decay* (Penguin, 1973)

Social Welfare Law (Ed. by D.W. Pollard) (Oyez) paras. C. 3126 – C. 3160, C. 4445 – C. 4739 and F. 2601 – F. 2916

The Better Way: An Approach to Gradual Renewal in Leeds (Community Housing Working Party, 1978)

First Report from the Environment Committee Session 1979 – 80, HC 714, 24 July 1980

From Failure to Facelift (Birmingham Community Development Project, 1980)

The Planning and Implementation of a General Improvement Area (School of Planning, Kingston Polytechnic, 1975)

The Poverty of the Improvement Programme (National Community Development Project, 1975)

Priorities for Housing Action (North Islington Housing Rights Project) (Shelter, 1973)

Street by Street — Improvement and Tenant Control in Islington (North Islington Housing Rights Project) (Shelter, 1976)

Tomorrow in Upper Holloway (North Islington Housing Rights Project) (Shelter, 1973)

Holmes, C., 'Islington's Tough Approach Works', *Roof*, May 1977, pp. 81 – 83

Karn. V. and Whittle, B., 'Birmingham's Urban Cosmetics', *Roof*, November 1978, pp. 163 – 164

Paris, C., 'Housing Action Areas' *Roof*, January 1977, pp. 9 – 14

Wintour, J. and Franey, R., 'Are Improvement Grants Tied Up in the Town Halls?', *Roof*, May 1978, pp. 81 – 83

Wintour, J. and Van Dyke, S., 'Housing Action Areas: But Where's the Action', *Roof*, July 1977, pp. 105 – 113

'Housing in Housing Action Areas', *Roof*, September 1979, pp. 151 – 153

Chapter 11

Multi-occupancy and overcrowding

Introduction

Multi-occupation and overcrowding occur together in sufficient cases to convey an impression that they are always associated evils. In fact, as has been shown by David Smith and Anne Whalley in *Racial Minorities and Public Housing* (PEP Broadsheet No. 556) p. 99, the problem of overcrowding is not restricted to multi-occupied dwellings, nor even primarily associated with them. Nor should it be assumed that conditions in all multi-occupied houses are necessarily bad. Nevertheless it is the case that a combination of poor amenities and overcrowding is nowadays most often found in multi-occupied houses. This must always be born in mind even though it must also be remembered that not every multi-occupied house is overcrowded, and that overcrowding can occur even in a single small one-family dwelling-house.

Multi-occupation and overcrowding can arise for totally different reasons in different areas of varying housing types. In the past the typically overcrowded house was the small 'two-up-and-two-down' house situated in industrial towns and cities. Frequently such houses stood together in yards, courts or terraces and shared lavatories and water supplies with other similar houses. They were overcrowded either because of the sexual composition of the families occupying them, with brothers and sisters frequently having to share bedrooms until the eldest ones left home to get married, or because the houses were simply too small to be able to accommodate properly the large families occupying them. The law relating to overcrowding was developed primarily to deal with situations of the above kind. In our own day the nature of the problem has altered. Anyone who is familiar with the urban geography of the nation will be aware that one of the great unanswered problems of housing policy is what to do with the very large Victorian and Edwardian houses found in inner suburban areas.

As Professor J.B. Cullingworth says in *Essays on Housing Policy*, p. 65: 'Commonly, the houses which today are in multiple occupation are the socially obsolete Victorian piles designed for an age when the distribution of wealth allowed rich families to live in large houses which could be serviced by a plentiful supply of cheap domestic labour. Properly converted they can provide reasonable accommodation, particularly for smaller households, of which there are great numbers in the centre of large cities. This demand, particularly from newly formed households, migrant newcomers (British and foreign), single and child-less people and the aged can — and does — result in abuses which have been forced on public attention in recent years. Unlike the nineteenth-century situation, the problem is not simply one of poverty: though the households in the worst conditions are those with the lowest incomes and those with average incomes but large families, the situation is made more difficult because of "competition" from newcomers and from those with higher incomes'.

These large, old and once proud houses are obviously ripe for con-version into multi-occupation. Where the conversion is sympathetically and well done the result is the provision of much useful accommoda-tion. However, unscrupulous owners have indulged far too often in unsatisfactory divisions, failing to provide proper cooking and sanitary facilities, and frequently resorting to overcrowding the individual units of accommodation provided as a way of extracting the maximum financial return from their properties. The result has been the pro-duction of squalor. It is in properpties such as these that multi-occupation and overcrowding occur together.

Local authorities have many powers available to combat such unsatis-factory housing conditions. These powers confer a great deal of discretion on authorities, and their use is, in any case, subject to two major constraints:

1) a lack of staff and other resources necessary to implement the powers fully;

2) the fact that an energetic use of the available powers usually means a reduction of overcrowding and the closing of houses which cannot be brought up to the required legal standards, leading to increased demands upon the already limited stock of municipal housing.

An authority making the fullest use of its powers to combat both over-crowding and multi-occupation would have to accept either an increase in its housing waiting list or a cut back in its clearance programme. Few authorities are prepared to accept such consequences. So the problems continue, frequently exacerbated by administrative systems which separate public health supervision of multi-occupied houses and housing management and allocation into distinct departments with little liaison between the two. It must also be admitted that the law relating to these issues has traditionally been negative in its approach to the problems. There has been little articulation in the past of a legal policy to encourage good quality conversions. However, as we have seen the amendments to the law relating to special grants for houses in multiple occupation made by the Housing Act 1980 do go some way to rectifying this omission. The existence of purely negative powers of control has encouraged local authorities to take little action because these powers, by their very nature, offer little or no way of transforming the worst multi-occupied properties into acceptable accommodation. They can, of course, prevent the use of such properties for accommodation purposes but this only leads to increased housing demand being placed on the already overstretched public sector of housing.

The supervision of multi-occupation by planning control

Under planning law 'development' may not in general be carried out without a grant of planning permission from the local planning authority. Can local authorities use their planning powers to prevent the inception of undesirable multi-occupation developments? Section 22(1) of the Town and Country Planning Act 1971 defines development as:

'the carrying out of building, engineering, mining or other operations in, on, over or under land, or the making of any material change in the use of any buildings or other land'.

Section 22(2)(a) excludes from this definition:

'the carrying out of works for the maintenance, improvement or other alteration of any building, being works which affect only the interior of the building or which do not materially affect the external appearance of the building'.

But section 22(3)(a) goes on to provide:

'For the avoidance of doubt it is hereby declared for the purposes of this section — the use as two or more separate dwelling-houses of any building previously used as a single dwelling-house involves a material change in the use of the building and of each part thereof which is so used'.

Unfortunately doubt in this area of the law has not been avoided, and it is not entirely certain whether a change from single residential to multi-occupied use inevitably constitutes an act of development by virtue of being either a material change of use or by falling within section 22(3(a) above, and so requiring planning permission. In *Ealing Corpn v Ryan* [1965] 2 QB 486, [1965] 1 All ER 137 a local planning authority alleged that unauthorised development had taken place in that the use of a house had changed from being a single dwelling to use as two or more separate dwellings. The house was found to contain several families who all shared a common kitchen, and presumably the lavatory and bathroom also. It was held that on such facts the house had not been divided into *separate* dwellings. Cases decided on the doctrine of sharing in relation to the Rent Acts were followed. Thus a house may be occupied by two or more persons living separately under one roof, without their occupying 'separate dwellings', provided they are sharing certain common living accommodation, which, following *Goodrich v Paisner* [1957] AC 65, [1956] 2 All ER 176, certainly includes kitchens. Multiple occupation by itself therefore is insufficient to bring section 22(3)(a) of the Town and Country Planning Act 1971 into operation. That provision is designed to deal with the situation where the new dwellings can be regarded as truly separate, self-contained and independent, in which circumstances the existence or absence of any form of physical reconstruction will be a factor of great importance.

But multi-occupation of a dwelling-house may still constitute development even though there has been no conversion into separate dwellings for the conversion may amount to a material change of use under section 22(1) of the 1971 Act. In *Birmingham Corpn v Minister of Housing and Local Government and Habib Ullah* [1964] 1 QB 178, [1963] 3 All ER 668 three former singly-occupied houses were let in parts to a number of occupants each paying a weekly rent. The local planning authority alleged unauthorised development, which the minister refused to accept as he considered that there was no change of use: the houses remained solely in residential use. The Divisional Court held otherwise, and pointed out that there had been a change of use in that the houses, which had previously been used as single family accommodation, were being used for gain by their owner letting them out as rooms. The material change of use is constituted by the real change from family/residential to commercial/residential use.

It had been argued from *Duffy v Pilling* (1977) 33 P & CR 85 that where a single person owns or rents a house and lives there with lodgers, generally providing meals for them but sometimes allowing them to provide for themselves, there is no change of use unless there is some form of physical division between the parts each person occupies. This decision is generally agreed to be most unsatisfactory, and the better view of the law is that a material change of use occurs as soon as a predominantly single family use alters into a predominantly non-family use. Once the lodgers predominate then a change of use has taken place. Certainly in *Lipson v Secretary of State for the Environment* (1977) 33 P & CR 95 a change of use of premises from self-contained flats to individual bed-sitters was found to be a material change of use. The test that emerges from the decisions is to ask a simple question of fact in each case: 'who has control over the property?' If control is in the hands of one person who has a small number of others living with him there is no material change of use. On the other hand if the effective control of the property has been 'parcelled out' amongst a number of individuals, the best evidence of which is a physical partitioning of the premises, then a multi-occupancy will have arisen and will constitute a material change of use for which planning permission will be required.

It is questionable how far a local authority may go in using its planning powers in order to prevent the spread of undesirable multi-occupation. An outright policy of refusing any application for planning permission to convert premises to multi-occupation would undoubtedly be an illegal fetter on discretion. Nor would it appear generally proper for a local authority to take into account the character of the person applying for planning permission. Even an applicant who had a long history of abuse in relation to his tenants, for example convictions for harassment, etc., under the Protection from Eviction Act 1977, or of mismanagement in relation to other multi-occupied properties owned by him, could not be refused planning permission merely because of his misdeeds as they are matters relevant to other areas of law and do not raise real issues of planning as such. Neither could an authority impose restrictive conditions designed to regulate future behaviour on a grant of permission to such a person for the whole thrust of the cases is that a planning condition must always relate fairly to the physical development, and not to the subsequent use by the developer of his powers of letting and management.

In *Chertsey UDC v Mixnam's Properties Ltd* [1965] AC 735, [1964] 2 All ER 627 a local authority attempted to use powers conferred by the Caravan Sites and Control of Development Act 1960 to impose requirements on a site owner that would have required them to give caravan occupiers, inter alia, security of tenure equivalent to that enjoyed by tenants protected by the Rent Acts. It was held that the authority had no power to impose such requirements. On the basis of ministerial decisions on planning appeals the proper factors to be taken into account by a local planning authority in these situations include: the density of housing; the possibility of overcrowding; the amenities of the neighbourhood; any prevailing shortage of accommodation in the locality; the suitability of the premises for conversion; architectural considerations and, occasionally, the problems that might arise from an increase in the number of cars that incoming residents might wish to park in the area. All these are, of course, proper land use considerations.

The supervision of multi-occupation under the Housing Acts

The foregoing paragraphs show that the control of the spread of multi-occupation by means of planning law is no easy matter. Nevertheless local authorities have been urged by Ministry of Housing and Local Government Circular No. 16/62 to take a positive rôle in relation to proposed conversions of houses to multi-occupation to secure, by collaboration with the owners, good standards of work and adaptation. Sadly many conversions have been carried out which are way below any acceptable standard, and in relation to these properties local authorities have wide ranging *powers* of management and control.

The definition of multi-occupation

The Housing Act 1969 s. 58(1) provides that a multi-occupancy arises when a house 'is occupied by persons who do not form a single household'. Unfortunately the word 'household' is itself not defined by law and this has given rise to litigation. In *Wolkind v Ali* [1975] 1 All ER 193, [1975] 1 WLR 170 Mr Ali occupied certain premises which he used as a lodging house. Under their statutory powers the local authority served on him a notice prescribing the number of persons who could lawfully sleep in certain rooms. These restrictions were observed by Mr Ali until he was joined by his large family from abroad. Thereafter the premises were occupied solely by the family. Mr Ali was subsequently charged with exceeding the prescribed numbers of persons allowed to sleep in certain rooms in the house. The Divisional Court held that Mr Ali was not guilty of the offence with which he was charged. The local authority's multi-occupancy powers did not apply to this house as it was being used only by a single household.

On the other hand it was held in *Okereke v Brent London Borough Council* [1967] 1 QB 42, [1966] 1 All ER 150 that, once a property is divided between separate households, it makes no difference whether the multiple occupation arises from a physical division of the building or not. Here a house built originally for occupation by one family had been converted into separate self-contained dwellings. The basement and ground floor were each occupied by one family and the first floor by two or more families, who shared a bathroom, water closet and kitchen. The second floor was unoccupied and unfit for occupation. It was held that the house as a whole was multi-occupied.

Thus where there is a clear division of control over a house between two or more households the multi-occupancy powers apply. Likewise (as has been argued previously in relation to the cases that have arisen as a result of the use of planning control with regard to multi-occupation) where a person lives in or occupies a house, and there caters for lodgers on a *substantial* scale, and shares control with them, as a commercial enterprise, a multiple occupation of that property arises.

But what of the situation where persons live together freely and communally in a house? This situation faced the courts in *Simmons v Pizzey* [1979] AC 37, [1977] 2 All ER 432. Here Mrs Pizzey occupied a property in a London suburb as a refuge for 'battered women'. The local authority fixed, under their statutory powers, a maximum number of persons who might lawfully occupy the house, and Mrs Pizzey was subsequently charged with a failure to comply with the local authority's direction. Her defence was that the house was not multi-occupied as all the residents lived there communally as one household. The House of Lords rejected this argument and laid down a number of tests to be applied in deciding whether a group of persons do or do not form a single household.

1) The number of persons occupying the property, and the place of its location, must be considered. Where, for example, 30 or more persons occupy a suburban house they can hardly be regarded as forming a single household.

2) The length of time for which each person occupies the property must be considered. A fluctuating and constantly altering population is a clear indication that the property is multi-occupied.

3) The intention of the owner of the property has to be taken into account. Mrs Pizzey, for example, never intended to set up a permanent community of women. Her intention was to provide a place of refuge for women who had been maltreated by their husbands. Some of the women simply needed time to get away from their homes to let the domestic violence spend itself, while others had no intention of ever returning to their husbands but wished to go to friends, relatives or to set up their own new homes.

This approach to the definition of 'household' was followed by the Court of Appeal in *Silbers v Southwark London Borough Council* (1978) 122 Sol Jo 128. Here a common lodging house was used for accommodating some 70 women, some of whom were alcoholics while others were mentally disturbed. They stayed there for varying periods or indefinitely. It was held that such a fluctuating group of residents could not be regarded as forming a single household. It is not necessary for persons to have exclusive possession of different parts of the property for them to form individual households and for a multi-occupancy to arise. Indeed it seems from dicta in *Milford Properties v Hammersmith London Borough Council* (1978) JPL 76 that a multi-occupancy can arise even where some of the occupiers are in the premises unlawfully, for example as unlawful sub-tenants.

Local authority powers

Management orders

By virtue of section 13 of the Housing Act 1961, as amended, the

Secretary of State has power to make a code to ensure proper standards of management in houses in multiple occupation. This code is contained in the Housing (Management of Houses in Multiple Occupation) Regulations 1962 (S.I. 1962 No. 668). Where it appears to a local authority that a multi-occupied house is in an unsatisfactory state as a consequence of failure to maintain proper standards of management they may by order under section 12 of the 1961 Act apply the management code to that house. Orders under this provision come into force on the date on which they are made, though within seven days from their making the local authority must serve a copy of the order on the owner of the house, and on every person whom they know to be a lessee of the house, and also post a copy of the order in some conspicuous place in the house where it is accessible to the inhabitants. Such orders are local land charges. Persons on whom copies of the order have been served have a period of 21 days (or such longer period that the local authority may by writing allow) from the service of the copy to appeal against the order, on the ground that it is unnecessary, to the magistrates. Should an appeal be made the court is to take into account the state of the house, both at the time of the making of the order as well as at the time when the appeal was instituted: merely temporary improvements are thus to be disregarded. Once a management order is made it remains operative until revoked by the local authority on the application of any person having an estate or interest in the house. Should an authority refuse such an application, or fail to notify an applicant of their decision within 35 days, there is a further right of appeal to the magistrates' court, who may revoke the order if they feel there has been a substantial change in the circumstances since it was made and that it is in other respects just to order a revocation.

A management order imposes certain duties on 'the manager' of the house in question. He is defined in the management regulations as a person who, being an owner or lessee of a house, receives rents or other payments from tenants of parts of the house or who are lodgers therein, and also any person who receives such payments on behalf of an owner or lessee as a trustee or agent. The actual duties of the manager are:

1) To maintain in good repair and proper, clean working order all means of water supply and drainage;

2) To maintain and keep in proper order and repair installations for the supply of gas and electricity, and for lighting and heating the common parts;

3) To keep safe and unobstructed, clean and in good order all common parts and facilities;

4) To make certain that at the commencement of a period of letting the rooms, facilities and service installations are clean and in good repair and order;

5) To maintain all means of ventilation in good order;

6) To maintain proper means of escape from fire;

7) To maintain in correct order all outbuildings, yards, forecourts or gardens in common use, together with any boundary walls and fences thereto;

8) To make available an adequate supply of rubbish bins, and not to allow refuse and litter to accumulate in the premises;

9) To take reasonable precautions to prevent injury to the occupants as a result of any structural defects, and

10) To display within the premises a printed copy of the regulations, and also a notice giving the manager's name and address.

The Regulations also require that the local authority maintain a register of the names and addresses of managers of houses in multiple occupation subject to the management code. Persons served with copies of the management order are also required to give the local authority details of their interest in the house, of its occupation, and also of any agents or trustees. They may also be required to supply details of any other person with an interest in the house, and the name and address of the manager. It should also be remembered that the regulations require the occupants of multi-occupied houses to co-operate with managers and not to hinder them.

A failure to comply with or a knowing contravention of the management regulations is an offence punishable on summary conviction by a fine of up to £200, Housing Act 1961, s. 13(4) as amended by the Housing Act 1980, Sch. 23.

Powers to require the doing of further works

If in the opinion of a local authority a house in multiple occupation is defective because of neglect in complying with the management regulations or other failure to observe proper standards of management or maintenance corresponding to those in the regulations, they may serve a notice under the Housing Act 1961 s. 14 on the manager specifying the works necessary to make good the defects and requiring their execution. The notice must allow at least 21 days for the doing of the works, though this period may be extended from time to time with the written permission of the authority. Information of the service of the notice must also be served on all other persons who are known to the local authority to be owners, lessees or mortgagees of the house. Following the service of the notice the person on whom it has been served has a period of 21 days (or such longer period as the local authority may allow) to appeal against the notice to the magistrates' courts. The grounds on which such an appeal is made are:

1) that the condition of the house did not justify the local authority in requiring the execution of the specified works;

2) that there has been some material error, defect or informality in, or in connection with, the notice;

3) that the authority have refused unreasonably to approve the execution of alternative works, or that the works required are otherwise unreasonable in character or extent or are unnecessary;

4) that the time allowed for the doing of the works is not reasonably sufficient, or

5) some person other than the appellant is wholly or partly responsible for the state of affairs, or will benefit from the doing of the works, and therefore ought to bear the whole or part of the cost of the works.

Further powers to require the doing of works are conferred by section 15 of the 1961 Act. If a local authority, having regard to the number of individuals or households accommodated in a multi-occupied house, consider that it is so far defective with regard to a number of listed particulars that it is not reasonably suitable for occupation by the individuals or households, they may serve a notice specifying the works which, in their opinion, are necessary to make the premises reasonably suitable for occupation, and requiring the execution of those works. The particulars the local authority may consider are: natural and artificial lighting; ventilation; water supply; personal washing facilities; drainage and sanitary conveniences; facilities for the storage, preparation and cooking of food, and for the disposal of waste water, and installations for space heating or for the use of space heating appliances. The notice must allow at least 21 days for the doing of the works, but this period may be extended by written permission. The notice is to be served either:

1) On the person having control of the house, i.e. the person who receives the rack rent of the property, or who would receive it if it were so let, or

2) On any person to whom the house is let at a rack rent, or an agent or trustee for such a person, and who receives rent or other payments from tenants or lodgers in the house.

Where a section 15 notice is served the local authority must also inform any other person who is known to them to be an owner, lessee or mortgagee of the property of the service. The notice may be withdrawn in writing if the local authority are satisfied that the level of occupation of the house has been reduced, and will remain reduced, to such a level as to render the doing of the works unnecessary.

With regard to fire, new rules replacing section 16 of the 1961 Act are contained in Schedule 24 to the Housing Act 1980. Where a local authority consider a house in multiple occupation is not adequately supplied with means of escape from fire they may exercise their powers under the schedule. They *must* do so if the house falls within a description of houses specified in an order by the Secretary of State. One serious limitation under the new law is that Schedule 24, paragraph 12 states: 'the functions of a local authority under this Schedule shall not be among those referred to in section 70 of the 1969 Act'. This means that the periodic reviews of housing conditions required by the 1969 Act will exclude reviewing the condition of houses in multiple occupation with regard to the means of escape from fire, and there will be no general obligation to seek out properties with inadequate fire escape provision. The Housing Act 1980, Sch. 12, paragraph 17 makes the payment of a special grant for the installation of fire escapes mandatory, provided that an application for such a grant follows a notice served under Schedule 24 to the Act. But this still leaves the initiative for doing repairs with the owner of the property in question, and places no obligation on local authorities *to search out* those properties that are deficient in respect of fire escapes. It has been argued that the Secretary of State should use his powers under Schedule 24, paragraph 1 to specify certain categories of houses in multiple occupation in relation to which local authorities would be under a duty to enforce effective fire precautions. These categories should include any house or hostel:

1) with more than two storeys, or

2) containing more than three households or eight individuals.

See Nick Beacock, 'Playing with Fire', *Roof*, September/October 1980, p. 149.

The new powers are otherwise quite extensive. The local authority may serve a notice on any person on whom they may serve notice under section 15 of the 1961 Act specifying the works required to provide the necessary means of escape from fire, and also requiring the execution of that work within a period of not less than 21 days from the service of the notice. This period may be extended from time to time. The fact of service must also be communicated to all other persons known by the local authority to be owners, lessees or mortgagees of the house.

Where it appears that the means of escape from fire would be adequate if part of the house ceased to be used for human habitation, the local authority may secure that. Alternatively they may secure the closure of part of the house while serving notice specifying those works necessary to supply the rest of the house with adequate fire escapes. In the execution of these powers they may accept undertakings from owners or mortgagees that part or parts of houses will not be used for human habitation without the consent of the local authority. It is an offence to use, or to permit the use of, any part of a house subject to a closing undertaking. Where such an undertaking is not accepted, or if one accepted is found to be broken, the local authority may make a closing order on the relevant part of the house. That part of the house closed will lose any protection under the Rent Act 1977, but displaced residents will fall within the rehousing obligations under section 39 of the Land Compensation Act 1973. Where a closing order is made it must be determined *provided* the local authority are satisfied that the means of escape from fire are adequate (owing to a change of circumstances) and will remain so if the closed part of the house is made available for human habitation.

The term 'means of escape from fire' was given a wide meaning in *Horgan v Birmingham Corpn* (1964) 108 Sol Jo 991 to include not just fire escapes as such but also ancillary matters such as screens operating to keep escape routes clear of smoke.

A person on whom a notice is served under either section 15 of the 1961 Act or Schedule 24 may, within 21 days of service (or within such longer period as the local authority allow in writing) appeal against the notice to the county court. The grounds on which an appeal can be made are similar to those relating to appeals made under section 14 which have been discussed above. If a notice under sections 14 to 16 (as replaced) is not complied with, or if the person on whom it was served informs the local authority in writing that he is not able to do the works, section 18 of the 1961 Act allows the authority to do the work themselves. They may then recover their reasonable expenses from the person on whom the notice was served, or where an agent or trustee was served, in whole or in part from the person on whose behalf the agent or trustee was acting. Recovery may be by action in the county court. It should also be noted that a *wilful failure* to comply with a notice issued under sections 14 – 16 (as replaced) of the 1961 Act is, by virtue of section 65 of the Housing Act 1964 as amended by Schedule 23 to the Housing Act 1980, an offence punishable by a fine of up to £500. By virtue of section 61 of the Housing Act 1969, where a person is initially convicted of the offence created by section 65 of the 1964 Act, he commits a further new offence if he then wilfully fails to leave the work undone. Furthermore this provision lays down that the obligation to do works created by a notice served under sections 14 to 16 of the 1961 Act is a continuing one, despite any expiration of the time limits set by the notice, thus a failure to comply with the *continuing* obligation itself constitutes a continuing offence. The meaning of 'wilful failure' was stated in *Honig v Islington London Borough* [1972] Crim LR 126 to include voluntary omissions to act, irrespective of motive. It appears that the only allowable reasons for not acting are force majeure, accident or impossibility.

The Housing Act 1980, Sch. 23 creates a new section 26A of the Housing Act 1961. This applies where any person, being an occupier, or owner of premises, and having received notice of intended action under Part II of the 1961 Act prevents the carrying into effect of the proposals. A magistrates' court may order such a person to allow the doing of what is necessary. If he fails to comply with their order he is liable on summary conviction, to a fine of up to £200, and to a further fine of £20 a day for every day on which his failure continues.

Power to prevent overcrowding in multi-occupied houses

Where a notice, or further notice, under section 15 of the Housing Act 1961 could be served the local authority may use their powers under section 19 of the Act to make a direction fixing the highest number of individuals or households or both who may occupy the house in its existing condition. At least seven days before making such a direction the local authority must serve on the owner and every known lessee notice of their intention, and also post a copy of this notice in the house in some place where it is accessible to the occupants. A right solely to make representations is given to those on whom such a notice is served. The direction once given makes it the duty of 'the occupier', who is any person entitled or authorised to permit individuals to take up residence in the house (Housing Act 1974, s. 67(5)), to keep the number of persons in the house within the permitted number. Copies of the direction must be served, within seven days of its making, on the owner and known lessees of the house, and also posted within the house in some place where the occupants can have access to it. It is an offence knowingly to fail to comply with a direction. On summary conviction the penalty is a fine of up to £500, see the Housing Act 1961, s. 19(11) as amended by the Housing Act 1980, Sch. 23.

A section 19 direction can only be issued at a time when the house to which it applies is multi-occupied, and further multiple occupation of the premises at the time of the alleged offence is an essential requirement for liability. However, it seems from *Simmons v Pizzey* [1979] AC 37, [1979] 2 All ER 432 that once a direction is validly given a temporary cessation of multiple occupation does not end the direction but merely suspends its operation; it will revive and be applicable as soon as the house is again multi-occupied. It is a mitigating circumstance when consideration is given to the penalty to be imposed for contravention of a section 19 direction that the accused committed the offence by providing accommodation for people in urgent and tragic need. There is no right to appeal against the giving of a section 19 direction as such. However, local authorities have power to revoke or vary such directions, following changes of circumstances affecting the house, or the execution of works there, on the application of anyone having an estate or interest in the house. An unreasonable refusal to exercise this power can form the subject of an appeal to the county court.

A new power to control overcrowding is given by section 146 of the Housing Act 1980, which replaces section 90 of the Housing Act 1957. Where it appears to a local authority that an excessive number of persons, having regard to the number of rooms available, is being, or is likely to be, accommodated in a house in multiple occupation they may serve on the occupier, or on the person having control or management of the house, or on both, an 'overcrowding notice'. This notice must state in relation to every room on the premises what the authority considers to be the maximum number of persons who can suitably sleep therein, if any. Special maxima may be included in the notice where some or all of the persons occupying the room are below such an age as is specified.

The local authority may require a number of courses of action from persons on whom such notice is served. The first such course is that he must refrain from:

1) knowingly permitting any room to be occupied as sleeping accommodation otherwise than in accordance with the notice, or

2) knowingly permitting the number of people using the premises for sleeping to rise so high that it is not possible to avoid persons of opposite sexes over the age of twelve (other than those living together as man and wife) sharing sleeping accommodation without contravening the notice, or using a non-room for sleeping accommodation.

The *alternative* course of action is that the person on whom the notice is served must refrain from:

1) knowingly permitting any *new* resident to occupy a room as sleeping accommodation otherwise than in accordance with the notice, or from

2) knowingly permitting a new resident to occupy part of the premises for sleeping if such permission *and* to avoiding of sexual overcrowding (as above) result in contravening the notice, or using a non-room for sleeping accommodation.

Not less than seven days before serving such a notice the local authority must:

1) inform the occupier of the premises, and any person appearing to have the control and management thereof, in writing of their intention to serve the notice, and

2) ensure, so far as reasonably possible, that every other person living in the house is informed of their intention.

its confirmation. A scheme made under the 1961 Act is *informatory* in character and empowers a local authority to seek particulars for registration from any person with an estate or interest in the house or living in it, and may also make it the duty of certain prescribed persons to notify the local authority that a house appears to be registrable. Occupiers of the house, its owners, lessees, mortgagees, those who receive its rents, and its managers may also be required to give information to the local authority under the Local Government (Miscellaneous Provisions) Act 1976, s. 16. This provision imposes a £400 fine for non-compliance with, or the wrongful supply of false information in answer to, their request. Section 22(4) of the Housing Act 1961, as amended by Schedule 23 to the Housing Act 1980, makes it an offence to fail to provide a local authority with information in connection with their section 22 enquiries. The penalty is a fine of up to £50. The 1969 Act, however, allows the insertion of *regulatory* or control provisions in a registration scheme where a house is occupied by *more* than two households, or by one household and four individuals. Thus a local authority may refuse to register a house: (a) on the ground that it is unsuitable and incapable of being made suitable for occupation; (b) because the person having control, or intended as the manager is not 'fit and proper'. They may also require the execution of works as a condition of registration. Written statements of reasons for refusing to register a house must be given, and there is a period of 21 days thereafter in which an appeal can be made to the county court, who may confirm, reverse or vary the decision of the local authority. It is an offence under section 64(7) of the Housing Act 1969 as amended by Schedule 23 to the Housing Act 1980 to contravene or to fail to comply with any provision of a registration scheme. Nevertheless it seems that though a number of local authorities have introduced such schemes that the worst sort of profiteering landlord ignores registration. Thus, unless an authority are prepared to search out unregistered houses in their area, or the residents thereof are prepared to supply information, which they may be too frightened or insufficiently informed to do, a registration scheme can be ineffective to eradicate unsuitable multi-occupancies.

Control orders

Because the powers under the 1961 Act were insufficient to deal with the problem of multiple occupation, the Housing Act 1964 granted powers to make 'control orders' which allow local authorities to take over the management of a house for up to five years and to act as if they were its owners. Under section 73(1) of the Housing Act 1964, as amended, a control order can be made:

1) if an order under section 12 of the Housing Act 1961 is in force, or a

notice has been served or direction given under sections 14, 15 or 19 of that Act; or

2) if it appears to the local authority that the state or condition of the house is such as to call for the taking of any such action, *and*

3) if it also appears to the authority that the state of the house is such that it is necessary to make a control order to protect the safety, welfare or health of the persons living in the house.

Control orders are designed to deal with the most squalid conditions and so there is no lengthy procedure as to their making. Such an order comes into force when made, and as soon as practicable thereafter the local authority must enter the premises and take such immediate steps as are necessary to protect the residents' health, welfare and safety. A copy of the order has to be posted in the house where it is accessible to the residents, and copies must also be served on every person who, before the order, was the manager of the house, or had control of it, or was an owner, lessee or mortgagee of the house. These copies of the order must be accompanied by a notice setting out rights of appeal against the order under section 82 of the 1964 Act (see below).

The effect of a control order

A control order transfers full possession and control of the house to the local authority and cancels any orders, notices or directions already made under the management provisions of the 1961 Act, but without prejudice to any liabilities incurred thereunder. The property will not fall within Part V of the Housing Act 1957. It is possible to exclude from control, by virtue of section 76 of the Housing Act 1964, any part of the house which is occupied by an owner or tenant of the whole house. Such an excluded part will be subject to the authority's right of entry for the purposes of survey, or to execute any works in any part of the house which is subject to the order. The authority may grant, under section 74 of the 1964 Act, weekly or monthly tenancies within the property, but rights and obligations of existing residents are protected by section 75, and this extends to any protection enjoyed by virtue of the Rent Acts. Section 77 lays an initial double duty on the local authority once they have control:

1) to maintain proper standards of management and take any action which would have been necessary under the management provisions of the 1961 Act, and

2) to keep the house insured against fire.

Thereafter section 79 requires them to prepare a scheme and to serve

1) an applicant for registration is unfit to be a keeper; or

2) the premises are unsuitable for use as a common lodging house, having regard to the sanitation, water supply, means of escape from fire, etc.; or

3) the use of the premises as a common lodging house would cause inconvenience or annoyance to persons in the neighbourhood.

A refusal to register must be given in writing and accompanied by reasons, and a person aggrieved by such a refusal may appeal to the justices, see sections 238 and 239 of the Public Health Act 1936. The period of registration may be for up to thirteen months. Despite these provisions many common lodging houses are unregistered because many 'keepers' do not realise that they should apply for registration.

The keeper's duties. By section 241 of the 1936 Act the keeper or his duly registered deputy must be on duty between 9.00 pm and 6.00 am as well as maintain general management over the house and its inmates. The keeper must supply to the local authority, on their request, a list of persons who occupied the house during the day or night preceding the request. Keepers must also allow the local authority's duly authorised officers to have free access to all parts of their houses. Under section 242 keepers must immediately give notice of any case of a person suffering from an infectious disease within their houses, see Public Health (Infectious Diseases) Regulations (S.I. 1968 No. 1366), as amended.

Supervisory powers of local authorities

Sections 243 and 244 of the 1936 Act enable local authorities to apply to a justice of the peace for a warrant to enable them to enter a common lodging house and there to examine the inmates to see whether any of them are suffering or have recently suffered from a 'notifiable disease'. A person suffering from such a disease may be removed to a hospital. A common lodging house which has housed such a person may be closed by the court until it is certified as free from infection. Section 343 of the Act of 1936 lists the 'notifiable diseases' as: cholera, plague, relapsing fever, smallpox and typhus. Local authorities also have power under section 240 of the Act to make byelaws:

1) for fixing the maximum number of persons allowed to use a common lodging house, and to provide for the separation of the sexes;

2) for promoting cleanliness and ventilation;

3) to provide for precautions against the spread of infection in common lodging houses, and

4) generally to secure the well ordering of such premises.

Model byelaws have been issued by the Department of Health and Social Security. The Model Byelaws Series III (1938) provide:

'The keeper of the lodging house shall ensure that each lodger has 40 square feet of floor space (30 square feet if lodger under ten years old). If the height of the room is less than eight feet, the floor space per person is increased by five square feet for every foot or part of a foot less than eight feet'.

Local authorities, however, do not always enforce the standards of the 1936 Act because some keepers, if proceeded against, would simply close down their houses, thus imposing an increased number of homeless persons on the authorities. Nevertheless by section 246 of the Act any person who:

1) contravenes or fails to comply with any provision of Part IX, or

2) fails in his duty as a keeper to maintain the premises in a fit state to be used as a common lodging house, or

3) deliberately misleads the local authority in relation to an application for registration,

commits an offence. Where a keeper is convicted of such an offence, or contravening a byelaw relating to common lodging houses, the court may cancel his registration and may disqualify him from registration for such period as it thinks fit, Public Health Act 1936, s. 247.

Overcrowding

We have already seen how, historically, overcrowding was a problem principally associated with areas of poor court and terrace houses, but that today it can also occur in multi-occupied premises. Our present concern is with overcrowding in separate dwelling-houses.

One initial problem is that local authority powers with regard to overcrowding exist principally under Part IV of the Housing Act 1957, and, by virtue of section 87 thereof are confined to premises 'used as a separate dwelling by members of the working class or of a type suitable for such use'. The expression 'working class' has never been legislatively defined. Judicial statements in *Guiness Trust (London Fund) v Green* [1955] 2 All ER 871, [1955] 1 WLR 872 and *Chorley Borough Council v Barratt Developments (North West) Ltd* [1979] 3 All ER 634 indicate that 'working class' is nowadays to be interpreted as that group of people who are in the low income range *and* who are in unskilled occupations. The sort of houses 'suitable' for such persons would seem to be, though such a statement must sound archaic and class prejudiced, mainly the smaller older type of houses found generally in inner city areas.

The definition of overcrowding

Section 77 of and Schedule 6 to the Housing Act 1957 provide:

'A dwelling-house shall be deemed for the purposes of this Act to be overcrowded any time when the number of persons sleeping in the house either —

(a) is such that any two of those persons being persons ten years old or more of opposite sexes and not being persons living together as husband or wife, must sleep in the same room [this is known as sexual overcrowding]; or

(b) is, in relation to the number and floor area of the rooms of which the house consists, in excess of the permitted number of persons as defined in the Sixth Schedule to this Act'. [This provides that the permitted number is to be calculated as follows:

(a) Where a house consists of:

one room . . . . 2 units
two rooms. . . . . 3 units
three rooms . . . . 5 units
four rooms . . . . 7½ units
five rooms. . . . . 10 units with an additional 2 units
for each room in excess of five

(b) Where the floor area of a room is:

110 sq ft or more . . . . 2 units
90 − 100 sq ft . . . . 1½ units
70 − 90 sq ft . . . . 1 unit
50 − 70 sq ft . . . . ½ unit
under 50 sq ft . . . . Nil]

Rules for the measurement of rooms in order to obtain the permitted number are found in the Housing Act (Overcrowding and Miscellaneous Forms) Regulations 1937 (S.R. & O. No. 80) reg. 4, the principal effect of which is to *exclude* from the measured floor area any part of the floor over which the ceiling height is less than five feet.

A child under one year old is a nil unit, a child between one and ten years counts as half a unit and a person over ten years is a whole unit. To calculate the permitted number both the above tables are used and the lowest figure found is the permitted number for any given house. Overcrowding occurs where there is either sexual overcrowding or a breach of the permitted number standard. It should be noted that *all* persons who use the house as their home should be counted when deciding whether there is overcrowding, and not just those who are sleeping there at any given time. If this were not so the law could be ignored by persons sleeping on a shift or 'Box and Cox' basis. In *Zaitzeff v Olmi* (1952) 102 LJ 416 (county court) a daughter away at a boarding school was held to be living at home for the purposes of the permitted number standard. It should also be noted that the only rooms that can be taken into account when deciding the issue of overcrowding are those normally used in the locality either as living rooms or bedrooms, Housing Act 1957, s. 87.

Section 80 of the 1957 Act permits local authorities to license an occupier to exceed the permitted number standard, but only up to the number specified in the licence and only for a period of up to twelve months. Within that period the licence may be revoked by the authority giving the occupier one month's notice. Licences may be granted to take account of seasonal increases of population in a district, for example to allow for the accommodation of migratory agricultural workers or holiday makers, or in other 'exceptional circumstances', an undefined phrase that might cover the sheltering of wives and children driven from the homes by matrimonial disputes or other persons rendered homeless by disaster.

Offences

These are principally defined by section 78 of the Housing Act 1957, and can be committed by the occupier of a dwelling-house and by the landlord where the property is let. If the occupier or the landlord of a dwelling-house cause or permit it to be overcrowded an offence is committed for which the penalty is a fine on summary conviction of £5, plus a fine of up to £2 for every day on which the offence continues. However, an *occupier* commits no offence if the persons sleeping in the house lived there on the appointed day (which is a reference to the Housing Act 1935, and effectively refers to various appointed day orders made for various parts of the country between 1936 and 1938) and have lived there continuously since, or are children born after that day of any of those persons, *unless*:

1) suitable alternative accommodation has been offered to the occupier and he has failed to accept it; or

2) suitable alternative accommodation has been offered to some person living in the house who is not a member of the occupier's family (e.g. a lodger) and whose removal is reasonably practicable in all the circumstances and the occupier has failed to require his removal.

Likewise an occupier commits no offence merely because a child attains a sufficient age to be counted as either a full or half unit for the purposes of determining whether there is overcrowding, provided he applies for suitable alternative accommodation to the local authority, and also provided that all the persons sleeping in the house are persons who were living there at the date when the child reached the relevant age and have lived there continuously since, or are themselves children born after that date to any of those persons. Again this immunity is lost if the occupier fails to avail himself of an offer of suitable alternative accommodation, or otherwise fails to take reasonable steps to secure the removal of persons who are not members of his family from the house. A mere visit by a member of the occupier's family who normally lives elsewhere which causes temporary overcrowding is not an offence, and this circumstance is excluded from criminal liability by section 78(4) of the Housing Act 1957.

Section 87 of the 1957 Act defines 'suitable alternative accommodation' as a dwelling-house as to which the following conditions are satisfied, that is to say —

1) the house must be a house in which the occupier and his family can live without causing it to be overcrowded;

2) the local authority must certify the house to be suitable to the needs of the occupier and his family as respects security of tenure and proximity to place of work and otherwise and to be suitable in relation to his means; and

3) 'if the house belongs to the local authority, they must certify it to be suitable to the needs of the occupier and his family as respects accommodation . . . and they shall treat a house containing two bedrooms as providing accommodation for four persons and a house containing three bedrooms as providing accommodation for five persons, and a house containing four bedrooms as providing accommodation for seven persons'.

So far as a *landlord* is concerned, he will commit an offence and be deemed to have caused or permitted overcrowding if:

1) after receiving notice from the local authority that his house is overcrowded he fails to take reasonable steps to abate the overcrowding, or

2) he let the house having reasonable cause to believe that it would become overcrowded, or if he failed to make inquiries of the proposed occupier as to the number, age and sex of persons who would be allowed to sleep in the house.

To aid the landlord in the abatement of overcrowding section 101 of the Rent Act 1977 takes away any security of tenure enjoyed by a tenant in a house which is so overcrowded that the occupier is guilty of an offence. But to prevent families from being dispossessed and made homeless, Ministry of Health Circular No. 17/49 makes certain recommendations. First, occupiers whose houses have become overcrowded merely by the natural increase of children, and who have not deliberately aggravated the situation by taking in additional persons, such as lodgers, should be encouraged to apply for suitable alternative accommodation to the local authority, thus terminating their own criminal liability and so escaping from dispossession under section 101 of the 1977 Act . Second, local authorities have been advised to use their powers to license over-crowding under section 80 of the Act of 1957 so as to prevent criminal liability falling on an occupier. A landlord is under a duty by virtue of section 83 of the Housing Act 1957 to inform the local authority within seven days of overcrowding within any of his houses that has come to his knowledge.

In order to inform occupiers of their rights, section 81 of the 1957 Act requires that a summary of sections 77, 78 and 80 of the Act shall be contained in any rent book or similar document given to the tenant, together with a statement of the permitted number of persons in relation to the house. A local authority are under an obligation to inform either the occupier or the landlord, if either apply, of the permitted number of persons in relation to the house in question. With regard to tenancies where rent is payable weekly a landlord is under an obligation to supply his tenant with a rent book by virtue of section 1 of the Landlord and Tenant Act 1962.

Enforcement and remedial powers and duties of local authorities

The Housing Act 1957, s. 85 makes it the duty of the local authority to enforce the duties relating to overcrowding, and only they may prosecute. Where the local authority itself is responsible as landlord for overcrowding they can themselves be prosecuted by another person but only with the consent of the Attorney-General. To aid them in discharging their obligation a local authority may serve notice on an occupier requiring him to give them within fourteen days a written statement of the number, ages and sexes of the persons sleeping in the house. Failing to comply with this request or deliberately making a false return will involve the occupier in criminal liability, for which he can be fined up to £2 on summary conviction, see Housing Act 1957, s 85(3).

Section 85(2) grants a power to the local authority to commence possession proceedings in respect of a privately rented overcrowded house. If they notify an occupier in writing that overcrowding exists and require him to abate it within fourteen days, and if he takes no action, or having taken action allows overcrowding to recur, within three months, then they may apply to the county court for possession to be given to the landlord. According to Jenkins LJ in *Zbytniewski v Broughton* [1956] 2 QB 673 at 688, [1956] 3 All ER 348 at 356: 'the position crystallises at the end of the period of three months, and, provided the house is still overcrowded at the date when the complaint is made to the court . . ., then the order for possession must go'. Any expenses incurred by the local authority under this power may be recovered by them summarily as a civil debt from the landlord. Tenants displaced in consequence of the use of this power do not fall within the scope of the local authority's rehousing obligations under the Land Compensation Act 1973.

Local authorities are also under a general duty under section 76 of the 1957 Act to investigate overcrowding within their areas of which they become aware, to make a report to the Secretary of State of their findings, and of the number of new houses needed to relieve the overcrowding. The Secretary of State may direct an authority to make such an investigation and report.

Further reading

Garner, J.F., *Alteration or Conversion of Houses* (Oyez) (4th edn., 1975) pp. 15 – 20

Smith, D., *Racial Disadvantage in Britain* (Penguin, 1977) pp. 230 – 242 and 270 – 274

Smith, D. and Whalley, A., *Racial Minorities and Public Housing* (PEP Broadsheet No. 556) pp. 99 – 106

Social Welfare Law (Ed. by D.W. Pollard) (Oyez) paras. C. 5500 – C. 6089 and C. 6400 – C. 6441

Wolmar, C., 'Overcrowding in Southall', *Roof*, July/August 1980, pp. 117 – 118

Chapter 12

Municipal housing: the rôle of the Commission for Local Administration

We have already seen how local authorities are the second main provider of homes in Britain, and that municipal housing is a scarce resource with an insufficient supply to meet the demands of society. Its allocation can therefore often give rise to disputes with feelings of anger at real or imagined injustices. It must be remembered that local authorities have an almost total discretion as to the disposal and transfer of their housing stock — a discretion with which the courts are reluctant to interfere. For this reason the existence of an independent body such as the Commission for Local Administration (the 'local ombudsman') is extremely important for those who rely on administrative discretion to obtain accommodation. In *Landlord and Tenant* Martin Partington discusses these discretionary powers of local authorities, and refers to a Justice Report *The Citizen and his Council* (Stevens 1969) which stated: 'complaints are made about local authority maladministration, some of which may allege some element of maladministration, while others may be concerned with the merits of a discretionary decision. In our examination of this subject we found that complaints of both kinds are commonest in relating to such topics as the allocation of "benefits" of various kinds [such as] . . . the granting of tenancies of council houses . . . in these and similar cases, a complaint about maladministration is not, we feel, always redressed'. In his comment (at page 371) Partington states that the Commission for Local Administration 'may develop a useful role in resolving difficulties in the housing area'. It is now necessary to consider the role of that 'local ombudsman' principally in relation to housing authorities, though it is impossible to divorce housing from other aspects of the Commission's work. Housing authorities fall within the scope of that work under section 25(1)(a) of the Local Government Act 1974.

The creation of the Commission and its terms of reference

Established by the Local Government Act 1974, Part III, the Commission for Local Administration in England came into being in April 1974 and was modelled on the Parliamentary Commissioner, who had no jurisdiction over the actions of local government. The Commission is charged with investigating complaints from members of the public about injustice caused by maladministration in local government. In its booklet *Your Local Ombudsman*, which sets out details of the scheme, the Commission states: 'Maladministration is not defined in the Act and it will be for Local Commissioners to decide whether it has occurred. But it refers for example to the way in which an authority's decision has been taken. Maladministration may be taken to cover administrative action (or inaction) based on or influenced by improper considerations or conduct. Arbitrariness, malice or bias, including unfair discrimination, are examples of improper considerations. Neglect, unjustifiable delay, incompetence, failure to observe relevant rules or procedures, failure to take relevant considerations into account, failure to establish or review where there is a duty or obligation on a body to do so or the use of faulty systems are examples of improper conduct. The Commissioner has no power to question the merits of a decision taken without maladministration'.

The Local Government Act 1974, s. 34(3) provides that nothing in the Act authorises or requires a Local Commissioner to question the *merits* of a decision taken without maladministration by an authority in the exercise of a discretion vested in it. This does not prevent the *investigation* of the merits of a decision, but it prevents the Commission from criticising a decision as *wrong in substance* when there was no procedural flaw in the process leading up to the decision. The maladministration must, by virtue of section 26(1) of the 1974 Act, arise 'in connection with action taken *by or on behalf of* a local authority. This is wide enough to cover the acts and decisions of members, officers and other employees, and also agents of an authority.

It is possible to arrive at a working definition of 'maladministration' by reading the Commission's published decisions, and by assigning the subject matter of the complaint to a classified complaints system. It has to be admitted that in some cases this process is somewhat arbitrary as many reports raise multiple issues and allegations cutting across neat category boundaries. The most useful system of categorisation seems to be, so far as housing matters are concerned: delay; bias and victimisation including unfair treatment; complaints arising out of planning and building regulation powers and also related to housing; inefficiency, including bad or non-existent administrative procedures, failures to fulfil statutory obligations and broken promises; repair problems, including heating, and covering both public and private sector tenants; health complaints, especially with regard to cases arising out of failures to allocate council housing despite medical evidence of need; grant and home loss payment disputes; and, finally, miscellaneous. On this basis most complaints seem to arise out of allegations of general inefficiency, with problems relating to repairs and those arising from delay coming quite a close second and third respectively. On the other hand an examination of the reports shows that a complaint based on inefficiency has less chance of succeeding than one in either of the two other large categories.

The complainant must also claim to have sustained injustice in consequence of maladministration. 'Injustice' is not defined in the legislation but covers a wide range of matters from loss consequent upon a refusal to make a financial grant through to annoyance, disturbance or frustration caused by maladministration. No actual financial loss need be proven.

Procedure before the Commission

There is a strict procedure, laid down in section 26 of the Local Government Act 1974, to be followed before a complaint will be entertained and failure to comply with the procedure set out in the Act is responsible in some measure for the large number of complaints which are not accepted for investigation. The Local Commissioner will not investigate any complaint until it has been brought to the attention of the authority complained against, either by the person aggrieved (or his personal representative) or by a member of the authority on behalf of that person, and until the authority has had a reasonable time in which to reply to the complaint. A complaint intended for reference should be made in writing to a member of the authority complained against with a request that it should be sent to the Local Commissioner. It should state the action which it is alleged constitutes maladministration. If the member does not refer the complaint to the Commissioner, the person aggrived may ask the Commission to accept the complaint direct. A complaint should not be addressed directly to a Local Commissioner in the first instance.

When a complaint is received direct the Commission advise the complainant on the correct procedure. In appropriate cases the Commission will inform the Chief Executive of the Authority of the direct complaint regardless of whether it might be within a local ombudsman's jurisdiction if it were properly referred. The Chief Executive is asked to consider whether the complaint can be settled locally and it is known that local settlement is achieved in some such cases.

The actual procedure for an investigation is set out in the booklet published by the Commission, *Your Local Ombudsman*, pp. 11 and 12:

'When a complaint is received it will normally be handled as follows:
(a) It will be examined to decide whether it is within the Commissioner's cope. [Some 80 per cent of complaints are not investi-

gated, largely because many relate only to the *merits* of a decision.]

(b) If it proves to be outside his scope, a letter of explanation will be sent to the complainant and to the member who referred the complaint.

(c) If a complaint is received directly from a member of the public, or if further information about the complaint is needed, the matter will be taken up in correspondence.

(d) Before beginning to investigate a complaint, the Commissioner will tell the complainant and the member that he has accepted it for investigation. He will also notify the authority and any person named in the complaint as having taken or authorised the action complained of, giving them the opportunity to comment on any allegations contained in the complaint. [The Commission may, by section 29 of the 1974 Act, require *any* person to furnish information and produce documents. A Commissioner enjoys the same powers as the High Court in respect of the examination of witnesses and the production of documents.]

(e) If at any stage in the investigation the Local Commissioner decides that the action complained of also concerns a government department or part of the National Health Service (e.g. a hospital) he will consult the Parliamentary Commissioner or the Health Service Commissioner as the case may be. If he thinks it advisable that the complainant should ask for an investigation by either of those other commissioners he may inform him of the steps necessary to do so.

(f) When the investigation is completed a report giving the Local Commissioner's finding will be sent to the complainant, the member, the authority or authorities concerned and any person complained against. A report will not normally give the name or other identifying details of the complainant or of any other person involved in the matter'.

An investigation, once it has been undertaken, usually involves a visit by an officer of the Commission to the authority concerned where the relevant files are investigated and the officers, the complainant, members and any other person considered to have information bearing on the matter complained of will be interviewed. Interviews are held in private, and interviewees may be accompanied by a friend, a trades union adviser or a legal representative. Where a junior local government officer is involved chief officers are not allowed to be present, neither may an officer be represented by a lawyer in the employment of his local authority. These practices are followed to ensure candour in the investigative process. Before a report is issued on an investigation it is sent in a draft form to the complainant and the local authority for their comments.

Revised operating procedures

During 1979/80 the Commission reviewed their operating procedures with the aim of providing a fairer and more economic service to complainants and authorities. As a result certain changes are to be made early in 1980/81. In the past only about 20 per cent of all properly referred complaints have been described as being 'investigated'. But about half the remaining complaints have been subject to inquiries which have gone well beyond consideration of the material submitted by the complainant. These inquiries have usually included a request to the Chief Executive of the Authority for preliminary comments on the complaint, or for some specific information, and may have included an interview with the complainant, or examination of the authority's files.

For the future the definition of 'investigation' will include all dealings with a complaint which is within jurisdiction and has been properly referred. As in the past, the depth of investigation will vary according to the particular complaint. The detailed procedures will be:

1) in many cases the Chief Executive of the Authority will be asked for comments on a complaint on the understanding that these may be sent to the complainant;

2) if the Local Commissioner then feels, after considering the complaint submitted and the comments, that he should not investigate further, a copy of the letter giving the Chief Executive's comments will generally be sent to the complainant in support of that decision. The complainant will then be able to submit reasons why the investigation should continue;

3) in those cases where the investigation continues, the authority will be asked if they have any further comments to make on the complaint;

4) the local commissioner may decide not to investigate further at a later stage in the process (for example, after an authority's files have been seen it may become clear that there was no maladministration). In many such cases it will be possible to put this decision in a letter which will not require publication as a report, or in a short report discontinuing the investigation. In the remaining cases investigation will continue and a formal report will be issued;

5) the Commission's published statistics will show as investigations all those cases where some investigation has been made, including those where the Local Commissioner decided not to investigate to the point of a formal report.

Certain matters are excluded from the ambit of the Commission's investigations; for example the Commission cannot normally investigate the matter if the person has or had a right of appeal or a right to go to the courts but has not used it, Local Government Act 1974, s. 26(6).

Similar exclusions apply where there is a right of appeal, reference or review to any statutorily constituted tribunal, or where there is a right of appeal to a minister. But all these exclusions are subject to the proviso that the Commission may conduct an investigation if satisfied that in the particular circumstances it was reasonable for the complainant not to have used his other legal remedies. The Commission will exercise their discretion where, for example, the cost of pursuing a remedy in the High Court would be prohibitively high. The Commission has a general discretion to investigate complaints. The circmustances of the exercise of that discretion were considered by the Court of Appeal in *R v Local Commissioner for Administration for the North and North East Area of England ex parte Bradford Metropolitan City Council* [1979] QB 287, [1979] 2 All ER 881.

The Court of Appeal's decision confirmed:

1) that although a Local Commissioner cannot question the merits of a decision taken without maladministration, he can investigate a complaint about the decision to see whether there was maladministration in the process of making it;

2) that the fact that a complaint is about the exercise of 'professional judgment' does not prevent investigation by the Local Commissioner to determine whether there was maladministration;

3) that the Local Commissioners should not be rigid in enforcing the section 26(4) requirement that a complaint should have been made to a member of the authority within twelve months from the date when the complainant first knew about the matter alleged in the complaint where justice requires that the time be extended and the complaint heard;

4) that a complainant (who of necessity cannot know what took place in the council offices) should not have to specify any particular piece of maladministration. It is enough if he specifies the action of the local authority in connection with which he complains there was maladministration;

5) that because the complainant might be able to voice the complaint in court proceedings, a Local Commissioner is not barred from investigating questions of injustice and maladministration which will not be directly at issue in those proceedings.

[This case arose out of an alleged failure by a local authority to use their statutory powers and resources to help a woman look after her children before they were taken into care.]

The Commission will not investigate an action which affects all or most of the inhabitants of the area of the authority concerned, section 26(7). Apart from these restrictions there are other drawbacks implicit in the procedure for referring complaints: the lack of direct access and the need to exhaust local complaints procedures (if they exist) mean that any complaint takes a long time to process. According to the Commission's Annual Reports the average time taken from the receipt of a complaint to completion of the investigation rose from 41.4 weeks in 1976/77 to 47.6 weeks in 1977/78 but fell in 1978/79 and 1979/80 to 43 weeks. This figure can be compared with that for the year ended 31 March 1976 where the average for the first twenty investigations completed was 24.65 weeks and for the last twenty completed during the year 35.25 weeks.

Apart from the delay in actually completing each investigation there are other facts which have become apparent since the inception of the scheme which suggest that the Commission — albeit through no fault of its own — is not achieving all that it might. The largest number of complaints received has been in the planning field. In 1975/76 31 per cent of complaints received related to planning matters with housing problems next at 22 per cent: the figures for 1976/77 were 31 per cent and 23 per cent respectively, for 1977/78 34 per cent and 23 per cent, for 1978/79 34 per cent and 27 per cent and for 1979/80 36 per cent and 31 per cent respectively. These figures suggest that the complaints procedure is used more readily by land developers, who are by definition in the higher income brackets, although the number of completed investigations in the housing field is almost the same for those concerned with planning matters.

The effectiveness of the Commission in providing a remedy

There is no obligation for a local authority to heed a Commissioner's report. One Commissioner, Mr F.P. Cook, has said in his annual report for 1976: '[t]here must be cause for concern at an authority's apparent disregard of one of the Commission's investigations and at their failure to remedy an injustice'. In the Annual Report for the year ended 31 March 1978 the same Commissioner states that in his opinion 'the success of the service will rest ultimately on acceptance and consent, not on narrow legalism'. It is to be hoped that the longer the complaints procedure is in operation the more it will be accepted as a legitimate part of local government and that local authorities everywhere will act on the Commission's findings.

On the other hand a complainant does not go to the Commission for *redress* as he would go to a court, he goes for a *finding* as to whether or not there has been maladministration. The Commission may find such maladministration but cannot insist on its being remedied. All they have power to do, under section 31 of the Local Government Act 1974, is to make a report of findings to the authority concerned, who must then consider it and notify the Commission of the action they have taken or propose to take. If no such notification is received, within a reasonable time, or if the Commission is not satisfied with the action taken or proposed they may make a second or further report indicating what they consider would be appropriate. Generally, therefore, the *absence* of a second report is good evidence that the problem complained of has been dealt with to the satisfaction of all the parties. In fact very few second reports have been issued in relation to housing complaints. Second reports do not have to be considered by local authorities and there is nothing that can be done if an authority resolves to do nothing after such a report has been issued. However, it is exceptionally rare for a second report to be disregarded. It should also be remembered that sometimes though maladministration is found the Commissioner states that no injustice was caused, or that a mere apology on the part of the authority concerned would be sufficient. From the evidence to hand it would seem that most cases where maladministration causing injustice was found were remedied satisfactorily. The general rarity of further reports also indicates that the activities of the Commission have some effect on local housing authorities and may contribute to the better administration of discretion in this area of the law. Against this it should be said that some local housing authorities have from time to time been made the subject of multiple complaints by numbers of individuals. The evidence here suggests that there may well be pockets of resistance to the introduction of good housing administration policies.

Remedial action taken following the issue of a report in which maladministration causing injustice is found is likely to fall under one, or more, of the following four headings: the giving of an apology; the redressing of the actual grievance; the making of a compensatory payment; and the improvement of administrative procedures. Where an authority apologises to a complainant it is the easiest and cheapest form of redress which should, at least, appease ill feeling and make for better relationships without necessarily removing all cause for complaint. Where steps are taken that redress the cause of the complaint this will satisfy the complainant. However, there are times when correcting one wrong may well cause other problems. An example of this is where rehousing a complainant raises allegations of unfair treatment in relation to other persons awaiting municipal accommodation. In such circumstances a local authority would seem justified in considering the wider issues and their implications before deciding what response to make to the Commission's findings.

In some cases making a monetary payment may be the best course of action. Before the Local Government Act 1978 local authorities had, in the absence of express statutory permission, to seek the sanction of the Secretary of State to make *ex gratia* payments in those cases where such compensation was considered appropriate. Section 1 of the 1978 Act now allows a local authority subject to investigation by the Commission to make payments to or provide other benefits for persons who have suffered injustice because of maladministration. This, of itself, does not remove all the difficulties. It may not always be easy to satisfy the loss caused by maladministration. Legal costs and damage to property are easily reduced to cash terms, but injury to health, or inconvenience and discomfort are not so easily quantified. Some authorities have resorted to the services of an independent expert to quantify the amount of payments to be made. Such an independent assessment is likely to be fair and unbiased and acceptable to all the parties. An alternative solution is to make an analogy with damages in tort and to make such payments as will put the complainant in the position in which he would have been had the maladministration not taken place. Such an approach to the problem should not be pursued in too legalistic a fashion, otherwise the compensation payment might well approach the level of tort damages. In 'Local Authority Response to the Local Ombudsman' (1979) JPEL 441 Christine Chinkin reveals that sums of up to £20,000 have been paid as compensation. Before making a compensatory payment an authority must consider the general duty they owe to their ratepayers not to impose over heavy burdens on the general rate fund, and also the need to avoid uncomfortable precedents. Further advice on the making of payments under the 1978 Act is contained in Department of the Environment Circular No. 54/78. Recently the Commission has become more willing to make specific suggestions in reports as to the best way to satisfy them that the act of maladministration has been remedied.

The receipt of a finding of maladministration causing injustice may, of course, lead to a change or improvement in an authority's administrative workings so as to minimise the risk of future complaints. Such a response may be particularly appropriate where the complaint arose out of unjustifiable delay on the part of an authority. Some authorities have gone so far as to set up schemes to monitor their future performance in relation to their statutory functions, and others have created special subcommittees to deal with specific problems. But excessive caution in relation to administrative matters could bring the wheels of local government to a halt. Furthermore, local authorities are unlikely to be able to devote considerable resources to changing their practices at a time of general financial stringency. The Annual Report of the Commission for 1979 reports the findings of a survey of complaints carried out by Justice. This revealed that a substantial majority of complainants who had been subject to injustice caused by maladministration were dissatisfied with the remedial action taken by the authorities concerned. There is still, therefore, room for improvement on the part of local authorities in relation to their practices and procedures.

Another difficulty with the present system for investigations was highlighted in *Re a complaint against Liverpool City Council* [1977] 2 All ER 650, [1977] 1 WLR 995. A Commissioner requested the Council to produce certain relevant records for the purpose of the investigation. The Council refused to do so and the Commissioner issued a subpoena requiring production. The Council replied by serving a notice under section 32(3) of the Local Government Act 1974 claiming that it would be against the public interest for them to disclose the records (which related to action taken concerning children in the care of the Council) and applied to the court for the subpoena to be set aside. The court granted the application. The Commissioner had a further right under section 32(3) of the Act to apply to the Secretary of State to discharge the notice but decided not to do so on the basis that the logical solution would be to amend the Act to bring the procedure into line with that governing the Parliamentary Commissioner. Section 11(3) of the Parliamentary Commissioner Act 1967 provides that a minister may serve a notice claiming that it would be prejudicial to the safety of the State or against the public interest to disclose certain documents and the effect of such a notice is to prevent the Parliamentary Commissioner communicating to any other person the information contained in such documents. Unlike the position under section 32(3) of the Local Government Act 1974 the Parliamentary Commissioner is therefore entitled to see the documents specified in the notice. In the *Bradford* case the Secretary of State's powers were, however, invoked in order to secure production of local authority records.

An assessment of the work of the Commission

The general consensus of opinion as to the performance of the 'local ombudsmen' during their first few years of operation would seem to be that there has been a worthwhile achievement both in terms of individual complaints remedied and in relation to general improvements in administrative practices. An example of such an achievement was the joint issue in 1978 by the Local Authorities Associations and the Commission of a Code of Practice for local authorities to adopt when dealing with complaints made to them. Amongst other matters this code urges all local authorities to have a standard written procedure for dealing with complaints, irrespective of the particular department or action against which any given complaint is directed. The Code also counsels authorities to ensure that their members are fully aware of and conversant with the complaints procedure. It also makes the telling point that complaints and queries can be minimised if the public are given adequate information in advance about the activities and problems of local authorities. The complete text of the Code can be found in Appendix 9 of the

Annual Report of the Commission for 1978. There is, however, no obligation on any authority to adopt and use the code.

Future reforms

There have been a number of suggestions made for improvements in the powers and practices of the Commission. The annual report for 1979 disclosed that research carried out by Justice on the social background of complainants had revealed that the majority came from the professional, managerial or skilled working classes, that they were likely to be middle-aged and also to have received more than an average formal education. The implication is that younger, semi-skilled or unskilled persons with only average educational achievements do not use the services of the Commission, though complaints about *housing* were slightly more likely to come from manual workers than other groups.

These findings explain various other features of the complaints processes discovered by Justice. Most complainants (64 per cent) went to the council office first with their complaint although there was a slight tendency for complainants from non-manual households to go first to a councillor. A third of all respondents to the survey reported that nothing happened after they had made their complaint to the council. These were more likely to be manual workers and/or young and/or with less formal education than the population generally. The importance of the media in learning about the local ombudsman emerged. But the importance of radio, television and newspaper declined as one moved down and social scale. Friends, relatives, workmates and the council or councillor were slightly more important than the media in informing those in the central classes of junior non-manual and skilled manual workers. Citizens Advice Bureaux played a smaller role than might be imagined — only 7 per cent heard of the local ombudsman through them. CABs were not often the source of information for professional and managerial workers but they increased in importance down the social scale and 15 per cent of semi- and unskilled workers had learned of the Commission from them. Most respondents (88 per cent) had seen the Commission's booklet.

A decision on whether to accept a complaint for investigation took more than three months for about a quarter of the complaints covered by the survey. Decisions on housing and rating complaints were made marginally more quickly, whilst decisions on social services and education complaints took slightly longer. Amongst those whose complaints had been investigated, one-third said the investigation was too slow and this response reflected social class. Where the complainant was a professional or managerial worker, the investigation tended to be quicker possibly because such complainants are better at selecting facts and presenting them in writing. Difficulty in putting the complaint in writing was to some extent related to social class and education but even a third of those in social class 1 complained of difficulties. Overall 41 per cent of complainants said they found it difficult. Most of the respondents stated that they considered a meeting with the Commission's staff to be helpful.

Dissatisfaction with the Commission's service was understandably higher among those whose complaint had not been accepted for investigation. However, only 30 per cent of the respondents said they would not use the service again. More than half of respondents whose complaint had been investigated were satisfied with the way in which the investigation was conducted and many were complimentary about the way in which the investigation had been done and the calibre of the Commission's investigators. Dissatisfaction amongst the investigated complainants was not only related to whether maladministration and injustice had been found. Three-quarters of those where injustice had been found were not satisfied with the action taken by the council. Those who had withdrawn their complaints were the most satisfied because in most cases action had been taken by the council to settle the matter — hence the withdrawal. Most of this group (91 per cent) thought that the council had taken action because of their complaint to the local ombudsman.

More personal contact was the most frequent improvement mentioned by those whose complaint had been rejected. Lack of personal contact was particularly resented by respondents who were relatively poorly educated. Other changes were also mentioned by some respondents. More power to enforce findings and more 'teeth' were the main improvements mentioned by those whose complaint had been investigated, and quicker investigations were mentioned by one in five people whose complaint had been investigated.

The Commission has attempted to meet some of these criticisms by reducing the length of time taken to consider and investigate complaints, and also by increasing the number of complainants seen by a member of staff before the taking of any decision whether or not to investigate. It has also been accepted that more publicity is needed to acquaint the general public with the existence of the Commission, and that specially designed and written publicity material is most important where an attempt is made to contact socially disadvantaged groups within society.

There have been other calls for the powers of the Commission to be increased and for it to be given a greatly increased rôle in solving disputes and conflicts between citizens and local authorities. In 1978 the Commission itself reviewed its powers under Part III of the Local Government Act 1974 and produced certain modest proposals for reform. (These can be found in detail in the Commission's Annual Report for

1978, pp. 16 to 27.) The Secretary of State gave his reply to these proposals, and this is contained in the Annual Report for 1979, pp. 94 to 106. The Secretary of State rejected any proposals for giving the Commission a wider rôle as either a conciliatory or investigative agency. Nor is it likely that the Commission will be given power to enforce its findings and recommendations. There is an understandable reluctance on the part of all those connected with the work of the Commission to see its investigations becoming formalised and akin to proceedings in court. It is thought that granting executive powers might foster such a tendency.

The recommendations which the Secretary of State accepted were as follows:

1) That the 1974 Act should be amended to enable authorities to make a payment to, or provide some other benefit for, a person who has suffered injustice arising from maladministration. (This recommendation was given effect by the Local Government Act 1978.)

2) That, subject to prior presentation to the Representative Body, the annual, report should be published by the Commission and not, as sections 24(b) and (5) of the 1974 Act provide, by the Representative Body.

3) That authorities should be required by section 30(4) of the 1974 Act to supply copies of investigation reports to the public and the media at a reasonable charge, and be given two weeks instead of one under section 30(5) to advertise that a report is available for inspection.

4) That authorities should be required under section 31 of the 1974 Act to consider further reports in the same way as first reports.

5) That section 32(1) of the 1974 Act, which deals with the law of defamation, should be amended to include officers as well as members of the Commission.

6) That section 32(3) of the 1974 Act should be amended to ensure that local commissioners have an unrestricted right of access to such information and documents as are relevant to the conduct of their investigations. Authorities would be able to claim that in the public interest the publication of the information provided should be restricted. (Legislation to amend the law on this point has been repeatedly promised since 1977.)

The Secretary of State also agreed to consider whether New Town Development Corporations and the Commission for New Towns should be brought within the Local Commissioners' jurisdiction and that appropriate arrangements should be made to ensure that these bodies meet a share of the Commission's costs in the light of any recommendation which may be made by the Select Committee on the Parliamentary Commissioner for Administration. No legislation to implement any of these proposals has yet been forthcoming.

The Commission's Report for 1979/80 contains the following comment on possible changes in the law.

'In December 1979 the Government published *Patients First* a consultative paper on the structure and management of the National Health Service in England and Wales. The paper made proposals for changing the structure of the National Health Service and referred to the need for effective links between health authorities and local authorities. Commenting on the paper the Commission stressed a point which they had already brought to the attention of the Department of Health and Social Security and the Department of the Environment. Their concern is that the revised arrangements proposed should clearly provide that an officer of a health authority should be appointed a proper officer of the local authority for advising a local authority on housing matters in the same way that the Government propose that District Medical officers should be appointed proper officers for other purposes, for example in respect of education and social services matters.

The investigation of some housing complaints has proved difficult where the responsibility of the medical officer advising the local authority, for example on whether there are medical reasons for housing priority, has not been clear. The new legislation provides the opportunity to clarify the situation and remove the source of difficulty'.

Overseeing the overseers

The Commission for England does not work in isolation. There are similar bodies for Scotland and Wales under the Local Government Acts 1974 and 1978 and the Local Government (Scotland) Act 1975. There are regular meetings between the Commissioners, and also between the Commission and the Department of the Environment and the Local Authority Associations. The Commission has to present its annual report to the 'Representative Body' set up under section 24 of the Local Government Act 1974. This body represents the authorities subject to investigation by the Commission and there are presently eleven members representing the Association of County Councils, the Association of District Councils, the Association of Metropolitan Authorities, the Greater London Council and the National Water Council. The Commission's report has to be presented annually for the year ending 31 March, and there is generally a brief introductory section wherein the Representative Body comment on the report. They may make such other comments as seem to them appropriate from time to time, which they did in the 1978 report as part of the Commission's review of its powers.

Further reading

Foulkes, *The Local Government Act 1974* (Butterworths) Chap. 3

Lewis and Gateshill, *The Commission for Local Administration: A Preliminary Appraisal* (Royal Institute of Public Administration, 1978)

Williams, *Maladministration: Remedies for Injustice* (Oyez, 1976)

Local Ombudsman 1980 (a report published by Justice)

Social Welfare Law (Ed., by D.W. Pollard) (Oyez) paras. I. 501 – I. 620

Reports of the Commission for Local Administration in England (published annually by the Representative Body from 1975 to date, and available from 25 Buckingham Gate, London, SW1E 6LE)

Chinkin, C., 'Local Authority Response to the Local Ombudsman' (1979) JPEL 441

Chinkin, C., 'The Power of the Local Ombudsman Re-examined' (1980) JPEL 87

Hoath, D.C., 'Council Tenants' Complaints and the Local Ombudsman' (1978) 128 New LJ 672

Hughes, D.J. and Jones, S.R., 'Bias in the Allocation and Transfer of Local Authority Housing; A Study of the Reports of the Commission for Local Administration in England' (1979) 1 JSWL 273

Williams, D.W., 'Social Welfare Consumers and Their Complaints' (1979) 1 JSWL 257

Index

Abatement notice
 sub-standard house, as to, 236 – 239
Accommodation
 suitable, definition of, 105, 106
Aged
 homeless
  duty as to, 193
  priority need of, 172, 173
Allocation
 council houses, of. *See* COUNCIL HOUSING
Arrears
 rent, of. *See* RENT

Battered women
 homelessness of, 173
 housing for, 140 – 144
Blind person
 homelessness of, 173
Building societies
 co-operation of, with local authorities,
  152 – 155

Capital
 expenditure control, new system of,
  14 – 16
 local authority house building, for,
  11 – 14
 receipts, example of increased,
  16 – 18
Children
 homeless
  duty as to, 193
  priority need of, 172, 173
Clearance procedures
 back-to-back dwellings, 252, 253
 clearance order, by, 251
 compensation
  assessment of, 261
  disturbance payments, 267, 268
  expenses of acquisition of new
   dwelling, 268

Clearance procedures—*contd.*
 compensation—*contd.*
  home loss payments, 269, 270
  purchase price of the land, 261 – 263
  well maintained payments
   amount of, 265 – 267
   meaning of well maintained, 265
   provisions as to, 264, 265
 compulsory purchase, by
  acquisition of the land, 258 – 260
  clearance area
   declaration of, 251 – 255
   method of dealing with, 255, 256
  compensation. *See* compensation,
   above
  entering upon the land, 260
  general vesting declaration procedure, 260, 261
  notice to treat, service of, 258, 259
  procedure, 256 – 258
  purchase price of the land, 261 – 263
 development of the law, 249, 250
 disturbance payments, 267, 268
 fate of land acquired, 270, 271
 home loss payments, 269, 270
 rehabilitation
  houses, of, in clearance areas,
   272 – 275
  order, making, 273 – 275
 rehousing displaced residents, 253, 254,
  271, 272
 well maintained payments, 264 – 267
Closing order
 sub-standard house, as to
  appeals procedure, 229, 230
  provision for, 227, 228
Commission for Local Administration
 assessment of work of, 344, 345
 creation of, 335 – 337
 effectiveness of, 341 – 344
 future reforms of, 345 – 348
 importance of, 2

351

Commission for Local Administration —
  contd.
  procedure before the, 337 – 341
  report to Representative Body, 348,
    349
  role of, generally, 335
  terms of reference of, 335 – 337
Common lodging houses
  local authority powers as to, 327 – 329
Compensation
  compulsory purchase, for
    assessment of, 261
    disturbance payments, 267, 268
    expenses of acquisition of new
      dwelling, 268
    home loss payments, 269, 270
    purchase price of the land, 261 – 263
    well maintained payments
      amount of, 265 – 267
      meaning of well maintained, 265
      provisions as to, 264, 265
Compulsory improvement. *See*
  IMPROVEMENT POLICIES
Compulsory purchase
  clearance area, as to. *See* CLEARANCE
    PROCEDURES
  compensation. *See* COMPENSATION
  disturbance payments, 267, 268
  home loss payments, 269, 270
  houses, of, 44, 45
  land, of
    ancillary rights as to, 43, 44
    confirmation of, 42
    planning permission requirements,
      42, 43
    price paid, 261 – 263
    procedure for, 41, 42
    provisions as to, 41 – 43
  well maintained payments, 264 – 267
Control orders
  multi-occupied houses, as to
    appeals against, 326, 327
    effect of, 325, 326
    finances of, 326
    making of, 324, 325
Council flat. *See* COUNCIL HOUSING
Council housing
  allocation of
    appeals against decisions, 95, 96
    housing registers, 88 – 93
    management policies, 86, 87
    mobility schemes, 89, 90
    points system, 91 – 93
    racial discrimination, 96 – 99
    reform, 95, 96

Council housing — *contd.*
  allocation of — *contd.*
    residence qualifications, 88 – 90
    selection schemes, 91 – 95
    sexual discrimination, 96 – 99
    waiting lists, 88 – 93
  Commission for Local Administration.
    See COMMISSION FOR LOCAL
    ADMINISTRATION
  convert buildings into, 39
  declining condition of, 8
  enlarge, power to, 35
  improve
    power to, 35
    sale, for, 82
  management of
    allocation. *See* allocation, above
    secure tenancy. *See* tenancy; tenants,
      below
    subletting, 108, 109
    tenant participation in, 107, 108
    tenure, as to, 99 – 101
  marriage
    break-up of
      problems arising out of, 146, 147
      rights of the parties, 144 – 146
    domestic violence
      homelessness, causing, 173
      housing for battered wives,
        140 – 144
    matrimonial home, as, 138, 139
  repair. *See* REPAIR AND MAINTAIN
  sale of. *See* SALE OF COUNCIL HOUSES
  serfs or citizens issue, 5 – 9
  sub-standard house, individual. *See*
    SUB-STANDARD HOUSE
  tenancy, secure
    definition of, 99 – 101
    periodic tenancy, 101
    possession orders, grounds for,
      103 – 107
    publicity regarding, 110, 111
    rights as to, 99, 101 – 103
    successor tenant, 101, 102
    variation of terms, 110, 111
    See also tenants, below
  tenants
    grading of, 6, 7
    legal position of, 6
    paternalistic attitudes to, 7, 8
    sale of council houses to. *See* SALE
      OF COUNCIL HOUSES
    secure
      eviction, position as to, 126
      improvements by, 109, 110

Council housing — *contd.*
  tenants — *contd.*
    secure — *contd.*
      new, right to buy, of, 71
      participation in housing manage-
        ment, 107, 108
      rights of, 99, 101 – 103
      subletting, 108, 109
      successor tenants, 101, 102
      See also tenancy, above
    tenure of, 99 – 101

Deaf person
  homelessness of, 173
Demolition. *See* also CLEARANCE
    PROCEDURES
  order, sub-standard house, as to
    appeals procedure, 229, 230
    provision for, 226, 227
    well maintained payments, 230
Disabled
  housing for, 35
Disturbance payments
  compulsory purchase, in cases of, 267,
    268
Domestic violence
  homelessness, causing, 173
  housing for battered wives, 140 – 144
Dumb person
  homelessness of, 173

Fire
  homelessness, causing, 172
  insurance, multi-occupied houses, for,
    325
  means of escape from
    house renovation grants for, 283,
      294, 295
    multi-occupied houses, as to
      local authority powers as to, 318,
        319
      maintenance of, 316
      special grants for, 283, 294, 295
First time buyers
  improve older houses for, 82
  local authority home purchase
    assistance for, 157 – 159
  starter home schemes, 81, 82
Flats
  council. *See* COUNCIL HOUSING
  definition of, 60
Flood
  homelessness, causing, 172

Freehold terms
  sale of council houses under, 71, 72,
    73 – 75

General improvement areas
  compulsory improvement powers in,
    301
  effect of, 300
  generally, 299, 300
  priority neighbourhoods, 300, 301
Greater London
  Council, housing management powers
    of, 32 – 34
  sub-standard house in, position of, 247

Homeless
  accommodate, duty to, 186 – 188
  aged
    priority need of, 172, 173
    residential accommodation for, 193
  battered woman, 140 – 144, 173
  blind person, 173
  causes of being, 164 – 169
  challenging decisions made under Act,
    190 – 192
  children
    duty as to, 193
    priority need as to, 172, 173
  deaf person, 173
  disaster, as a result of, 172
  domestic violence, causing woman
    to be homeless, 173
  dumb person, 173
  duties owed to
    differing, 174, 175
    enforcement of, 190 – 192
    intentionally homeless, 175 – 182
    statutory provisions as to, 174
    unintentionally homeless, 174,
      182 – 186
  fire, as a result of, 172
  flood, as a result of, 172
  infirm, residential accommodation for,
    193
  intentionally
    acts causing, definition of, 175
    duties owed to, 175 – 182
    meaning of, 175, 176
    reasons for being, 176
  local authority, initial contact with,
    171 – 174
  mentally ill or handicapped, 172, 173
  notification, duties of, 188, 189
  numbers of, 164 – 169

Homeless — *contd.*
  offences, 189
  physical disability, those with, 172, 173
  pregnant woman, 172, 173, 178, 179,
    180
  priority need for accommodation, with,
    172, 173
  property of, protecting, 190
  reception centres (now resettlement
    units), provision of, 166, 167,
    169, 192
  residential accommodation, provision
    of, 169, 192, 193
  squatting, 167
  unintentionally, 174, 182 – 186
  wandering, resettlement units for,
    166, 167, 192
  who they are, 169 – 171
Home loss payments
  compulsory purchase, in cases of, 269,
    270
House of Commons Environment
    Committee
  first report, conclusions of, 25, 26
House renovation grants
  applications for, 283 – 285
  availability, general conditions as to,
    283 – 285
  certificates of future occupation, 285,
    286
  conditions
    enforcement of, 289, 290
    residence, 287
  fire, means of escape from, for, 283,
    294, 295
  improvement grants, 283, 290 – 292
  intermediate grants, 283, 292 – 294
  payment of, 286, 287
  percentage of grant payable, 285
  repair grants, 283, 295, 296
  special grants, 283, 294, 295, 310
  standard amenities, for, 290 – 295
Housing. *See also* COUNCIL HOUSING; SALE
    OF COUNCIL HOUSES; SUB-STANDARD
    HOUSE
  acquisition of
    houses, 35, 39, 40
    land for, 37 – 41
  Act of 1980, discussion of, 9, 10
  action areas. *See* HOUSING ACTION AREAS
  alter houses, power to, 35
  authorities, 32 – 34
  back-to-back dwellings, 252, 253
  battered wives, for, 140 – 144, 173
  building, local authority
    capital for, 11 – 14

Housing — *contd.*
  building, local authority — *contd.*
    loans for, 11, 12
    Parker Morris standards, 18 – 20
  clearance areas, in
    rehabilitation of, 272 – 275
    rehousing displaced residents, 253,
      254, 271, 272
    See also CLEARANCE PROCEDURES
  compensation for compulsory purchase.
    See COMPENSATION
  compulsory improvement of, powers as
    to, 301 – 304
  compulsory purchase of. *See* CLEARANCE
    PROCEDURES; COMPULSORY PURCHASE
  conversion of leasehold, 36
  convert buildings for, power to, 35
  disabled, for, 35
  duty to provide, 34 – 36
  enforcing duties of local authorities, 45
  expenditure, control of recurrent, 20, 21
  first time buyers. *See* FIRST TIME BUYERS
  home loss payments, 269, 270
  house, definition of, 60, 252
  house renovation grants. *See* HOUSE
    RENOVATION GRANTS
  Investment Programmes, 13, 14, 25
  large houses, conversion of, for multi-
    occupation, 308 – 310
  law, introduction to, 1 – 26
  local authorities
    powers and duties of, 31 – 48
    providers of homes, as, 1 – 3
  multi-occupied. *See* MULTI-OCCUPIED
    HOUSES
  new areas, provision in, 45, 46
  overcrowding. *See* OVERCROWDING
  ownership, advantages and disadvan-
    tages, 5, 6
  registers, 88 – 93
  repairs. *See* REPAIR AND MAINTAIN
  Repairs Account, 114, 115
  Revenue Account, 113 – 115
  Services Advisory Group, 88, 89
  starter home schemes, 81, 82
  statistics, 2, 3
  subsidies
    new system, 21 – 24
    role of, 20, 21
  tenements, 323, 324
  tenure, argument on, 4, 5
  unsatisfactory
    numbers as to, 280 – 282
    renovation, figures for rate of, 282

Housing Action Areas
compulsory improvement powers in,
301
declaration of
consequences of, 298, 299
procedure, 297, 298
generally, 296, 297
priority neighbourhoods, 300, 301
Improvement grants
introduction of, 276, 277
payment of, 283, 290 – 292
Improvement policies
area improvement, 296
assessment of, 305, 306
compulsory improvement
notices
issue of, 302 – 304
local authority mortgages, where,
156
outside improvement areas, 304, 305
powers as to, 301 – 304
provisional notice as to, 301, 302
general improvement areas
compulsory improvement powers in,
301
effect of, 300
generally, 299 300
generally, 276
grants
house renovation
applications for, 283 – 285
availability, 283 – 285
certificates of future occupation,
285, 286
conditions
enforcement of, 289, 290
residence, 287
individual, 290 – 296
payment of, 286, 287
percentage payable, 285
improvement
introduction of, 276, 277
payment of, 283, 290 – 292
intermediate, 283, 292 – 294
repair, 283, 295, 296
special, 283, 294, 295, 310
standard amenities, for, 290 – 295
history of, 276 – 280
housing action areas
declaration of
consequences of, 298, 299
procedure, 297, 298
generally, 296, 297
priority neighbourhoods, 300, 301

Improvement policies – *contd.*
unsatisfactory houses
number of, 280 – 282
renovation, figures for rate of, 282
Infirm
homeless, duty as to, 193
Intermediate grants
payment of, 283, 292 – 294

Land. *See also* CLEARANCE PROCEDURES
acquisition of
clearance area, in
fate of, 270, 271
procedure, 258 – 260
housing, for, 37 – 41
compulsory purchase of
ancillary rights as to, 43, 44
clearance area, in, 258 – 260
confirmation of, 42
planning permission requirements,
42, 43
price paid, 261 – 263
procedure for, 41, 42
provisions as to, 41 – 43
See also COMPULSORY PURCHASE
disposal of, by local authorities
provisions for, 37 – 39, 78
starter home schemes, for, 81, 82
register of, 38
Leasehold property
conversion of, 36
repairs and maintenance of, 216
sale of council houses under long lease,
71 – 73
Loans. *See also* MORTGAGE
first time buyers, local authority
assistance for, 157 – 159
local authority house building, for,
11, 12
Local housing autonomy
erosion of, 10, 11
future role of, 24 – 26
London Boroughs
housing duties of, 32 – 34

Maintenance. *See* REPAIR AND MAINTAIN
Management orders
houses in multiple occupation, as to,
314 – 316
Marriage
break-up of
problems arising out of, 146, 147
rights of the parties, 144 – 146
council house as matrimonial home,
138, 139

Marriage — *contd.*
  domestic violence
    homelessness, causing, 173
    housing for battered wives, 140 – 144
    non-tenant wife, rights of, 139, 140
    pregnant woman, homelessness of, 172,
      173, 178, 179, 180
Mentally ill or handicapped
  homeless, priority need of, 172, 173
Mortgage
  council house sale, for
    right to a
      amount to be left outstanding, 68
      exercising, 69, 70
      provisions for, 67, 68
      terms of, 70, 71
  local authority
    compulsory improvement notices, to
      persons subject to, 156
    co-operation with building societies,
      152 – 155
    guarantee powers, 155, 156
    home purchase assistance powers,
      157 – 159
    interest rates, 149, 150
    large, guarantees for, 162
    lending in practice, 150 – 152
    option mortgages
      end of, 162
      extension of right to opt, 161
      object of, 159
      right to opt for subsidy, 160, 161
    powers as to, 147 – 149, 156, 157
  option, local authority. *See* under
    local authority, above
  shared ownership schemes, for, 83, 85
Multi-occupied houses
  common lodging houses, 327 – 329
  conversion of large houses for, 308 – 310
  definition of multi-occupation, 313,
    314
  fire insurance of, 325
  fire, means of escape from
    local authority powers as to, 318, 319
    maintenance of, 316
    special grants for, 283, 294, 295
  local authority powers as to
    common lodging houses, 327 – 329
    control orders
      appeals against, 326, 327
      effect of, 325, 326
      finances of, 326
      making of, 324, 325
    further works, requirement for,
      316 – 320

Multi-occupied houses — *contd.*
  local authority powers as to — *contd.*
    management orders, 314 – 316
    prevention of overcrowding,
      320 – 322
    registration, 323, 324
    supplementary, 322, 323
    tenements, 323
  management orders as to, 314 – 316
  overcrowding and, 308 – 310
  reasons for having, 308 – 310
  registration of, 323, 324
  repairs and maintenance of, 315, 316
  special grants to, 283, 294, 295
  supervision of
    Housing Acts, under, 312, 313
    planning control, by, 310 – 312
  tenements, 323

National parks
  resale of council houses in, restrictions
    on, 78
New towns
  Commission for the, 50, 51, 52
  development corporations
    role of, 49
    transfer schemes, 49 – 52
  development of, 46, 48, 49
  housing management powers in, 52
  ownership of housing in, 49 – 51
  provisions for, designation of, 48
  'right to buy' provisions, 52, 53
  transfer of housing
    effect of, 51, 52
    provisions for, 50, 51
Notice of determination to purchase
  sub-standard house, as to
    appeals procedure, 229, 230
    provision for, 228
    well maintained payments, 230
Notice to treat
  service of, 258, 259
Nuisance order
  sub-standard house, as to, 237 – 239

Option Mortgages
  local authority. *See* MORTGAGE
Overcrowding
  multi-occupied houses
    association of, 308 – 310
    local authority powers to prevent,
      320 – 322
  separate dwelling-houses, in
    definition of, 330, 331

Overcrowding—*contd.*
  separate dwelling-houses, in—*contd.*
    enforcement powers and duties as to,
      333, 334
    offences as to, 331–333
    problems of, 329
    remedial powers and duties as to,
      333, 334

Parker Morris standards
  conforming to, 18–20
Physical disability
  homelessness of those with, 172, 173
Planning permission
  compulsorily purchased land, for, 42, 43
Possession orders
  grounds for, 103–107
  suitable accommodation, definition of,
    105, 106
Pregnant woman
  homelessness of, 172, 173, 178, 179,
    180
Purchase
  notice of determination to. *See* NOTICE
    OF DETERMINATION TO PURCHASE

Racial discrimination
  allocation of council houses, as to,
    96–99
  local authority mortgages, as to, 148
Rehabilitation order
  procedure for making, 273–275
Rent
  arrears
    administrative practices as to, 128
    distress
      meaning of, 122, 123
      procedure for levying, 123–125
    eviction, 125–128
    figures as to, 119, 120
    National Consumer Council recom-
      mendations, 120, 121
    problem of, 119, 120
    reasons for, 119, 120
    rent action, 121, 122
  Housing Repairs Account, 114, 115
  Housing Revenue Account, 113–115
  increasing, 118, 119
  pooling, 115–117
  reasonable, 117, 118
  rebates
    administrative procedures concer-
      ning, 134–136

Rent—*contd.*
  rebates—*contd.*
    calculation of, 132, 133
    examples, 133, 134
    generally, 129, 130
    model scheme, 130–132
Repair and maintain
  landlord's obligation to
    Building Regulations, liability for
      breach of, 205
    contract, in
      common law, at, 205–210
      statute, under, 210–218
    council houses and flats sold
      leasehold, 72, 73
    Defective Premises Act, under,
      201–204
    generally, 197, 198
    liability under Occupiers Liability
      Act, 204, 205
    tort, in
      common law, at, 198, 199
      statute, under, 199–204
  multi-occupied houses
    further works, local authority powers
      as to, 316–320
    management orders as to, 315, 316
  power to, 35
  'self-help' by tenants, 207, 208
Repair grants
  payment of, 283, 295, 296
Repair notice
  sub-standard house, as to, 223–225
Residential accommodation
  homeless, for, 192, 193
Resettlement units,
  homeless, for, 166, 167, 169, 192

Sale of council houses
  completing the transfer, 67
  former law, 54, 55
  freehold sales, terms of, 71, 72, 73–75
  general consents for, 79–81
  improvements for, 82
  leasehold terms of
    landlord's repairing covenants, 72, 73
    provisions for, 71–73
  local authority estimates of, 84
  modern law, background to, 57–60
  moneys from, 16, 26
  mortgage
    right to a
      amount to be left outstanding, 68
      exercising, 69, 70
      provisions for, 67, 68

Sale of council houses — *contd.*
mortgage — *contd.*
terms of, 70, 71
policy as to
background to modern, 57 – 60
history and development of, 55 – 57
politics of, 3, 54
powers of local authorities, 78 – 81
price to be paid, 63 – 65
provisions for, 9, 10
resale, restrictions on, 75 – 77, 78
'right to buy'
change of landlord, where, 71
exceptions, 61
exercising the, 66, 67
Housing Act 1980, under, 9, 10,
60 – 63
joint tenancy, where, 62, 63
new secure tenants, by, 71
new towns, effect on, 52, 53
provisions as to, 9, 10, 60 – 63, 66, 67
qualification period, 60 – 62
withdrawal by tenant, 71
Secretary of State, powers of, 77, 78
shared ownership schemes, 83, 85
Secure tenancy. *See* TENANCY
Service charges.... 73 – 75
Sexual discrimination
housing allocation, as to, 96 – 99
local authority mortgages, as to, 148
Slum
clearance. *See* CLEARANCE PROCEDURES;
COMPULSORY PURCHASE
Special grants
payment of, 283, 294, 295, 310
Squatters
proceedings against, 167
Standard amenities
compulsory improvement powers to
provide, 301
grants to provide, 290 – 295
Starter home schemes. *See also* FIRST
TIME BUYERS
sale of housing land for, 81, 82
Subletting
secure tenant, by, 108, 109
Subsidies
new system of, 21 – 24
role of, 20, 21
Sub-standard house
abatement notice, service of, 236 – 239
architectural interest, of, 227
closing order, issue of
appeals procedure, 229, 230
provision for, 227, 228
dangerous building, 246, 247

Sub-standard house — *contd.*
demolition order, issue of
appeals procedure, 229, 230
provision for, 226, 227
well maintained payments following,
230
notice of determination to purchase
appeals procedure, 229, 230
provision for, 228
well maintained payments following,
230
Greater London, in, 247
historic interest, of, 227
Housing and Public Health Acts,
relationship between, 241
infested
rats and mice, with, 244, 245
vermin, other, with, 245, 246
legislation, mandatory character of
requirements of, 231, 232
listed, 227
local authorities, duties of, 222 – 228
made fit at reasonable expense
can be, 223 – 225
cannot be
appeals procedure, 229, 230
closing order, 227 – 230
demolition order, 226 – 230
duty as to, 225 – 228
notice of determination to
purchase, 228 – 230
'time and place' notice, 225, 226
well maintained payments, 230
miscellaneous powers to deal with,
244 – 247
modern council-built, 243, 244
nuisance order, issue of, 237 – 239
obstructive building, 246, 247
older, owned by local authority, 242,
243
prevention of houses becoming unfit,
232 – 234
private ownership, in, 241, 242
problems and remedies, generally, 220,
221
repair notice, issue of, 223 – 225
standard of fitness, 221, 222
statutory nuisance
definition of, 235, 236
taking action in respect of
abatement notice, service of,
236 – 239
nuisance order, issue of, 237 – 239
private citizens, by, 239, 240
procedures for, 236 – 239

Sub-standard house—*contd.*
'time and place' notice to discuss, 225, 226

Tenancy
joint, 'right to buy' where, 62, 63
non-tenant wife, rights of, 139, 140
periodic, 101
rent of. *See* RENT
repairs and maintenance, 'self-help' duties as to, 207, 208
'right to buy'. *See* SALE OF COUNCIL HOUSES
secure
definition of, 99 – 101
eviction, position as to, 126
housing management, participation in, 107, 108
improvements by, 109, 110
new tenant, right to buy of, 71
periodic, 101
possession orders, grounds for, 103 – 107
publicity regarding, 110, 111
rights as to, 99, 101 – 103
subletting by tenant, 108, 109
successor tenant, 101, 102

Tenancy—*contd.*
secure—*contd.*
variation of terms, 110, 111
shared ownership schemes, 83, 85
Tenements. *See also* MULTI-OCCUPIED HOUSES
local authority powers as to, 323
meaning of, 323
registration of, 323, 324
Towns
development of, provisions for, 46 – 48
new. *See* NEW TOWNS
new areas, provision of housing in, 45, 46

Waiting lists
council houses, for, 88 – 93
Wandering homeless
resettlement units for, 166, 167, 192
Well maintained payments
clearance area, as to
amount of, 265 – 267
provisions as to, 264, 265
individual sub-standard house, as to, 230
meaning of well maintained, 265